Enterprise Agility

by Doug Rose

Enterprise Agility For Dummies®

Published by: **John Wiley & Sons, Inc.,** 111 River Street, Hoboken, NJ 07030-5774, www.wiley.com

For general information on our other products and services, please contact our Customer Care Department within the U.S. at 877-762-2974, outside the U.S. at 317-572-3993, or fax 317-572-4002. For technical support, please visit https://hub.wiley.com/community/support/dummies.

Wiley publishes in a variety of print and electronic formats and by print-on-demand. Some material included with standard print versions of this book may not be included in e-books or in print-on-demand. If this book refers to media such as a CD or DVD that is not included in the version you purchased, you may download this material at http://booksupport.wiley.com. For more information about Wiley products, visit www.wiley.com.

Library of Congress Control Number: 2018930061

ISBN 978-1-119-44613-2 (pbk); ISBN 978-1-119-44610-1 (ebk); ISBN 978-1-119-44609-5 (ebk)

Manufactured in the United States of America

10 9 8 7 6 5 4 3 2 1

Enterprise Agility

by Doug Rose

Enterprise Agility For Dummies®

Published by: **John Wiley & Sons, Inc.,** 111 River Street, Hoboken, NJ 07030-5774, www.wiley.com

For general information on our other products and services, please contact our Customer Care Department within the U.S. at 877-762-2974, outside the U.S. at 317-572-3993, or fax 317-572-4002. For technical support, please visit https://hub.wiley.com/community/support/dummies.

Wiley publishes in a variety of print and electronic formats and by print-on-demand. Some material included with standard print versions of this book may not be included in e-books or in print-on-demand. If this book refers to media such as a CD or DVD that is not included in the version you purchased, you may download this material at http://booksupport.wiley.com. For more information about Wiley products, visit www.wiley.com.

Library of Congress Control Number: 2018930061

ISBN 978-1-119-44613-2 (pbk); ISBN 978-1-119-44610-1 (ebk); ISBN 978-1-119-44609-5 (ebk)

Manufactured in the United States of America

10 9 8 7 6 5 4 3 2 1

Contents at a Glance

Table of Contents

Introduction

To survive and thrive in a fast-moving economy, enterprises must work to improve their agility; they need to be able to pivot quickly to respond to new technologies, emerging opportunities and threats, and ever-evolving customer demands. However, many organizations are built more like cruise ships than jet skis. They're designed to command and control, making decisions at the top and passing them along the chain of command to the employees who do the work. Even when these organizations manage to change direction, they're either too late to market or too far off course to stay ahead of the competition.

An agile enterprise is lean and nimble. Product developers collaborate closely with the organization's leaders and management and with customers to optimize value. Decision-making is distributed throughout the organization, and employees are encouraged to take the initiative, experiment and innovate, and continuously learn and improve. Agile organizations ride the waves of change instead of being tossed and turned by external factors beyond their control.

However, a large-scale agile transformation is no small feat, especially when it develops complex products that traditionally involve a great deal of up-front planning. How do you transform a large organization with deeply entrenched functional areas into a collection of small, closely aligned teams without sinking the ship? In this book, I answer that question.

About This Book

Over the past ten years, I've helped a number of large organizations become agile enterprises. Most organizations that succeed follow the same three-step approach:

1. Review the top enterprise agile frameworks.
2. Identify the organization's existing culture.
3. Create and execute a strategy for making big changes.

Those that fail never do so from a lack of trying. They fail from *doing* agile instead *being* agile. They create teams that do everything agile teams are supposed to do, but they continue to function as they always did — making decisions at the top, issuing commands, and expecting employees to follow orders. They just don't try to change their *mindset*. As a result, they fall short of creating a culture of mutual trust and respect in which employees and customers collaborate closely to deliver innovative products. These organizations look like agile enterprises, but they never reap the full benefits of agility.

In this book, I take a three-pronged approach to transforming organizations into agile enterprises so they can both *be* agile and *do* agile:

- **Being agile:** To achieve enterprise agility, everyone in your organization must have a shared understanding of what it is and its purpose. If your teams understand agility, but your executives and managers don't, you'll end up with teams that merely do what they're told instead of coming up with creative solutions. In Part 1, I bring you up to speed on the agile mindset, describe agile at the team level, and present the Simple Lean-Agile Mindset (SLAM), which provides a high-level understanding of enterprise agility.
- **Doing agile:** In Part 2, I introduce the top enterprise agile frameworks — Scaled Agile Framework® (SAFe®), Large-Scale Scrum (LeSS), Disciplined Agile Delivery (DAD), the Spotify Engineering Culture, Kanban, and Lean. Most organizations begin their agile transformations by choosing one of these frameworks and then tailoring it to meet their needs. Others may use the frameworks to generate ideas for their own custom enterprise agile framework.
- **Making the transformation:** In Part 3, I lead you through the process of transforming your organization to improve your enterprise agility. Here, you evaluate your organization's existing culture, choose a top-down or bottom-up approach to executing the transformation, and then follow my detailed ten-step transformation process. (Keep in mind that enterprise agility is an ongoing process of continuous improvement, not a one-time event. Your organization will evolve over time.)

Foolish Assumptions

A key component of enterprise agility is empirical process control. As such, its practitioners frown upon making detailed plans. Instead, teams are encouraged to "think, build, release, and tweak," through empirical, data-driven decisions. However, because I don't know you personally (although you seem nice), I had to make several assumptions about you when writing this book:

- You're probably an executive or manager in a large organization who has heard of enterprise agility and you want to learn more about it. Or you have decided already that you want to make your organization an agile enterprise.

(Or you may be an employee who sees the value of enterprise agility and you want to enlighten others in your organization.)

- Your knowledge of agility ranges from knowing nothing about it to actually working as a part of an agile team. In other words, you can benefit from this book whether you know a lot or a little about enterprise agility.
- You're interested primarily in *enterprise* agility, not *business* agility. Enterprise agility pertains to product development, while business agility has a much broader scope that permeates an organization. While I touch on business agility in several chapters, my focus in this book is on using enterprise agility to optimize *product delivery*.
- You're committed to adopting an enterprise agile mindset. That is, you're not just interested in making your organization more agile, but also you want everyone in your organization to collaborate as autonomous, closely aligned teams to deliver awesome new products.

Icons Used in This Book

Throughout this book, icons in the margins highlight different types of information that call out for your attention. Here are the icons you'll see and a brief description of each.

REMEMBER

I want you to remember everything you read in this book, but if you can't quite do that, then remember the important points flagged with this icon.

TECHNICAL STUFF

Throughout this book, I stick to the bare essentials — what you need to know to conduct a successful enterprise agile transformation. If I dig any deeper into a topic, I warn you with this icon. If you're looking for an in-depth discussion, dig in; otherwise, you can safely skip ahead.

TIP

Tips provide insider insight. When you're looking for a better, faster way to do something, check out these tips.

WARNING

"Whoa!" Although enterprise agility encourages learning through experimentation and failure, learning without the failure is always preferred. When you see the warning icon, proceed with caution. I've seen many organizations make critical mistakes that have slowed or derailed their attempts at becoming more agile. Learn from *their* mistakes.

CASE STUDY

Throughout this book, you'll find plenty of real-life case studies that provide valuable insight into enterprise agile transformations (successes and failures), so if you're the type of person who commonly skips sidebars, I strongly encourage you to break that nasty habit — at least for this book.

Beyond the Book

In addition to the abundance of information and guidance on enterprise agility that I provide in this book, you get access to even more help and information online at `Dummies.com`. There you can find a free, access-anywhere Cheat Sheet that gives you even more pointers on how to embark on an enterprise agile transformation. To get this Cheat Sheet, simply go to `www.dummies.com` and search for "*Enterprise Agility For Dummies* Cheat Sheet" in the Search box.

Where to Go from Here

You're certainly welcome to read this book from cover to cover, but I wrote it in a way that facilitates skipping around. If you're new to agile, I recommend you read Chapters 1 and 2 to get up to speed on the topic. Chapter 3 is also essential reading, but you *could* hold off on reading Chapter 3 until you review the different enterprise agile frameworks in Part 2. Chapter 3 provides a conceptual understanding of enterprise agility that highlights common themes among all the frameworks.

In Part 2, I cover the top enterprise agile frameworks, so feel free to skip around in that part — the chapters aren't sequential. I describe each of the frameworks, so you can make a well-informed choice of which framework to start with.

When you're ready to embark on your enterprise agile transformation, turn to Part 3. In this part, the chapters are sequential, so read Chapters 9, 10, and 11 in that order. Chapter 11 is most important, because it outlines a specific ten-step process for transforming your organization into an agile enterprise.

With enterprise agility, failing is okay, as long as you learn from it and persevere. The danger is that failing often leads to discouragement. When an agile transformation doesn't meet expectations, organizations often conclude that greater agility isn't the right solution and they give up. In nearly all cases, improving agility *is* the right solution — it's the transformation process that fails. Approach enterprise agility with the conviction that it's the right solution as long as everyone in your organization adopts an agile mindset. If you're struggling to overcome obstacles, look for and address issues in the transformation process, which can almost always be traced back to pockets of resistance in the organization — people who haven't accepted the agile mindset.

1

Getting Started with Enterprise Agility

IN THIS PART . . .

Get up to speed on what's involved in making your organization an agile enterprise and begin to appreciate the crucial role that culture plays in any enterprise agile transformation.

Explore the key differences between agile at the team level, enterprise agility, and business agility, and recognize the importance of starting on a smaller scale.

Start to gauge just how receptive or resistant your organization will be to the big changes you're about to implement.

Take a quick look at the 1-2-3 process of transitioning your organization's product delivery to enterprise agility, and start thinking about the approach you will take to transform your organization.

Brush up on agile basics at the team level, so you have a fundamental understanding of various agile frameworks, such as Scrum, Extreme Programming, Lean Software Development, and Kanban.

Get to know the principles that drive agile product development and the common practices many agile teams use in the product delivery process.

Understand the challenges you're likely to face as you scale agile to develop and deliver enterprise-level products, and start thinking about ways to meet these challenges.

» Defining enterprise agility

» Distinguishing enterprise agility from business agility

» Transforming your organization with the 1-2-3 approach

Chapter 1
Taking It All In: The Big Picture

When you're getting ready to tackle a complex topic, such as enterprise agility, having a general understanding of the topic and what it entails is a great place to start. In this chapter, I give you that eye-in-the-sky view of enterprise agility. Here you develop a general understanding of agile and enterprise agility and the key distinction between the two. You discover how to build an agile enterprise without making the common mistake of trying merely to scale up agile frameworks to your entire organization. And I introduce you to some commonly used agile frameworks that I cover in greater detail in Part 2.

Defining Agile and Enterprise Agility

Because you're reading a book about enterprise agility, I assume you're familiar with the topic, but readers may have different levels of understanding and different ideas about what "agile" and "enterprise agility" mean. In this section, I define the two terms and explain the key differences between them.

Understanding agile product delivery

According to the Agile Alliance, *agile* is "the ability to create and respond to change in order to succeed in an uncertain and turbulent environment." Instead of relying on extensive up-front planning, "solutions evolve through collaboration between self-organizing, cross-functional teams utilizing the appropriate practices for their context." (*Self-organizing* means the teams manage themselves. *Cross-functional* means each team has all the expertise and skills required to complete its work.)

Small teams (typically fewer than nine people) are empowered to collaborate and make decisions as opposed to being subject to intensive planning, rigid processes, and consulting management for direction and approval. The goal is to remove the management obstacles that commonly get in the way of competent people doing their jobs.

Agile frameworks originated in the context of software development, an area subject to rapid change — changes in end-user needs, technologies, and even the tools and processes used to develop software. To be effective, developers needed to be agile. They had to be able to make decisions locally instead of having to wade through the bureaucracy of traditional management matrixes.

The Agile Manifesto

In 2001, 17 software developers gathered at The Lodge at Snowbird ski resort in the Wasatch mountains of Utah and talked about why companies were having difficulty developing software. They represented some of the newer methods in software development — Scrum, Extreme Programming, the Crystal Methods, and continuous integration. After some discussion, they identified what was common among all these approaches: They were all lightweight compared to the complexities of the popular software development approaches at the time, including IBM's Rational Unified Process (RUP) and the manufacturing-inspired waterfall approach. They didn't want to become known as a bunch of "lightweights," so they settled on calling their approach "agile." Together they formed the Agile Alliance.

The word "agile" implied that software developers needed to be quick and flexible and able to change course quickly to take advantage of new ideas, changing customer needs, and emerging technologies. Many of the first articles and books on the topic included drawings of cheetahs.

After they settled on a name for their workgroup, a few of the members drafted the *Manifesto for Agile Software Development*. The Agile Manifesto, as it has come to be called, provides insight into the mindset agile embraces (from `agilemanifesto.org`):

We are uncovering better ways of developing software by doing it and helping others do it. Through this work we have come to value:

- **Individuals and interactions** over *processes and tools*
- **Working software** over *comprehensive documentation*
- **Customer collaboration** over *contract negotiation*
- **Responding to change** over *following a plan*

That is, while there is value in the italicized items on the right, we value the bolded items on the left more.

After the group came down from the mountain, they decided to continue to work together. In the weeks and months following their return, they added 12 agile principles they deemed to be consistent with the Agile Manifesto's four values and exemplary of the kinds of operating principles one could expect to observe in an agile group.

Agile principles

Agile is based on the following 12 guiding principles:

- Our highest priority is to satisfy the customer through early and continuous delivery of valuable software.
- Welcome changing requirements, even late in development. Agile processes harness change for the customer's competitive advantage.
- Deliver working software frequently, from a couple of weeks to a couple of months, with a preference to the shorter timescale.
- Business people and developers must work together daily throughout the project.
- Build projects around motivated individuals. Give them the environment and support they need, and trust them to get the job done.
- The most efficient and effective method of conveying information to and within a development team is face-to-face conversation.
- Working software is the primary measure of progress.
- Agile processes promote sustainable development. The sponsors, developers, and users should be able to maintain a constant pace indefinitely.
- Continuous attention to technical excellence and good design enhances agility.
- Simplicity — the art of maximizing the amount of work not done — is essential.

» The best architectures, requirements, and designs emerge from self-organizing teams.

» At regular intervals, the team reflects on how to become more effective, then tunes and adjusts its behavior accordingly.

WHAT DOES IT MEAN TO BE "AGILE"?

Agile is an organizing concept for orchestrating software development or other work. It has never been or tried to be a unified engineering system for developing software. Since its birth, it has become more like an empty truck bed gathering new ideas (after being accepted as common practice) as it travels through time. Soon after the Agile Manifesto was written, several books and articles were added to the truck bed of ideas collectively regarded as "agile":

- In 2002, *Test-Driven Development: By Example* by Kent Beck, encouraged developers to think about what the software would accomplish before starting to code.
- Around the same time, James Grenning published an article entitled "Planning Poker or how to avoid analysis paralysis while release planning," to help agile teams create group estimates for the time they thought the work would take to complete.
- In 2003, *Lean Software Development: An Agile Toolkit*, by Mary and Tom Poppendieck, argued that software was pulling the wrong ideas from manufacturing. Instead of using a one-phase-at-a-time waterfall approach, agile teams should work to maximize value to the customer by making their processes leaner — a concept inspired by Toyota's manufacturing process, the Toyota Production System (TPS).
- In 2006, *Agile Retrospectives: Making Good Teams Great*, by Esther Derby and Diana Larsen, introduced the concept and practice of team retrospectives.
- In 2010, *Kanban: Successful Evolutionary Change for Your Technology Business*, by David J. Anderson, explained how to use Lean principles to visualize work and maximize workflow.

The ideas presented in those books and others like them were not written into the original Agile Manifesto, although many of those ideas represent practices known to the Manifesto's authors. Today most agile teams consider them to be a core part of their work. The takeaway message here is that even agile is agile — subject to change "in an uncertain and turbulent environment." To become agile, you need to understand the accepted values, principles, and practices and then apply them in a way that works for you and adapt whenever necessary. What works for one organization may not work for another, and the agile of tomorrow may not look anything like what the writers of the Agile Manifesto had envisioned in 2001.

Agile frameworks

To facilitate their product development process, agile teams use different methodologies, referred to as "frameworks," such as the following:

- **Extreme Programming (XP):** A team of contributors, formed around a business representative called "the customer," operates according to certain basic values including simplicity, communication, feedback, courage, and respect. Through high customer involvement, close teamwork, rapid feedback loops, and continuous planning and testing, teams strive to deliver working software at frequent intervals (generally one to three weeks).
- **Kanban:** A team uses a "Kanban board" to track and visualize workflow. The board divides product development stages into columns, such as To Do, In Progress, and Done. Each work item is described on a "Kanban card" (index card or sticky note) and cards are arranged in the To Do column in order of priority. As team members are able, they pull work items from the To Do column and perform the work required. When they're done, the card is moved to the Done column. It gets more complicated, and the Kanban board can have many columns, but that's the general idea. Kanban strives to minimize work in progress (WIP), eliminate bottlenecks, and minimize waste (increase efficiency).
- **Lean Startup:** The Lean methodology follows a "Think it, build it, ship it, tweak it" approach with data driving ideas that lead to the development of code. The framework calls for a close connection with customers and frequent tests that drive a never-ending cycle of improvement.
- **Scrum:** A *product owner* provides a prioritized wish list of features, fixes, and so on, called a *product backlog.* A *development team* draws from the top of that list (a *sprint backlog*), decides how to implement those items, and estimates the amount of time it will take to complete that work in the form of a potentially shippable product (typically 30 days or fewer). The development team meets daily to assess progress and discuss issues. A *Scrum Master* functions as the servant-leader for the Scrum team — more in the capacity of facilitator than project manager. There is a clear separation of concerns as the product owner prioritizes *what* must be done next, and the development team figures out *how* to get those things done.

See Chapter 2 for more about these team-level agile frameworks.

Agile practices

Agile practices are specific applications of agile, as opposed to more general theories and principles. Here are just a few of the many agile practices:

- **Planning poker:** A game for estimating product backlogs. The product owner describes a product feature or function, and each player (team member) draws a card from her own deck with a value, such as 1, 2, 3, 5, 8, 20, 40, or 100 to estimate the time or work required. After all players have chosen their cards, they flip their cards over at the same time. If everyone's estimate is the same, that becomes the estimate; otherwise, players discuss the reasons for their estimates until consensus is reached or the team determines that more information is needed.
- **Product backlog:** A prioritized list of work items that must be completed to deliver a product.
- **Stand-up meetings:** Daily meetings during which everyone stands as a clear message that the meetings cannot extend past 15 minutes.
- **User story:** A description of a product feature from the user's perspective such as, "Customers can pay with credit cards, debit cards, or PayPal."
- **Work-in-progress (WIP) pull board:** Kanban uses a WIP pull board designed to limit WIP and encourage collaboration among team members. Seeing a WIP item on the board, the team can address the issue and remove the item. The notion of "pull" is key; instead of having work pushed on them, which often produces traffic jams and delays, team members pull work items from the board as they're able to do the work.

WARNING

Don't equate agile with a framework or a set of agile practices. Agile is more of a culture or shared mindset among team members that influences the way team members think about their work and impacts the way they work individually and together as a team. Having a shared understanding and appreciation of the agile concept is far more important than having shared practices. For example, mutual respect, trust, and a spirit of innovation are far more important than user stories and stand-up meetings.

Defining "enterprise agility"

Enterprise agility is agile for big products — typically one that requires many different teams throughout the organization that coordinate with many different departments and stakeholders.

While agile involves one or two teams working on a *part* of a product, enterprise agility may involve dozens or even hundreds of teams working on a *whole* enterprise solution. When you have that many teams working on a single enterprise solution, you start running into alignment issues and creating a lot of dependencies. Although you may want to remain agile, you need to start with at least a unified vision and have a system in place that enables the teams to communicate, coordinate, and collaborate efficiently and effectively to bring the vision to fruition and improve on the vision through innovation.

While agile team frameworks, including Scrum and Extreme Programming, work well on a small scale, they can lead to chaos when you attempt to scale up. To resolve this issue, the agile community has developed a number of enterprise agile frameworks — systems to help align the efforts of teams working together on a big product and reduce the number of dependencies.

WARNING

Don't confuse enterprise agility with business agility. *Business agility* applies the agile mindset to the entire organization, which is sometimes referred to as "diffusion of IT-based innovations." Business agility deals with all domains, including those outside of product development, such as adaptive leadership, organizational design, human resources (HR) or personnel, and budgeting. This book's focus is on enterprise agility, *not* business agility (but I do include a brief section on business agility near the end of this chapter).

However, for enterprise agility to work in your organization, everyone in the organization must adopt an agile mindset. Otherwise, the traditional management practices that are common in a culture that values predictability and failure avoidance will clash with the agile values of experimentation and innovation. You won't get the full benefit of agile if agile teams are merely doing what they're told.

REMEMBER

Few organizations that consider themselves agile enterprises have the culture and mindset to make that claim. What typically happens is that an organization will have five or six agile teams that practice Scrum, Extreme Programming, Kanban, or Lean Startup. The teams may achieve some degree of success — the organization may produce higher-quality software and the developers may be happier — but until the agile mindset permeates the entire organization, it's not an agile enterprise and will not reap the full benefits of enterprise agility.

TRACING THE RISE OF "ENTERPRISE AGILITY"

After witnessing the success of agile software development teams, people in the agile community began to wonder whether the concept could be scaled to large organizations that develop enterprise solutions. After all, what organization would not want to be more *agile?*

(continued)

(continued)

But large organizations aren't designed to be nimble. As much as everybody celebrates disruptive entrepreneurship, being big has its rewards. Large organizations do a lot of interesting work, and there are real advantages to their size, scale, and deliberation. Most of these organizations focus on steady incremental improvements. The challenge is to help such organizations reap the benefits of agile without losing the benefits of being big.

Enter, enterprise agility. As agile software development was hitting its stride around 2007, the agile community started talking about how to put fast-moving agile teams into larger, more established organizations by "scaling agile." Two early books on the topic were *Scaling Software Agility: Best Practices for Large Enterprises* by Dean Leffingwell (2007) and *Scaling Lean & Agile Development: Thinking and Organizational Tools for Large-Scale Scrum* by Craig Larman and Bas Vodde (2008). At about the same time, Scott Ambler had introduced his Agile Unified Process, but he has since stopped working on it to work on Disciplined Agile Delivery (DAD).

However, the notion of scaling was never accurate. Scaling an agile team would turn the team into a lumbering hippopotamus instead of an agile cheetah. A more effective and realistic solution is to find the sweet spot between fast-moving teams and the slow, deliberate enterprise. At the same time organizations were looking to become more agile, the role of enterprise software in an organization's success was growing, so large organizations needed their software development teams to become more agile. Yet, they needed a buffer zone between agile and the rest of the enterprise.

Enterprise agile transformations created a whole new genre of articles, books, and consultants. In a few short years, the number of people who changed their LinkedIn profile to "agile coach" went from hundreds to tens of thousands as the demand for experts who could help large enterprises navigate their transformation to enterprise agility soared. Many of the authors of these scaling agile ideas started to create their own enterprise agile frameworks. These frameworks proliferated like diet and exercise programs, and large organizations couldn't get enough of these pre-packaged solutions.

These frameworks were so enticing that by 2016 nearly half of all enterprise agile transformations were using (or actively considering) an enterprise agile framework. Just a little over a quarter were considering building their own. The little over a half that were using an enterprise agile framework generally settled for one of the top five frameworks I cover in this book: Scaled Agile Framework® (SAFe®), Large-Scale Scrum (LeSS), Disciplined Agile Delivery (DAD), the Spotify Engineering Culture, or Kanban and Lean.

Even when organizations try to build their own enterprise agile frameworks, they often rely on one of these pre-packaged frameworks as a template. So, while there is no standard enterprise agile framework, a consensus is forming around a standard set of ideas.

Checking out popular enterprise agile frameworks

Just as agile has several different frameworks for structuring the way teams function, enterprise agility has a selection of frameworks that provide direction for how teams work together on enterprise solutions. Currently, about a dozen well-established frameworks are available, and each one takes a different approach. Collectively, these methodologies form a cafeteria of ideas from which organizations can choose based on the organization's existing culture and the culture it wants to establish moving forward.

Following are five of the most popular frameworks:

- **Disciplined Agile Delivery (DAD):** A *process decision framework*, DAD encourages you to make certain choices at different points in product delivery, but doesn't prescribe any specific process to follow to make your organization agile. Instead of prescribing a process, it offers general guidance such as, "Here are the goals, and here are a few approaches for meeting each of those goals, and here's some guidance to help you choose the best approach." You're free to choose any framework and practices to mix and match, or create your own. (See Chapter 6 for details.)
- **Large-Scale Scrum (LeSS):** A framework that contains many of the elements familiar in Scrum at the team level, including sprint planning, backlogs (prioritized lists of work items), sprints (the basic unit of development that results in an iteration of the product), daily sprint meetings, and a sprint retrospective (a sort of post-mortem meeting). The primary distinction between LeSS and Scrum is that with LeSS, you have several teams working in different "lanes" on different sprints, sometimes coordinating and collaborating between lanes. (See Chapter 5 for details.)
- **Lean Product Delivery:** A system for reducing waste in products and processes by eliminating anything that's unnecessary, including excessive steps (in a process) and functionality (in a product) that don't bring value to a customer. The focus is on minimizing waste and maximizing value. (See Chapter 8 for details.)
- **Kanban:** A system in which team members pull work items from a list of prioritized items on a Kanban board to work on them as their capacity allows. Kanban (signal) cards are used to indicate when a work item is ready for the next stage in the process. A buildup of Kanban cards in any stage of the process signals a bottleneck that must be addressed. The emphasis is on maintaining a smooth and continuous workflow. (See Chapter 8 for details.)

- **Scaled Agile Framework (SAFe):** A collection of frameworks, principles, and practices that attempts to combine the best of top-down management with the best of agile. Teams work together as teams of teams (called "agile release trains," or ARTs) and as teams of teams of teams (called "solution trains") to achieve the enterprise's vision. SAFe is one of the more complex frameworks, adding numerous processes, layers, roles, and tools to solution delivery. (See Chapter 4 for details.)
- **Spotify Engineering Culture:** A mashup or composite of agile frameworks and practices that's anchored by a strong culture of mutual respect, trust, and innovation. Teams (called "squads") and teams of teams (called "tribes") are encouraged to experiment freely, release products frequently, and tweak their products and processes for continuous improvement. Failure is not punished, and learning from failure is revered to encourage squads to experiment. (See Chapter 7 for details.)

Practicing as much agile as your organization can tolerate

The downside of some of these enterprise agile frameworks, with the exception perhaps of DAD and the Spotify Engineering Culture, is that they try to "productize" your transformation. (To *productize* is to take a concept like agile and turn it into a pre-packaged solution.) It's like getting a suit off the rack when you really need something that's tailored to your organization.

The suit off the rack isn't really how most enterprise agile transformations are done. There won't be a day when you cross the agile finish line. Your organization will never reach an agile end state. Instead, much like a fitness program, you try to integrate these new ideas into the way you already work. It is a long process of small adjustments and continuous improvement, which is why you should think of your enterprise agile transformation as your organization accepting as much agile as it can tolerate. It's about how well your organization accommodates change.

TIP

Before you even think about where you want to be on the agile scale, look at where you are. How much change can your organization tolerate? Think of it almost like a room in which you can only put so much furniture. If your organization can tolerate only small changes, then think of the highest priority agile practices that you can try to implement.

WARNING

Don't try to go too big too soon. Many enterprise agile frameworks require that you make several big changes simultaneously. The hope is that if your organization can tolerate big changes, you can quickly reap the benefits of your transformation. However, your organization will likely snap back if you try to make too many big changes too quickly, especially if your organization has a low change tolerance. Consider a more gradual approach — starting with a few teams, reviewing the results, and then building on your success. Build the desired culture in one small corner of your organization and, if successful, it will spread, as long as you remove any obstacles.

REMEMBER

Large organizations usually have a change tolerance — how much change they can stomach without too much grumbling. If you exhaust everybody's ability to change, transformation is likely to grind to a halt. Everyone will go on working, but don't expect any more progress in the change department.

CASE STUDY

A FAILED ATTEMPT

I once worked for one of the largest retailers in the United States. Its business was centered around home improvement and construction. The way it worked made it one of the fastest-growing companies in the world. It wasn't a high-tech business, but it needed technology as a way to improve the organization.

The solution it decided on consisted of replacing all managers in the information technology (IT) department with managers from high-tech businesses. One of the first changes these managers wanted to make was to transform the retailer into an agile enterprise.

The organization was filled with project managers and business analysts, many of them with construction backgrounds, who approached software as they would any other construction project. They were used to a detailed plan, and it was their job to make sure there were no surprises. They valued predictability over innovation.

When the new managers introduced enterprise agility, the business analysts and project managers thought that it sounded like a plan for total chaos, but they didn't want to be singled out as the resident foot-draggers. After all, the organization just removed a lot of its long-time IT managers. Instead, they made a series of symbolic changes. They changed their titles to make them sound more like agile roles, and they stood during meetings. They didn't make any substantive changes. After a few years, the frustrated IT managers drifted off to jobs at different organizations, and the organization ran as it always had.

The moral of this story is this: If you want to make any major changes to an enterprise organization, you need to change minds first.

Achieving Enterprise Agility in Three Not-So-Easy Steps

The best way to implement enterprise agility in your organization is to take the following three steps:

1. Review the top enterprise agile frameworks.
2. Identify your organization's existing culture.
3. Create a strategy for making big changes.

REMEMBER

This three-step process isn't really unique to enterprise agile transformations; it's pretty standard for making any large-scale organizational changes. You want to better understand the changes you're proposing, then understand the environment in which you're making the changes, and finally figure out how to apply these changes to your environment.

Step 1: Review the top enterprise agile frameworks

The first step toward an enterprise agile transformation is to understand what being agile means and get a sense of what different manifestations of agile look like. The fact is that you can achieve enterprise agility in an infinite number of different ways, just as you can use different health and fitness programs, mix-and-match programs, or develop your own program to become healthy and fit.

A great way to start is to look at the top enterprise agile frameworks I describe in Part 2: SAFe, LeSS, DAD, the Spotify Engineering Culture, Kanban, and Lean. Collectively, they provide several frameworks and include numerous agile principles and practices. Simply by exploring the different frameworks, you will start to develop a more agile mindset and begin to appreciate the full scope of enterprise agility.

TIP

As you explore the enterprise agile frameworks in Part 2, try to look beyond each framework to understand the rationale behind it. If you can understand what the developers of each framework were thinking and the problems they were trying to solve, you will be well on your way to making the right decisions and choices for your organization. Remember, pulling a framework off the shelf may work fine, but be open to the possibility of tailoring it to your organization. No framework is a one-size-fits-all solution.

Step 2: Identify your organization's existing culture

One of the biggest reasons organizations fail in their transformation effort is that they don't take their existing culture into account. The problem is worst when an organization with a firmly embedded traditional management matrix tries to become more agile, because strong management tends to clash with some of agile's emphasis on self-organizing teams.

Organizations don't intentionally ignore culture. They're just so immersed in it that they no longer notice it. Culture is sort of like the air that surrounds us; we don't notice the air until a cold front sweeps in. We don't notice culture until it comes in contact with another culture, at which point cultural differences become readily apparent. You may not notice your organization's culture until you try to change it to something that's very different.

I don't want you to make the common mistake of ignoring your existing culture, so I encourage you to size up your culture before attempting to transform it. Following are four common corporate culture types:

- **Collaboration culture:** Common in schools and professional training organizations, collaboration cultures are run like family businesses, with leaders acting as decision-makers, team builders, and coaches. Managers work closely together like a small group of friends, and the closer you are to the head of the organization, the more authority you have. These organizations are typically more open to change than those with a control or competence culture, so they tend to adopt an enterprise agile mindset more readily. However, in a collaboration culture, leadership may have a difficult time allowing decisions to be made at the team level.
- **Competence culture:** Those with the highest level of expertise rise to the top, become managers, and create and delegate tasks. A meritocracy. The management style is task-driven; it's all about who can do the best job at finishing the work. People in competence cultures often become highly specialized in their areas of expertise, because expertise is what is valued and rewarded. If they excel in more than one area, they're likely to be given too many tasks and become quickly overwhelmed, so they specialize. They also don't like to share their knowledge, because it places them at risk of losing some of their authority.
- **Control culture:** This culture is authoritarian with alpha managers setting the direction and beta managers following close behind. Leadership gives orders and demands compliance. Only a few individuals in the organization have

decision-making powers; others must seek approval or permission, making the organization slow to respond to change. Such organizations favor order and certainty and rely on large management systems that ensure predictable outcomes.

- **Cultivation culture:** Employee growth and development form the cornerstone of the organization. Managers seek to bring someone into the organization, hold them up, and then build them up. Charismatic individuals quickly rise to the top, and generalists commonly do well. These organizations tend to be more democratic and transition more easily to an agile mindset, but decision-making can be slow as consensus is sought among large groups of individuals.

TIP

Consider choosing a framework that's a closer match to your current culture than a match to the culture you want for your organization, so the transformation won't be too much of a stretch. Some frameworks are much more agile than others. For example, Spotify's approach gives teams a lot of autonomy, and that may strike you as the way you want your organization to be. However, Spotify's approach works for Spotify, because it's not a huge organization. Spotify has nurtured a collaborative culture from its inception, and the company redesigned its product's architecture to make it more modular, so a squad can work on one feature without having to integrate its work with a lot of other squads and tribes. If your organization has a strong control culture, making the leap to Spotify's approach may be as challenging as trying to jump across the Grand Canyon on a motorcycle.

Instead, SAFe may be the better choice, because it has more practices for top-down decision-making. It allows for some agility while giving managers deep insight and control over the organization.

REMEMBER

An organization may fit into more than one category; for example, its engineers may be driven more by a competence culture, whereas marketing is run more in line with a cultivation culture.

The famous management consultant Peter Drucker once said that "Culture eats strategy for breakfast." This holds true for enterprise agility. Whatever strategies you pick for your enterprise agile transformation, they won't succeed without the support of a culture that values people, respect, trust, and innovation.

CASE STUDY

POOR CHOICE, POOR OUTCOME

I once worked for an organization with a strong competence culture. Management consisted of engineers who were easily persuaded by other engineers. Everyone worked hard to lock up his own expertise. Individuals knew their competence increased their standing and authority in the organization.

This competence culture made working in teams difficult. Everyone wanted to be a superhero and show that he or she was who carried the rest of the team. No one wanted to collaborate or share information with the other team members. Nobody cross-trained; people simply learned more about what they already knew. On top of that, everyone was working long hours to show his commitment to the product. In the end, leaders had to abandon their agile transformation. They couldn't create the kind of collaborative teams they needed to improve the product.

They would have had a better outcome if they had tried something like Kanban, which would have allowed them to track their workflow and introduce the value of collaboration more subtly. Such an approach also would have helped them visualize their workflow and begin to realize how much time they were wasting by not cross-training people.

Step 3: Create a strategy for making big changes

As you think about your strategy for making big changes, look for the sweet spot between your organization's acceptable and unacceptable change, as shown in Figure 1-1. Finding that sweet spot is more art than science. Identify areas you want to change and areas where you're likely to encounter resistance. Try to understand *why* you may encounter resistance in certain areas. Your organization probably has gravitated toward a particular culture for good reasons, so you can decide whether and how an area needs to be changed. If a certain area is less agile for good reason, you may want to let it be.

After you've found your sweet (and not so sweet) spots, you're ready to start adopting the agile frameworks, processes, and principles you choose.

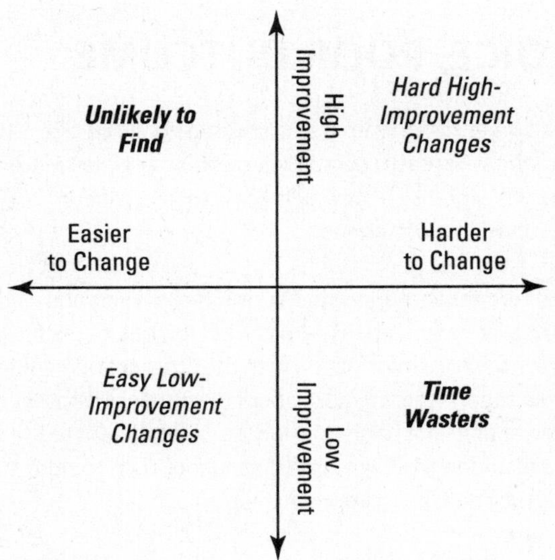

FIGURE 1-1: The change sweet spot.

Choosing a top-down or bottom-up strategy

When you're ready to start your enterprise agility adoption journey, you basically have two big-change strategies from which to choose:

- **Fearless Change:** A bottom-up approach, which can be driven by a few employees. Fearless Change tends to work better in competence, cultivation, and collaboration cultures. Fearless Change may also be effective in smaller, newer organizations that don't yet have a deeply entrenched hierarchy.
- **Kotter approach:** An eight-step, top-down process driven by a change leader, who can be a manager or an outside consultant. The Kotter approach tends to work better in control cultures — the most common culture in large organizations, which typically have a well-defined hierarchy.

See Chapter 10 for more about these two options.

TIP

Whichever strategy you choose, look for opportunities to make smaller, realistic changes. Instead of trying to force change on your organization all at once, win the war gradually, battle by battle. Pick the low-hanging fruit. Giving teams shared workspaces and providing agile training can get the culture ball rolling. Then, build on the momentum of your success.

Mapping out your plan

After you've thought about which approach is likely to work best, map out your plan. As you develop your change management plan, you're likely to end up with an odd combination of general and specific. You'll have specific deadlines of when to expect real improvement. Maybe you'll have a concrete objective to have all your business analysts sit with your team in a shared workspace. But then you'll have general guidelines on how to reach that objective. You may decide to have everyone in that shared workspace receive coaching on the benefits of sitting together. You could also just make it a simple matter of rearranging desks.

This combination of specific and general guidance gives your plan enough structure to be useful, but enough flexibility to allow teams to adapt. No change management plan will survive implementation; that is, your plan will change as you implement it, and that's okay. The trick is to spend just enough time planning to make your organization more agile, but not so much that you steal away time from the implementation or make your plan so restrictive that it undermines the agile mindset.

Setting the stage for business agility

A growing movement among businesses is to extend enterprise agility from product delivery to the entire organization in order to achieve *business agility.* This movement is really about "agile management" — taking agile ideas that have worked well for product development and using them to run an entire organization. Business agility is about "agilizing" every part of your organization.

The best way to think about the relationship among agile, business agility, and enterprise agility is to look at them as three levels of agile implementation (see Figure 1-2):

- **Agile (at the team level):** You have one-or-two agile teams working on a part of a larger product. In Chapter 2, I introduce you to the various frameworks, principles, and practices that drive agility at the team level, such as Scrum and Extreme Programming.
- **Business agility:** The entire organization adopts an agile mindset and a set of agile principles that guide the way everyone works independently and together.
- **Enterprise agility:** You have dozens or hundreds of agile teams working in concert on a single large product — an enterprise-level product. Some enterprise agile frameworks are simply expansions of team agile approaches; for example, SAFe is Scrum only with more Scrum teams and additional roles and structure to coordinate their work.

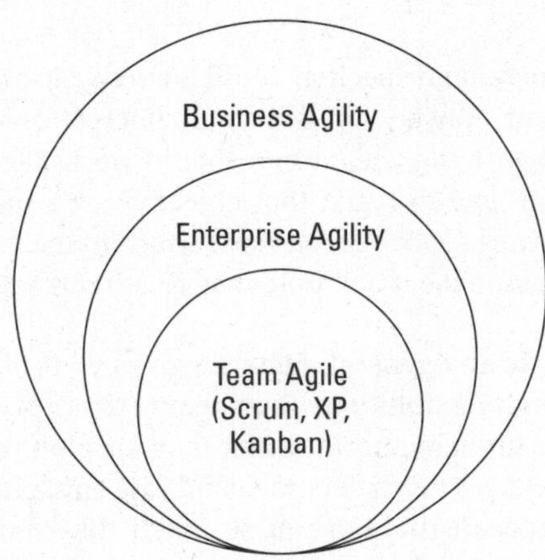

FIGURE 1-2: The three levels of agility.

In general, business agility deals with all domains, including those outside of product development, such as adaptive leadership, organizational design, and budgeting. While the more robust frameworks, including SAFe, touch on these domains, they offer little guidance to help you extend agile into these domains. It's a little like old maps that put dragons in place of uncharted territory with the caption "there be dragons here." They suggest that agility involves changes in other domains, but they don't explicitly describe the changes or offer guidance on how to make those changes.

WARNING

Resist the urge to tackle all three circles at once. Start with a few agile teams. After finding success with those teams, try enterprise agility with a larger product. As you gain success with several teams working together to deliver a whole enterprise solution, you can begin to start thinking about using agile methodologies to rework your entire organization. Don't try to rework your whole organization until you have a proven strategy for delivering enterprise-level products.

REMEMBER

Enterprise agility is *not* business agility. Enterprise agility is about delivering product. All the changes that you make to your organization in terms of frameworks, roles, processes, and practices should sit neatly within the realm of product development. Any changes you make to the overall organization or to organizational leadership will be in the realm of culture and mindset — to make management more receptive to an agile mindset and supportive of the big changes you're introducing to product delivery. Stay focused on delivering better products and not on creating a better organization. Certainly, success in product delivery may lead to an expansion of agile to the entire organization, but start with product delivery and work your way up.

You may find it strange to use practices that were designed for software development to run domains such as human resources, sales, marketing, or legal, but advocates of business agility argue that the accelerating pace of change demands that the entire organization become agile.

Practicing shuhari

Many of the agile and enterprise agile frameworks are influenced by Japanese manufacturing models developed to minimize waste and optimize workflow. Another common agile practice that comes from the Japanese is *shuhari*, a martial arts model of learning and honing one's skills:

- **Shu:** Follow the rules and learn the basics.
- **Ha:** Start to break the rules and put your own learning in context.
- **Ri:** Create your own rules and find your own way.

As you transition your organization's product delivery to enterprise agility, follow the shuhari approach. Here's how:

- **Shu:** Explore the top enterprise agility frameworks, principles, and practices to gain knowledge and wisdom of the commonly accepted approaches to enterprise agility. In other words, learn from the masters.
- **Ha:** Start thinking about how these approaches to enterprise agility would look in your organization. Think about them in the context of what's already in place and in the context of your organization's existing culture. What ideas make sense to you? Where do you think the developers may be wrong? Which ideas are likely to work well (and not so well) in your organization?
- **Ri:** Using all the knowledge and wisdom you've acquired, create your own custom framework tailored to your organization. Adopt the principles and practices that work best for your organization, mix and match, modify, and create your own.

REMEMBER

No two organizations are identical, and none of the enterprise agile frameworks is a one-size-fits-all solution. Use what works, toss what doesn't, and keep your eye on the prize — delivering value to your customers while achieving your business goals. That's what agile is all about.

» Getting up to speed on agile team frameworks, including Scrum and XP

» Improving workflow transparency and management with Kanban

» Launching new products with Lean Startup

Chapter 2
Reviewing Agile Team Practices and Frameworks

Before you can begin to scale agile practices and frameworks to the development of enterprise software, you need to understand what agile is all about on a smaller scale — the agile team. All enterprise agile frameworks, including the five covered in Part 2, are built on the foundation of agile teams, the principles that guide them, and the practices they engage in.

In this chapter, I bring you up to speed on agile team practices and frameworks, including Scrum, Extreme Programming, Lean Software Development, and Kanban. By developing an understanding of agile at the team level, you'll be better prepared to understand the scaled-up frameworks presented in Part 2.

Exploring Common Agile Practices

Most of this chapter introduces you to the common agile frameworks, the most popular of which are Scrum, Extreme Programming (XP), Lean Software Development, Kanban, and Lean Startup. An *agile framework* is a method for working collaboratively and creatively in small teams to develop products incrementally as opposed to doing a lot of up-front planning. Although each of these frameworks is different, they all share common practices, such as writing user stories and epics, estimating size through the use of planning poker or affinity estimation, managing workflow to eliminate bottlenecks, and eliminating waste (such as unproductive meetings and having to wait for management approval).

By understanding these practices, you'll be better prepared to approach the discussions of the various agile frameworks presented in the later sections.

REMEMBER

These practices may or may not be a part of any given agile framework, but are common practices among agile teams regardless of which framework they follow. For example, Scrum doesn't require or recommend user stories, but most Scrum teams start their product development by writing user stories.

Starting with user stories, epics, and themes

As I explain in Chapter 1, a *user story* is a description of a product feature from the user's perspective; for example, "As a mobile phone user, I need to know whether the cell signal is strong enough so that I'm sure to have a clear conversation when I place the call." The most common format for user stories is this:

> As a <user type>, I want <some goal> so that <some reason>.

The last part of the user story is actually the most important, because it describes the pain point the product needs to address and indicates the value that the feature must deliver to the customer. In the example of the mobile phone user, what's most important to the user is that the cell signal is strong enough to support a clear conversation. The user story is general enough to give the developers room to come up with various ways to deliver this value to the user. For example, the developers may decide to display bars or dots on the screen to indicate signal strength, they may tweak the software to improve the audio compression, or they may even develop a better way for the phone to lock in a signal.

REMEMBER

The purpose of a user story is to spark a conversation about *how* to meet that need and deliver value to the customer. Prior to user stories, developers were given well-defined software requirements that ended conversations and stifled innovation. Management told the developers what to do and how to do it. With user stories, customers tell developers *what* they want, and the developers determine *how* to deliver it. The developers may deliver what the customer wants in ways that the customer and management never would have imagined.

In addition, user stories get customers more involved in the product development process, because they enable customers to describe what they want without having to know anything about the technology.

WARNING

Don't confuse a user story with a *use case*, which is a much more detailed description of how the user interacts with the software and how the software behaves and interacts with other systems. While user stories are often one or two sentences written on an index card, a use case is typically a page or more of functional requirements. Perhaps more important, user stories are intended to start conversations, whereas use cases tend to shut them down.

CASE STUDY

A TERRIBLE WAY TO APPROACH USER STORIES

I once worked for an organization that was just getting started with user stories. The product owner, a former business analyst, was put in charge of creating all the user stories. The organization had a 40-page list of software requirements, so he just copied and pasted the bullet points from that document into fields in a spreadsheet and added labels off to the side: "As a," "I want," and "so that."

It was the worst of both approaches. It had neither the coherence of a requirements document nor the conversational language of a user story. The spreadsheet items left nothing open to discussion. The product owner wasn't interested in having a conversation; he was just looking for a quick way to clear that task off his desk. He was doing the opposite of what the Agile Manifesto promoted by putting "tools and processes" over "individuals and interactions."

When creating user stories, avoid the urge to save time by transforming requirements into user stories. You're usually better off starting from scratch with customer input.

A couple terms related to user stories are *epics* and *themes:*

- **Epic:** A big user story; for example, "As the owner of an appliance repair shop, I need to automate my inventory system so that I always have the parts available to complete a repair."
- **Theme:** A collection of related user stories, such as all user stories related to inventory management or all user stories related to producing monthly reports.

Estimating with story points

Instead of following a detailed plan and schedule to deliver product, agile teams work to continually create product iterations that gradually integrate more and more value into the product. For example, a team may start with a list of user stories, prioritize that list, and then work in two- to three-week time blocks to complete each story. Instead of a detailed plan, agile teams work off of something that looks more like a to-do list. Instead of using milestones or deadlines that are often subject to change (because nobody knows exactly how long certain work items will take to complete), agile teams use various collaborative estimation techniques to give ballpark estimates that reflect the relative sizes of work items, such as the following:

- **Animal sizing:** I often recommend agile teams go to a toy store and purchase a deck of cards with animal pictures on them, such as horses and ducks, so that they focus less on trying to score jobs and more on using the cards to open up a discussion of what each job entails. Animal sizing is similar to using a Fibonacci sequence; using animal pictures instead prevents the team from focusing on numbers. Some teams are tempted use Fibonacci numbers as days or hours. The animals keep your team focused on sizing.
- **Big, uncertain, and small:** For super-fast estimation, consider using three categories of work — big jobs, small jobs, and uncertain jobs that are tough to estimate because they may have uncertainties that can result in delays.
- **Fibonacci sequence:** A *Fibonacci sequence* is a series of numbers in which each number is the sum of the preceding two numbers (for example, 1, 2, 3, 5, 8, 13, and 21). These numbers represent level of effort, not hours or days. A two is roughly twice as difficult as a one. And eight is roughly four times as difficult as a two.
- **T-shirt sizing:** Agile teams may use T-shirt sizes, such as XS (extra-small), S (small), M (medium), L (large), XL (extra-large), and XXL (extra-extra-large).

REMEMBER

However you choose to rank items, keep in mind that ranking reflects more than just the estimated amount of time required to complete a job. Rankings should consider the amount of work, complexity of work, coordination of any external dependencies, the risk or uncertainty involved (which may result in delays), and the time/duration.

Agile teams use a variety of estimation techniques, including the following:

- **Affinity mapping:** The team groups items that are similar in whatever dimension they choose, such as degree of difficulty, duration, or uncertainty. After grouping the items, the team can then assign a number or other size designation to each group.
- **Bucket system:** The team creates a number of "buckets" to represent difficulty levels. Then the team assigns relative estimates to these buckets. You could use 0, 1, 2, 3, 4, 5, 8, 13, 20, 30, 50. Someone selects a work item randomly from the stack of work items that need to be completed, reads it to the group, and sticks it in the middle bucket. In this case, the bucket with the number 5. The team estimates the remaining items relative to the middle bucket while discussing the placement with other team members. The team then does a "sanity check," where team members can discuss any disagreements they have over placements and reach consensus on the placement of all items. The bucket system is fast, and it's a great technique to use when you have a considerable number of work items.
- **Planning poker:** Everyone on the team has a stack of playing cards with numbers on them that indicate the relative difficulty of a work item. Each person chooses a card, and then everyone flips his card over when the facilitator gives the signal. If all "scores" match, that becomes the estimate for the work item. If the cards have different scores, team members explain the reasons for their scores, and voting repeats until the team reaches consensus or has bid three rounds without converging (in which case the work item is set aside for further refinement). The most important factor is the rapid learning (from each other) that takes place during these discussions.

  Most agile teams use a deck with a modified Fibonacci sequence. This typically has a number sequence, such as 0, ½, 1, 2, 3, 5, 8, 13, 20, 40, 100. (The sequence is close to being exponential in order to reduce disagreement; getting a group to decide between a 5 and an 8 is easier than getting them to agree between 7 and 8.) Each person usually has a card with a question mark and another with a coffee cup that are to be used sparingly to indicate uncertainty or to ask for a break.

THE BIRTH OF PLANNING POKER

A year after the release of the Agile Manifesto, James Grenning wrote a paper describing a practice he called "planning poker." Grenning based his technique on a much earlier technique called Wideband Delphi, which involved a panel of experts who were forced to give their opinions on a subject before they could hear from the other experts. Prior to sharing their thoughts, each expert wrote his or her opinion on a sheet of paper. Then a facilitator presented everyone's ideas to the group. The idea of Wideband Delphi and planning poker is to allow people to express their honest opinions without being influenced by the opinions of others.

Whatever technique you use, approach it more as a group discussion technique. Don't push for consensus on a number at the expense of having a good discussion. And don't promote an average of the scores. Teams create bad estimates when they don't have a shared understanding of what it takes to deliver the story. It's that shared understanding that's the most important part of any estimation technique.

The purpose of planning poker and other agile estimation techniques is to limit any bias that may influence the estimates. Group decision-making often suffers from the following sources of bias:

- **Anchoring:** The group supports the first opinion expressed by someone in the group who has a strong personality. That first opinion serves as an anchor that makes it difficult for anyone else to change direction, because in order to do so, members must first prove that the opinion expressed is wrong.
- **Dunning-Kruger effect:** The loudest person in the group — who's usually wrong — drives the group's decision. David Dunning and Justin Kruger, two social scientists, found that the people who are wrong typically have the strongest opinions and are most vocal in expressing them. The people who are quieter and less confident are more likely to be correct.
- **Groupthink:** To avoid the messiness of confrontation, people refrain from expressing their honest opinion, because they think it will lead to conflict.

Estimation techniques, including planning poker and the bucket system, require that all members give an opinion without knowing what their other team members think. Team members with strong opinions or those who are more vocal than the others can still drive the team in a certain direction, but at least the discussion begins with less biased views.

CASE STUDY

A BOTCHED ATTEMPT AT ESTIMATION

I once worked for an organization that struggled with estimates. The teams would go from completing 30 story points over a certain time frame to completing 80 over the same time frame.

I asked to sit in on one of their estimation sessions. The first thing I noticed is that they completely neglected the group discussion part of the process. The facilitator would present a user story and then ask one developer for her estimate. The facilitator would say something like, "Sally, you're our lead testing developer; how long do you think it'll take to complete the story?" Then she would give an estimate that was higher than what she thought, so she'd have a buffer in case she was wrong.

When the time came to present their work, they only had about half of the stories completed with the other half partially completed. They pushed the partially completed items into the next few weeks, and because those items were already half done, their story-point completion for those few weeks soared. This pattern repeated with alternating three-week periods of very low and very high numbers of story points being delivered.

Queuing up work

Every agile framework employs queueing theory to manage workflow. (*Queueing theory* is the mathematical study of how items move through a sequential system.) The idea is to reduce bottlenecks that often result when you try to push large batches of items through production. To improve workflow and reduce cycle times (the time to complete work items), agile teams try to create batches of work that are uniform in size and can be completed over the course of a single production cycle (which is why they employ estimation techniques, such as those described in the previous section).

Although different agile frameworks approach queuing in different ways, they typically start with a *product backlog* (a prioritized list of items that must be completed to deliver the product). They draw items from the top of the product backlog to create a list of items that the team is reasonably sure it can complete within the given time frame, and then the team uses a system, such as a Kanban board, to track work in progress. As I explain in Chapter 1, a Kanban board has several columns that represent stages in the development process, such as "To Do," "In Progress," and "Done." A description of each item is written on a sticky note or index card and placed in the first column, and then as the team works on and completes the item, it moves the note or card to the next column. (For more about Kanban, see Chapter 8.)

Conducting stand-up meetings

To reduce the time wasted in unproductive meetings, agile teams usually conduct daily 15-minute meetings in which all team members stand around in a circle to sync up with each other and coordinate their game plan for the next 24 hours. They stand to reinforce the notion that these meetings must remain brief and crisp, just enough to make sure everyone is "on the same page" together. Traditionally, team members may use a round-robin approach and take turns addressing questions. (See "Standing up for the Daily Scrum" later in this chapter for more details.)

The daily stand-up meeting is typically conducted in the morning to help transition into the day's work and to avoid interrupting work later in the day. However, it is up to each self-organizing development team to optimize its daily routine by choosing the time slot that works best for it.

Shifting to test-driven development

Agile teams often take a *test-driven development* (TDD) approach to creating new software — writing a test case, designed to fail, that defines an improvement or new function and then writing just enough code to enable the software to pass the tests. The team then *refactors* the code to clarify and simplify the design. TDD encourages developers to think about what the software will accomplish before they begin coding. It also encourages writing lots of tests to improve the quality of the software. A typical test-driven developer will add a test, run the test, write the code, rerun the test, refactor the code, and repeat if necessary.

TDD enables teams to focus solely on developing a product that passes a specific test rather than on the product as a whole, thus increasing productivity and delivering cleaner code that's less buggy. TDD also supports the practice of continuous integration, discussed next.

Developing product iterations through continuous integration

Continuous integration (CI) is the practice of merging code changes into a share repository several times each day to achieve the following two objectives:

- Minimize the duration and effort required to integrate new code into existing software.
- Develop a version of a product (a product iteration) that's suitable for release at any time during the development process.

To understand the concepts of continuous integration and product iterations, compare traditional product development with agile development as they may be applied to building a car. With a traditional approach, developers might start with a wheel and then create a chassis, add a body, and then add seats, a steering wheel, and an engine, as shown in the top of Figure 2-1. In contrast, an agile team may start with a user story that is something like, "As an employee, I need a vehicle, so that I can get to work faster." The team would then set out to create various iterations of a vehicle that would get the employee to work faster than if the employee had to walk, as shown in the bottom of Figure 2-1. The first vehicle may be a skateboard, the next is a scooter, and then a bicycle, a motorcycle, and finally a car. Each iteration would be a fully functioning vehicle.

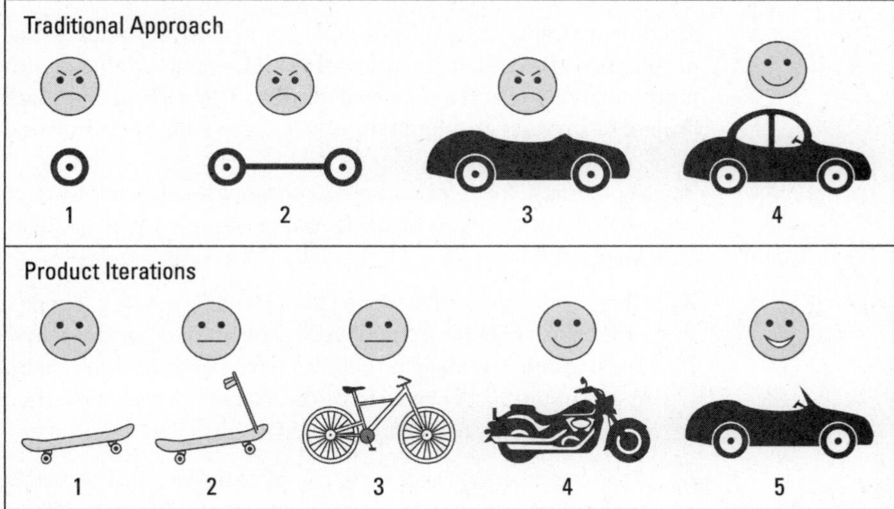

FIGURE 2-1: Delivering in product iterations.

This iterative approach offers many advantages, including the following:

- Every iteration results in a potentially deliverable product.
- The team has many opportunities to inspect and adapt the product over the course of development. Team members could even decide at some point to create a flying vehicle to help the employee avoid traffic.
- The team learns along the way and develops knowledge and skills to improve the quality and value of the product. In this example, by the time the team is working on the motorcycle, it has probably learned a great deal about wheels, structural design, and transportation.
- The customer has the opportunity to opt out at any time; for example, if the customer falls in love with the motorcycle, he may decide that the expense to engineer a car isn't worth it.

Transitioning from a traditional approach to product iterations is often challenging, because it requires transforming the company from one that's organized around functional areas to a team-based, cross-functional model. For example, in a typical organization, marketing may have an idea for a product; developers build the product, and then quality assurance tests it. Many companies have trouble imagining an approach for delivering a smaller version of a completed product with marketing, design, development, and quality assurance all baked in at the team level.

Delivering Products with Scrum

Scrum is a simple, lightweight agile framework for addressing complex evolving problems while delivering innovative high-value products. Although it was originally created for software development, it's a great approach for any complex project or product development effort. Here's how Scrum works:

1. A product owner creates a *product backlog* — a prioritized list of user stories or work items that must be completed to create a potentially deliverable product increment.
2. The Scrum team gathers for a sprint planning meeting, during which it pulls a small batch of items from the top of the product backlog to create a sprint backlog and determine how to complete the items it selected. (A *sprint backlog* is a prioritized list of items to be completed in a given time frame — a *sprint* — which is typically two to four weeks.)
3. Team members collaborate to complete the work in the team's sprint backlog with the goal of creating a potentially deliverable product increment at the end of the sprint.
4. The team members meet with the product owner and other stakeholders for a *sprint review* to discuss the product increment they created and adjust the product backlog, if necessary. The purpose of the sprint review is to discuss what should be done next to optimize value for the customer.
5. The team members gather for a *sprint retrospective*, during which they discuss possible improvements to the way they work together on future sprints. While the sprint review focuses on improving the product, the sprint retrospective is more about improving the process.

WHY "SCRUM"?

The word "scrum" comes from rugby, where it's used to describe the method of restarting play after a stoppage in the game. Team members from each of the opposing teams lock arms to form two packs facing one another. The ball is thrown into the tunnel formed by the two packs, and they push against one another in an attempt to gain control of the ball and advance it toward the opponent's goal.

The developers of Scrum applied the analogy to software development, because they liked the idea of a largely self-managed team, with team members working together with a shared sense of purpose to achieve a common goal. They contrasted it to the traditional method of software development, which was run more like a relay race with the product passing through different stages, such as requirement gathering and analysis, design, coding, testing, deployment, and maintenance. With Scrum, a self-managed, cross-functional team develops software in small increments designing, coding, testing, and deploying throughout the development process.

Wrapping your brain around Scrum theory

REMEMBER

Scrum is an empirical process framework, as opposed to a model framework. "Empirical" means data-driven — gaining knowledge from direct observation and experience and basing decisions on what is known. Instead of engaging in a lot of up-front planning that's often based on conjecture, Scrum teams experiment, inspect, and adapt, relying on empirical data to drive their decisions.

As an empirical process framework, Scrum is built on the three pillars of transparency, inspection, and adaptation, as explained next.

Transparency

One of Scrum's key benefits is that it exposes flaws in your current processes so that you have an opportunity to improve. According to Ken Schwaber, one of Scrum's creators, "Scrum is like your mother-in-law; it points out ALL your faults."

In practice, Scrum encourages team members to be transparent about their work — to freely admit mistakes and point out limitations in products and processes. Scrum teams know they will fail. Instead of trying to avoid failure, they place more value on learning from it.

To promote transparency, Scrum encourages team members to develop a common language when discussing their process and to agree on a *definition of "done"* (DoD) — a set of criteria that must be met for a product to be considered satisfactorily completed. For example, a DoD may state that "done" means a feature has been tested and successfully integrated into a working version of the product.

Inspection

Scrum calls for frequent inspections by skilled inspectors at the point of work (while work is in progress). Inspection focuses on *scrum artifacts* (items created and used during development, such as the product backlog and sprint backlog) and progress toward the sprint goal to detect undesirable variances that need to be addressed.

Scrum teams deliver products incrementally, working iteratively in short cycles to create plenty of checkpoints throughout the development process, thus maximizing opportunities for gathering feedback and adapting processes along the way.

Adaptation

If inspection reveals a deviation in the process that's outside of acceptable limits or that will result in an unacceptable product, the Scrum team makes adjustments as soon as possible to minimize further deviation. Scrum uses four formal inspection and adaptation events to minimize deviation:

- Sprint planning
- Daily Scrum
- Sprint review
- Sprint retrospective

See the section "Stepping through Scrum events" later in this chapter for details.

Getting up to speed on Scrum values

Scrum stipulates five values every Scrum team should embrace:

- **Commitment:** Every team member must be personally committed to achieving the team's goals.
- **Courage:** Team members must have the courage to do the right thing and tackle difficult problems.
- **Focus:** Everyone on the team must focus on the work and on achieving the sprint goal.
- **Openness:** All team members and other stakeholders agree to be open about their work, mistakes, limitations, expectations, and obstacles. Think of openness as transparency at the team level.
- **Respect:** Scrum team members respect and trust one another as capable members of a community.

Working in a Scrum team

Every Scrum team has a product owner, a Scrum Master, and a development team, and every team is *self-organizing* and *cross-functional:*

- **Self-organizing:** Instead of being managed by someone outside the team, the team members decide the best way to accomplish their work.
- **Cross-functional:** The members of each team have all the knowledge and skills to accomplish their work without having to rely on others.

Setting direction with the product owner

In traditional software development, the product owner, typically a business analyst, creates a list of software requirements and then "throws it over the wall" for the development team to deliver. In Scrum, the product owner is an integral member of the team, collaborating with the customer, the Scrum Master, and the development team to optimize value for the customer. The product owner has the following responsibilities:

- **Maximize the value of the product and the work of the development team.** This responsibility is intentionally vague, because how the product manager meets this responsibility varies across organizations.
- **Maintain the product backlog (a prioritized list of work items).** Although the product owner may share product backlog maintenance with the rest of the team, the product owner is ultimately responsible for ensuring the following:
  - Product backlog items are clearly described.
  - Items in the product backlog are arranged to best achieve goals and missions.
  - The product backlog is visible, transparent, and clear to everyone on the team.
  - The development team fully understands each item in the product backlog.
- **Serving as the sole point of contact for the team.** In other words, the product owner prevents anyone else in the organization from assigning work to the team or changing the software requirements. All work items funnel through the product owner to the team.

REMEMBER

The product owner must be one person, not a committee. She may represent a committee's interest in the product, but she ultimately decides what gets passed along to the team. By acting as the single source of authority on the product, the product owner enables the team to make real-time product decisions instead of having to seek management approval, which often introduces delays.

Mastering Scrum with the Scrum Master

The Scrum Master is the team's servant-leader and coach. The term "master" doesn't imply that the Scrum Master is in charge of the team. The Scrum Master is actually in charge of making sure everyone in the organization is aligned with Scrum theory, practices, and rules. Think of her more like a Jedi Master who gets her power from an understanding of the Force. The Scrum Master serves three groups:

- **Development team:** The Scrum Master helps the development team by coaching it in self-organization and cross-functionality, assisting the team in creating high-value products, removing obstacles, facilitating scrum events, and providing additional coaching and training.
- **Organization:** The Scrum Master serves the overall organization by leading, planning, and facilitating Scrum adoption and implementations; suggesting changes within the organization to increase Scrum team productivity; educating leadership and employees on Scrum theory, practices, and rules; and collaborating with other Scrum Masters to make Scrum more effective.
- **Product owner:** The Scrum Master helps the product owner acquire the knowledge, skills, techniques, and tools for more effectively managing the product backlog and clarifying product backlog items to the development team. The Scrum master may also facilitate Scrum events and educate or train the product owner on Scrum theory and practices, including how to plan products in an empirical environment.

REMEMBER

A good Scrum Master spends most of her time training others on the team and across the organization. For example, when a team is just getting started, the Scrum Master may provide training on how to write user stories. The Scrum Master may also attend a stand-up meeting or a session of planning poker to provide feedback on how the team can engage in these agile practices more effectively.

WARNING

Be careful when training project managers to become Scrum Masters, because they often have a traditional management mindset that's counterproductive to the servant-leader role of a Scrum Master.

Getting it done with the development team

The development team consists of three to nine developers (excluding the product owner and Scrum Master) who are in charge of creating a potentially deliverable product increment at the end of each sprint. (The trend is toward smaller development teams, typically four or five.) As mentioned earlier in this chapter, each Scrum team is self-organizing and cross-functional. Nobody, not even the product owner or Scrum Master, tells the development team *how* to do its job.

Although team members may have specialized skills and areas of focus, all team members are referred to as "developers." Teams do not have specialized roles or titles, such as database engineer, user interface developer, back-end developer, or tester. In fact, team members are encouraged broaden their knowledge and skill sets through cross-training. This doesn't mean that every tester will become a skilled developer. What it means is that all people on the team should constantly be developing new skills and increasing their breadth of knowledge. You don't want the work to come to a halt because the only person who knows how to complete a certain task calls in sick.

TIP

Generally, the product owner focuses on *what* gets done, and the development team focuses on *how* it gets done, but the dividing line can get fuzzy. For example, the product owner may have a strong opinion about a certain tool or technology used during the previous sprint and insist that the team use something else. Likewise, the development team may want to work on lower-priority items in the product backlog first, for whatever reason. In such cases, the Scrum Master may step in to help the team reach consensus.

Stepping through Scrum events

Scrum has five events that provide some regularity throughout the product development process while minimizing time spent in meetings:

- **Sprint planning:** A two-part meeting devoted to *what* must get done during the sprint (the first part) and *how* to get it done (the second part).
- **Sprint:** A two- to four-week time frame in which the development team completes its list of work items.
- **Daily Scrum:** Brief daily team meetings to report progress and discuss impediments.
- **Sprint review:** A post-sprint meeting to discuss the current state of the product and what needs to be done in future sprints.
- **Sprint retrospective:** A post-sprint meeting in which the team discusses ways to improve the way the team functions.

All events are time-boxed, meaning each event has a maximum duration. For example, the Daily Scrum has a maximum duration of 15 minutes.

I describe these events in greater detail in the following sections.

TIP

Prioritization is one of the keys to successful use of time boxes. The team focuses on the most important items first. That way, if the team should run out of time, it can be confident that it made the best use of the time box.

Delivering in sprints

Product development occurs over a series of sprints. Each *sprint* is a two- to four-week time box in which a team creates a useable and potentially deliverable product increment. The sprints are all the same length. Within each sprint is a period of sprint planning, Daily Scrums, the development work, the sprint review, and the sprint retrospective. Scrum has several rules that govern a sprint:

- No changes can be made that would compromise the team's ability to meet the sprint goal.
- You can't skimp on quality by easing up on the quality goals.
- The product owner and development team may renegotiate and clarify the scope of the sprint as they learn during the development process.

A product owner may cancel a sprint at any time when pursuing the sprint's goal no longer makes sense (for example, if a change in the market makes a particular feature obsolete). However, sprint cancellations are rare.

Planning a sprint

Prior to each sprint, the Scrum team engages in sprint planning, which is a two-part meeting:

- **Part 1:** The product owner, Scrum Master, development team, and other stakeholders meet to decide which items in the product backlog the team will complete during the sprint. On many Scrum teams, the product owner writes user stories for the work that needs to be completed. The team may perform a quick round of planning poker to get a general idea of how much work it can complete within the sprint. At the end of the first part of the meeting, the development team has a *sprint backlog* — a list of work items it has planned to complete by the end of the sprint.
- **Part 2:** The development team meets to figure out how it will complete its sprint backlog and to determine its higher-level *sprint goal*. The team will usually identify "tasks" (to-do's) for each story, possibly including estimated

hours for each task. The team may use that for an initial "sanity check" on its planned capacity for the sprint. Many teams write their work items on sticky notes or index cards and affix them to a task board that they clear off at the end of each sprint. They may also use a Kanban board (see Chapter 8) to track work in progress.

Standing up for the Daily Scrum

The Daily Scrum is a daily planning meeting for the development team that's time-boxed to 15 minutes. Traditionally, teams stand during the meeting to reinforce the need to keep the meetings short (see the earlier section "Conducting stand-up meetings"). The purpose of this meeting is to enable team members to coordinate their work and to plan for the next 24 hours. During the meeting, members of the development team might take turns answering the following three questions outlined in the official Scrum Guide:

- What did I do yesterday that helped the development team meet the sprint goal?
- What will I do today to help the development team meet the sprint goal?
- Do I see any impediment that prevents me or the development team from meeting the sprint goal?

It is up to each development team to optimize its performance by reflecting and adjusting its practices accordingly. If you were to visit some of the highest performing teams today, you might discover that they have transformed their Daily Scrum agenda. For example, instead of an individualized round-robin check-in, they may "walk the wall" (or Kanban board) together, focusing discussion on their sprint backlog and its stories, rather than team members and their tasks. They'll likely concentrate on work in progress (WIP) first, then touch on the remaining sprint backlog if needed, addressing stories in their prioritized order. For such teams, they'll more likely be thinking and speaking in team- and story-centric terms:

- What did WE do yesterday, to move this STORY forward?
- What are WE going to do today, to get this STORY done?
- What do WE need, versus impediments to OUR progress today?
- What have WE learned that changes how WE move forward?

A fairly common practice for teams is to reserve 25 to 30 minutes for the Daily Scrum, building in a "parking lot" buffer for immediate follow-up. In the first 5 to 10 minutes, they'll walk the wall or board (sprint backlog), "parking" any issues or discussions until they've addressed the stories. Then they'll take up any issues, parking-lot items, or general announcements in the remaining time, adjourning the meeting before their time box expires. After the Daily Scrum, the team or certain team members may have additional meetings to have more detailed discussions on issues raised during the Daily Scrum.

REMEMBER

The Daily Scrum is for development team members. They should be talking *to each other* as peers, not "reporting status" to the product owner or Scrum Master. The Scrum Master's role is only to ensure that the daily meetings are being held and to coach the team on how to have an effective meeting within the 15-minute time box.

Reviewing the sprint

At the end of each sprint is a *sprint review*, during which the Scrum team, customer, and other stakeholders meet to review the product increment delivered at the end of the sprint and determine what must be done to improve the product in future sprints. The time box for a sprint review is generally one hour per week of sprint, so a three-week sprint should have a sprint review that lasts no longer than three hours.

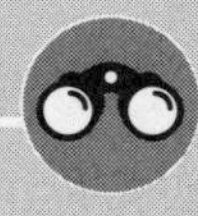
CASE STUDY

A SCRUM REVIEW IS NOT A BEAUTY CONTEST

I once worked for an organization where the Scrum team gave a lengthy sprint demo at the end of every sprint. Instead of a collaborative session with stakeholders, it was just a beauty contest, in which the team showed off all the great things the product could do and talked about how hard it worked during the last sprint to improve the product. The meeting usually ran much longer than the scheduled time box, giving customers little time to ask questions or provide feedback.

After a few sprints, the Scrum team had trouble getting any of the customers to attend. When the Scrum Master followed up with some of the customers, they said that they were too busy to attend the meetings. A few said that they were bored watching the team members celebrate their work every two weeks.

The Scrum Master worked with the product owner to change how the team ran the meeting. They decided to spend more time discussing instead of demonstrating the product. When the customers offered feedback, the team members made sure the product owner followed up with them to show that their ideas had an impact. After a few sprints, the attendance picked up. The customers realized they had a real opportunity to work with the team to develop the product.

Some organizations refer to the sprint review as a sprint demonstration (or "sprint demo" for short), but this term has fallen out of favor, because it implies that the Scrum team is staging a performance to show off the work it has done. However, the purpose of the meeting is to support the three pillars of Scrum: *transparency, inspection, and adaptation*. Ideally, the Scrum team, customer, and other stakeholders discuss what they like and dislike about the product and what they would like to see improved in future program increments.

Improving the process with a sprint retrospective

After the sprint review and before the next sprint planning meeting, the team members perform a *sprint retrospective* to discuss ways to improve their process and work together more effectively as a team. The time box for the sprint retrospective is three hours for a four-week sprint and less for shorter sprints. During the retrospective, the team should:

- Discuss how the sprint went in relation to people, relationships, process, and tools.
- Identify areas that went well and areas for potential improvement, and prioritize the list of improvements to be made.
- Create a plan or list of action items to make improvements; for example, if the team decides it could improve its user stories, members may ask the Scrum Master to schedule a training session.
- Consider ways to improve product quality by adapting the team's definition of "done."

While the sprint review focuses on how to improve the product, the sprint retrospective is more about improving the team and the relationships, processes, and tools used to create the product. The Scrum retrospective is a time for team members to be transparent about their work and to inspect and adapt to improve the way they work together, looking for ways to "raise the bar" — even in the smallest details — again and again.

If a Scrum team works together for several years, members may decide to limit the amount of time they spend on process improvement, but most teams can always find ways to improve. The key is to not just use the meeting as a way to identify challenges, but also use it as a way to make concrete improvements.

Producing Scrum artifacts

Scrum specifies that teams produce the following four artifacts to provide transparency and to support inspection and adaptation:

- **Product backlog:** A prioritized list of work items to be completed to create the product.
- **Sprint backlog:** A prioritized list of work items to be completed over the course of a single sprint to deliver a potentially shippable product increment.
- **Product increment:** A fully functioning rendition of the product.
- **Definition of "done":** A set of requirements that indicate when a product increment is considered finished.

In the following sections, I describe each of these artifacts in greater detail.

Prioritizing the work with a product backlog

The product backlog is an evolving prioritized list of everything that must be done to create a given product, including all features, functions, requirements, enhancements, and fixes in future releases. Changes in customer needs, business requirements, market conditions, technologies, and other factors that impact the product often initiate changes in the product backlog.

REMEMBER

As long as the product exists, its product backlog should continue to evolve and grow to represent an exhaustive list that identifies everything the product needs to be appropriate, competitive, and useful.

Allocate about ten percent of each sprint to refining the product backlog. For a two-week sprint (ten business days), the Scrum Master, product owner, and development team should spend about one day with the customer and other stakeholders to do the following:

- Consider what to add to or remove from the product backlog.
- Clarify items in the product backlog.
- Break down user stories into more manageable work items.
- Reprioritize items in the product backlog.

Although the product owner is ultimately responsible for managing the product backlog, the development team and Scrum Master should be involved along with customers and other stakeholders. The development team may want to do a quick round of planning poker to estimate work items. Refining the product backlog makes the next sprint planning meeting go much more smoothly, because everyone involved will have a clearer idea of the work to be done.

Moving items into a sprint backlog

The sprint backlog is the subset of work items from the product backlog that the team commits (in the first half of the sprint planning meeting) to completing over the course of a single sprint. Typically, all the development team does during the first half of the sprint planning meeting is move items from the top of the product backlog to its sprint backlog. However, team members often must engage in some sort of estimation exercise, such as planning poker, to ensure that they don't commit to completing more work than they can handle over the course of the sprint. The team then uses the sprint backlog to formulate a *sprint goal* — a high-level commitment to the product owner and the rest the organization.

TIP

Consider using a Scrum board, task board, or Kanban board (see Chapter 8) to visualize workflow and provide transparency into work status. These boards are usually columnar, with each column representing a workflow state for work items. A simple board might have three columns, typically labeled "To Do," "Work in Progress," and "Done." Team members write a description of each work item (such as a user story or task) from their sprint backlog on a separate index card or sticky note and arrange them in order of priority in the To Do column. When they begin working on an item, they move the item's card or note to the Work in Progress column, and when they complete their work on the item, they move the card or note to the Done column.

More advanced boards may add cross-cutting rows known as "swim lanes." Each swim lane could represent a level of service such as an expedited lane and a normal lane. Swim lanes can be used to group collections of related work items, like those belonging to a certain feature or product increment.

The team usually updates the board and the sprint backlog in real time, as work flows throughout the day. Some teams do board updates during the Daily Scrum meeting. Either way, the team can literally *see*, in a glance, how close it is to finishing all the work in the sprint backlog. And that's not just for the team members. Everyone with an interest can look and see a near get a real-time update of the team's progress toward reaching its sprint goal. You'll have 24/7 access to unfiltered "status" without having to ask.

TIP

As far as Scrum and Kanban boards go, think big, visible, and always on. You'll want your boards to serve as "information radiators" rather than "information refrigerators." If your teams are tracking work items on the wall, consider hanging a high-res camera over each board and broadcasting live — like traffic cams — on an easily accessible website. On the other hand, if your teams are using an electronic system for tracking, you could increase visibility by putting up a few big-screen displays or lighting up the hallways with live projection displays.

Pumping out product increments

At the end of the sprint, your Scrum team needs to deliver a useable product increment that includes all product backlog items that the team integrated into the product during the sprint. The new increment must conform to the team's definition of "done" (explained next).

Only the product owner can decide when a product is ready for release. The development team may conduct several sprints and produce a series of product increments before the product owner decides that the product is ready to be released to the customer. However, because each sprint delivers a useable product, the customer can decide at the end of any sprint that the product is good enough to meet its needs, in which case the product owner can decide to release it.

Defining "done"

The definition of "done" is a set of requirements that the product must meet in order for it to be considered potentially shippable. For example, a team's definition of "done" may stipulate the following criteria:

- The code has been fully tested.
- The code has been checked back into the continuous integration server.
- More than one person has inspected the code.
- There's no immediate need to make improvements or changes.
- The product increment has cleared an internal review.
- The product has met all regulatory criteria.
- There's no need for further documentation.

Your team should agree on its DoD before starting any work, so everyone on the team can easily tell when the product has achieved shippable status.

During a sprint, a product owner or Scrum Master or one of the members of the development team may express a need to "stop starting and start finishing," which means the team needs to focus more on completing its work in progress than on starting new items. The team can then look to the definition of "done" to figure out what it needs to do next with work in progress (WIP) items to move them to the Done column.

Growing Scrum

Because of Scrum's popularity, Scrum teams are included in nearly all enterprise agile frameworks, which puts the developers of enterprise agile frameworks in a bind. On the one hand, they celebrate the simplicity of Scrum, which is what made it appealing to so many organizations. On the other hand, they must argue that Scrum is not enough so that they can justify the need for a larger framework.

TIP

When you see Scrum included in an enterprise agile framework, ask yourself whether it's really Scrum. Some enterprise agile framers create their own version of Scrum, while others scale up Scrum by adding extra roles and processes. Still others create a new network of different practices as a way to connect several Scrum teams.

Each of these approaches adds a lot of external baggage to a simple framework. Remember that the three pillars of the Scrum framework are *inspection, adaptation, and transparency,* which means that any good Scrum team must use any expanded practices as a way to inspect and adapt. You don't want to add anything that weakens the three pillars. You don't want to grow Scrum to the point where you're losing the advantages of working as a small, self-directed Scrum team.

CASE STUDY

GOING TOO BIG WITH SCRUM

I once worked with an organization that was trying to scale up its Scrum teams to work on an enterprise-level product. They tried to do something called the Scrum-of-Scrums. It was a few layers of added practices that helped several strong teams coordinate their work.

One of the practices they tried was having a Daily Scrum meeting with all the teams. Five Scrum teams (30 people) met for a shared stand-up meeting. They realized they couldn't have a 20-minute meeting with 30 people. So they expanded the meeting to an hour. They also realized that they couldn't have everyone standing for an hour, so they made it a sit-down meeting.

At the beginning of each day, 30 people sat in a room and gave a progress report, which was a total waste of time, because at the end of the meeting, nobody could recall even one of the status reports. They had scaled up their Scrum practice to the point at which it wasn't even recognizable as a Scrum event. They called it Scrum but they weren't getting any of the benefits of working as a small adaptive team.

When you're scaling Scrum, make sure you don't expand it to the point where it's no longer Scrum. Sometimes it's better to start an entirely new process than it is to try to hammer Scrum into a place it may not fit.

Developing Better Software with Extreme Programming

Extreme Programming (XP) is an agile framework that emphasizes collaboration to achieve customer satisfaction. Kent Beck, one of XP's co-creators, describes it as "a style of software development focusing on excellent application of programming techniques, clear communication, and teamwork." Like Scrum, XP builds features into a product through iterations to address the customer's current needs, enabling developers to respond to changes in customer requirements during the development cycle. Like all agile frameworks, XP is built on a team concept with managers, customers, and developers collaborating as equal partners.

In this section, I describe XP's values and practices and explain how many companies combine XP with Scrum to form a hybrid approach to agile.

Checking out XP's values

Like most agile frameworks, XP is driven by a set of values that its practitioners embrace to work in harmony with one another and in alignment with personal and corporate values. Its creators suggest starting with the following five values and adding values to reflect your organization's implementation of XP:

- **Communication:** Developers, customers, and other stakeholders are all part of a team that communicates face-to-face daily and collaborates on everything — from writing user stories to writing code. Communication is a key factor in developing the right solution to any problem.
- **Courage:** XP operates in a culture of transparency, with team members telling the truth about estimates, status, obstacles, and mistakes. Team members don't make excuses or blame others, but instead focus on solving problems. The team fears nothing, because nobody ever works alone.
- **Feedback:** XP calls for short development cycles that produce frequent program iterations, so the team can demonstrate the software early and often and obtain regular feedback.
- **Respect:** Everyone involved in product development does her job in a culture of mutual respect. Developers and customers respect one another, while management respects the team's authority over its own work.
- **Simplicity:** XP is a minimalist approach to programming. Developers are encouraged to "do what is needed and asked for, but no more" to optimize return on investment (ROI). XP programmers should always ask themselves, "What's the simplest thing that could possibly work?" They take small steps and address challenges as they arise.

Following XP's software engineering practices

XP's creators combined XP's values with a dozen practices that the team commits to over the life of the project. Some of these practices are just for the development team, while others include the customer and other stakeholders. Here's a list of XP's software engineering practices:

- **The planning game:** A quick, high-level activity that determines the scope of the next release by discussing business priorities along with technical estimates. The plan is not designed to be written in stone. If something changes, the team should update the plan.
- **Small releases:** Start with a simple system and then build up new versions in smaller future releases. Don't go for a Big Bang product delivery. Instead put something small into production and then look for ways to improve.
- **Metaphor:** Help the development team understand the whole system by creating a shared story of how everything should work together. Use metaphors such as shopping carts, checkout lines, and parking lots to describe complex technical concepts.
- **Simple design:** Don't set out to develop something complex. Instead focus on creating the simplest system and then build in complexity only when absolutely necessary. Always look for ways to remove extra complexity from the system.
- **Testing:** A big part of the programmer's job is to write his own tests, which the product must pass with every update to the system. Customers should also write tests to verify that the features meet their expectations.
- **Refactoring:** Programmers should expect to restructure the program to remove duplication or to simplify or add flexibility to the whole system.
- **Pair programming:** Programmers develop software in pairs, with two programmers in front of a single workstation. One programmer "drives" (writes the code) while the other observes, navigates, makes suggestions, and checks the work. The two switch roles frequently.
- **Collective ownership:** Anyone on the team can change code for the whole system at any one time. Parts of the product shouldn't be hidden or inaccessible to the programming team.
- **Continuous integration:** The team should use a server to automatically integrate new code and build the program several times throughout the day, each time a major task is completed.

Partly because of the influence of XP, most agile teams now use something called a continuous integration server. This server allows the entire team to check in and check out all or parts of a software product in a centralized code repository. The server automates the process of testing the software when you check in any new code. This improves quality by ensuring that changes don't "break the build."

- **40-hour week:** Programming is a creative problem-solving skill. You can't increase productivity by having your team work overtime. No one on the team should work more than 40 hours per week. Never have the team work overtime two weeks in a row.
- **Onsite customer:** The team requires that customers participate with the developers and are available full time to answer questions. They should be part of the team and share some responsibility for delivering the product.
- **Coding standards:** All of the code should be written to help emphasize communication and collaboration. Individuals shouldn't write code that only they can recognize.

Noting the similarities between XP and Scrum

After publication of the Agile Manifesto, XP and Scrum started to become more similar as teams adopted whichever practices worked best for them from the two frameworks and from others. Similarities between XP and Scrum include the following:

- **Continuous integration:** Continuous integration got its start long before XP, but it quickly became an integral part of XP, due to XP's focus on making continuous, incremental improvements to products. Now, continuous integration servers are widely used in nearly every agile framework.
- **Planning poker:** Both XP and Scrum adopted planning poker as a way to estimate job sizes early in their development.
- **Product owner versus customer representative:** While Scrum has a product owner who represents the customer and maintains the product backlog, XP has a customer representative who is much more directive, telling the team what it should work on during the next iteration. Both of these roles own the "what next" prioritization for the team's work.

- **Scrum Master versus XP Coach:** Both XP and Scrum require that every team have a servant-leader coach. Scrum refers to this role as Scrum Master, whereas XP uses the term "XP Coach."
- **Sprints versus iterations:** Both XP and Scrum develop software through a series of short development cycles. Scrum focuses on the cycles themselves (the sprints), whereas XP focuses on the product delivered at the end of each cycle — the program iteration.
- **Test-driven development:** Test-driven development (TDD) has been around since the 1960s, but was given a rebirth in XP, where the manual approach became automated. Now, TDD is common practice among all agile frameworks.
- **User stories:** While XP introduced the user story as part of its planning game, almost all agile teams rely on user stories instead of detailed requirements documents.

The most important distinction between XP and Scrum is that Scrum is a product delivery framework, which means you can use Scrum to deliver products that aren't software. XP is explicitly for software development; it prescribes specific software development practices, such as continuous integration, simple design, and pair programming. Scrum can include these practices but doesn't explicitly require them.

Mixing and matching agile frameworks

Some of the enterprise agile frameworks mix elements from both Scrum and XP. The Scaled Agile Framework® (SAFe®), discussed in Chapter 4, goes one step further and creates its own agile team referred to as ScrumXP — similar to a Scrum team but incorporating many of XP's software engineering practices.

Since the Agile Manifesto, proponents of XP have done a great deal to increase its footprint. In *Extreme Programming Explained: Embrace Change*, Second Edition, Kent Beck includes new sections on the philosophy behind XP and some techniques for scaling. He also ties XP together with the Toyota Production System and Lean Software Development — some of the earlier ideas that led to Kanban and Lean Startup, discussed later in this chapter.

Most of XP's contribution to enterprise agile has been at the team level, because its focus on software development has prevented it from becoming an attractive option for overall organizational change.

Learning from Manufacturing with Lean Software Development

Lean Software Development applies Lean Manufacturing principles and practices, specifically from the Toyota Production System (TPS), to software development, summarizing Lean thinking into four basic values:

- **Add nothing but value:** Always look for ways to eliminate waste ("muda" in Japanese).
- **Center on the people who add value:** Respect everyone and encourage mutual trust.
- **Flow value from demand:** Delay commitment to deliver until you have enough demand.
- **Optimize across organizations:** Always look for ways to improve the entire system. A Lean organization engages in continuous improvement ("kaizen" in Japanese) of processes, practices, personal efficiency, and so on.

In Lean Manufacturing, value is what your customers are interested in buying. Everything else is waste, and all waste needs to be eliminated. In TPS, the seven sources of waste are:

- **Defects:** The need to conduct inspections and address problems or defects
- **Extra processing steps:** System inefficiencies
- **Inventory:** Storing unfinished products
- **Motion:** Unnecessary or inefficient physical movement
- **Overproduction:** Producing more than is needed to serve demand
- **Transportation:** Moving product from one place to another
- **Waiting:** Lack of productive activity primarily due to bottlenecks or interruptions in production

Lean Software Development translates these sources of wastes in manufacturing to the software development process:

- **Defects:** Software defects often introduce inefficiencies, because they require that developers stop what they're doing to address the defects. The problem is worse when defects aren't detected until the very end, because the developer may then need to do a great deal of rework, and problems may be compounded due to dependencies.

- **Extra processing steps:** In software development, extra processing steps are mostly those related to having to relearn a solution to a problem, which can happen when a solution isn't logged or when work is handed off from one developer to another and the learning must also be passed along.
- **Inventory:** Partially done work that just gets in the way or is discarded later because it's no longer needed.
- **Motion:** Inefficiencies in motion are often introduced through hand-offs, where both the work and the training or knowledge needed to complete it must be transferred and through task-switching, where a developer must invest extra time and effort to switch from one task to another.
- **Overproduction:** Unnecessary features.
- **Transportation:** Handoffs between different functional areas in the organization, such as between development and testing, can cause additional delays.
- **Waiting:** Waiting at any stage in the development process; for example, waiting to receive requirements, waiting for approval, waiting for testing to be completed, waiting due to dependency on work done externally.

To help streamline processes and eliminate waste, Lean Software Development uses *value stream mapping* (see Chapter 8) that involves tracing all steps required to deliver value to the customer. Some enterprise agile frameworks refer to value stream mapping as "taking a product from concept to cash." After tracing all steps required to deliver value to the customer, you eliminate any steps that don't bring value, such as unproductive meetings.

STIRRING THE AGILE STEW

Lean Software Development never set out to be a practical method for delivering software like Scrum or XP. It was presented as a set of ideas — a key part of the agile mindset. Recently, Lean thinking has become fully mixed in with the top enterprise agile frameworks covered in Part 2. All of these enterprise agile frameworks have adopted value-stream optimization, improving the whole system, and pushing responsibility and authority to act down to the teams.

Now that the agile stew has been bubbling for years, it's nearly impossible to extract each ingredient to analyze its contribution to the recipe. It's safe to say that Scrum, XP, and Kanban were inspired by Lean Manufacturing, and that Lean Software Development connected the ideas much more closely. As agile moves up to higher levels in the organization, these Lean ideas are reemerging and reasserting themselves. You see them much more expressly laid out in enterprise agility and even at higher levels in overall business agility.

TIP

Even though a lot of enterprise agile frameworks emphasize optimizing customer value and eliminating waste, newer Lean thinking places much more emphasis on continuous improvement and respect for people. Lean Software Development focuses a great deal on empowering the team and amplifying learning.

Managing Workflow with Kanban

Kanban is a method for continually delivering products without overburdening the development team. Team members use a "Kanban board" and cards to track and manage workflow. A very basic Kanban board may have three columns labeled "To Do," Work In Progress," and "Done." Each Kanban card contains a description of a work item. As work is done, team members move the Kanban card for the work item to the column that represents its flow state in the process. (See Chapter 8 for details about creating and using Kanban boards and cards.)

The Kanban method enables team members to pull work through the process as their capacity to complete the work allows instead of having work pushed into the process — an approach that often leads to bottlenecks and increases stress among team members. The Kanban board increases visibility, making it easier for everyone to see the status of work items and to identify backups and delays. Kanban enables teams to break down jobs into smaller work items and smaller batches of items to keep work items moving through the system, rather than trying to tackle big jobs, which often leads to delays.

At the team level, Kanban is an effective way to increase transparency and improve processes. It doesn't require explicit practices, such as iterations, TDD, or user stories. It also doesn't require the creation of additional roles, such as a product owner or Scrum Master. You can use Kanban in any situation in which you need to track work items or tasks, whether you're developing products, managing a help desk, maintaining an editorial schedule, or streamlining hiring practices. Many of the top enterprise agile frameworks covered in Part 2 include a Kanban component for tracking and managing workflow.

TIP

Think of Kanban less as an agile framework and more as a tool that's used within various agile and enterprise agile frameworks to facilitate workflow management and to help coordinate everyone's efforts.

Innovating Quickly with Lean Startup

Lean Startup is about using the Lean mindset to quickly deliver innovative products. The idea behind it is that companies that are just starting out don't have the money to invest in market research and product development. So instead, these companies should focus on quickly getting their product into the customer's hands, gathering and analyzing customer feedback, and adjusting accordingly. Otherwise, the startup is likely to invest a great deal of time and effort to launch a product that customers really don't care about, and the startup fails.

TIP

Although Lean Startup has been developed for small startup companies, many large firms, including General Electric and Intuit, use it to launch new products.

Using a build-measure-learn feedback loop

Lean Startup uses a build-measure-learn feedback loop based broadly on the plan-do-study-act (PDSA) cycle that was originated by Walter A. Shewhart and championed by W. Edwards Deming and influenced Lean Manufacturing, Scrum, and XP:

- **Plan:** Specify objectives
- **Do:** Implement the plan
- **Study:** Gather and analyze data
- **Act:** Adapt your process based on what you learned

The PDSA loop is an empirical process that emphasizes experimentation and evaluation, and you can see its influence on many agile frameworks, including Scrum, Lean Software Development, and XP.

Lean Startup modifies the loop slightly to emphasize learning (see Figure 2-2):

- **Idea:** Your customer has a need and you have an idea to meet that need.
- **Build:** You build a specific solution that has an impact on meeting that need.
- **Product:** You create a *minimum viable product* (MVP) — a product with just enough features to appeal to early adopters.

TECHNICAL STUFF

  Many agile software teams use the MVP model, although they may refer to it as something else, such as a "product increment." In Lean Startup, the MVP offers the most opportunity for validated learning with the least amount of effort. For example, if you were considering opening up a restaurant, you may start with a sandwich stand to test the demand for your sandwiches and to fine-tune your recipe to the consumer's tastes.

- **Measure:** You measure the impact that your product had on your customer.

- **Data:** You create a list, based on your measurements, of actionable data points.
- **Learn:** You compare your data points to the original plan and figure out what you need to change to improve value to the customer.

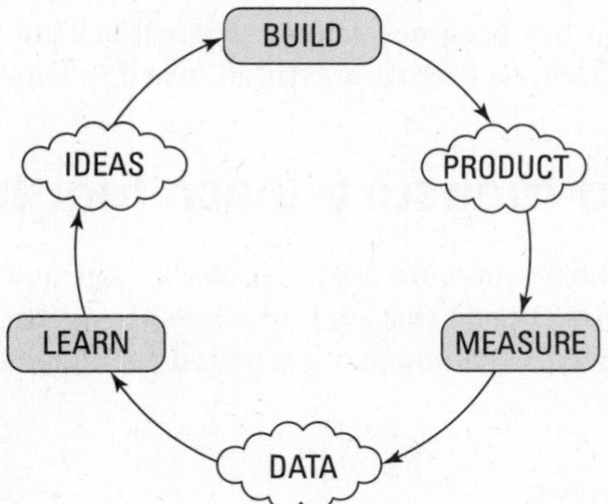

FIGURE 2-2: Lean Startup's build-measure-learn cycle.

Focusing on the one metric that matters

Lean Startup relies heavily on metrics as a way to learn, which doesn't mean you should bury yourself in data or fall victim to analysis paralysis. Instead you should focus on the *one metric that matters* (OMTM). Remember that you're trying to work with an MVP, which should provide you with a minimum number of data points to analyze. For example, if you have a sandwich stand, you don't necessarily need to examine the various condiments people order; you may need to know only which sandwich seems most popular.

You pick a single OMTM at a time, measure the results, learn from the data, and make improvements. Then, repeat the process in the spirit of continuous improvement.

Mixing Lean Startup with enterprise agile frameworks

Although Lean Startup is a separate and distinct agile framework, you can see elements of it in many agile frameworks and in the enterprise agile frameworks covered in Part 2. All agile teams engage in experimentation and deliver software iteratively in small product increments that result in short feedback loops that drive continuous improvement. In many ways, agile teams function as small startups. Their objective is to get working products in the hands of customers and then learn and adapt along the way.

» Seeing how product delivery fits into business agility

» Identifying common ideas among all enterprise agile frameworks

Chapter 3
Simplifying Lean Agility with SLAM

After graduating college, one of my first jobs was with Northwestern University's academic computer lab. Early each morning on my way to work, I'd pass by a house with a small wooden fence. Behind the fence was a dog that would scratch, claw, and bark at me. It was our daily routine — something the dog and I shared. Some days, I'd even see its glossy brown head pop up above the top of the fence.

One morning the dog was unusually motivated, so much so that the gray fence planks rumbled like a concert speaker with the dog struggling to get through. This time it actually managed to get one of its front legs over the fence, and then it flipped over to the other side. We looked at each other with mutual shock and neither of us really knew what was next.

I think about this incident when I see organizations transitioning to enterprise agility. Many organizations do the equivalent of scratching and clawing at the fence in an attempt to get to the other side. They adopt agile practices, such as small teams, stand-up meetings, and planning poker. They think that if they can scratch and claw their way through these key practices, then they're sure to become a more agile enterprise. However, achieving enterprise agility takes more than merely adopting agile practices. Organizations must make the leap; they need to adopt an agile mindset.

In this chapter, I present the Simple Lean-Agile Mindset (SLAM) that can help your organization adopt the shared understanding of enterprise agility that your organization needs to make the leap.

REMEMBER

With enterprise agility, a shared understanding of agile is more important than shared practices. A shared understanding of agile is the surest way for your organization to get real benefits from your enterprise agile transformation. This chapter provides the conceptual overview of enterprise agility that can help your organization develop that shared understanding.

Introducing the Simple Lean-Agile Mindset (SLAM)

The Simple Lean-Agile Mindset (SLAM) is a conceptual construct for understanding how agile enterprises function regardless of which enterprise agile framework they adopt (see Figure 3-1). Think of SLAM as an overall description of a game, such as Monopoly, and look at the enterprise agile frameworks (see Part 2) as various ways to play the game. SLAM is a high-level view of what the different enterprise agile frameworks and practices are trying to accomplish.

SLAM breaks down enterprise agility into the following four areas (starting at the bottom of Figure 3-1):

- **System-level optimization:** A collection of eight methods for improving the way people work alone and together in an organization to achieve any given objective and to engage in continuous improvement.
- **Strategic vision and execution:** The organization's unifying vision, along with the three-step process for executing that vision: (1) Break it down, (2) prioritize, and (3) pull work into the teams.
- **Empirical process control:** The system for ensuring continuous improvement: (1) Deliver in small batches and (2) gather and respond to feedback.
- **Business agility:** The extension of agility throughout an organization. While enterprise agility focuses on product delivery, business agility makes every part of the organization more lean and agile, including human resources, accounting, marketing, sales, purchasing, and production. Small teams, autonomous but aligned, work toward delivering the highest value to the customer and to the organization.

REMEMBER

Note the arrow on the right side of Figure 3-1 labeled "Continuous Improvement (Kaizen)." Your organization should always look for ways to reduce waste, improve efficiency, and eliminate defects. Many of the items listed under System-Level Optimization support continuous improvement, including shortening the cycle time, clearing communication channels, encouraging transparency, working in cross-functional teams, and removing fear of failure.

SIMPLE LEAN-AGILE MINDSET (SLAM)
BUSINESS AGILITY
EMPIRICAL PROCESS CONTROL
Get Feedback
Small Batch Delivery
Enterprise Agility
INNOVATION
PRODUCT
OPERATIONS
Ideas
Features
Tasks
Pull work into the teams
Prioritize
Break it down
Strategic Vision
Continuous Improvement (Kaizen)
SYSTEM-LEVEL OPTIMIZATION
Shortening the Cycle Time
Clearing Communication Channels
Value-stream Budgeting
Encouraging Transparency
Timeboxing
Working in Cross-Functional Teams
Respecting People
Removing Fear of Failure

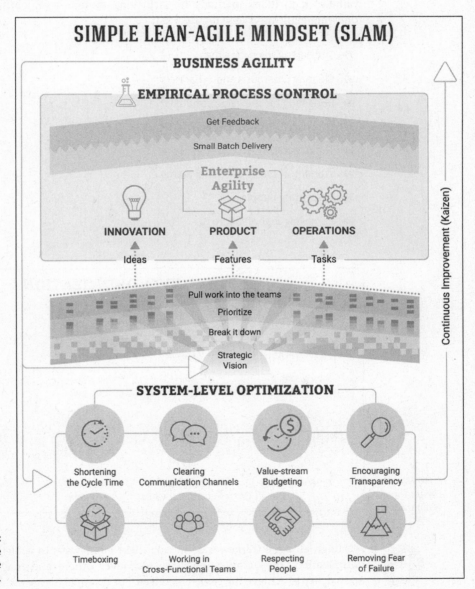

FIGURE 3-1: The Simple Lean-Agile Mindset (SLAM).

Starting at the Bottom with System-Level Optimization

System-level optimization involves improving the way people work alone and together to execute the organization's strategic vision. Every enterprise agile framework includes methods for achieving system-level optimization in the following eight ways (see Figure 3-2):

- Shortening the cycle time
- Clearing communication channels
- Budgeting for the value stream
- Encouraging transparency
- Timeboxing
- Working in cross-functional teams
- Respecting people
- Removing fear of failure

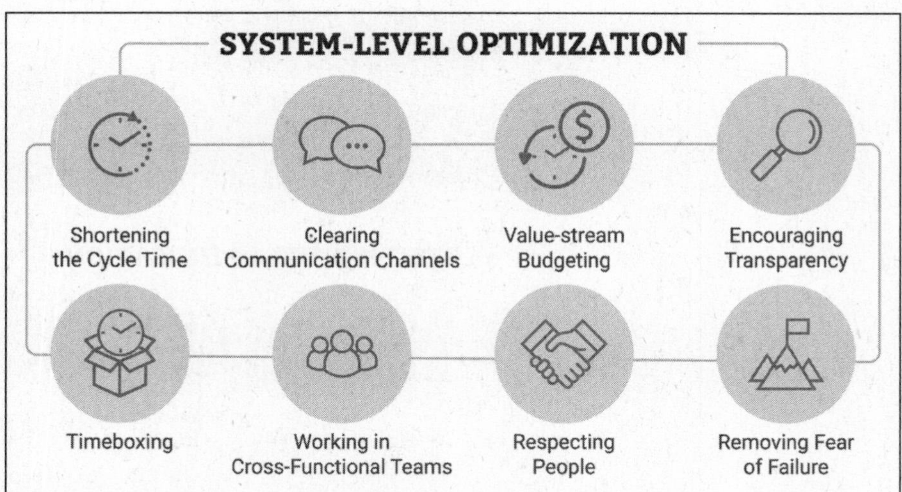

FIGURE 3-2: System-level optimization.

REMEMBER

Although all agile frameworks include these eight ways to achieve system-level optimization, they may emphasize some over others and may take different approaches to achieve the same objectives. For example, Large-Scale Scrum (LeSS) (see Chapter 5) removes the fear of failure by encouraging experimentation, whereas the Spotify Engineering Culture emphasizes the importance of celebrating failure and capturing what teams have learned from their failures (see Chapter 7).

Shortening the cycle time

All enterprise agile frameworks put a lot of emphasis on shortening product development cycles to optimize workflow, improve transparency, and ensure continuous incremental improvement. However, each framework uses a different approach. Here are a few examples:

- The Scaled Agile Framework® (SAFe®) (see Chapter 4) uses a concept called value streams — the steps between "concept and cash." You want to optimize the stream to deliver working program increments (PIs) in the shortest possible time.
- LeSS (see Chapter 5) puts a lot of emphasis on queueing theory to reduce the cycle time by putting the smallest batches of work through the system.
- Kanban (see Chapter 8) breaks work into smaller work items and encourages teams to complete work items in small batches and reduce work in progress (WIP) to optimize workflow.

TIP

To illustrate the efficiency of processing work items in smaller batches, play the penny game, as I explain in Chapter 11. Keep in mind, however, that everyone in the system must batch work into the same size. Otherwise, a team that batches its work into larger sizes will create a bottleneck that slows down all the other teams both upstream and downstream. Having just one or two well-run agile teams isn't going to improve the way your entire organization delivers products; all teams must process work at the same pace.

Clearing communication channels

One key area all the frameworks touch on is open and honest communication among everyone involved in product development, including team members, customers, management, and the organization's leaders. All frameworks have different ways to encourage and facilitate communication, as illustrated in the following examples:

- With Kanban (see Chapter 8), teams use a Kanban board that anyone in the organization can look at to determine product development status, find out what the teams are working on, and even gain insight into workflow issues.

- LeSS (see Chapter 5) calls for numerous meetings, including sprint planning 1 and 2, product backlog refinement, daily team scrums (15 minutes maximum), sprint reviews, retrospectives, and overall retrospectives. (A *sprint* is a two- to four-week product development cycle that ends with a working version of the product — a *program increment*.)
- SAFe (see Chapter 4) has engineers that act as servant leaders for each of their areas of responsibility, including a Solution Train Engineer (STE), who communicates the solution to several teams, and a Release Train Engineer (RTE), who focuses on the releases.

In addition, all enterprise agile frameworks involve small teams that work closely together, often within talking distance of one another to promote close communication and collaboration among team members. All frameworks also encourage and facilitate communication between customers and the product development team to ensure that the people delivering the solution have an intimate understanding of the customers' needs.

Budgeting for value streams

The third value of the Agile Manifesto is "Customer collaboration over contract negotiation." In the past, customers would contract with an organization to provide a product with a detailed list of features. With enterprise agility, customers collaborate with the organization instead, so budgets need to be more flexible. Instead of budgeting for projects, you budget for value streams, and your teams integrate functionality into the product incrementally based on the customer's priorities (see Chapter 11). The customer receives as much value as he's willing to pay for, and he can decide at any point in time that the product is good enough.

REMEMBER

With enterprise agility, traditional budgeting (for a project) doesn't work. You can't come up with an innovative solution during development if all solutions must be agreed to in advance. You can't add something new when you've already budgeted for the features everyone agreed to, and the customer can't change his mind without having to pay for the extra work.

Most enterprise agile frameworks create a budget around customer value; for example:

- SAFe (see Chapter 4) provides strategies for Lean Budgets. You create a budget for a value stream and then assign that value stream to an agile release train (ART). A Lean Budget ensures that each ART works only on what delivers value to the customer.

» Disciplined Agile Delivery (DAD) (see Chapter 6) recommends rolling-wave budgeting. Instead of funding projects, you allocate funds in waves of product development.

REMEMBER

Agile projects typically don't have a set scope or a detailed list of requirements. You work with your customer to build up the scope over time. To develop a budget, look at the product backlog (the prioritized list of features) and have your teams estimate the amount of work and time required to complete the work. Based on the time required for developing each program increment (for example, the duration of a sprint) and the number of teams required, you can develop an overall budget. As your teams complete the work, you collaborate with the customer to reevaluate the budget and future work. The product's budget and scope evolve as the teams complete the work.

TIP

Budgeting in enterprise agility is like buying a car. You figure out how much you're willing to spend, you choose a car within your budget, and then you choose any options you can afford, such as Bluetooth, a backup camera, heated seats, and keyless entry. If you can't afford any options, you still have a product that meets your most essential needs. The key is to focus on the value (getting around) and not focus on specific functions and features (Bluetooth, cameras, and heated seats).

Encouraging transparency

A key part of continuous improvement is making sure your teams are transparent about what's working and what's not. Transparency can be a real challenge in many organizations. Strong control cultures (see Chapter 9) favor certainty and focus on accountability. These organizations want their managers and leaders to minimize risk and make accurate predictions. Leadership doesn't want to hear about problems, so employees often cover up problems or pass them along to someone else.

The top enterprise agile frameworks emphasize the importance of transparency in driving continuous improvement:

» SAFe (see Chapter 4) lists transparency as one of its four core values. Prior to each sprint, teams set and communicate their sprint goals, and at the end of each sprint, they evaluate whether they achieved their goals.

» LeSS (see Chapter 5) includes transparency as one of its ten principles.

» DAD (see Chapter 6) has as its fourth principle for effective agile delivery governance, "Transparency into teams provides better insight than status reports."

- The Spotify Engineering Culture (see Chapter 7) uses retrospectives, captured learning, and improvement boards to identify and address issues in the product and the process for creating it.
- Kanban (see Chapter 8) has "visualize the workflow" as the first of its core practices. A Kanban board provides real-time insight into work in progress.

All of these frameworks have different roles and practices in place to encourage and facilitate transparency. Most involve some form of iterative product delivery (small and frequent releases) that provide teams, customers, management, and other stakeholders with greater visibility into the product development process and make it easier to spot problems.

Timeboxing

Timeboxing involves allocating a fixed amount of time to any given activity. All enterprise agile frameworks and certain agile practices rely on timeboxing to ensure predictability and eliminate waste. For example, stand-up meetings are limited to 15 minutes, and sprints are often limited to two to four weeks. You fit whatever you can into the box, but you can't break the box to get more to fit, such as by letting a meeting run over or extending a deadline.

All the top enterprise agile frameworks have some form of timeboxing:

- SAFe has program increments (PIs).
- The Spotify Engineering Culture has a minimum viable product (MVP).
- LeSS has sprints.
- Kanban has WIP limits.

Even though these names are different, they all limit the amount of time or work allocated. Teams deliver whatever they can within that constraint.

DON'T BREAK THE BOX

What happens if you do "break the box"? You may set off a chain reaction in an otherwise well-orchestrated cadence of events and commitments. It's a lot like toppling a line of dominoes just by knocking the first one over. Breaking the box is a form of disrespect for others and adds uncertainty to their plans. (Ever been hungry and waited for someone at a restaurant?) *Don't break the box!*

REMEMBER

Agile enterprises favor predictability over planned outcomes, so teams should deliver predictably within set time boxes. A time box can be every two weeks or eight weeks, you can call them sprints or program increments, but what's important is that teams deliver increments according to a predictable pattern.

Working in cross-functional teams

Many organizations are structured according to functional areas, such as marketing, engineering, operations, software development, quality assurance, and business analysis. Each area focuses on its own slice of the project. The business analysts work closely with the customer and then communicate what they learn to software developers. Then software developers create the product and hand off their work to a quality assurance team. Each handoff adds a wait time to the project and requires functional areas to coordinate their work.

To eliminate handoffs, agile frameworks favor cross-functional teams. (*Cross-functional* means the team has all the expertise required to deliver the product.) But cross-functional teams are not just about bringing people together from different functional areas. Instead, team members work collaboratively on the product and often develop skills that cross the traditional functional boundaries; for example, a software developer may do some work related to business analysis or testing. Ultimately, having a sufficient breadth of *intra-team* skills among multi-skilled team members will enable any cross-functional team to avoid most of the queueing problems such as scheduling complexities and wait times that go hand-in-hand with *inter-team* functional dependencies.

Each enterprise agile framework has a version of the cross-functional team. For example:

- SAFe (see Chapter 4) uses agile release trains (ARTs) — long-lived cross-functional teams that focus on delivering the value stream.
- LeSS (see Chapter 5) uses feature teams — cross-functional teams that have all the expertise required to deliver a given feature. Instead of one person working on a slice of the product (such as database, coding, or user interface), the whole team focuses on a feature that combines all these different slices.
- The Spotify Engineering Culture (see Chapter 7) uses squads that can work together in product-focused tribes to develop specific feature sets.

REMEMBER

Each of these approaches attempts to accomplish the same objectives — eliminate handoffs and improve communication and collaboration.

Respecting people

A core principle of the Lean-Agile Mindset is respect for people. In practice, respect for people involves the following:

- Listening and giving due consideration to everyone's opinion. While some people may have a higher level of expertise in some areas, innovative ideas often spring from conversations among people with expertise in different areas.
- Letting people do their jobs instead of micromanaging. All enterprise agile frameworks are built on the foundation of autonomous but aligned teams. Management may provide direction on what to do, but teams decide how to do it.
- Encouraging people to achieve their full potential through cross training and continuing education.
- Rewarding people for innovation and for revealing and correcting weaknesses in the organization. Encouraging experimentation without the threat of punishment for failures.

REMEMBER

The first value in the Agile Manifesto is "Individuals and interactions over processes and tools" (see Chapter 1). Respect for people is the glue that holds together all other system optimization initiatives and ensures continuous improvement.

All the top enterprise agile frameworks promote and facilitate respect for people through similar practices, including self-organizing teams or squads, retrospectives, communities of practice, customer collaboration, and so on. While many organizations retain a traditional role hierarchy, with enterprise agility the product development practice is largely democratic.

Removing fear of failure

To drive innovation and continuous improvement, organizations must promote a fearless culture. Here are a few ways you can reduce the element of fear in your organization:

- Take a collaborative, problem-solving approach to dealing with performance issues. For example, instead of threatening or punishing a team for missing a deadline or milestone, work with the team to figure out ways to improve the process.
- Encourage and reward employees for speaking out and being honest about weaknesses in the organization.

* Encourage and reward employees for taking the initiative and experimenting, even when it leads to failure. Employees shouldn't think that job security is simply a matter of not screwing up.
* Strive to improve employee retention. In organizations with high turnover due to firings and layoffs, employees often have a constant fear of losing their jobs, which discourages innovation and initiative.
* Discourage the common urge to blame others when something goes wrong.
* Nurture a creative workplace, where employees are having too much fun creating awesome products to be afraid of anything.

Don't use fear to motivate employees. This includes fear of missing deadlines and a fear of questioning the status quo. Fear may appear to work in the short term, but it actually degrades the system over time. The top enterprise agile frameworks approach fear in different ways:

* The eighth principle of SAFe (see Chapter 4) encourages organizations to "unlock the intrinsic motivation of knowledge workers."
* LeSS (see Chapter 5) focuses on using engineering practices such as continuous integration to encourage developers to take risks. Lean leaders are responsible for giving employees autonomy and encouraging them to work without fear.
* The developers of DAD (see Chapter 6) emphasize the importance of creating a culture of *psychological safety* in which employees can function without fear.
* The Spotify Engineering Culture (see Chapter 7) values trust over control and recommends "limiting the blast area," so teams can fail more safely.

You want your employees to feel as though they can tinker with all levels of the process and the product. They need to feel comfortable running experiments and learning from their success and failures. This approach may be difficult for organizations that have a strong control culture and low risk tolerance, but fear and agility don't mix.

Setting and Executing a Strategic Vision

Because enterprise agility involves scaling up agile team practices to work on enterprise-level products, it requires *strategic vision* — top-down guidance regarding what the organization will be and will do in the foreseeable future. As illustrated earlier in Figure 3-1, strategic vision comes from the organization's business agility, which is a high-level understanding of the following three factors:

- The organization's needs
- The customers' needs
- Enterprise agility in product development

An organization's strategic vision specifies the organization's unifying goal and its overall strategy for achieving that goal. For example, you could say that Spotify's strategic vision is to help people listen to whatever music they want, whenever they want, and wherever they want by creating an online music platform that allows them to easily listen to and share music that's free, accessible, and legal.

REMEMBER

Notice what's absent from that strategic vision — any indication of *how* the company will achieve that vision. The vision stops short of providing a detailed list of requirements or setting milestones. Instead, leadership provides a statement of what it must do to be successful and to serve its customers' needs. Leadership leaves it up to the rest of the organization to figure out how to achieve the strategic vision.

The organization then turns that strategic vision into tactical work through a three-step process, as shown in Figure 3-3:

1. **Break it down.** Everyone in the organization collaborates to break down the work required. In the Spotify example, the work may involve marketing, obtaining licensing for the music, building a platform, developing partnerships with social networking platforms, and so on.
2. **Prioritize.** Work is prioritized to deliver the most essential and highest value items first.
3. **Pull the work into the teams.** Teams can then pull work from the system to complete it.

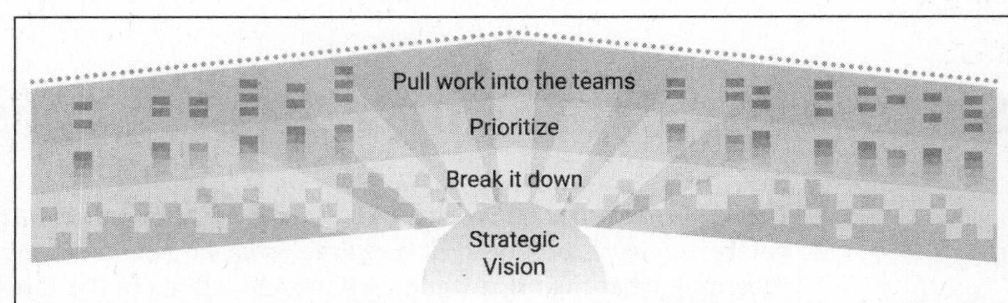

FIGURE 3-3: Turning a strategic vision into tactical work.

Each enterprise agile framework has its own approach to setting and executing the strategic vision; for example:

- SAFe (see Chapter 4) recommends executives create high-level *strategic themes* based on the organization's budget and goals and on customers' needs. These themes help the Lean Portfolio Management group decide which of the initiatives (or value streams) gets funding from the organization. SAFe puts a lot of emphasis on organizational alignment.
- LeSS (see Chapter 5) has a head of the product group, who creates a prioritized list of work items that a product owner distributes to different teams. The head of the product group may create the strategy for the entire organization and dozens of individual teams.
- DAD (see Chapter 6) encourages teams to develop a common vision, where executives, managers, and stakeholders collaborate with the teams on high-priority goals.
- Spotify's approach (see Chapter 7) distributes the vision among different product owners. They can work together to find common goals, but it's up to them to do what works for their teams (squads).

Breaking it down

After your organization's leaders establish a strategic vision, the rest the organization breaks it down into something that can be delivered. For example, suppose an organization's strategic vision is to create a version of its product that runs on smartphones. This vision doesn't specify any of the particulars for implementation. Does it mean *all* smartphones or only Android and iOS smartphones? Should it be an app or just a mobile version of the website? These are questions the executives may not know the answers to and that the teams should answer in collaboration with customers and other stakeholders.

To implement the strategic vision, the organization must transform into something more tactical. This transformation is a higher-level version of Scrum's divide between the "what" and the "how" (see Chapter 2). The strategic vision is the "what." Breaking it down provides the "how," which is up to the product development teams to decide. The teams work closely with the customer to figure out what the customer would find most useful — a mobile app, a web-based version of the product, or something else entirely.

Each enterprise agile framework has its own approach to breaking down the work:

- SAFe (see Chapter 4) breaks down strategic themes into epics, which can be broken down further into user stories and delivered over multiple program increments (PIs).
- LeSS (see Chapter 5) does something called an *initial product backlog refinement* (PBR), during which the product owner works closely with the team to refine the backlog into something that can be delivered. Together, they create a shared idea of what the customer wants and how the team can implement the vision.
- Kanban (see Chapter 8) breaks larger work down into work items recorded on Kanban cards. Work items may be written as user stories (see Chapter 2).

REMEMBER

Breaking the work down serves three purposes:

- It transforms a strategic vision into tangible deliverables.
- It increases innovation by providing an opportunity for those who work most closely with the product (the developers) to provide input on the best solution for achieving the strategic vision.
- It optimizes workflow; smaller work items flow more smoothly through the development process. (See the sidebar in Chapter 11 called "Playing the penny game.")

Prioritizing the work

Prioritizing the work is a key aspect of enterprise agility because it ensures the most essential and high-value work is completed first, providing the organization and its customers with the most value as early as possible. Teams strive to "stop starting and start finishing," so they can produce potentially shippable product increments.

Each of the top enterprise agile frameworks has its own approach to prioritizing the work:

- SAFe (see Chapter 4) has several different levels of prioritization. At the top (portfolio) level, managers and executives prioritize their epics on a portfolio Kanban board. Then middle managers prioritize the work in program and solution backlogs. Finally, individual teams have their own product backlogs. Each of these steps is a way to zero in on the highest priority solution.

» LeSS (see Chapter 5) relies on frequent product backlog refinement (PBR) meetings. The initial PBR breaks down the work. Then subsequent PBRs prioritize the work based on customer feedback.

» DAD (see Chapter 6) includes prioritizing the work as an agile best practice — a part of each of its different delivery lifecycles. Agile teams deliver the highest value product as a way to increase the customer's return on investment (ROI). Customers get more of what they want earlier.

REMEMBER

Breaking down and prioritizing the work supports system optimization (see the earlier section "Starting at the Bottom with System-Level Optimization") in several ways:

» It shortens cycle times by diving the work into smaller units.

» It clears communication channels and promotes transparency by encouraging collaboration among the organization's leadership, customers, and teams.

» It supports respect for people, because everyone can provide input on which work items are likely to bring the most value.

Pulling work into the teams

Unlike traditional product development, in which management *pushes* work onto teams, lean agile has teams *pulling* the highest priority work items from a product backlog or similar list to complete the work at a pace within their capacity for completing the work.

REMEMBER

The pull method prevents the bottlenecks, delays, defects, and anxiety that often result when too much work is pushed onto a team. When too much work is pushed onto teams, the teams either work overtime or get discouraged by the lack of progress. They may feel like they're shoveling snow in the middle of a snowstorm. The pull method produces continuous and measurable progress and makes delivery more predictable.

The pull method also supports several system-level optimizations:

» **Encourages timeboxing.** Teams develop a better sense of how much work they can complete within a given time box, so they can deliver at a predictable pace. If a team's pace is being set by another team pushing work onto the team, it may never have a clear idea of its own capacity for work.

» **Shortens cycle times.** Teams develop a better sense of the workflow and have an easier time spotting issues that are slowing the workflow. Think of it in terms of rowing a boat; a team that's too busy rowing may not notice or have the time to fix the leaks in the boat that are slowing it down.

- **Supports respect for people.** You're not asking teams to work overtime or deal with undue stress. In fact, too much work often slows people down as opposed to motivating them to finish quickly.

Each of the top enterprise agile frameworks has its own way of pulling work through the system. For example:

- SAFe (see Chapter 4) recommends using Kanban boards at every level of the organization. You pull portfolio epics based on the budget. Then you pull different parts of the product across a Kanban board and into an agile release train (ART). Finally, each agile team has its own Kanban board to manage its capacity to complete the work.
- LeSS (see Chapter 5) focuses on pulling work through the teams by applying queueing theory. Queueing theory suggests that you can increase the flow of work through the system if you break things down into smaller batches, as I explain in Chapters 8 and 11.
- Kanban (see Chapter 8) is the most straightforward. You create a simple swim-lane diagram on the wall or on a board that shows the team's capacity. Then, you pull work across the board as you complete it.

Taking an Empirical Approach to Products, Operations, and Innovation

Heavily influenced by Scrum (see Chapter 2), enterprise agility encourages an empirical approach to products, operations, and innovation — experiment, learn, and adapt. This approach is in response to the traditional method of speculating or assuming what will work best and investing considerable time planning a solution only to discover, upon delivery or implementation, that the solution doesn't work or the product doesn't deliver what the customer wants or needs. With an empirical approach, a team has an idea, tries it out on a limited scale, and gathers feedback before investing more time and effort. The empirical approach is consistent with Agile Manifesto's fourth value: "Responding to change over following a plan."

TECHNICAL STUFF

An *empirical approach* is based on evidence and observation instead of theories and reasoning. A classic example is the scientific method; you formulate a hypothesis based on observations, perform an experiment to test that hypothesis, analyze the results, and draw a conclusion. For example, instead of assuming customers would prefer a certain website layout, you may try three different layouts and collect data on how users interact with the site. Based on that data, you can pick which layout is best or perhaps gain insight into different aspects of each layout users prefer.

Enterprise agile frameworks break the empirical process into two stages (see Figure 3-4):

1. Pulling in ideas, features, and tasks.
2. Delivering small batches to gather and analyze frequent feedback.

I explain these steps in greater detail in the following sections.

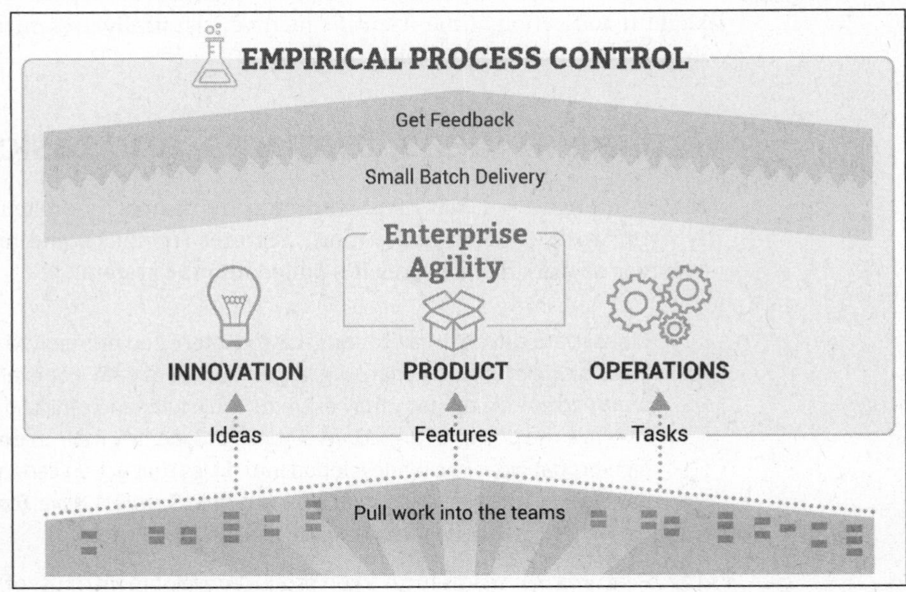

FIGURE 3-4: Following an empirical process.

All the top enterprise agile frameworks support the empirical process:

» A key part of SAFe's leadership training (see Chapter 4) centers on encouraging teams to innovate, experiment, and even fail. Teams need to experiment as a way to innovate and continuously improve.

» LeSS (Chapter 5) is one of the most enthusiastic about running experiments. In fact, the official LeSS documentation is packed with dozens of different experiments you can try to improve enterprise agility.

» DAD (see Chapter 6) focuses on lifecycles, including a disciplined agile continuous delivery (or "Lean") lifecycle that you can use for tasks, an agile lifecycle for adding features to products, and an exploratory "Lean Startup" lifecycle for testing ideas. All of these lifecycles encourage a more experimental mindset.

» While other enterprise agile frameworks, including SAFe and LeSS, have set roles, meetings, and practices, Kanban (see Chapter 8) lets you tinker with the whole process. You can add roles, eliminate formal meetings, split teams, and make other changes to optimize workflow.

REMEMBER

The empirical process aligns with the Lean-Agile Mindset and its focus on continuous improvement. In fact, early Lean Manufacturing was inspired by the "Shewhart cycle," originated by Walter A. Shewhart and popularized by W. Edwards Deming. This cycle encouraged teams to "plan, do, study, act" (PDSA), which is a slight modification of the scientific method, classically presented as "hypothesis, experiment, evaluation, conclusion."

Pulling in ideas, features, and tasks

Notice in Figure 3-1 that "Pull work into the teams" is broken down into three types of work — ideas (innovation), features (product), and tasks (operations). The type of work dictates how it's pulled into the system:

» **Ideas:** Data-driven organizations may be interested primarily in mining new ideas by collecting and analyzing large volumes of data. For example, a pharmaceutical company may examine molecular and clinical data and leverage the power of predictive modeling to identify molecules that have a high probability of being developed into drugs that act on certain biological targets. For more on this topic check out *Data Science: Create Teams That Ask the Right Questions and Deliver Real Value* by Doug Rose.

» **Features:** For teams focused on product development, most of the work being pulled into the system is in the form of features, epics, or user stories. Teams select the highest priority features and work toward integrating them into an enterprise-level product.

» **Tasks:** If you're primarily focused on operations, such as a help desk or development and operations (DevOps), work orders are in the form of tasks. Many help desks, for example, use something similar to a Kanban board (see Chapter 8) to track workflow. They may have color-coded tickets, such as red, orange, and yellow to prioritize items. DevOps may use a similar approach to manage infrastructure — creating a prioritized list of tasks that must be completed to perform a major operation, such as installing a new server or creating a testing environment.

All the enterprise agile frameworks have ways to pull features into the teams:

- SAFe (see Chapter 4) starts with strategic themes at the enterprise level that are broken down into solutions by Solution Train Engineers (STEs) and then broken down further into release trains by Release Train Engineers (RTEs), which are then passed along to various agile teams.
- LeSS (see Chapter 5) has one product owner who maintains an evolving product backlog from which the agile teams pull their work.
- DAD (see Chapter 6) has a three-phase delivery lifecycle, during which the teams plan their work (inception), do the work (construction), and release their work to the rest of the organization (transition).
- The Spotify Engineering Culture (see Chapter 7) follows a "think it, build it, ship it, tweak it" approach that leaves it up to the teams to pull work and complete it.
- Kanban (see Chapter 8) relies on a Kanban board, which serves as a to-do list for teams. Many enterprise agile frameworks use Kanban boards to create a prioritized list of work items (commonly referred to as a *backlog*) that teams use to manage their workflow and communicate work status to the rest of the organization.

Getting real-time feedback by delivering in small batches

The success of empirical process control hinges on delivering work in small batches, collecting and analyzing feedback frequently, and making adjustments. With small batches, teams learn from their successes and failures and can apply that learning to improve the product and the process for creating it.

REMEMBER

Note that delivering in small batches and obtaining frequent feedback helps to drive system-level optimization and continuous improvement (kaizen):

- It shortens cycle time by delivering frequent product iterations.
- It clears communication channels by giving teams frequent opportunities to evaluate the product and process and obtain customer feedback.

- It requires teams to timebox by breaking work into smaller batches that they have a limited time to complete.
- It encourages transparency; completing work in small batches provides greater visibility into any problems that arise.
- It removes fear of failure by giving teams more opportunities to learn from and correct mistakes and address inefficiencies.

All the top enterprise agile frameworks have practices that drive small batch delivery and tight feedback loops. Here are a couple examples:

- In SAFe (see Chapter 4) cross-functional teams, or ARTs, deliver in program increments (PIs) that can be further divided into product iterations. At the end of each of increment or iteration, teams can gather customer feedback. After each PI is a system demo, and after each iteration is an iteration review.
- LeSS (see Chapter 5) conducts a multi-team sprint review after each sprint, during which the team collaborates with the customer to identify areas for improvement. Each sprint is timeboxed (typically two to four weeks), to ensure small batch delivery and frequent feedback.

REMEMBER

A key selling point of enterprise agility is that it enables teams to quickly pivot and take advantage of new information and emerging technologies and methods. Delivering in small batches and obtaining feedback frequently gives teams ample opportunities to change direction. When batches are too large, teams tend to become invested in suboptimal solutions, making it difficult to change direction. The team tends to substitute its ideas for the customer's, relying on speculation or assumption instead of empirical evidence to make its decisions.

Think of the small batch delivery and feedback loops as the engine of your empirical process. This engine enables your teams to frequently experiment with the product and the process and zero in on the best solutions, resulting in both a better product and a better process. It also encourages a culture of continuous improvement, which is a key factor to improving your overall enterprise agility.

Building Toward Business Agility

While enterprise agility focuses on product delivery, business agility applies to the entire organization. This book focuses on enterprise agility, but over time, your organization may want to expand the scope of its agility — to, in effect, scale enterprise agility. As shown in Figure 3-4, empirical process control can be applied to innovations and operations, just as enterprise agility applies it to product.

Currently, Disciplined Agile (DA) (see Chapter 6) is the enterprise agile framework that offers the clearest options for scaling the framework to business agility. Specifically, DA offers the Disciplined Agile Enterprise (DAE) "process blade," which operates according to the following four principles:

- People must be agile
- Optimize your value streams
- Don't focus solely on practices
- Sense, respond, learn, and adapt

However, the other enterprise agile frameworks, including disciplined agile delivery (DAD), have enterprise-level decision-makers playing a key role in product delivery:

- LeSS (see Chapter 5) has the head of the product group create the strategic vision. The product owner helps to break down that strategic vision into something that can be developed by the teams.
- SAFe (see Chapter 4) has strategic themes created at the very top of the organization by directors and executives.
- DAD (see Chapter 6) has a group of stakeholders that helps to establish strategy and good governance.

As each of these high-level groups of people works to align products with the organization's strategic vision, it contributes to the organization's business agility. To extend its efforts to business agility, the organization must extend agile beyond product to innovation and operations.

2

Reviewing the Top Enterprise Agile Frameworks

IN THIS PART . . .

Scale agile to enterprise-level products layer by layer, from agile teams to teams of teams (agile release trains) to teams of teams of teams (solution trains) by using the Scaled Agile Framework® (SAFe®), which gives leadership greater control over setting the vision.

Scale Scrum to enterprise-level product delivery by using the Large-Scale Scrum (LeSS) framework and its layered approach to sprint planning and reviews to align and coordinate the work of dozens or even hundreds of Scrum teams working together on a single large product.

Increase your options with Disciplined Agile Delivery (DAD) — a process-decision framework that encourages you to set goals, explore your options for achieving those goals, and gain the insight required to make well-informed decisions.

Give your teams more autonomy to innovate and make decisions locally, while maintaining close alignment with the product's vision and individual team missions by adopting the Spotify Engineering Culture — a framework anchored in a strong community and a culture of creativity, mutual respect, and trust.

Improve workflow speed and efficiency through Kanban by using Kanban cards to track work items from process beginning to end, enabling your teams to visualize workflow, coordinate their efforts, and prevent and identify bottlenecks.

Minimize waste with a Lean approach that encourages you to eliminate anything and everything that doesn't serve the purpose of delivering value to customers and supporting your organization's business goals and objectives.

» Seeing how SAFe aligns your team with management

» Mapping your team's work to solution trains

» Focusing on delivering value with agile release trains

» Delivering a product with multiple agile teams

Chapter 4
Joining the Big Leagues with the Scaled Agile Framework

The *Scaled Agile Framework*® (SAFe®) is a modular, scalable system for orchestrating alignment, collaboration, and delivery for large numbers of agile teams. It got its start when Dean Leffingwell and his collaborators (now known as Scaled Agile, Inc.) began looking at how some of the largest organizations deliver software. What they found was a mix of Lean thinking, agile practices, and traditional top-down decision-making. The Scaled Agile team then consolidated and distilled these common practices to form SAFe.

In this chapter, I introduce you to SAFe in principle and in practice. I bring you up to speed on the SAFe framework and principles, offer guidance on how (and how not to) implement SAFe, and step you through the framework's various management layers so you can determine whether SAFe is the right framework for your organization. If you decide it is, this chapter can help you begin to envision your organization with SAFe and start taking the steps necessary to transform your organization into a SAFe enterprise.

SAFe is a little more prescriptive than other enterprise agile approaches. These practices are often closely related and presented in layers. They start with a few high-level Lean principles and practices for management and then work their way down to the team level. SAFe relies heavily on its infographics. This could be a little overwhelming at first when you look at graphics such as the SAFe full-framework graphic (Full SAFe), shown in Figure 4-1.

WARNING

Scaled Agile, Inc., controls the SAFe graphics, and these graphics are subject to change. While this chapter may not track exactly with the latest Full SAFe graphic, it will track closely enough with it for you to gain the understanding you need to determine whether this framework is right for your organization and to start formulating your plan to transition your organization to SAFe. You can always get the most current version of the SAFe graphics at `www.scaledagileframework.com`, where you will find an open repository of diagrams backed by detailed definitions and descriptive content.

Getting Your Head in the SAFe Game

Whenever you first encounter a complex model consisting of numerous parts, you can often benefit by stepping back to look at the whole before digging down into the details. In this section, I take you a few steps back to present SAFe in principle and in practice, so you have a general idea of what it is and how it's used to make large organizations agile.

Here, I introduce the SAFe framework and principles, explain the benefits of its modular approach, and encourage you to view SAFe as a compromise between traditional top-down management and team-based agile. I also steer you clear of the common mistake of focusing too much on SAFe practices without getting a handle on the overarching concepts.

Meeting the SAFe framework and principles

Looking at the Full SAFe graphic (refer to Figure 4-1), you see right away that it's a beast. It's designed for hundreds of developers and dozens of teams that are either working on one big product or several smaller products. The product(s) might have millions of lines of code that must be updated regularly across the enterprise. But when you step back for a moment and look at the whole and consider it in the context of the SAFe principles, it all begins to make sense.

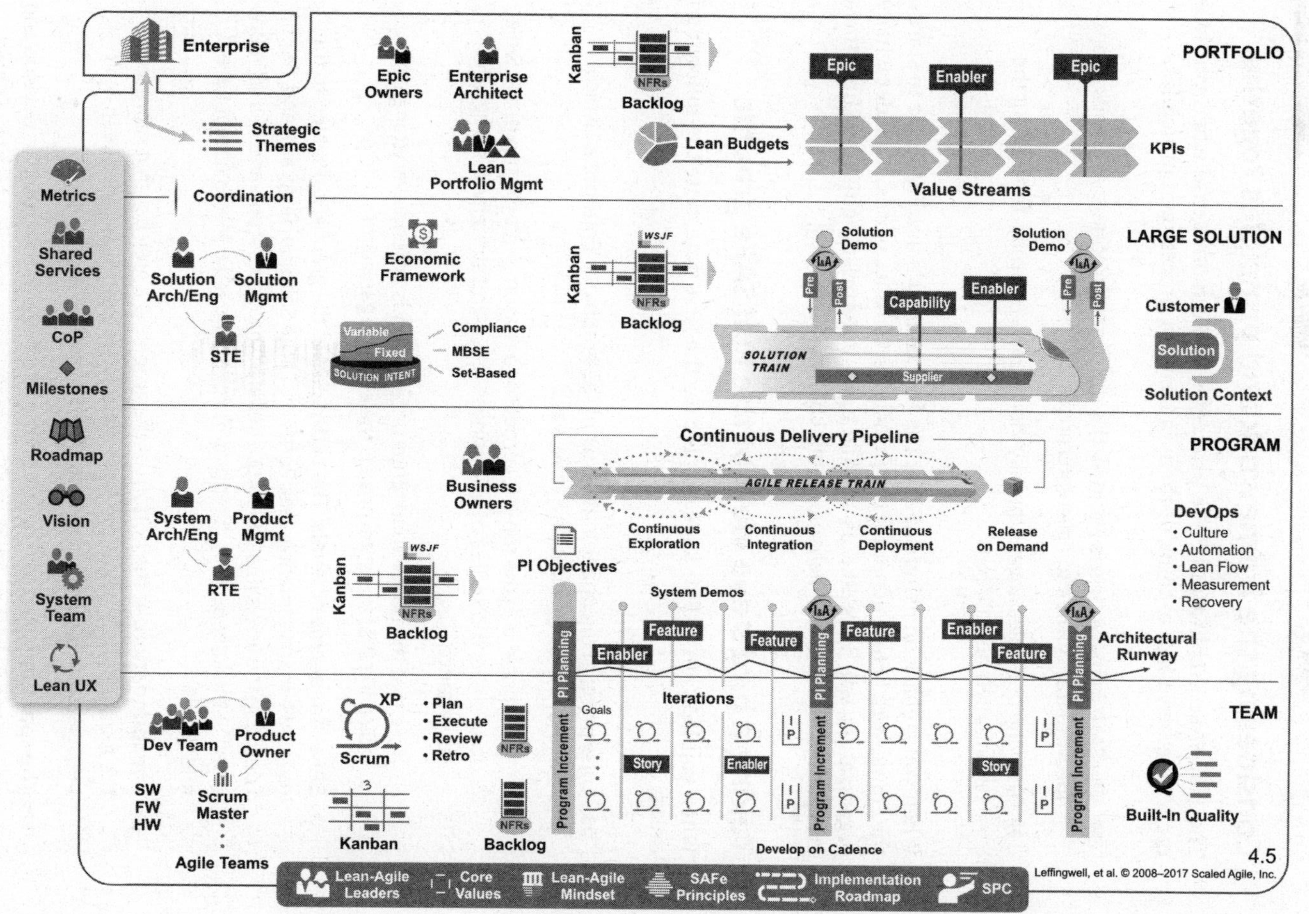

All SAFe content reproduced with permission from © Scaled Agile, Inc. (www.scaledagileframework.com).

FIGURE 4-1:
The Full SAFe graphic.

Considering the framework and principles together

The Full SAFe graphic and SAFe principles make more sense when you look at them together. I like to think of them in terms of process and principles:

- The SAFe framework (see Figure 4-1) is the overall process that organizations follow to transform into agile enterprises.
- The nine principles govern the way individuals and teams throughout the organization do their jobs.

When you embark on using SAFe for the first time, it's usually better to start with the framework before adopting the principles. In other words, consider what your organization will look like as a SAFe agile enterprise before tackling the way everyone's mindset and behaviors will change.

Taking a bird's-eye view of the Full SAFe graphic

When you look at the Full SAFe graphic for the first time, note the following four areas:

- **Enterprise:** In the upper-left corner of the graphic is "Enterprise," which represents the organization in two ways:
  - "Enterprise" is in the top-left corner for a reason — it's the top of the SAFe food chain, the source of all business vision and strategy, funding, and governance.
  - Note that the box around "Enterprise" extends around everything else, indicating that the enterprise is the entire organization.
- **SAFe management levels:** The better part of the graphic is devoted to the four SAFe management levels: Portfolio, Large Solution, Program, and Team. I describe the levels in a little more detail in the next section and in a lot more detail in the later section, "Stepping Through the SAFe Management Layers and Levels."
- **The foundation:** At the bottom of the graphic is a gray bar that represents the foundation on which the SAFe framework rests. It includes Lean-Agile Leaders, Core Values, Lean-Agile Mindset, and SAFe principles.
- **The spanning palette:** The bar on the left contains tools used to develop and deliver products through the SAFe methodology, including Metrics, Shared Services, Milestones, Roadmap, and Vision. For more about the spanning palette, see the later section, "Filling in the background with the SAFe spanning palette."

Brushing up on SAFe framework fundamentals

The Full SAFe configuration is divided into the following four management levels:

- **Portfolio:** At this level, you find the principles, practices, and roles for creating and managing value streams. A *value stream* is a series of steps for building solutions that deliver value to a customer continuously. The people and processes that reside in the Portfolio level are responsible for building solutions that enable the enterprise to meet its strategic objectives.
- **Large Solution:** This level contains the roles, activities, and *artifacts* (byproducts of the development process, such as a user story) to build large-scale solutions beyond the scope of what a single *agile release train* (ART) can develop.

  REMEMBER

  An ART is a team of teams, which you find at the Program level (discussed next). At the Large Solution level, you find *solution trains* (teams of teams of teams). A solution train may have dozens of ARTs, each having 5 to 12 agile teams.
- **Program:** At the Program level are the roles and activities necessary to deliver solutions continuously via ARTs. This is where agile teams, key stakeholders, and other resources conduct their ongoing mission to develop and deliver solutions. Each ART is composed of 5 to 12 agile teams. (The "train" in ART is based on the idea that this train is always moving on time; you can pile features into the backlog, and the train will fit them into the product incrementally, so no team needs to wait for another team to complete its work.)
- **Team:** At this level, each team (five to nine team members) is dedicated to defining, developing, testing, and delivering a quality end product. Every team at this level is part of an ART at the Program level.

For more detailed coverage of these four layers, see the later section, "Stepping Through the SAFe Management Layers and Levels." Here's how the framework functions in practice:

1. At the **Portfolio level,** high-level business leaders break down value into a *backlog* (a prioritized list what's needed to deliver the desired value), which is then broken down into *epics* (high-level business cases); for example, "create a version of our software that works with Apple products." (A single epic may spawn more than one product or solution.)
2. At the **Large Solution level,** engineers work with the customer to deliver large and complex solutions. This might be a software program with several different areas of functionality. The teams work together to create a solution train that helps align people to a common vision, mission, and backlog.

3. At the **Program level,** leaders break down the epic from the portfolio backlog to create a *program backlog* (a prioritized list of product features). A feature may require one team or several teams based on its size and complexity. If several teams are required, they function within the construct of an ART.

4. At the **Team level,** each agile team pulls projects from its program backlog in order of priority and completes them within a specified period of time.

With SAFe, an organization's value to the customer is defined at the enterprise level and broken down into smaller and smaller units of value at each level of the framework from portfolio (at the top) to team (at the bottom). Each of these levels refines the epic to ensure that the organization continuously delivers the highest value to the customer.

Getting to know the nine SAFe principles

SAFe has nine principles that govern the way everyone in the organization approaches product development:

1. Take an economic view.
2. Apply systems thinking.
3. Assume variability; preserve options.
4. Build incrementally with fast, integrated learning cycles.
5. Base milestones on objective evaluation of working systems.
6. Visualize and limit WIP, reduce batch sizes, and manage queue lengths.
7. Apply cadence, synchronize with cross-domain planning.
8. Unlock the intrinsic motivation of knowledge workers.
9. Decentralize decision-making.

WARNING

Don't focus on these principles just yet. Their significance and application may be difficult to grasp at this point. It's a bit like looking at the lyrics of a song before you decide if you like the music. Consider reviewing the principles after you have a better understanding of the framework.

Picking and choosing what to use

At first glance, the framework graphic looks like a subway map for the most confusing city on Earth. But fear not. You may not need all four levels of Full SAFe, and you may not use all the little pieces of whichever SAFe configuration you use. The framework tries to show you everything that you *can* do, not everything you *must* do. Remember, it's modular.

The first choice you need to make is which SAFe configuration to use. Each of these configurations includes only the management levels that are appropriate for that solution. Four are provided:

- **Full SAFe:** This is the most comprehensive Scaled Agile Framework. It's intended to be used for complex solutions that can have hundreds of people and dozens of teams working to deliver the product.
- **Portfolio SAFe:** This is for organizations that are primarily interested in aligning their agile development to one or two value streams and just one or more agile release trains.
- **Large Solution SAFe:** This is for large and complex solutions that don't need the type of portfolio management like other SAFe configurations. This is for industries where you wouldn't need SAFe to govern portfolio of projects. Instead you'll have one or two complex projects that may take dozens of teams to deliver. This configuration is more common for industries such as aerospace and defense. Here most of the focus is on the product and not necessarily on governance.
- **Essential SAFe:** This is the most stripped-down version of the Scaled Agile Framework. Consider it SAFe lite. This version has the most crucial elements of the framework and can be a building block for some of the larger configurations. It includes key concepts such as the agile release train, and it helps align teams to a common solution.

TIP

Choose the smallest configuration you think will work best for your organization. You can easily upsize to a larger version of the framework, if necessary, but if you start with too large a configuration, you may make your efforts more complicated than they need to be and encounter needless resistance and frustration.

TECHNICAL STUFF

The earlier versions of SAFe had collapsible levels and tabs on each side of the diagram. The idea was that you could collapse and tab your way through the graphic to create something customized. So, you had to show or hide the different parts of the one big graphic to make it fit your organization. Now SAFe uses these configurations as a way to provide the "out-of-the-box" configuration that's appropriate for your environment. You don't have hidden layers, which can become confusing.

REMEMBER

SAFe is a template, suitable for tailoring. It's not intended to be used exactly as presented. In fact, it's modular, and you're encouraged to use the elements that work best for you and be aware of the rest if you need them. You can freely mine the framework for ideas and practices that you think might help your organization.

FUNNY, BUT TRUE

Here's an old joke I like to use to introduce the Scaled Agile Framework (SAFe):

> A manager wants to try skydiving, so he goes to the classes and suits up for his first jump. The trainer says to him, "Don't worry; you'll have a very experienced pilot. Besides, everyone gets a big parachute and one backup parachute. When you land, there'll be someone waiting for you in a van to take you back to the center."
>
> The manager is nervous, but he gets on the plane. Just as he's about to take off, he notices that the pilot looks like a kid. The pilot says not to worry and assures him that he's done this more than a few times.
>
> The ride to the top is a little bumpy, but the manager gathers his courage and jumps off the plane. After a few seconds, he pulls the ripcord for his big parachute, but nothing happens. Then he remembers what the trainer said. So, he rolls onto his back and pulls the cord from his backup parachute, but it breaks off in his hand.
>
> At this point he's really frustrated and thinks to himself, "Great! I bet there's not going to be a van either."

This joke often reminds me of SAFe, because it gives you so many practical steps that you can easily overlook the fact that you've jumped into an organizational change.

SAFe's flexibility and it numerous options make it a popular starting point for organizations interested in making the leap to enterprise agility, but those qualities also pose a challenge — it's easy to get lost in the process and lose any sense of the ground below.

Approaching SAFe as a practical compromise

The Agile Manifesto (see Chapter 1) was a battle cry against large processes and heavy systems. In fact, the very first value in the Agile Manifesto is "individuals and interactions over processes and tools." Teams are supposed to focus on delivering software, not on the overwhelming process of doing so. Looking at the SAFe diagram, you'd have a hard time imagining the founding agile workgroup accepting this framework as part of the agile mindset. It's an overwhelming process filled with dozens of tools.

Many people in the agile community feel that SAFe subverts the benefits of being agile. The framework takes away much of the self-directed power of agile teams. It does this in favor of giving management greater visibility and control. In a sense, SAFe takes the agile teams that were designed to own all the aspects of the product and forces them to align with a larger organizational goal.

TRACING SAFe'S ORIGIN

The Scaled Agile Framework has stimulated a lot of great discussion in the agile community. Its creator, Dean Leffingwell, was part of the team that created IBM's Rational Unified Process (RUP), so SAFe comes from a world of big frameworks designed for large enterprises.

A lot of the ideas for SAFe came out of Leffingwell's blog posts and his book on agile software requirements. Much of his work was centered on gathering requirements for larger frameworks, sometimes referred to as "waterfall-style frameworks."

One of the controversies around SAFe is that agile has always seen itself as a group of small, lightweight frameworks — frameworks like Scrum, Extreme Programming, and Kanban. Each of these had only a few rules and left it up to the team to figure out how to work together. SAFe, on the other hand, involves a good deal of top-down management.

In theory, SAFe may contradict agile, but as I explain in the following sections, it's more of a compromise that makes sense in terms of a large-scale enterprise product.

Reinterpreting "lightweight"

At first glance, SAFe may appear too big to be agile, but its size serves a practical purpose. If you have a large product with hundreds of developers, then coordinating dozens of agile teams becomes increasingly difficult. Also, if you have several smaller products that all depend on each other, then you need some way to communicate a common vision. You don't want one product to be completely different from every other product you're delivering.

If you're a large organization, and you're stumbling through a hybrid approach, attempting to combine agile with traditional top-down management (see "Avoiding water-agile-fall" later in this chapter), then SAFe's guidance can be useful.

Being realistic

The reality is that many organizations already have one foot in waterfall (top-down management) and another in agile (bottom-up management). What SAFe does (and does really well) is offer a shared set of best practices for what such an organization is already doing. In one sense, SAFe normalizes this water-agile-fall approach, even though this approach may not be benefiting your organization. On the other hand, SAFe may be the only form of the agile mindset that your organization will accept — the only way to infuse some creativity into a large rigid process.

Either way, SAFe is very reasonable in the context of the problem it's trying to solve. The framework assumes that your teams can't deliver an enterprise-level product using the bottom-up approach that's inherent with an agile team. In a sense, SAFe is built on the premise that a cross-functional, self-organized agile team doesn't scale well when you're developing larger products.

Giving managers more authority

The solution to the problem of trying to develop large, complex products with small, self-organized agile teams is to take some authority and self-direction away from the teams and create communities of teams that work together and follow a common path. Manager-style roles in these communities can help prioritize work and set direction.

SAFe is a compromise; it's not just another top-down process to control your teams, nor is it fully consistent with an agile mindset. The framework contains plenty of fixes to help decentralize management, which helps it avoid the top-down, command-and-control approach in waterfall frameworks. SAFe also features plenty of practices to help ensure agile teams have as much creative flexibility as possible.

If you see this framework as a set of compromises, then your teams can get a lot of value from following SAFe. The framework gives you the convenience of trying to fit agile into your enterprise instead of the other way around. For many organizations, SAFe is the best place to start.

Avoiding water-agile-fall

If you've worked on a large enterprise project, then you've probably heard of the *waterfall approach*. In 1970, Dr. Winston Royce described a method for "managing large software developments" based on his personal experience in the development of ground systems for spacecraft mission planning, control, and post-flight analysis. The approach, as he described it, is delivered in seven sequential phases (including analysis and coding), cascading like a waterfall from system requirements to operations. Royce introduced five additional process features or steps "to eliminate most of the development risks." Interestingly, the fifth step Royce added was to "involve the customer" in a number of reviews at critical phases in the waterfall sequence.

Take automobile manufacturing as an example. To develop a new vehicle, you would first envision the type of car you want, such as an SUV hybrid with all the trimmings. Designers would draw the car, then engineers would figure out which parts were needed and how to fit them all together, then analysts would determine how to build it and how much that would cost. After it's built, experts would test the car for safety, drivability, and so on. Based on the test results, you would probably need to go through the process several times until you had the product you wanted. Finally, you'd sell the completed product to dealers who would sell it to their customers.

Royce applied this approach to software development. He said to create software you needed to plan out all the features. Then, high-level software architects would create a design for the whole product. Then teams of software developers would work to code the product. A quality assurance group would test-drive the software, bugs would be fixed, and then you'd ship the completed software to your customer.

In this section, I explain the fundamental flaw in this approach to product development, particularly software development, and explain why combining the waterfall approach with agile, a common practice, can be a recipe for disaster, if it's not done right.

Recognizing the flaw: Planning over adapting

Software developers who tried Royce's waterfall approach soon discovered that it was fundamentally flawed. During the planning, software features changed so frequently that many companies ended up delivering a product that was completely different from the idea they started with. All the time and effort spent planning was wasted.

Mixing the worst of both worlds

To address this weakness in the model, many organizations began encouraging a more agile mindset so that the software development teams could quickly pivot and modify the product to better fit their customers' needs. However, most organizations that embraced the more responsive agile approach refused to let go of the more predictable waterfall approach. As a result, many organizations ended up with a hybrid, often referred to as *water-agile-fall*. You might hear it called the "hybrid approach" or "mixed methodology," but the construct is the same: You have a waterfall organization with agile teams.

This hybrid approach allows development teams to have much more flexibility to design, code, and test even when much of the product has already been planned and analyzed. However, these same teams are pressured by the top brass to deliver a well-planned product on a specific release date. A team might be free to create the minimum viable product, but that well-planned product must be delivered on time and within a set budget.

REMEMBER

In many ways, water-agile-fall is the worst of both worlds. Time spent planning is wasted, because everything is subject to change, and developers have a tough time being agile when the product is (or is perceived to be) inflexible.

Introducing a "SAFer" approach

Even though water-agile-fall is less than ideal, many organizations insist on it. This is where SAFe really shines, because it gives organizations the best of both worlds. It accepts the reality of how most large organizations approach agile. Then it takes the best practices of this mixed approach and bundles them into a comprehensive enterprise framework.

As you can imagine, this hybrid approach has a lot of compromises. In many cases, most large enterprises would do better either transitioning to agile or trying to improve their existing waterfall arrangement. For organizations that are currently following a water-agile-fall approach, SAFe is a more effective model that's easier to transition to. Large organizations have no reason to reinvent the wheel when they have so many best practices and compromises bundled into SAFe. The SAFe team has worked for years to fine-tune its framework to deal with the exact challenge these water-agile-fall organizations struggle with. Why not take advantage of the team's hard work?

Differentiating doing agile from being agile

At its heart, enterprise agile is a radical change; it's a difficult change to embark on, and it's even more difficult to see through to its finish. SAFe offers organizations the comfort of having a structured plan for their transformation, but it doesn't confuse this plan with the groundwork required for transformational change. Such change requires that people think about their work in a different way, so don't fall into the false comfort of the promise of a structured plan.

REMEMBER

There's a big difference between *doing* agile and *being* agile. Standing up in a meeting (a common Scrum practice described in Chapter 1) is easy, but communicating with one another on a true, cross-functional team and communicating across teams is much more difficult. With SAFe, you can encounter similar distinctions but on a much larger scale. (For more about the importance of changing mindsets and culture, see Chapter 9.)

Wait a minute: Is SAFe the right solution?

An old joke keeps floating around the Internet: If you want to look smart at meetings you should ask, "How do we bring this idea to scale?" "Scale" has become a corporate buzzword. No one really knows what it means. Does it mean you want to make something bigger? Or does it mean you just want something to be more widely used?

This lack of understanding only makes companies think wrongly that they need to use scaling to tackle many of their challenges. The fact is, the *Scaled* Agile Framework has benefited from including these buzzwords. It has both "scale" and "agile" in its name, so it seems like a ready-made, pre-packaged solution for any large company. It lends itself well to marketing; if you're a large organization, and you want to try agile, then you'll need the Scaled Agile Framework.

CASE STUDY

A POOR FIT

SAFe is not the best solution for every large organization. A prime example is an organization I once worked with that was just starting its agile transformation. The company had a team in one state, three teams in its home office, and two teams offshore. Altogether, it had about 25 software developers.

The organization didn't even consider having small agile teams. Instead it went directly for the Scaled Agile Framework. The organization created its agile release trains and had a release train engineer who coordinated six teams.

The company also brought in people throughout the organization to fill in roles on the Portfolio and Program levels. It ended up having more managers than developers on its SAFe teams. The Scaled Agile Framework creates these roles as a way to coordinate larger groups of people. When you don't have these larger groups of people, you end up with a lot of managers.

I remember asking the chief information officer (CIO) why he decided to start with the Scaled Agile Framework. He seemed almost annoyed with the question. He said, "We're a Fortune 100 company. We have developers and technical employees on three continents. Simply running a few agile teams would never be enough. We needed to go right to scale."

What he was saying was that it was a big company, big companies have scaling issues, and so it needed to start with the top-of-the-line framework.

It ended up being a little ridiculous in practice. The company had only about 25 people working on three different products and could've easily accomplished everything it wanted with a few well-run agile teams. Too many managers believe that big companies need big solutions. From that perspective, the Scaled Agile Framework is the only option — even when it isn't.

Before you embrace SAFe, ask yourself whether it makes sense for your organization. If you have only 25 people in charge of developing and delivering new solutions, SAFe probably isn't the right solution. You can figure that out just by looking at the SAFe graphic. Skim down the left side of the graphic, and you'll see a lot of new roles: Epic Owners, an Enterprise Architect, Lean Portfolio Managers, Solution Architects and Managers, System Architects, Product Managers, Product Owners, Scrum Masters, and more. Start adding all that management to a small group of people, and just imagine what will happen. Your organization will have more managers than developers.

REMEMBER

Don't assume that because you're big, you need a big framework. Right now, it seems as though most SAFe implementations are a mismatch between what organizations have and what they need. It's almost like an oversized jacket on the shoulders of a few small development teams.

Stepping Through the SAFe Management Layers and Levels

The Full SAFe configuration graphic (see Figure 4-1) has four management levels and an underlying layer, the foundation layer, on which those levels rest. In this section, I guide you through the foundation and the four management levels and provide some guidance on how to put the framework into practice.

Bottom up: Starting at the foundation

At the bottom of the Full SAFe graphic is a gray box that represents the foundation on which the framework rests (see Figure 4-2). A line extends from the left and right sides of the box to surround the four management levels, indicating that the foundation layer applies to all four levels and to the entire enterprise. The foundation contains the following items:

- **Lean-Agile Leaders:** The people responsible for the successful adoption of SAFe and its outcomes.
- **Core Values:** The four fundamental beliefs that are key to SAFe's success (see Figure 4-3):

FIGURE 4-2: The foundation.

All SAFe content reproduced with permission from © Scaled Agile, Inc. (www.scaledagileframework.com).

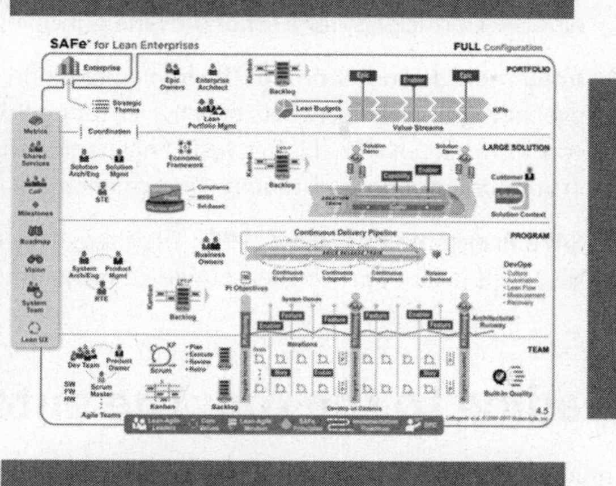

FIGURE 4-3: The core values.

- *Alignment:* Unlike team agile (see Chapter 2), in which solutions are built from the bottom up, in SAFe, top-level management formulates and communicates the vision, and all others must align their efforts with that vision. SAFe teams then have some flexibility on how to deliver the product.
- *Built-in quality:* All the work that comes out of the system must be ready for production. No time is set aside at the end for testing and reworking.
- *Transparency:* Everyone on the team should feel comfortable sharing problems and challenges. At no time should team members sense that they'll be penalized for making mistakes. In software development, mistakes happen, but, much like politics, "It's not the crime, it's the cover-up" that causes the most problems. All the teams should develop a shared sense of trust to avoid unknown mistakes that may impact the quality of the software.
- *Program execution:* Bottom line, deliver the goods.

» **Lean-Agile Mindset:** The beliefs, assumptions, and actions that comply with the Agile Manifesto and with Lean thinking. Think of the SAFe mindset as a culture defined by merging agile and Lean principles.

- **SAFe Principles:** Nine directives that govern how the organization thinks, acts, and interacts around what it does. See the earlier section "Getting to know the nine SAFe principles" for a list of the nine principles.
- **Implementation Roadmap:** The implementation roadmap consists of an overview graphic and 12 sets of activities for implementing SAFe. Don't concern yourself with this yet. Just keep in mind that at some point, everyone in your organization will require SAFe orientation and training.
- **SAFe Program Consultant (SPC):** The change agent in the organization is responsible for improving its software and systems development processes.

Heading to the top: The enterprise

In one respect, the enterprise is the entire organization; it encompasses executive leadership and all four process management levels. In another respect, it sits at the top of the SAFe food chain as the source of all the business strategy, funding, and overall governance of the organization.

SAFe takes a practical view of the enterprise — as the entity that hires people who provide their expertise or service to the organization. The relationship is very transactional. The enterprise provides employees with a salary, and, in return, they execute the enterprise's strategic themes and product delivery.

In its role as the head of the organization, the enterprise works with others in the organization to develop strategic themes that the rest of the organization is then responsible for executing. Execution begins at the Portfolio level, discussed next.

Visioning at the Portfolio level

As the head of the organization, the enterprise collaborates with top-level managers at the Portfolio level (see Figure 4-4), where managers much reach a consensus on many of the decisions around a product. At this level, management sets the direction for the entire enterprise by creating value streams that align with the enterprise's strategic themes.

TECHNICAL STUFF

As you recall from earlier in this chapter, a *value stream* is a series of steps that provide value to a customer. For example, you enter a restaurant, you're seated at a table, and the server brings you a menu, a place setting, and a glass of water; takes your order; and delivers your order to the kitchen. The cooks prepare your order (which involves additional steps), and then the server brings your food to you. All of these steps comprise the value stream.

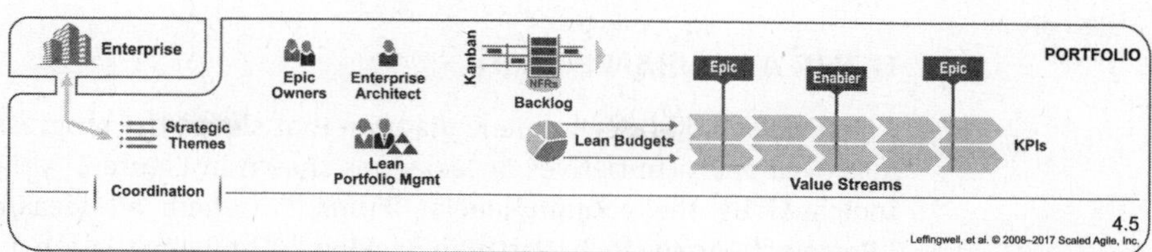

FIGURE 4-4: The SAFe Portfolio level.

All SAFe content reproduced with permission from © Scaled Agile, Inc. (www.`scaledagileframework.com`*).*

In this section, I take you on a tour of the Portfolio level, where you meet the people who drive the process and develop an understanding of the purpose of this level and how it functions.

Meeting the key players

The Portfolio level includes three distinct roles (which can be held by several people):

- **Epic owners:** Define, coordinate, and facilitate implementation of high-level *epics* (business cases, such as introducing a new product, merging with another company, or responding to marketplace changes).
- **Enterprise architects:** Provide the strategic technical direction, which may include recommending the development and delivery of technology stacks, application programming interfaces (APIs), and hosting strategies, and facilitating the reuse of ideas, components, services, and proven patterns across a portfolio's solutions.
- **Lean portfolio management:** Typically the business managers and executives who are responsible for the highest level of decision-making and financial accountability related to the portfolio's success.

Prioritizing epics and adding them to the backlog

The Portfolio level is where management formulates large business initiatives for the organization, considering such things as new business opportunities, mergers and acquisitions, problems with existing solutions, marketplace challenges, and so forth. Here, all big ideas are welcome. Ideas are then reviewed, analyzed, and added to the portfolio backlog (a prioritized list of major initiatives) for execution.

Portfolio managers use a Kanban board, as explained in the next section, to help determine what gets added to the backlog.

USING A KANBAN BOARD

A *Kanban board* is a swim-lane diagram that shows the progress of proposed and approved epics (initiatives or tasks), as shown in Figure 4-5. Progress is usually indicated by the column labels "Funnel" (where all ideas/epics are listed), "Review," "Analysis," "Portfolio Backlog," "Implementation," and "Done." (See Chapter 8 for more about Kanban.)

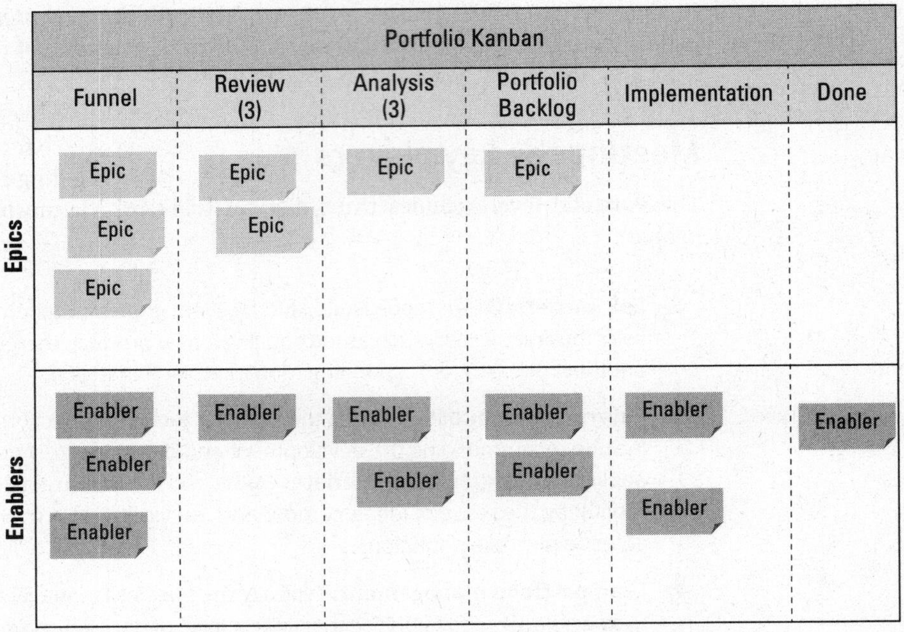

FIGURE 4-5: A typical Kanban board.

In SAFe, you break down the work into the smallest possible chunks. At this stage, these chunks are epics. You can then prioritize the epics to decide where to place them in the backlog.

STARTING THE WEIGHTED SHORTEST JOB FIRST

A common way to prioritize items in the backlog is to do the *weighted shortest job first* (WSJF). To determine which is the weighted shortest job, calculate the cost of delay (CoD) and divide that by the job duration. For example, if you're working on a product that will generate $50,000 per month for the company, CoD is $50,000 per month, because the company will lose $50,000 every month the product is delayed. (You could divide that figure by 4 to determine the weekly CoD or by 30 to calculate the daily CoD.) To determine WSJF, you divide that figure by the duration of the project, so if the CoD is $50,000 per month, and the project will take eight months:

$$WSJF = \frac{CoD}{Duration} = \frac{50,000}{8 \text{ months}} = 6,250$$

If you have two 12-month projects, one of which will generate $5 million in revenue and the other $500,000 in revenue, the CoD for the first project has a much greater return for the same duration, so its weight is also greater and you do that job first.

Unfortunately, the expected economic impact may be unknown. Fortunately, the WSJF criteria can be relative. All you need is relative scoring to support prioritization. It's similar to the relative estimating you do for Scrum projects (see Chapter 1). You can balance a bunch of elements, including business value, time pressure, and risk reduction or opportunity enablement, to come up with a cost of delay. Then you divide that by the job size to determine its relative weight. So, in general, the highest priority job would take very little time to complete and add a lot of business value.

TIP

Some organizations like to use the same planning poker group decision-making process you see in Scrum to come up with the cost of delay and job size (see Chapter 1). Others may use a spreadsheet to come up with ballpark estimates and may even break down their estimates into CoDs for several areas, such as business value, time pressure, and risk removal. Some just use two estimates: one for CoD, the other for duration, and the two together to calculate WSJF using the earlier formula.

ADDING NONFUNCTIONAL REQUIREMENTS TO THE BACKLOG

Nonfunctional requirements (NFRs) are constraints or restrictions that apply to all items in the backlog (see Figure 4-6). For example, an NFR may be that all items must comply with the Healthcare Insurance Portability and Accountability Act (HIPAA) security standards or that all software must be written in a certain version of Java.

You can see that NFRs are a constraint on the backlogs at all of the management levels. SAFe is reminding you that you can't spend all of your adding features. The framework forces you to also consider reliability, performance, and supportability. In a sense, you shouldn't always be focused just on cooking the meal. Sometimes you need to spend a little more time setting the table.

CASE STUDY

CHARTING THE WAY TO WSJF

I once worked for a large retail company that was rolling out a SAFe implementation. One of the biggest challenges was how to prioritize the work in its value streams. Teams worked hard to optimize their workflow by thinking about queueing theory and Little's Law (see the later section "Streamlining the value stream"). The teams broke down their work into smaller chunks, and they did a great job. Now, they had to prioritize these small chunks.

I asked the staff to try to calculate the cost of delay for each one of the work chunks. Most of the employees weren't accustomed to taking an economic view of the software — either the product owner determined the priority or workers simply tried to finish the easiest chunks first.

They created a simple two-dimensional diagram that had the cost of delay along the y-axis and the duration along the x-axis. The diagram looked like a ski slope, similar to the following figure. Chunks of work were clustered at the top and on the downward slope. That meant that a few chunks of work had a substantial cost of delay but would take a short time to finish. When they looked at the chart, the product solution managers quickly realized that this work was the highest priority.

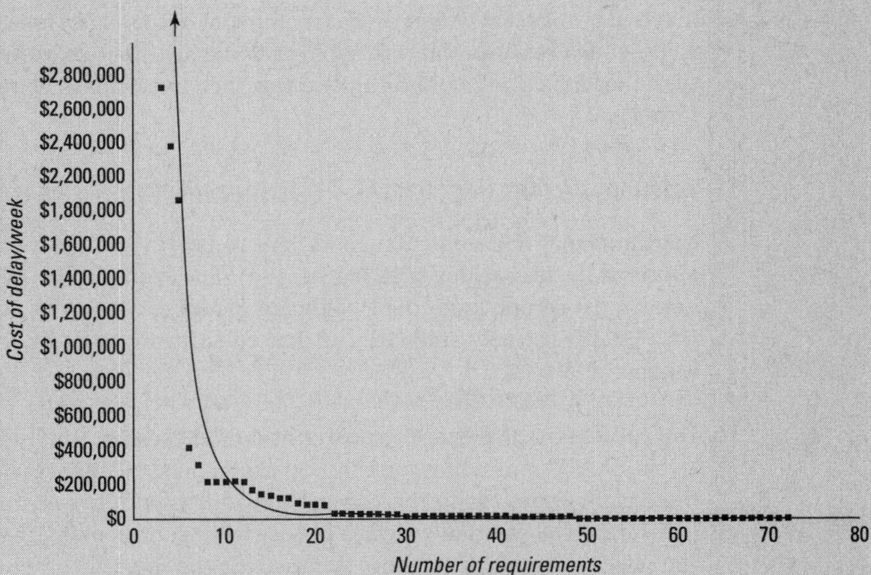

In SAFe language, they took an economic view and determined the weighted shortest job first. Then they knew how to prioritize the work in their value stream.

FIGURE 4-6: Constraints on the backlog.

All SAFe content reproduced with permission from © Scaled Agile, Inc. (www.scaledagileframework.com).

Financing value streams with Lean Budgets

Another way portfolio managers prioritize work and prevent any team from becoming inundated is through *Lean Budgets* — a set of practices for funding value streams rather than projects (see Figure 4-7). Remember that SAFe takes a transactional view of how people work in an enterprise. So, when the portfolio management team assigns a budget to a value stream, what it's really saying is, "You're welcome to work on whatever you want, but this is the only thing we're going to pay you for."

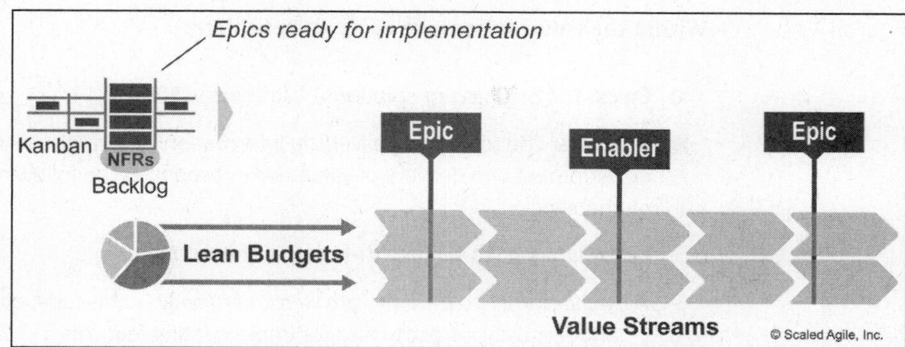

FIGURE 4-7: Prioritizing items in the backlog using Lean Budgets.

All SAFe content reproduced with permission from © Scaled Agile, Inc. (www.scaledagileframework.com).

Shifting the focus from projects and products to value streams

While the Portfolio level has many components, its primary focus is on the value stream. The steps involved vary depending on the product and how the organization delivers the product to the customer, but it's triggered by some event such as the customer placing an order, and it ends when the customer receives the product or some other value (see Figure 4-8). The steps in the middle are the actions the team needs to take to deliver that value. Maybe the team must meet to develop a vision for the product and then develop, test, and tweak the product before releasing it. Each of those actions is a step in the value stream.

FIGURE 4-8: A value stream.

All SAFe content reproduced with permission from © Scaled Agile, Inc. (`www.scaledagileframework.com`).

Value streams are a central part of Lean budgeting, which focuses the attention of everyone in the organization on financing these value streams. In addition, all key performance indicators (KPIs) are tied to value streams, so performance is measure by the value delivered to customers and how efficiently and cost-effectively that value is delivered.

Within the value stream are epics and enablers:

- **Epics:** The products or solutions customers value.
- **Enablers:** The tools that deliver the information and insight in support of the development and delivery of value. SAFe recognizes the following four types of enablers:
  - *Exploration:* To validate the need or the solution
  - *Architectural:* To pave the *architectural runway* — the code, components, and technical infrastructure for implementing features
  - *Infrastructure:* To develop, test, and integrate initiatives
  - *Compliance:* To prepare compliance activities

Making value streams Lean

SAFe relies heavily on Lean thinking, which emphasizes minimizing waste while maximizing value, or finding the most efficient path to deliver what customers value. Making a value stream Lean is a two-step process:

1. Identify what the customer deems most valuable.
2. Optimize the process for delivering that value to the customer.

REMEMBER

Lean is a concept that came out of the Toyota Production System and was originally used in automobile manufacturing. Software developers later adapted it and created Lean Software Development.

FINDING WHAT THE CUSTOMER DEEMS VALUABLE

Finding what customers value can be easy or difficult, depending on how your organization creates its product. For example, if your company sells running shoes online, then determining what customers value should be pretty easy; they want quality shoes at a reasonable price that are easy to find and order, are delivered quickly, and are free and easy to return if they don't fit. However, if your company develops an accounting application, finding out what the customer values can be more difficult. You may even have several different customer types — home users, small-business users, and corporate accounts.

Having a conversation early on about what the customer values is a key benefit to using SAFe. The portfolio-level practices encourage executives to help the rest the organization define what high-level value they need to provide to their customers. The SAFe enterprise strategic themes get the ball rolling, then the managers have to turn these themes into actual value streams with dedicated budgets.

STREAMLINING THE VALUE STREAM

After you've identified a customer and the value you deliver to that customer, it's time to streamline your value streams, which you can do in several ways, including the following:

- Remove unnecessary steps from the value stream.
- Make existing steps in the value stream more efficient.
- Reduce queue time by breaking the steps into their smallest possible components and distributing them.

You can see examples of value stream optimization by standing in line at your local grocery store. In the past, the checkout clerks had to key in the prices of each item. With the use of barcodes and scanners, that step has pretty much been eliminated. The step of having to weigh produce hasn't been completely eliminated, but it has been made more efficient by building a scale into the scanner mechanism. And if lines start to get too long, a manager will open additional lanes to move customers through the checkout process faster. All of these are ways to optimize the value stream.

Amazon's grocery stores have streamlined the value stream even more by completely eliminating checkout lines. A customer logs in to the store by tapping her smartphone on a turnstile when she enters the store, and as she adds items to her cart, they're entered into the customer's virtual cart app, which then totals the bill and charges it to the shopper's credit card as she exits the store.

TECHNICAL STUFF

In SAFe, value-stream optimization is based primarily on queueing theory, specifically Little's Law, which postulates that the best way to get something through a complex system is to split it up into the smallest possible chunks. The idea is that several short lines will go through a system faster than one long line.

Imagine that your work was set up like the water tank pictured in Figure 4-9. The "L" represents the water in the tank. You can think of it as the work in progress (WIP). The "λ" is the spout coming out of the tank. It's your team's throughput — the amount of work the team can finish (your constraint). The "W" is the lead time. This is the amount of time it takes for work to go through the whole system.

Imagine that your team's throughput "λ" is two gallons per day. That means five gallons in the tank will give you a lead time of 2.5 days:

$$W = \frac{L}{\lambda} = \frac{5 \text{ gallons}}{2 \; gallons \,/\, day} = 2.5 \; days$$

Now image that there are 30 gallons in the tank. This will give your team a lead time of 15 days:

$$W = \frac{L}{\lambda} = \frac{30 \text{ gallons}}{2 \; gallons \,/\, day} = 15 \; days$$

A shorter lead time will make your work more predictable and give your customer a greater opportunity to provide feedback. That means you want to break your work down into the smallest possible chunks and have it flow through the system at a protectable pace. In this case, you wouldn't want to keep any more than five gallons of work in the tank at any one time.

FIGURE 4-9: Illustration of Little's Law.

WARNING

Don't try to cram big chunks of work, especially unplanned work, into the value stream. Doing so may make you feel as though you're getting a lot done, but this will cause bottlenecks that can grind development to a halt. Just look at what happens on a highway when a few drivers try to rush to the front of the line and merge in front of everyone else. Some entrance ramps even have traffic "metering" lights for flow control to prevent a line of traffic from trying to merge all at once or trying to enter the highway at a rate that would overwhelm the road's capacity. Although the idea of having a stoplight might seem to contradict the SAFe concept of continuous movement, the idea of adding work gradually to the system to prevent bottlenecks is fundamental to the SAFe concept.

Tackling big jobs at the Large Solution level

If you're a large organization, you may have several teams of teams that must be coordinated to deliver large solutions. SAFe accommodates such scenarios with its Large Solution level (see Figure 4-10).

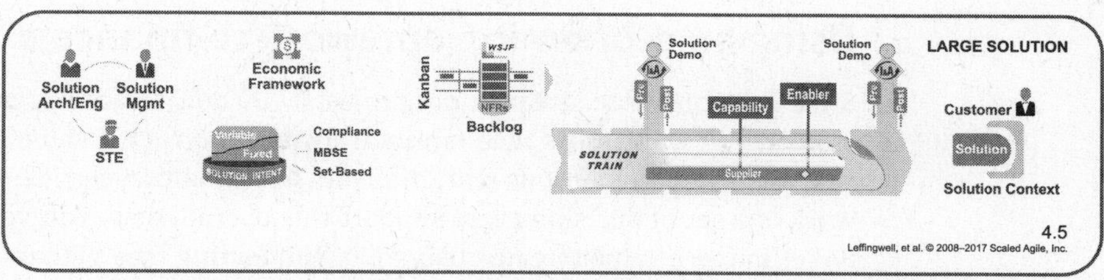

FIGURE 4-10: The SAFe Large Solution level.

All SAFe content reproduced with permission from © Scaled Agile, Inc. (www.scaledagileframework.com).

TECHNICAL STUFF

In the previous version of the Full SAFe illustration, the Large Solution level was called the value stream level. It was a collapsible management level between the Portfolio and the Program levels. The value stream level focused mostly on mapping solutions to value streams. The Large Solution level still retains a lot of that legacy, except here, instead of mapping value streams to agile release trains, you have a simpler *solution train*.

REMEMBER

In the large solution configuration of SAFe, the Large Solution level is at the top of the diagram. This configuration is for organizations that don't require the same level of portfolio management that you see in places that have a large project portfolio (or they're working on one big solution). You might use this for an organization such as a government agency or an aerospace or defense company. These organizations already have a robust built-in platform for managing their portfolio or are working on one solution — such as a rocket.

Meeting solution-level management

The solution-level employees are focused mostly on high-level solution governance. They capture requirements in a larger solution intent, and they work to coordinate several agile release trains around their larger solution train. The following people are part of the solution-level management:

- **Solution architect/engineer:** These people think about how well the solution maps to the organization's current architecture. They take a "system view" when they try to match the solution to various technical considerations.
- **Solution management:** This person works to make sure the solution aligns with the customer's expectations. They do this by creating a solution vision and roadmap. Then they prioritize the solution on a Kanban board.
- **Solution Train Engineer (STE):** This person makes sure the agile release trains align with the larger solution train. Each release should incrementally add value to the larger solution.

Using an economic framework to finance a solution

SAFe finances value streams, not projects. You don't want a focus on a car project; instead you want to finance family transportation. This value stream could have several different solutions (car, minivan, boat, motorcycle). The economic framework is a set of decisions that support this overall view. You've already seen how SAFe finances value streams using Lean budgeting (see "Financing value streams with Lean Budgets") and prioritizing based on the cost of delay (see "Starting the weighted shortest job first"). These ideas come into play in the decisions you make when you're delivering the best solution.

If you decided to create several family transportation solutions, you'd have to use an economic framework to make the best decisions. You could decide that a minivan would generate the most revenue and so that work would have the highest cost of delay. Using an economic framework, you may decide to make this the highest priority solution.

Planning with solution intent

According to Scaled Agile, Inc., *solution intent* is "the repository for storing, managing, and communicating the knowledge of current and intended Solution behavior." It "includes documented, fixed, and variable specifications and designs; reference to applicable standards, system models, functional and nonfunctional tests; and traceability." In simpler terms, solution intent involves answering two questions:

» What are we building?

» How are we going to build it?

REMEMBER

This word "intent," in this context, means a conscious, willful desire to do something, and it implies that some planning is involved. Think of it in terms of legal language; committing a crime with intent means you did it deliberately, not inadvertently. If you're an agile aficionado, you may find the concept of solution intent troubling because agile views software development as a continuous process of building an ever-changing product that requires frequent adaptations, not as a process of building a preconceived product. With solution intent, you have the well-established intent with only some flexibility to make changes.

SAFe addresses this concern by splitting the intent into fixed and variable specifications and designs (see Figure 4-11):

» **Fixed:** Required

» **Variable:** Flexible and adaptive

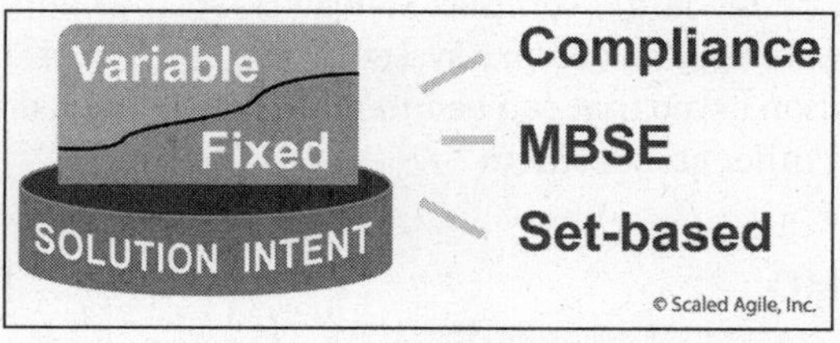

FIGURE 4-11: Solution intent.

All SAFe content reproduced with permission from © Scaled Agile, Inc. (www.scaledagileframework.com).

For example, suppose a restaurant manager makes the cooks responsible for creating the menu. It's a hamburger joint, and the manager tells the cooks they need to have six different specialty burgers. The only fixed requirement is that customers will be able to choose any of six different specialty burgers, but it's up to the cooks to decide what these burgers will be. They can decide based on variables, such as local customer preferences, what they like best to cook, and perhaps which ingredients are in season.

In such a case, the fixed/variable model works well, but what if the restaurant manager makes the six burger types a fixed requirement? In other words, management creates the menu, and the cooks must follow it. The only variable may be the actual recipes — how much of each ingredient to add. Now, the cooks have much less flexibility. If they know, for example, that people are flocking to other restaurants to order, say, an olive burger, they have no flexibility to add that burger to the menu, and the restaurant starts losing business.

WARNING

If you do decide to use solution intent, be careful how you use fixed and variable design. If you use too much fixed design, you're probably not getting that much value from your agile teams. If you use too much variable design, you're probably not getting that much value from your planning efforts.

Prioritizing solutions with a Kanban board and backlog

Like the Portfolio level (and every level in the SAFe framework), the Large Solution level uses a Kanban board. At the Large Solution level, the Kanban board is used to track solutions from the idea phase to completion. After ideas are reviewed, analyzed, and approved, they're added to the solutions backlog — a prioritized list of solutions that can then be developed and delivered by the solution train, discussed next. (For additional details about Kanban boards, backlogs, and methods used to prioritize work, see the earlier section, "Prioritizing epics and adding them to the backlog.")

Riding the solution train

The solution train is a coordinated team of teams of teams, along with suppliers, that designs and builds large, complex solutions, such as automobiles, software suites, banking systems, and defense systems. The purpose of the solution train is to produce a solution demo that can be integrated, evaluated, and made accessible to customers and other stakeholders.

SOLUTION DEMO

The solution demo is the product of the solution train's collective efforts. After it's produced, the solution demo can then be inspected by customers and other stakeholders and adapted.

FEATURES AND CAPABILITY

The solution train's focus is on building and integrating features and capabilities into the solution:

- **Features:** A *feature* is a system service that meets the need of a customer or stakeholder.
- **Capabilities:** *Capabilities* are whatever you need to do to deliver the value to the customer. The customer may not have asked for these capabilities and may never see them, but they're important to the success of the value stream, and they're typically available across all ARTs.

ENABLER

An *enabler* is supporting architecture or infrastructure that's not part of the value delivered to the customer, but is required to provide that value. For example, you may need a new server, a new testing environment, or a network upgrade to deliver value to the customer. All these items would be considered enablers.

REMEMBER

The enabler concept is a significant departure from Scrum at the team level. A Scrum team focuses on creating user stories that represent customer value. You wouldn't want to have a user story that says something like, "As a server, I need to be updated so that I can deliver more pages."

SUPPLIER

Suppliers are organizations (internal or external) that provide components, subsystems, or services to support the solution train's ability to develop and deliver solutions to customers. Suppliers are often used to reduce lead times and improve quality.

Considering the solution from the customer perspective

At the far right of the Large Solution level is the goal of the solution train — to deliver a solution that meets the customer's need in the context in which the customer will employ that solution:

- **Customer:** The one and only boss in the system.
- **Solution:** The products, services, or systems delivered to the customer (internal or external).
- **Solution context:** The operational environment for the solution, including its requirements, usage, installation, operation, and support. The solution context may be outside of the organization that develops and delivers the solution.

Making things happen at the Program level

The Program level (see Figure 4-12) is like the factory floor; it's where most of your teams and teams of teams (ARTs) work to develop and deliver the product. In this section, I introduce you to the various components that comprise the SAFe Program level and provide guidance on how to establish a Program level in your enterprise.

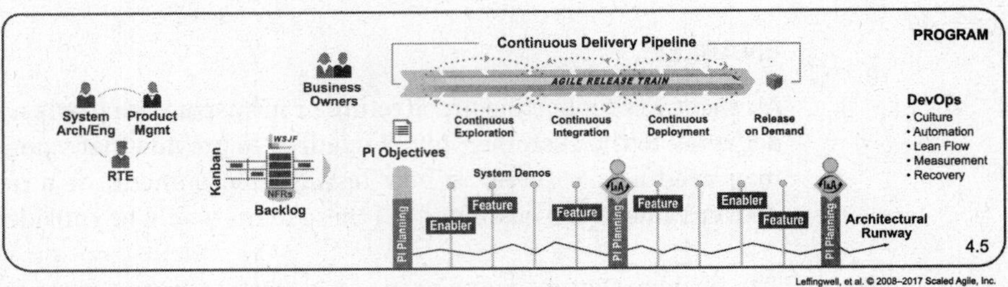

FIGURE 4-12: The SAFe Program level.

All SAFe content reproduced with permission from © Scaled Agile, Inc. (www.`scaledagileframework.com`*).*

Meeting the program leaders

At the Program level are several leadership roles:

- **System architect/engineer:** Defines the technical and architectural vision for the solution to be developed.
- **Product and solution management:** Identifies customer needs, prioritizes features, and develops the program vision and roadmap.
- **Release Train Engineer (RTE):** Coordinates, coaches, leads, and facilitates the teams that comprise an ART. Think of the RTE as the engineer that drives the train. If you're familiar with Scrum (see Chapter 6), think of the RTE as a super Scrum Master.
- **Business owners:** Ensure governance, compliance, and return on investment for each solution an ART develops.

Understanding program increments

The Program level delivers work in a *program increment* (PI) — a fixed period of time (typically 8 to 12 weeks) a team has to deliver the solution in the form of a working, tested product. If you're familiar with Scrum, you can think of this as a sprint of sprints. (See Chapter 1 for more about sprints.)

One of the RTE's most important duties is to manage and facilitate the program-increment-planning meeting. Prior to each PI, the RTE meets with her ART to formulate a plan for completing its work. This meeting may take a couple days, because each ART may have a hundred or more people working in dozens of teams. The RTE must get these teams to coordinate their activities and maintain close communication for the duration of the PI.

CASE STUDY

STRUGGLING AT THE PLANNING STAGE

The work at the Program level is some of the most difficult in SAFe. I once worked for an organization that really struggled getting this level to work. It had epics from the Portfolio level that were broad and communicated a larger vision. The RTE and the product team tried to break down these epics into something that a few dozen teams could work on.

The greatest challenge was getting a hundred or so people in dozens of different teams to coordinate their work. They needed everyone to commit to delivering their work at the end of the program increment. In their case, that was after ten weeks.

The RTE described it as trying to stage a different play every ten weeks. All teams had to know their parts, and if they forgot a line, it could make the entire production collapse. Every team depended on the others to complete the mission.

The most grueling part was the two-day product-increment-planning meeting. The meeting had to be flexible enough so that people learned something new, but it also had to be structured so it wasn't too noisy and chaotic. They tried many different techniques, but having more than one hundred people in a room communicating with each other always seemed unnatural.

This organization decided to break the PI planning meeting into two smaller meetings. Then the RTE worked to coordinate the information between these two events.

Remember that SAFe is a template. SAFe is being constantly updated to reflect new ideas. You shouldn't assume that every practice will work well in your environment. The key is to know the intended result for each practice. That way you can tweak it to fit your organization without losing the benefit.

Loading work into the backlog

RTEs work with product and solution management to pull epics from the top level and add them to their trains. Together, they use a Program-level Kanban board with columns to help prioritize and organize these epics and indicate what they want to implement now as well as other work that can wait.

Riding the ART through the continuous delivery pipeline

With Kanban board in hand, the RTE coordinates the agile release train (ART). According to Scaled Agile, Inc., an ART is a "cross-functional team-of-agile-teams, which along with other stakeholders, develops and delivers solutions incrementally, using a series of fixed-length iterations (building blocks) within a program increment (PI) time box." The idea is to maintain a continuous delivery pipeline with the following four traits:

- **Continuous exploration (CE):** The process of monitoring market and user needs and figuring out ways to address those needs.
- **Continuous integration (CI):** The process of developing, testing, integrating, and validating features taken from the program backlog.
- **Continuous deployment (CD):** The process of taking validated features, building them into the product, testing them, and preparing them for release.
- **Release on demand:** The process of placing features into production to be released to customers immediately or incrementally as driven by market demand.

The ART is the vehicle that delivers the organization's value streams (see Figure 4-13). Some value streams are small enough that one ART can deliver its intended solution. Other value streams are large enough that they require several ARTs to deliver a more complicated solution.

REMEMBER

These agile release trains also coordinate with larger solution trains. These solution trains deliver a solution demo at the end of every program increment. It's here that you get customer feedback on the new capabilities of the solution.

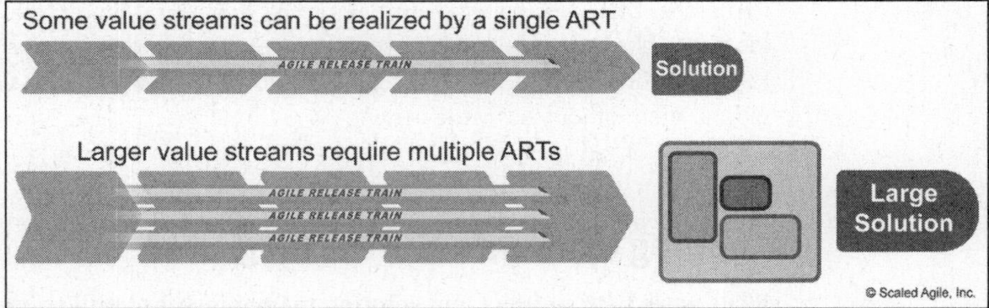

FIGURE 4-13: Map value streams to ARTs.

All SAFe content reproduced with permission from © Scaled Agile, Inc. (www.scaledagileframework.com).

The train analogy describes ideal workflow in SAFe product development. The train never stops running. As the cars pass by, the teams pull features from the backlog. Each team completes and delivers its work, where it can be picked up by another team to move it to the next stage in the process. Because the process is continuous, no team has to wait for another team to complete its work. If a team isn't ready to deliver, it doesn't hold up progress; it simply waits for the train to pass by again.

REMEMBER

You want trains to run without handoffs. (A *handoff* occurs when one team completes its work and passes it along to another team, so it can begin its work.) Because everyone is always working together on small tasks, you can limit handoffs and move the product through the system more quickly.

CASE STUDY

ELIMINATING HANDOFFS

I once worked for an organization that was using SAFe to create an inventory control system. The organization was trying to move away from its waterfall approach. The company had a strong control culture, so each department had its own area of responsibility. The project management office helped create the requirements, then they had business analysts design a project plan. Different development teams were assigned to each part of the application. One group worked on the database, another group did the software development, and another group performed testing and quality assurance.

Each one of these departments had its own handoff. The developers couldn't start until the database team finished. Then the quality assurance team couldn't test the product until the developers told them it was done. Each one of these handoffs made the system less efficient. One team had to wait for another to finish, and then the waiting teams were forced to work frantically to finish the part they were responsible for. Hurry up and wait then wait and hurry up.

It was more like an agile moving van. Each team had a set time at which it needed to get everything on its van. If teams missed the moving date, then their work wouldn't make it into the release. The organization had to work extra hard to map the value streams to agile release trains.

One of the first things the teams did was break their work into the smallest possible chunks that could easily fit into an agile release train. They learned from queueing theory that smaller chunks of work move more easily through the system. Then the teams systematically eliminated all the handoffs. The database teams, the developers, and the quality assurance teams all worked together on a small chunk of work. They didn't have to wait for each other to finish. Their agile release train was blasting through all their organizational barriers.

In the end, their agile approach improved product delivery. They didn't realize how much fat they had in their process. Even though each team was waiting for handoffs, it was continuously working on some part of the project. Using Lean thinking to form well-run ARTs leads to more consistent and predictable product delivery.

Breaking down silos with DevOps

Short for *development and operations*, DevOps is a mindset and collection of technical practices to improve communication and collaboration among everyone working in the Program level. DevOps consist of the following five elements:

- **Automation:** Developing and automating the continuous delivery pipeline increases the frequency and quality of deployment, stimulates innovation by making it safer to experiment, reduces time to market, shortens the lead time for fixes, reduces the frequency and severity of release failures, and improves recovery times.
- **Culture:** Everyone shares the responsibility of delivering value to the customer.
- **Lean Flow:** The Lean Flow concept has everyone looking for ways to visualize and limit work in progress (WIP), reduce batch sizes, and manage queue lengths to improve efficiency and speed of development and deployment.
- **Measurement:** DevOps mandates measurement and analysis over intuition in decision-making. Analysis is based on automated collection of real-time data regarding the performance of solutions.
- **Recovery:** DevOps stresses a proactive approach to recovery, based on the assumption that failures will happen rather than "failure is not an option." Teams are encouraged to plan for and rehearse failures, to be able to fix forward or roll back (to a prior working state), and swarm to fix a problem whenever one occurs (a stop-the-line mentality).

Transitioning to SAFe can be a monumental challenge for large enterprises with long-established departments for business analysts, project managers, product managers, system architects, hardware and software engineers, and software development, testing, and even deployment.

These separate departments are like vertical stacks that run through your organization (see Figure 4-14). That's why they're commonly referred to as "silos." Silos are tall, thin buildings that farmers use to store grain; they're designed to keep the stores of grain separate, not to share grain. Likewise, organizations with strict departmental divisions are not geared for close communication and collaboration.

In organizations such as these, creating and coordinating ARTs can be difficult. In a sense, you must create virtual organizations within your larger organization that cut across these silos. As you can imagine, that's not easy, especially in an organization with a strong control culture. If you're a manager in one of these silos, then you may feel as though your department and position are being threatened. The purpose of DevOps is to break down silos by creating communities with a shared mission, mindset, and methodologies.

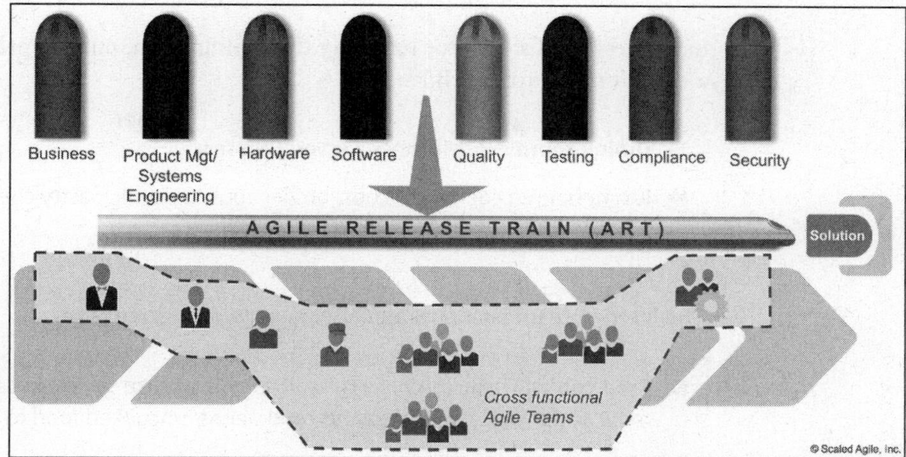

FIGURE 4-14: Creating ARTs across organizational silos.

All SAFe content reproduced with permission from © Scaled Agile, Inc. (www.scaledagileframework.com).

Forming ARTs

Performance at the Program level depends heavily on your team-building ability. The goal is to form teams that can work independently and together to deliver the greatest value to the customer the fastest. Here's one way to approach the challenge of forming ARTs:

1. List all the teams involved in developing and delivering your product.
2. Divide these teams into different value streams.
3. Create each train so it has the fewest dependencies. You don't want trains to depend on another to deliver their product. If you do then you'll just be adding more handoffs.

Think about how this might work in a restaurant. The value stream consists of all the steps necessary to take orders from customers, prepare their orders, and deliver the food and beverages to their table, preferably to everyone who's sitting at the table at the same time, so they can eat together. That's three steps: (1) Take orders, (2) prepare food and beverages, and (3) deliver food and beverages.

Now you could create teams around each of those steps, but then you'd have a team of servers to take orders and another team to deliver orders. In addition, you'd have a bottleneck at the kitchen, because they'd be preparing food and pouring drinks. A better approach is to start with the teams and then look at how those teams align with the value stream. For example, most large restaurants have three teams: one for handling the dining room, one for preparing food, and a third for preparing drinks:

- **Dining room:** Host/hostess, servers, bussers
- **Kitchen:** Prep cooks, grill cook, broiler cook, fry cook, pastry chef
- **Bar:** Bartenders

The kitchen team is commonly a team of two or three teams:

- **Prep cooks:** The prep cooks chop vegetables, make salads, cut and grind meat, weigh and mix ingredients, and deliver uncooked food to the cooks.
- **Cooks:** The cooks fry, grill, boil, broil, bake, deep fry, and then arrange the food on plates.
- **Expediter (Food Train Engineer):** Busy restaurants have an expediter who serves as the liaison between the cooks and servers, clarifying and arranging orders as they come in, making sure the food leaving the kitchen matches the order and is up to the restaurant's standards, ensuring that all orders for any given party are sent out at about the same time, and solving any complaints about the food that they receive from customers via the servers. Having an expediter enables the servers to focus on their customers and the cooks to focus on preparing the food.

Each of the teams functions independently but also must communicate and cooperate with at least one other team: Servers must communicate with the cooks (or the expediter) and bartenders. Cooks must communicate with the servers (or the expediter) and prep cooks. The bartenders must communicate with the servers (and perhaps directly with customers). But you've also eliminated a lot of the dependencies. No team should be waiting for the other to start its work. The bartender's free to make drinks while your cooks are working on meals. When each team delivers its product, it's scooped up by the wait staff and delivered to the customer. The expediter makes sure all the meals for any given table are sent out from the kitchen at the right time and that the server picks them up to deliver, so nobody at the table has to wait. In SAFe, this is described as the coordination of ARTs.

Taking off from the architectural runway

Near the bottom of the Program level, note that the agile release train runs on top of something called an *architectural runway*, which, according to Scaled Agile, Inc., contains "the existing code, components, and technical infrastructure needed to implement near-term features without excessive redesign and delay."

MIGRATING A DATA WAREHOUSE TO A BIG DATA CLUSTER

CASE STUDY

I once worked for an organization that was trying to use the Scaled Agile Framework to migrate its data warehouse into a big data cluster. The company really struggled with how to create agile release trains that could work within its existing organizational structure. It wanted to create three separate clusters: one cluster for testing, another for development, and finally one for production. The organization came up with many different ideas for how to create teams that would make up its ARTs.

First the organization wanted a train for each cluster, but then decided that wasn't really necessary because the work was so similar. It didn't want all three ARTs to have different teams working on the same product. That would be like a restaurant creating three separate ARTs that were all dedicated to making sandwiches.

In the end the organization decided to create one large ART called "database migration." Then it created three smaller ARTs. Each one of these smaller trains had its own destination. One train worked on data gathering, another train worked on data scrubbing, and the third train worked on uploading the data to the new cluster. The company got its inspiration from the classic extract, transform, and load (ETL) strategy used for data warehouses.

This setup was far from perfect. The trains struggled to keep their teams together. The larger database migration train was always trying to pull teams out of the smaller trains. Still, it was a good start, and it helped the organization focus on its value streams.

For example, in a restaurant, while servers, cooks, and bartenders perform the steps required to seat patrons, take orders, and deliver food and beverages, a great deal of infrastructure and equipment is required for them to do their jobs. Infrastructure may include the building itself; a website for advertising and taking orders; a phone system for communicating with customers, suppliers, and staff; a scheduling and payroll system; a system for accepting various methods of payment, and so on. Equipment may include dining room furniture, refrigerators, ovens, grills, deep fryers, plates, silverware, and dishwashers. All of this makes up the architectural runway that supports the restaurant's efforts to deliver value to its customers. Note, however, that the customers do not receive the value of this architecture directly.

In practice, the architectural runway is built and maintained the same way solutions are developed and delivered to customers — through the efforts of management-directed ARTs. The system or solution architect/engineer, serving as the product owner, helps to define and build out the runway. Typically, one or two ARTs perform most of the work and deliver the architecture as a solution over one or two iterations.

WARNING

Although the architectural runway is essential for executing solutions, don't pour time and focus on creating, maintaining, and extending it at the expense of developing and delivering value to customers. You should be spending no more than one or two iterations to implement and prove any new architecture.

Getting to work at the Team level

At the very bottom of the SAFe graphic is the Team level (see Figure 4-15), where the division of levels begins to blur. The Team level is actually an integral part of the Program level, because an agile release train at the Program level consists of teams. If you think about the Program and Team levels as two separate levels, then you might think a handoff must occur between the two levels, which is not the case. It's not as if the teams are feeding their work into the continuous delivery pipeline; they're performing their work *inside* the continuous delivery pipeline.

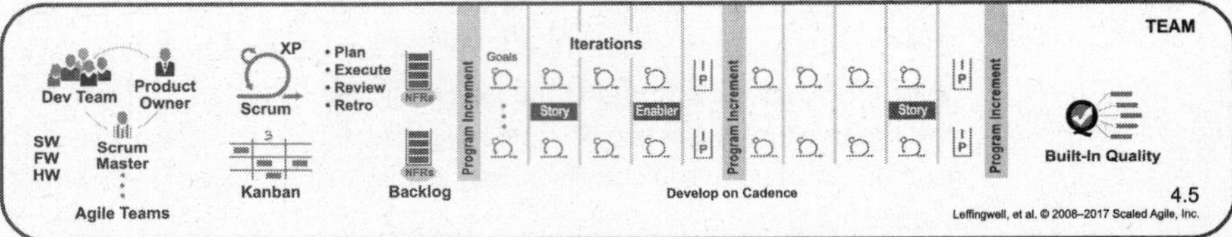

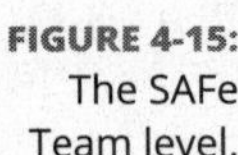

FIGURE 4-15: The SAFe Team level.

All SAFe content reproduced with permission from © Scaled Agile, Inc. (www.scaledagileframework.com).

In this section, I take you on a tour of the Team level, so you get to meet the people who work there and find out more about how they do their jobs.

Taking a SAFe agile team roll call

The core component of the Team level is the agile team. Each agile team has 5 to 12 members, including members in the following three roles:

- **Dev Team:** The Dev Team, typically comprised of software developers, testers, and engineers, develops and tests stories, features, or components. These teams are further distinguished with the letters SW, FW, and HW next to their team names to show whether they're working on software, firmware, and/or hardware solutions.
- **Scrum Master:** The Scrum Master leads and coaches the team; brings the team up to speed on Scrum, Kanban, SAFe, and Extreme Programming; facilitates the team's work; fosters a culture of high performance, continuous flow, and relentless improvement; and makes sure that the agile process and

SAFe principles and practices are being followed. Scrum Masters also help coordinate efforts among different teams. (For more about Scrum, see Chapter 5.)

- **Product owner:** The product owner is the team's content authority and customer representative, essentially serving as quality control to maintain the conceptual and technical integrity of the features and components the team is responsible for delivering. The product owner works with product management (outside of the team) to prepare the team's backlog and then manages that backlog. She's also responsible for prioritizing stories and is the only member of the team who has the authority to accept stories as done.

REMEMBER

At the Team level, product owners aren't true product owners in the sense that they own an enterprise-level product. Instead, they get their high-level guidance from a product manager and then translate their vision into a working product. The product is more like a solution owner; she doesn't spend time figuring out what to make, but helping the team figure out how to make it.

SAFe generally has two team types: ScrumXP and Kanban, both of which follow the Lean-Agile Mindset and self-organize and deliver their work in predictable chunks:

- **ScrumXP:** ScrumXP is a hybrid of Scrum and Extreme Programming. Scrum is an approach to software development in which teams of three to nine developers break their work into one- to four-week cycles, called sprints, conduct daily 15-minute progress meetings (standing up), and deliver working software at the end of each sprint. XP stands for Extreme Programming, which features more guidance on software engineering practices. ScrumXP differs from Scrum in other ways, as well:
  - Scrum Masters may handle several teams.
  - An extra sprint for innovation and planning enables teams to shift focus from delivery to come up with new ideas.
  - The product owner maintains the team backlog, which is pulled out of the product manager's program backlog.
- **Kanban:** While most teams operate in a Scrum environment, teams also have the option to use Kanban, which helps for visualizing and managing workflow and reducing work in progress. Kanban is a pull system, in which team members pull work from a queue when they have the capacity to do it. This approach may be best for system and maintenance teams. (See Chapter 8 for more about Kanban.)

Defining, building, and testing stories

Agile teams are dedicated to defining, building, and testing *stories* — small pieces of a product's functionality as told from the user's perspective. Pieces are sized so that they can be completed in a single *iteration* — a fixed period of time that an agile team has to complete its work. Teams engage in the following process to plan, execute, and review iterations:

- **Plan:** Team members meet to determine how many stories from their backlog they can deliver in the upcoming iteration, and they set their iteration goals.
- **Execute:** The team develops a high-quality, working, tested system (a program increment) within the allotted iteration time box.
- **Review:** The team inspects its program increment at the end of the iteration to evaluate progress and adjusts its backlog for the next iteration.
- **Retrospective:** The team looks back at the results of its iteration, reviews its practices, and considers ways to improve.

The goal is to maintain *develop on cadence* — a fast, rhythmic development flow that ensures important activities and events occur on a regular, predictable schedule.

Embracing the concept of built-in quality

Built-in quality, one of SAFe's four core values, is especially important at the Team level, where teams are actually building the solutions. Built-in quality makes everyone on the team responsible for the quality of its piece of the larger product to ensure a fast flow across the entire value stream and to build high-quality solutions. One of the key benefits of built-in quality is that testing is conducted during development instead of at the end of development, so problems can be fixed along the way instead of having numerous problems come to light near the end of a project and having to scramble to fix them.

Filling in the background with the SAFe spanning palette

The SAFe spanning palette (see Figure 4-16) contains a collection of tools you can use regardless of the level on which you're operating:

- **Metrics:** A key advantage that SAFe has over other waterfall approaches to management is that it contains far more measurables, especially backlogs, iterations, time boxes, and feedback. Using metrics to measure progress and outcomes ensures that the organization remains on track to achieve its business and technical objectives.
- **Shared services:** *Shared services* are people and resources teams need to do their job but that can't be dedicated to a particular team, such as security specialists, information architects, and technical writers.
- **Community of practice (CoP):** *Communities of practice* are informal self-organized gatherings of people who share a common interest and may benefit from meeting outside their respective agile teams. For example, all Scrum Masters may want to meet to discuss their challenges and share information and insight.
- **Milestones:** SAFe uses three types of milestones — program increment, fixed-date, and learning — to measure progress toward a specific goal or objective.
- **Roadmap:** A roadmap is a schedule of events and milestones that serves as a timeline for deliverables, typically program increments. The purpose of roadmaps is to provide some degree of certainty to an otherwise uncertain process.
- **Vision:** A *vision* describes the future state of the solution in a way that reflects customer and stakeholder needs and the features and capabilities required to meet those needs.
- **System team:** The system team is an agile team that supports the agile development environment and assists other teams with continuous integration, test automation, and deployment, providing end-to-end testing whenever necessary.
- **Lean User Experience (Lean UX):** Lean UX is a design mindset and culture that defines Lean-Agile principles and practices, including implementing functionality in increments and gauging success by measuring outcomes.

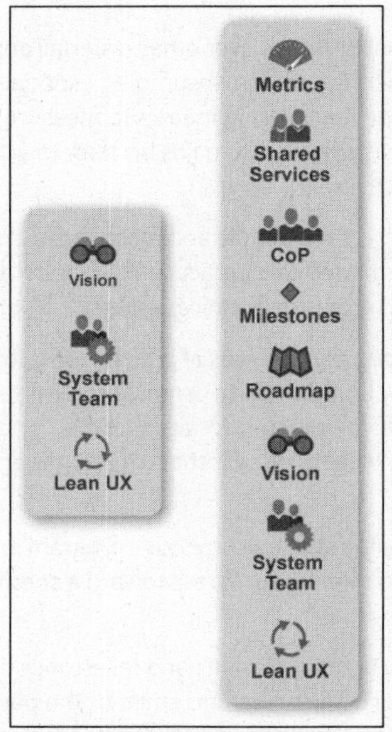

FIGURE 4-16: The SAFe spanning palette.

All SAFe content reproduced with permission from © Scaled Agile, Inc. (www.scaledagileframework.com).

Making Your Organization Agile with SAFe

It seems like everyone is running marathons. Every time I open up LinkedIn or Facebook, I see a picture of someone I know running a marathon. I had to know how these people got to this level of athleticism. I finally asked a runner I know, "How do you get to be a marathoner?" He looked at me and said, "I run a lot." I didn't expect such a simple answer.

The same can be said of the process of making an organization agile. The framework is generous about what a SAFe organization should look like. It has levels on top of levels, dozens of roles, and relationships between those levels and the roles. Yet the framework is stingy about what to do to make it work. You know where you need to be, but the system is not very clear about *how* to get there. And when you ask for clarification, SAFe's answers aren't very helpful:

- When you ask, "How do I build an agile release train when I have well-established departments?" SAFe says, "You just do."

- When you ask, "What are some different techniques for making the large release train meetings effective?" SAFe says, "You just figure it out."
- When you ask, "How can I use team story points to make enterprise-level estimates?" SAFe answers, "Somehow it just works."

You could easily forgive this missing information if SAFe were a lightweight framework like Scrum. Scrum has only three roles, three artifacts, and a few events. You're expected to figure out a lot on your own. However, with a large system, such as SAFe, you need more guidance.

In this section, I plug the gaps by providing guidance on how to transition your organization to SAFe, and I help you steer clear of the most common pitfalls.

Plugging the gaps

TIP

Some of the people who created SAFe would be likely to tell you that the secret to success is in building high-functioning agile teams. That's fine, but these teams still need some direction on making this large-scale organizational change. Following are some tips on how to make SAFe work for your organization:

- **Begin by choosing the SAFe configuration that's most relevant to your organization.** For example, Full SAFe, Large Solution SAFe, Portfolio SAFe, or Essential SAFe.
- **Try to understand the output of each of the key meetings.** If you can figure out what you need, then you may be able to adapt the meeting to fit your organization. Remember that SAFe is a template and it's frequently updated. If something doesn't work for you, look for ways to make it work or look for a different way to achieve the same outcome.
- **Approach agile teams as virtual organizations within your larger organization.** Think of each team having an objective and the personnel needed to achieve that objective. Engage existing management in a discussion of how agile teams break down silos and run across existing departmental boundaries.
- **Choose several people in the organization and get them trained as SAFe program consultants.** Eventually, you must train everyone in your organization, so all of them understand SAFe in principle and practice, but getting several people trained early on is a good start.

WARNING

Give it more time. When a person is trained as a SAFe program consultant he has a week to make the transition. The reality is that most organizations will need much more time laying the groundwork for such a big change.

- **Start your training by introducing the following three key concepts (in this order):**

  1. Queueing theory
  2. Value streams
  3. Agile release trains

  If you can get your organization to understand these key concepts, rolling out the framework will be much easier.

- **Develop a clear vision of how your organization will function with the SAFe framework.** Choose the pieces of the framework you need to bring your vision to fruition. Only when your vision is clear will you be able to explain SAFe to others in a way they'll understand.

Making your organization agile instead of fitting agile into your organization

SAFe is an attempt to fit agile into your organization, so the framework will feel as comfortable as an old pair of jeans. However, this can be a false sense of comfort that carries its own risks. It often seduces companies into embracing a water-agile-fall approach, which allows them to maintain a control culture they're reluctant to relinquish and simply adopt agile for a smattering of teams within the organization. For reasons given earlier in this chapter, in the section "Avoiding water-agile-fall," you won't reap the full benefits of agile by following this approach. Instead, you must make your organization agile.

To make your organization agile, you need to change its collective mindset, its culture, and you must break down the silos of clearly defined departments. Everyone in the organization needs to stop thinking so much about product and think more about process, and stop focusing so much on projects and shift his focus to value streams.

REMEMBER

Agile teams break down large initiatives into smaller chunks that can be delivered by cross-functional, self-organized teams. In practice, that requires pulling people out of their clearly defined departments and giving up a great deal of authority and control to teams. Such changes are the most difficult to make, but they deliver the greatest benefits — innovation, responsiveness, and value to the customer. So, if you like SAFe because it seems familiar and comfortable, you're probably liking it for the wrong reasons.

Starting communities of practice

A great way to maintain a SAFe mindset and culture is to start communities of practice (CoPs) within your organization. A *community of practice* is an informal self-organized group of people who share a common interest, typically in a specific technical or business area. The group meets regularly to collaborate, share information and insight, improve members' skills, and continuously advance their collective knowledge of their area of expertise. In other words, they "talk shop."

The good news is that in large organizations, such groups are likely to exist in various departments. For example, an organization is likely to have separate departments for software development, engineering, business analytics, information technology, accounting, and so forth. While these divisions may be challenged by the need to create agile teams, communities of practice enable and even encourage the divisions to persist.

However, CoPs need not be departmental. Sometimes developers create CoPs around a certain skill, such as Java development or programming in Python. They may even create a CoP around agile practices such as Extreme Programming or user stories.

While the primary goal of CoPs is to increase knowledge and skills in an area of expertise, a beneficial byproduct is that the groups can share their knowledge and experience of working in teams. In the process, their discussions can deepen their understanding and appreciation of SAFe and strengthen the SAFe mindset and culture.

As soon as you begin to form your agile teams and ARTs, start to encourage and facilitate the creation of CoPs. As soon as people in your organization receive their SAFe training and find out about CoPs, they're likely to take the initiative to start these groups on their own. A large part of encouraging them is to simply get out of their way. Let them schedule and manage their meetings. You can also encourage the formation of CoPs by allotting time during the normal day to conduct the meetings and perhaps by budgeting for snacks and beverages.

TIP

A CoP should have a loose format. Maybe a Scrum Master will give a short presentation about something that's worked very well for her team, or another Scrum Master may pose a question to the group that she needs help answering.

CASE STUDY

DISCOURAGING CoPs

I once worked for an organization that was hoping to create several communities of practice. After all the people in the organization received their SAFe training, they quickly self-organized into different interest groups. They struggled at first because the product managers didn't want to take time out of product delivery for informal meetings, so the managers put conditions on them. They said the groups could meet and discuss anything they wanted as long as it was after hours. As you can imagine, getting people to stay after work was difficult.

The teams worked around this restriction by calling their groups centers for excellence — a term that was more familiar and acceptable to the managers. The simple renaming did the trick. These groups were allowed to meet during normal business hours.

Several of these renamed CoPs popped up throughout the organization. There was one for database engineers and another for testers. Each one met on different days around 4 p.m. in a big conference room. Some of them were even able to convince management to budget for pizza and snacks.

These CoPs were some of the most successful meetings in their enterprise agile transformation. The only challenge was that as soon as the workplace became busy or chaotic, these meetings would disappear off the schedule. It was a classic problem about focusing on getting things done over doing things well.

It's a shame when that happens because these CoPs are actually the most useful when conditions are the most chaotic. Other people in your organization are often the most helpful when you're struggling with something on a tight deadline.

Don't be too concerned if a few of your CoPs fizzle out over time. They tend to have a natural lifespan that gives out when the need for them no longer exists (see Figure 4-17). Do be concerned if all your CoPs suddenly stop meeting. That usually means the people are spending too much time *doing* and not enough time *learning*.

TECHNICAL STUFF

The concept of communities of practice is born out of the Lean approach to software development. A core value of Lean organization is continuous improvement, which applies equally to people, solutions, and processes.

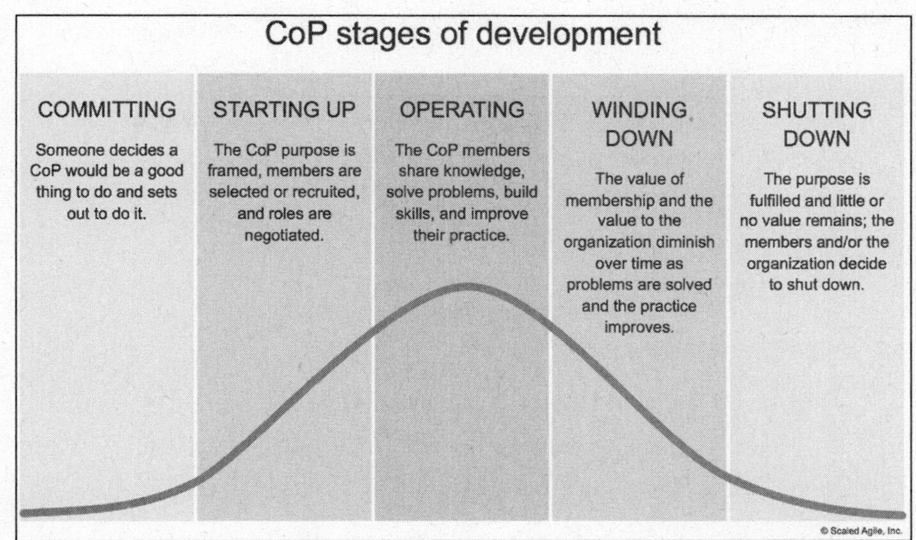

CoP stages of development
COMMITTING
Someone decides a CoP would be a good thing to do and sets out to do it.
STARTING UP
The CoP purpose is framed, members are selected or recruited, and roles are negotiated.
OPERATING
The CoP members share knowledge, solve problems, build skills, and improve their practice.
WINDING DOWN
The value of membership and the value to the organization diminish over time as problems are solved and the practice improves.
SHUTTING DOWN
The purpose is fulfilled and little or no value remains; the members and/or the organization decide to shut down.
© Scaled Agile, Inc.

FIGURE 4-17: Community of Practice lifespan.

All SAFe content reproduced with permission from © Scaled Agile, Inc. (www.scaledagileframework.com).

» Descaling your organization with LeSS principles and practices

» Meeting the product owner, Scrum Master, and other key players

» Transforming your organization to enterprise agility with LeSS

» Steering clear of common adoption pitfalls

Chapter 5

Growing Scrum with Large-Scale Scrum

To understand Large-Scale Scrum (LeSS), you first need to know Scrum basics. According to the LeSS Company, which manages the LeSS framework (`http://less.works`), "Scrum is an empirical-process control development framework in which a cross-functional, self-managing team develops a product in an iterative incremental manner." (*Empirical* in this context means that decisions are based less on up-front planning and more on experimentation and measuring outcomes. *Cross-functional* means a team contains all the people with all the knowledge and skills to create a product. See Chapter 1 for more about Scrum.)

LeSS is Scrum principles and practices applied to many teams working together to develop a single product. More important, perhaps, is what LeSS *isn't*. It's not a large Scrum team under the direction and supervision of a bunch of new managers.

In this chapter, I introduce you to LeSS in principle and in practice. I bring you up to speed on the LeSS framework and offer guidance on how (and how not to) implement LeSS. I also describe the framework in detail so that you can determine whether LeSS is the right framework for your organization and, if you decide it is, begin to envision your organization on LeSS and start taking the steps necessary to transform your organization into a LeSS enterprise.

REMEMBER

Although the LeSS framework has been stable for the last few years, like most enterprise agile frameworks, it continues to evolve. Visit `http://less.works` to check for updates and to download and print the latest full-size, colorized versions of many of the LeSS framework images included in this chapter.

Taking a Quick Tour of the LeSS Framework

At first glance, the LeSS framework graphic (see Figure 5-1) makes LeSS look a lot more fun than other agile frameworks. It almost looks like a theme park map. People appear to be standing in line at concessions booths. Some are juggling. Two people are even riding a teeter-totter! You can almost smell the popcorn.

On closer examination, you begin to see the LeSS product development process in action surrounded by a half-dozen key concepts. In this section, I take you on a tour of the LeSS framework graphic.

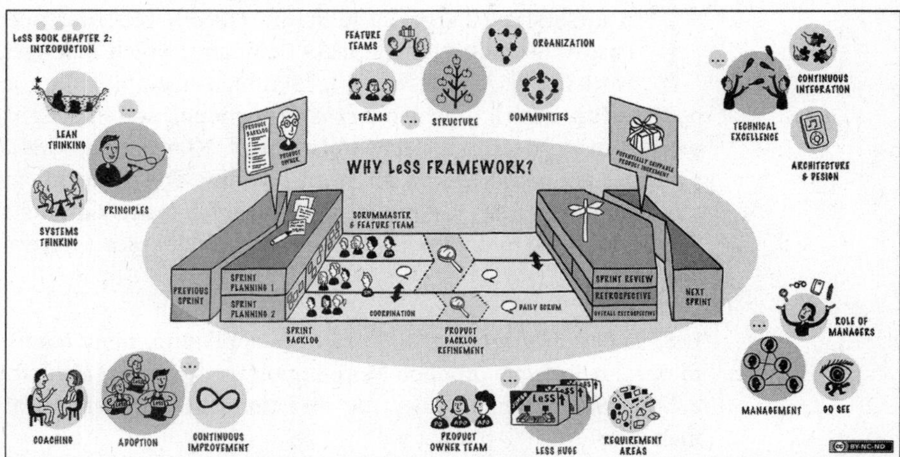

FIGURE 5-1: The LeSS framework.

Copyright © 2014–2017 The LeSS Company B.V. (`https://less.works`). Reprinted with permission.

Tracing the product development process

LeSS is based on the premise that Scrum is all an organization needs for individual teams to deliver quality products fast. However, it recognizes that some large enterprises don't have a culture or ability to deliver products with only one or two small teams. For them, LeSS is a good compromise because it creates a balance between concrete practices and the ability to inspect and adapt.

Smack dab in the middle of Figure 5-1 is the LeSS product development process, which begins on the left and continues indefinitely off to the right with three-dimensional structures shaped like arrows to point the way. Product development comprises a never-ending series of sprints, so although the process appears linear, it's actually circular and continuous. Imagine curling this page over so that the "Next Sprint" overlaps the "Previous Sprint," and you'll see what I mean. As soon as the Scrum teams complete a sprint, they start another sprint in a continual process that improves product value.

However, each sprint is linear with a clear starting and ending point. It begins with a product owner and product backlog and ends with a potentially shippable product increment. Here, I lead you through the process from beginning to end.

Product owner, product backlog, and sprint planning

On the left side of the LeSS product development process in Figure 5-1 is the product owner and product backlog. The product owner selects features from the backlog and engages in a two-stage sprint-planning process:

- **Sprint Planning 1:** The first stage of sprint planning centers on determining which items in the product backlog to work on and setting a goal for the sprint.
- **Sprint Planning 2:** The second stage of sprint planning involves determining how to get the work done — how to complete the selected items from the product backlog.

In other words, Sprint Planning 1 is about *what* to do, and Sprint Planning 2 is about *how* to do it.

Sprint backlog

One of the objectives of sprint planning is to develop a sprint backlog for the various Scrum teams. In Figure 5-1, the sprint backlog is depicted as the Jumbotron that all the team members are looking at. Each team draws items from its backlog and then works to complete those items in time allotted for the sprint.

Scrum teams

Over the course of a sprint, Scrum teams pull one or more items from the product backlog and work on completing them over the sprint. To complete their tasks, Scrum teams must collaborate with:

- Customers and end users to refine the definition of the product backlog item
- The product owner to prioritize product backlog items
- Other teams to coordinate and integrate their work to produce one whole product increment

Note in Figure 5-1 that the teams are divided into three lanes with a product owner who spans all three lanes. The product owner is about as close to top-level management as you will get in LeSS, and it's really not management at all. The product owner simply organizes the work to help the teams complete their sprints.

Scrum Masters

You may notice in Figure 5-1 that the three teams have only two Scrum Masters (designated by "SM" in the figure). One Scrum Master works with the two teams in the bottom two lanes. The other has her own team in the top lane. This shows that unlike team Scrum, LeSS permits different teams to share Scrum Masters.

Coordination

The double-headed arrows that cross the lanes dividing the teams represent the coordination required among teams to develop a single, unified potentially shippable product increment that's ready for shipment.

Daily Scrum

The dialogue bubbles in the graphic represent Daily Scrums. Every day, each team meets (without managers or a Scrum Master) to answer the following three questions:

- What did WE do yesterday?
- What will WE work on today?
- What is in OUR way?

Teams may meet together during Daily Scrums to spend some time coordinating their work.

Product backlog refinement

Teams are required to spend some time during their sprint (less than ten percent) to refine the product backlog for future sprints. Refinement (depicted by magnifying glasses in the graphic) may include one or more of the following:

- Splitting big items
- Adding detail about an item
- Estimating the time required to develop an item

Note that the teams in the top two lanes share a backlog refinement meeting. While in the bottom lane the team has its own meeting. (See Chapter 6 for details.)

Sprint review, retrospective, and overall retrospective

At the end of the sprint, various groups meet to discuss the outcome of the sprint and ways to improve the product and process:

- **Sprint review:** The teams, product owner, end users, customers, and other stakeholders meet to discuss what the team built along with changes and new ideas to decide the direction of the product. This is where each team demonstrates its work. You can see the little signpost on top of that meeting. That represents the feedback that the team gets so team members can inspect and adapt their product.
- **Retrospective:** Team members meet to share information and insight and discuss ways they can improve their work going forward.
- **Overall retrospective:** All teams meet with the Scrum Masters and product owners to discuss much broader process improvements, overall organization, and systemic problems within the organization.

See the later section, "Learning from achievements and mistakes: Continuous improvement" for details on how to conduct these three meetings.

Potentially shippable product increment

Every sprint ends with a potentially shippable product increment. Prior to that, during the sprint, the teams must collaborate to integrate their work and produce a whole product. The overall goal of developing a potentially shippable product increment is intended to:

- Keep the focus on the whole product
- Increase transparency and eliminate the possibility that any portion of the work remains undone
- Reduce work in progress
- Maintain short feedback cycles for continuous improvement

At the end of the sprint, you have a potentially shippable product increment, but that doesn't mean everyone stops working. As soon as the final review process is over a new sprint begins.

Brushing up on LeSS principles

At the core of LeSS is a set of principles that govern the way organizations apply LeSS in their specific context. While some enterprise agile frameworks, such as the Scaled Agile Framework® (SAFe®), provide more structure and more roles, LeSS calls for less structure and fewer roles, leaving decisions up to the organization itself as to how to implement LeSS. The guidance the framework offers comes more in the form of its ten principles. In this section, I introduce these principles.

Large-Scale Scrum is Scrum

LeSS creators stress that Large-Scale Scrum is no different from Scrum. Unlike SAFe (see Chapter 4), which adds processes and roles, Scrum simply provides principles, rules, and guides for the application of Scrum in a multi-team context. LeSS doesn't change the way Scrum teams function; it only provides guidance to facilitate how those teams scale or descale (see "More with LeSS") to larger enterprise-level products.

Transparency

The dictionary definition of "transparent" is "easy to perceive or detect." Transparency is a core concept in all agile frameworks, because it's what drives continuous improvement through discovery and adaptation. Product owners, Scrum Masters, team members, and other participants are expected to be open and honest with one another. In addition, the sprint model creates short feedback loops that dramatically increase visibility into problems in the product, process, team, and organization overall.

More with LeSS

The More with LeSS principle stresses simplicity over complex organizational solutions, such as increased layers of management and complicated structures and processes. The idea is that complicated solutions cause more problems than they solve. In this respect, LeSS is a *descaling* framework to remove large organization complexity. With LeSS, the emphasis is on developing greater insight into problems at the product development level and addressing them at that same level with simpler solutions.

Whole product focus

LeSS encourages cross-functional teams by focusing their efforts collectively on developing a whole product instead of having individual teams focus solely on whatever part of the product they're working on. Teams are advised to function according to the following guidelines:

- Your team's part has no value until it's integrated into the whole product.
- Your team isn't done until its part is integrated into the whole product.
- Given the choice to optimize the team or the whole product, optimize the whole product.

REMEMBER

Customers buy a product, not parts of it.

Customer centric

When multiple teams are involved in product development, each team tends to become so involved in developing its part that it forgets how the customer will use the product. LeSS encourages a closer connection between teams and customers by recommending that organizations do the following:

- Form feature teams instead of component teams to maintain a focus on end-user needs. (See the later section "Feature teams" for more about the difference between feature teams and component teams.)
- On very large products, group teams into customer requirement areas instead of architectural subsystems.
- Have the product owner connect teams directly with customers instead of serving as an intermediary.
- Have teams get most of the clarifications about the product directly from customers, which frees up more time for the product owner to focus on the big picture.
- Share the product backlog among all teams working on the product and continuously reprioritize the backlog to optimize the system for customer delivery.

Continuous improvement toward perfection

Continuous improvement toward perfection is one of the pillars of Lean thinking, the other being respect for people. The purpose of this principle is to encourage organizations to embrace change and for everyone in the organization to challenge everything and continue to develop his knowledge and skills. Improvement stops only when the product, the process for creating it, and the organization and the people who develop it have achieved perfection — which essentially means never.

Lean thinking

Lean thinking is a business methodology in which an organization's management is committed to continuously investing in its people and giving each employee the opportunity to identify problems in his own way of working, solve those problems, and make improvements. As you can see, the two principles of Lean thinking and continuous improvement toward perfection are closely aligned.

Systems thinking

Systems thinking is a management discipline that sharpens awareness of whole dynamic systems and how the components of those systems interrelate. Certain tools such as flow charts and simulation models are often used, but the scope of systems thinking often encompasses processes, limits, delays, behavioral patterns, and anything else that may affect the productivity of the system overall. With LeSS, systems thinking has two primary purposes:

- To ensure long-lasting systemic improvement in an organization through experimentation and empirical analysis instead of standard best practices and quick-fix solutions that commonly suffer from lack of insight or are based on false assumptions.
- To extend value beyond the product development teams and out to the entire organization to look at ways that the organization can be improved overall to deliver greater value to the customer.

Empirical process control

Empirical process control is an approach to product and systems development that relies less on up-front planning and more on experimentation, transparency, inspection, and adaptation. In short, teams are encouraged to innovate and experiment in order to continuously improve the product and the systems for building it.

Think of it this way: Every so often I'll get a contract to work in a different part of the city. I live in an area where it's extremely important to plan out your commute to work. If you come up with a bad plan, you could get stuck for hours in traffic. So I use an empirical approach to determine the best process for my commute to work. One day I try the bus, another day I try the train. I may try driving or riding my bicycle to the train station and then taking the train. Each time I try something new I record how long it takes for me to get to work. After a while I figure out the quickest commute.

That's how LeSS improves your enterprise agile approach. It encourages you to inspect and adapt how you deliver your product and find the way that works best. In many ways it takes the empirical approach of Scrum and applies it to the whole enterprise agile process.

Queueing theory

Queuing theory is a mathematical study of wait lines used to predict and reduce wait times. It's used in all agile frameworks to reduce wait times inherent in the traditional linear product development processes. In LeSS, many teams working in parallel and together, develop different parts of a product and then integrate the parts near the end of a sprint to create a potentially shippable product increment. See Chapter 4 for more about queueing theory and Chapter 8 for more about managing queues.

Getting up to speed on LeSS structure

Although LeSS is a framework for large organizations, it counters the traditional hierarchical structures found in many large organizations. The term "structure" is almost a misnomer. A better term might be "roles and teams." In this section, I introduce you to the various elements that provide some structure to this relatively unstructured development environment.

Scrum teams

A *Scrum team* is a self-managed, cross-functional group of three to nine people who do it all, from writing code to producing documentation, to creating a part of a product and integrating it into a functioning increment of the product. In LeSS, numerous teams work in parallel and together on a single product with the common goal of delivering a shippable product at the end of a given sprint. Each team has the following characteristics:

- Each team member is dedicated to only one team; a person can't be pulled off a team to work on another team.
- Teams are cross-functional, meaning each team contains all the skills needed to produce a shippable product.

» Members of each team work together in the same space to promote communication, cooperation, trust, and shared learning.

» Each team remains together for as long as possible to improve the ability of team members to work as a unit.

Feature teams

Feature teams are cross-functional, cross-component, stable, and long-lived. They take customer-centric features from the product backlog and complete them to deliver a potentially shippable product increment.

The "feature" in "feature team" highlights the difference between feature teams and component teams:

» **Feature teams:** A feature team has all the knowledge and skills required to build a *feature*, such as a feature in an accounting program for producing an accounts payable report (to show which customers owe money and how much).

TIP

Think of a feature team as a small, flat organization within the larger enterprise. Everyone on the team works together to deliver the product. Everyone in the rowboat rows, just as they do on any agile team.

» **Component teams:** Component teams handle various aspects of a feature. For example, to produce an accounts payable report, you may have a component team that works on the database, another that works on the user interface, and a third that focuses on presenting the data in a report. In this example, three component teams would be involved in delivering the feature, and they would need to work closely to coordinate their work.

The component team model results in a lot of dependencies, as shown in Figure 5-2 by the arrows from the items in the product backlog (in the column on the left). Because each work item requires two or more teams to complete it, one team may need to wait on another team to complete its work before it can move forward on that item. It also requires a great deal of cross-team coordination and communication, as shown by the double-headed arrows connecting the teams. No single team has the knowledge and skill set to complete a work item on its own.

In contrast, each feature team can choose one item from the product backlog and complete it without the help of another team. As you can see in the figure, none of the teams is connected to another. They all have the knowledge and skills required to work on each component of the product, so Team Wei can complete Item 1 by working on any and all Components A, B, or C, without depending on any other team to complete its work.

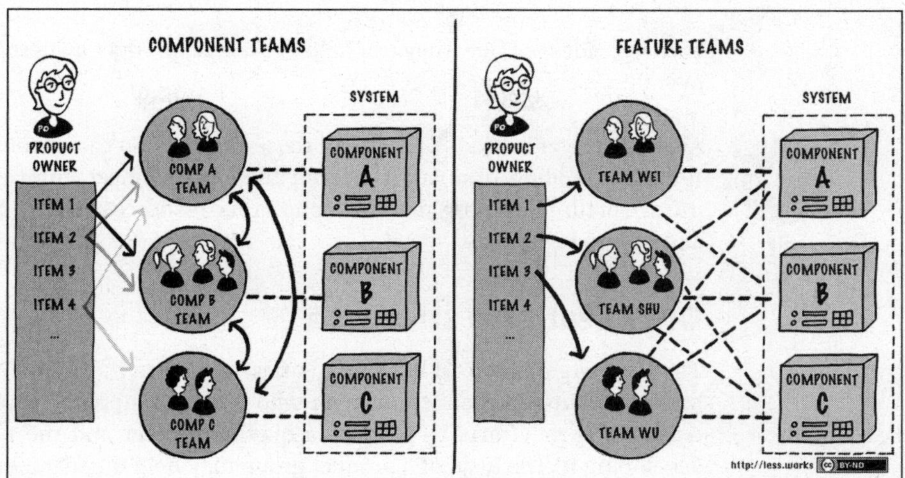

FIGURE 5-2: Component teams versus feature teams.

Copyright © 2014–2017 The LeSS Company B.V. (https://less.works). Reprinted with permission.

Scrum Master

The Scrum Master has a deep Scrum understanding to guide and coach the organization on Scrum principles and practices, so they have a better understanding of how to deliver value to customers. Each Scrum Master has four focus areas:

- Team
- Product owner
- Organization
- Development practices

WARNING

Don't think of the Scrum Master as team leader. The Scrum Master serves more of a role as advisor to bring everybody up to speed on Scrum, to educate and coach teams in self-management and shared responsibility, and to prepare product owners for their role and facilitate their interaction with their teams.

Communities of practice

Communities of practice (CoPs) are groups of people that gather informally around a certain functional area of expertise, such as software development, analysis, or testing, to share their knowledge and expertise and discuss their challenges. Essentially, they gather to talk shop. CoPs cross team boundaries, which can improve communication and cooperation across teams. For example, Scrum Masters may decide to meet as a group to share what they know about Scrum and exchange ideas of how they can help the teams, product owners, and organization overall.

TIP

Although organizations don't form these groups, you can encourage their formation by providing time and space for the CoPs to meet, information technology infrastructure, learning materials and other resources, and perhaps even snacks and beverages.

Organizational structure

The LeSS organizational structure is flat, as shown in Figure 5-3. The head of a product group is a product manager who works to support the product owner and teams in their efforts to produce a quality product and the perfect system for developing it. The head of a product group may help the team remove obstacles or improve its knowledge and skills.

Note that the organizational chart includes an Undone Department. Ideally, the nature of cross-functional teams makes this department unnecessary, but sometimes a team lacks the knowledge and expertise, such as testing, quality assurance, or business analysis, to complete a shippable product. When that happens, the undone department must complete the work.

For more about the various roles in the LeSS framework, see the later section "Getting to Know the Key Players."

FIGURE 5-3: A typical LeSS organizational chart.

Understanding the importance of technical excellence

Technical excellence comprises numerous agile engineering practices to help teams work in a continuous state of high quality and flexibility. In this section, I provide brief descriptions of these practices.

Continuous integration

Continuous integration is an approach to software development that involves making small changes that are integrated daily and tested frequently. Typically, each team member integrates his work at least once a day, which can result in several integrations over the course of a day. The emphasis is on developing a product in small batches and short cycles, which increases visibility into the process, thus increasing the quality of the system.

Continuous delivery

Continuous delivery involves keeping the product in a potentially shippable state at all times. The purpose of continuous delivery is to reduce the time, cost, and risk of delivering changes by allowing for more frequent updates to products in production. See Chapter 1 for details.

Acceptance testing

Acceptance testing checks a product to ensure that it meets the sprint goal and that the product is indeed potentially shippable. Acceptance testing includes a user-acceptance test and may also include functional or system testing.

Architecture and design

Architecture and design in LeSS involves less planning and more observation to see where the customer is going and then designing and building products accordingly. It's an approach to design that relies more on pull than push. (See Chapter 3 for more on "pulling" work.)

Clean code

Clean code is a term used in programming to describe a minimalist approach to programming. The goal is to use the least amount of code required for a feature or function, and that code should be easier for other programmers to read and extend. Writing clean code is especially important in LeSS, where you have so many teams of developers collaborating on a single product.

Unit testing

Unit testing involves running small, fast software programs to verify the functionality of a piece of code. Don't confuse a unit test with a bug test. A unit test determines whether a piece of code behaves as suspected in a variety of test cases. Unit testing is key in LeSS, which encourages frequent testing and adaptation.

Test-driven development

Test-driven development (TDD), as explained in Chapter 2, is a software development process that involves the repetition of a short development cycle. The developer writes a test case, designed to fail, that defines a desired function or improvement and then writes the least amount of code necessary for the program to pass the test and then refactors the code to acceptable standards. The main purpose of TDD is to reduce defect rates.

Thinking about testing

The notion of thinking about testing calls on team members to challenge their assumptions about testing, such as the following:

- Testing must be done at the end.
- Testing must be done by dedicated testers.
- Development must be complete before testing can start.
- Testing must be done according to plan.

By encouraging team members to challenge their assumptions, the thinking about testing approach encourages more innovative ways to test a product at any point in the development process.

Test automation

Iterative, incremental program development results in a continuously evolving product that must be tested at each iteration. In addition to testing the new code, the product must be tested to ensure that the old code still works after the new code has been integrated *(regression testing)*. In an agile development environment, manual testing can't keep pace. Testing must be automated as much as possible.

Specification by example

Specification by example (SBE) is a collaborative approach to defining requirements and developing test case scenarios for software products. The product owner and teams collaborate with end users and other stakeholders to develop realistic scenarios for how the product will be used.

Meeting LeSS management

LeSS management seeks to transition organizations from the traditional management-by-control to a managers-as-teachers-and-facilitators approach as promoted in Lean thinking. Most of management is delegated to self-managing teams that do most of the work and to product owners who decide (with team input) what the teams work on. In this section, I introduce some of the key concepts that drive management in a LeSS organization.

Role of manager

Traditionally, managers have been in charge of determining what needs to be done and how to do it. In a LeSS organization, the product owner (with team input) decides what needs to be done, and the Scrum teams figure out how to get it done. Management plays no role in either case and should resist any temptation to do so. Instead, managers function more as support personnel, ensuring that the product owner and teams have what they need to do their jobs and helping to remove any obstacles that may be getting in their way.

Go see

Go see is a method that closes the gap between management and product development to give managers greater visibility into what is happening in the organization. Managers are encouraged to sit with developers to find out what's really going on, so they can make better decisions and figure out ways to help.

Teaching problem-solving

While traditional managers are expected to solve problems, LeSS shifts the manager's role to teaching problem-solving and systems thinking and encouraging team members to think for themselves. The idea here is to move the problem-solving and decision-making responsibilities closer to product development, where they can be used more effectively to improve the product and the systems for creating it.

Self-management

One of the pillars of Lean thinking is respect for people. Instead of looking at employees as lemmings in need of strong leadership, Lean thinking sees them as highly motivated individuals who are able and willing to create high-quality products. Lean thinking encourages individuals and teams to be self-motivated and self-directed. As such, self-governing teams are expected to:

- Set their own direction
- Design the team and determine its role in the context of the organization
- Monitor and manage work process and progress
- Execute team tasks

Improvement service

Managers are in charge of developing an *improvement service* — a system for logging areas that need improvement and then addressing those issues. Following the LeSS framework, many organizations choose to create an improvement backlog. Managers consult with teams to determine areas of improvement and prioritize them. Teams can then choose items from the backlog to work on.

You may be able to find plenty of areas of improvement by looking at what comes out of the sprint review, retrospective, and overall retrospective at the end of each sprint (see the earlier section, "Sprint review, retrospective, and overall retrospective"). You may also consider conducting a workshop with the product owner, Scrum Masters, and teams to develop your initial improvement backlog.

Avoid adding items to the improvement backlog without first discussing them with the product owner, Scrum Master, and teams. Doing so will undermine the LeSS principle of self-management.

Manager as Scrum Master

The roles of manager and Scrum Master tend to overlap, so many organizations consider making the manager a Scrum Master. Is that a good idea? Well, that depends on the manager. If a manager is able and willing to relinquish control and authority to the teams and adopt a mindset of serving the team, such a move may make sense. If not, then it's a bad idea, because a Scrum Master who acts as a traditional manager will undermine the democracy of the team.

Supersizing your delivery with LeSS Huge

LeSS Huge is a second LeSS framework that's a step up from the framework you've been looking at so far — the framework shown in Figure 5-1. LeSS Huge is designed to scale up to many more teams and across the organization (see Figure 5-4).

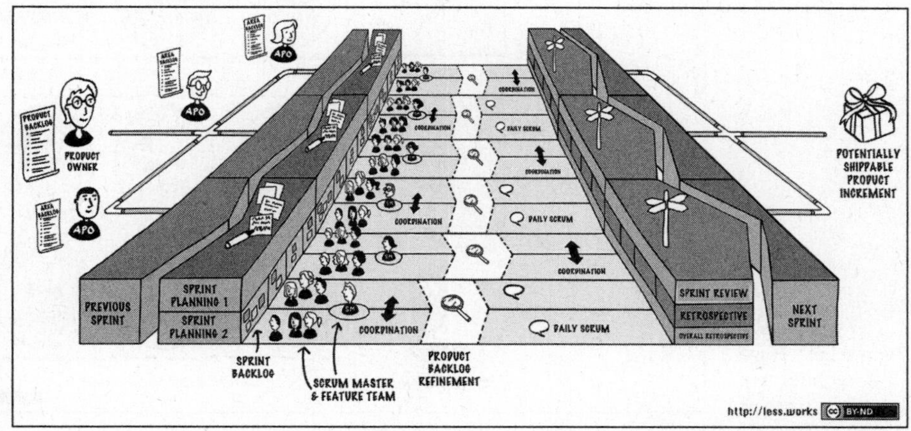

FIGURE 5-4: LeSS Huge is for even bigger products.

Even though this framework is larger and scarier than the standard LeSS framework, the emphasis remains on "less is more." The breadth of the framework is larger, but at its core are Scrum teams engaging in sprints. In this section, I highlight some of the differences in LeSS Huge.

REMEMBER

If you have eight or more teams, you can use the LeSS Huge framework, which provides additional structure through the use of requirement areas, explained next.

Requirement areas

Requirement areas are customer-centric categories of backlog items, often referred to as *product backlog items* (PBIs) (see Figure 5-5). For example, a website may have a separate requirement area for articles and advertisements. The product owner draws items from the product backlog and assigns each to a requirement area to create different views of the product backlog called area backlogs, discussed next.

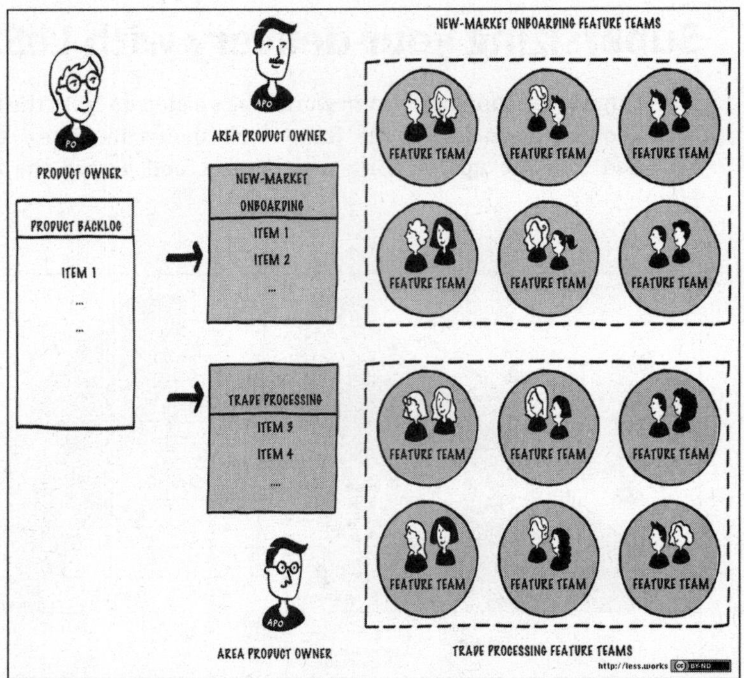

FIGURE 5-5: Typical LeSS Huge requirement areas.

Copyright © 2014–2017 The LeSS Company B.V. (`https://less.works`). Reprinted with permission.

Area product backlog

When working on a very large product, the product owner can easily become overwhelmed, and because LeSS focuses on optimizing the whole system, the product owner can become a bottleneck for all the feature teams. The best way to steer clear of this potential bottleneck is to break down the work into smaller batches. So the product owner breaks down the product backlog into smaller batches, each of which comprises an *area product backlog* assigned to its own area product owner.

REMEMBER

Lean thinking is about optimizing the whole and breaking down your work into smaller batches.

Area product owner

The *area product owner* maintains and prioritizes work items in a subset of the product backlog that pertains to a certain feature or a set of related features. Think of the area product owner as a product owner for a feature instead of for the entire product.

Organizational structure

The LeSS Huge framework is built on top of the regular LeSS framework, so it tries to add the minimum number of new roles and processes required to work on much larger products. Keep in mind that LeSS Huge is designed for eight or more teams, representing dozens, hundreds, or even thousands of developers. When you have that many people involved, you need an organizational structure to align their efforts. In LeSS Huge, the organizational structure, shown in Figure 5-6, involves the following areas:

- **Head of product:** The head of product provides the team with a unified vision of the product, communicating to everyone working on the product what it is and what it must do to serve the customers' needs.
- **Sites:** The two "Site" boxes on the left indicate the preference of grouping related teams and team members locally when an organization encompasses multiple sites across two or more buildings, cities, or countries. The purpose of having "teams in site," as the LeSS developers refer to this grouping, is to reduce the need for long-distance communication among teams.

  WARNING

  Although you want to keep your teams local to a given site, don't group teams according to requirements areas, because such an approach often results in making certain requirements areas more permanent than they need to be. Instead, look at these site groupings as a way to keep line organization local. (*Line organization* is traditional top-down, chain-of-command, department organization.)
- **Undone department:** In LeSS, "done" means a product increment is deliverable to a customer. A new team may not have the knowledge and skills required to create a product increment that's considered done, in which case the product enters the Undone department, where additional teams complete the work. The ultimate goal is to have no Undone department because, ideally, every team has the capacity to deliver potentially shippable product increments. However, the reality is that on large products, you'll probably have to spin up new teams that have trouble delivering product increments that meet the criteria for the definition of "done," so you'll need this department to complete their work until all teams have the capability to create deliverable product increments (which may never happen). (See Chapter 6 for more about the definition of "done.")
- **Support:** When teams are working on a huge product, they need more support in the form of configuration management, laboratory support, integration, and operations. On smaller products, regular LeSS teams can

usually take care of a lot of the environmental requirements to deliver their product; for example, they can spin up their own servers and software development environments.

WARNING

Try to keep your support "department" as small as possible and maintain its focus on supporting the teams, not controlling them or trying to set direction. They should be seeking ways to help, not ordering teams to "do it this way."

- **Product owner team:** The product owner team is made up of the product owner and area product owners, who work together to distribute work items and maintain and prioritize their respective backlogs.
- **Competence and coaching:** Products that need LeSS Huge can usually support full-time coaching and training staff. Some organizations create an agile center of excellence — typically a small group of coaches and trainers that thinks about ways to improve agile in the organization.

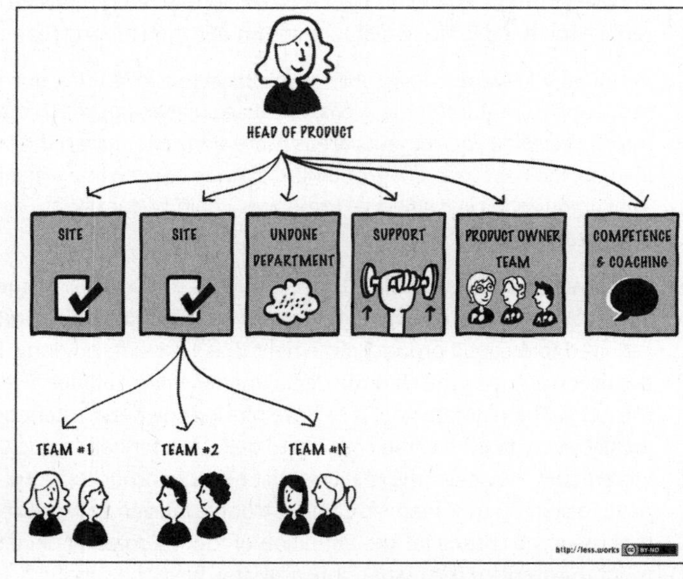

FIGURE 5-6: A typical LeSS Huge organizational chart.

Descaling Enterprise Agility

While most other agile frameworks scale up to enterprise agility, LeSS takes a different approach — it scales down. It steers you away from building up your teams and creating dozens of new roles, which is why LeSS creators, Craig Larman and Bas Vodde, often call their approach "descaling" enterprise agility.

WARNING

Larman and Vodde feel so strongly about the necessity for creating small, tight-knit teams that they start with a word of caution. They lay out three obstacles that commonly cause enterprise agile projects to fail:

- Making teams too large
- Having teams work at several different sites
- Offshoring one or more teams

The LeSS creators start out by saying these three obstacles will cause your projects to fail. It's almost as if they're saying, "Scaling agile will probably fail, but maybe not with LeSS." This is a very honest approach, but it's also very discouraging. Most organizations have all three obstacles. That's why they're looking for a scaled agile framework. They don't want to be told they'll probably fail; they want to be given something that ensures success.

Instead of giving up on these organizations, LeSS tries to enable large organizations that face these obstacles to scale with less risk of failure. It provides the framework, principles, and practices to help organizations overcome these obstacles and others.

Embracing the spirit of LeSS

Like Scrum, LeSS is intended to be a "barely sufficient methodology" to guide the product development process. Although the framework diagram described earlier in this chapter (see Figure 5-1) contains some details, LeSS is a minimalistic approach intended to provide just enough direction to get started and to encourage organizations to experiment on their own to find out what works best for them. This approach is captured in the LeSS Complete Picture diagram shown in Figure 5-7.

To provide a minimal amount of guidance and foster a culture of learning, questioning, engagement, and continuous improvement, LeSS replaces the notion of best practices with principles, rules, guides, and experiments:

- **Principles:** The principles govern the way organizations apply LeSS in their specific context. The purpose of the principles is to enable an organization to adopt a new mindset regarding product development. Many of these principles are just an upsized version of the agile mindset. Your teams need to be transparent about their work. They need to focus on the customer and inspect and adapt based on what they've learned or change requirements. (See the earlier section "Brushing up on LeSS principles.")

- **Rules:** The rules are key elements of the LeSS framework that support empirical process control and whole product focus. The rules are baked into the frameworks; for example, teams are required to conduct a retrospective at the end of each sprint.
- **Guides:** Guides provide direction on how to adopt the rules, and they provide a subset of experiments (discussed next).
- **Experiments:** Instead of prescribing best practices that would work for most organizations, the LeSS developers present experiments you can try to determine what works and what doesn't work in your organization. You can try these experiments on your own or use them to brainstorm ideas for your own experiments. See the later section "Experimenting to create your own approach" for details.

TIP

TIP

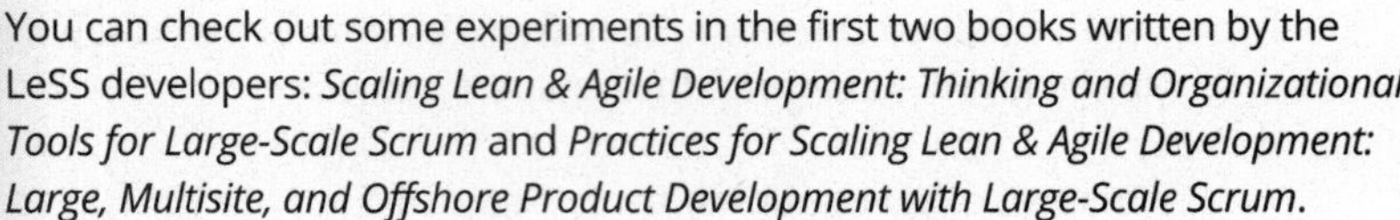

You can check out some experiments in the first two books written by the LeSS developers: *Scaling Lean & Agile Development: Thinking and Organizational Tools for Large-Scale Scrum* and *Practices for Scaling Lean & Agile Development: Large, Multisite, and Offshore Product Development with Large-Scale Scrum*.

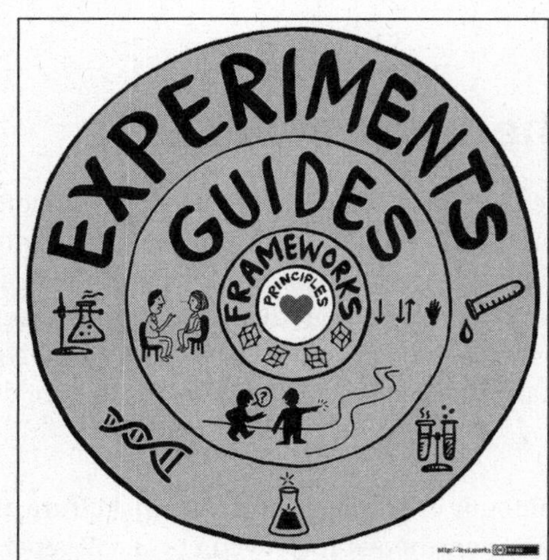

FIGURE 5-7: The LeSS Complete Picture.

Copyright © 2014–2017 The LeSS Company B.V. (`https://less.works`). Reprinted with permission.

Experimenting to create your own approach

LeSS encourages teams to experiment with their processes. From their perspective, an experiment is like a process recipe. It's something you can try at your organization and then evaluate the results. The creators of LeSS don't think in terms of best practices that work for every organization. Instead, they encourage organizations to be empirical — to experiment, measure the results, and make data-driven decisions.

The LeSS experiments usually begin with "Try . . ." or "Avoid . . .," so a LeSS experiment might be something like "Try . . . See root causes during causal modeling and retrospective workshops, with Five Whys and Ishikawa diagrams." These experiments range from small process tweaks to overall organizational structure. Here are few that have been pulled from the two books:

- "Avoid . . . test department."
- "Try . . . acceptance of test-driven development."
- "Try . . . product owner writes the tests."
- "Try . . . zero-tolerance on open defects."
- "Try . . . see the positive feedback loops in your system."

TIP

Start with the least amount of process and then experiment your way to an enterprise-level framework. Just enough. Just in time. In other words, start with less and then build your way up to a more robust framework.

Seeing software developers as craftsmen/women

Less incorporates Lean thinking, and one of the pillars of Lean thinking is respect for people. In LeSS, employees are treated as craftsmen/women who develop products. The creators of LeSS see software development as a rigorous intellectual pursuit. They cringe at the idea that software developers should get their requirements from business analysts and then make what they're told to make. Instead software developers should work to continually fine-tune their craft and, by extension, improve the product and the process for building it.

LeSS embraces the three-step *shuhari* model of learning and honing one's skills (see Chapter 1). The idea behind shuhari is that most software developers are stuck in "Shu." They only follow the rules and learn the basics (so called best practices). To reach the next level, developers must learn to break the rules and put their work into a larger context. Only then can they reach the highest "Ri" level where they actually make the rules and set their own path. It's at this level where software developers can unleash their creativity and help their organization build value. (See Chapter 1 for more on the shuhari model.)

LeSS is Scrum

As discussed earlier in this chapter, the LeSS creators are quick to point out that LeSS is Scrum. So what does this mean? Nearly all other enterprise agile frameworks include Scrum, which makes sense because Scrum is the most widely used of all the agile team frameworks. Yet what they're saying here is different. They're saying that LeSS *is* Scrum — it's not a new version of Scrum or something layered on top of Scrum.

Staying close to Scrum

One of the core ideas behind LeSS is that you don't have to add roles, events, rules, layers, and bureaucracy. You could take this lightweight Scrum framework and expand it out (wider but not necessarily deeper) to meet all your scaling needs. In other words, Scrum is all you need.

This approach differs significantly from how other enterprise agile frameworks deal with Scrum. The SAFe framework puts Scrum in the bottom corner of its diagram. Scrum is seen as just one of several agile practices you can use for your team. You could easily run SAFe without Scrum at all. (See Chapter 4 for more about SAFe.) All your teams could use Kanban, or Extreme Programming. They could even use a mishmash of agile methods such as ScrumBan or ScrumXP.

Disciplined agile (DA) also sees Scrum as a team-level set of practices. To deliver an enterprise-level product, you need to fill in the gaps that the lightweight Scrum intentionally leaves, which is why disciplined agile delivery (DAD) creates ten new roles to deliver agile enterprise software. (See Chapter 6 for more about DAD.)

Exposing flaws in processes

Like Scrum, LeSS sees itself as a way to expose flaws in processes. The combination of small teams and short development cycles enhances transparency, making failures more apparent. Again, other frameworks give you many more answers. Both SAFe and DAD add layers of new processes. While these layers provide additional guidance, they tend to obscure problems.

Staying simple

Above all, LeSS embraces Scrum's approach to simplicity. The creators of LeSS like to think of enterprise frameworks as having two extremes. On the one hand you have very process-heavy frameworks. These might include the rational unified process (RUP), traditional waterfall approaches (see Chapter 1), or even SAFe. On the other hand, you have very lightweight principles and ideas such as Lean Software Development and Kanban. LeSS positions itself between the two, providing just enough structure and guidance to create high-functioning teams that collaborate closely.

A SKEPTICAL VIEW OF ENTERPRISE AGILE FRAMEWORKS

Before you embrace (or adopt) an enterprise agile framework, consider where these frameworks come from. They're based on the observations and practices of a few agile coaches working at a couple large organizations who later decide to codify what they learned into a framework. The framework's success is measured according to its own success criteria. You may have no way of knowing whether the organizations actually benefited from the change.

The authors don't usually go back five or ten years later to check for long-term improvement. Even if they did go back, they have no reliable way to connect their work to the organization's success, and they have no impartial way to judge the long-term impact of their framework.

Many organizations discover that various frameworks are helpful and practical. The frameworks provide principles, guidelines, and structures to help you get started, but you shouldn't view them as rigorously tested and well-established.

One aspect of LeSS that may make it more attractive is that its creators don't view the framework as a one-size-fits-all solution. The framework provides a minimal amount of guidance and encourages those who adopt it to experiment and tailor the framework into something that works best for them.

REMEMBER

Scrum is simple and lightweight and designed to expose flaws. The creators of LeSS believe that's why Scrum is widely used. They want to take these ideas and apply them to large organizations without losing sight of what has made Scrum so successful.

Getting to Know the Key Players

Unlike some of the other enterprise agile frameworks, LeSS is careful to keep a shallow organizational chart. It doesn't add a bunch of new roles and layers to the development process. However, it does specify a few key players. In this section, I introduce you to these players and explain the role each plays.

TECHNICAL STUFF

OPERATING IN THE MATRIX

Matrix management was introduced in the 1970s as an early form of cross-functional product delivery. A typical organization would have projects that grouped specialists from different functional areas; for example, a developer from the engineering team and a tester from the quality assurance team. Most the people on the team would report to two managers — the project manager and the manager in their functional area. So a tester would report to both the project manager and the head of quality assurance. Sometimes this is referred to as "solid line and dotted line reporting." In this case, the solid line would lead to the functional manager and a dotted line would lead to the project manager.

Starting at the top: The head of product

Organizations that use LeSS commonly have a product manager, referred to as the "head of the product group," who serves the product owner of all the teams. Although this person is positioned at the top of the LeSS organizational chart (see Figure 5-6), she plays a supporting role, visiting the teams to find out about their challenges, helping teams remove obstacles, and facilitating their improvement.

REMEMBER

LeSS discourages *matrix management* — a management approach that has employees reporting to two or more managers, as explained in the sidebar, "Operating in the matrix." Each product group should have only one "manager" — the head of the product group — to whom all team members report.

Meeting the LeSS product owner

In team Scrum, the role of the product owner is one of most difficult. This one person sets direction and feeds the team the highest value work. The product owner also represents the customer and is the person ultimately responsible for ensuring that the product delivers the highest value to the customer.

LeSS upsizes this product owner role and gives it greater importance. Instead of coordinating with just one team, the product owner works with two or more teams, and must communicate and coordinate with customers and the head of product.

The product owner must manage the following five key relationships:

- Product owner and development teams
- Product owner and customers

- Developers and customers
- Product owner and higher management
- Product owner and Scrum Master

In this section, I explain what these relationships entail.

Working with the development team

The product owner has two primary responsibilities in regard to the development team:

- **Prioritization:** After analyzing information related to profit drivers, strategic customers, business risks, and other factors, the product owner prioritizes items in the product backlog.
- **Clarification:** To a lesser degree, the product owner clarifies items in the product backlog. I say "to a lesser degree," because this is a shared responsibility between the product owner and the teams. They work together to clarify features and functionality.

The product owner also ensures that what the teams build "hit the mark" and finds out what the teams need and how to meet those needs to remove any obstacles that may be hindering their efforts.

Teaming up with the customer

The product owner maintains a close relationship with the customer to deliver to the customer-centric solutions that meet their needs in a timely manner. She needs to know their goals and understand their key challenges and, when appropriate, challenge the customer if she envisions something beyond what the customer wants.

Facilitating communication between teams and customers

Ideally, customers and developers collaborate on solutions that best meet the customer's needs. The product owner must encourage and facilitate this open communication between the two. As their knowledge of the customer and product grows, developers often come up with interesting new ideas on their own. In many ways they understand the internals of the product better than anyone else. These teams will come up with the best ideas if they have an overall understanding of the customer's expectations.

CLOSING THE GAP BETWEEN DEVELOPERS AND CUSTOMERS

In many large organizations, two groups, each with a different focus, are involved in the product:

- **Outward focused:** Typically consisting of product managers and sales teams, this group is focused mostly on ensuring that the product meets the customers' needs. This group always wants to add features.
- **Inward focused:** This group comprises the developers and testers, who are mostly concerned with how to build the product. This group pushes for technical excellence. It wants to optimize what already works.

With LeSS, the lines between these two groups begin to blur, because product owners, Scrum Masters, and teams have direct contact with customers. However, the product owner has the greatest responsibility in this area. She must meet with customers directly and encourage and facilitate direct interaction between customers and teams. This differs from the traditional model in which product and project managers act as intermediaries between the customer and developers.

Collaborating with higher management

Although product owners are expected to maintain a productive relationship with higher management (portfolio managers and C-level executives and so on), it's really a two-way street that requires more from higher management than from the product owner:

- The product owner must understand and appreciate higher management's concerns for return on investment and market share and increase visibility into product development status.
- Higher management should respect the fact that the product owner's primary responsibility is to ensure product quality and customer satisfaction. For example, executives must not be pulling product owners and teams offline to attend to their pet projects. Higher management is also responsible for ensuring that the product owner has the information and resources to do her job.

Coordinating with the Scrum Master

The relationship between the product owner and the Scrum Master is one of student and teacher. Scrum Masters are expected to be aware of the product owner's challenges and concerns and provide helpful guidance while also educating the product owner about LeSS. The ultimate goal is to increase the product owner's knowledge and influence behaviors that facilitate product development in the LeSS framework.

Getting to know the LeSS Scrum Master

Scrum has no consensus on the role of the Scrum Master. Some teams think of their Scrum Masters as administrators, trainers, and facilitators who make sure the team has the computers, software, training, and other resources it needs. Scrum Masters may also schedule meetings or show the product owner how to add items to the backlog. The Scrum Master does her job and then gets out of the way, allowing the team to manage itself. The Scrum Master has no real authority to push the team in any direction.

Other Scrum Masters may take on a more managerial or team leadership role; they may push the team to meet deadlines or require status reports. Many of these Scrum Masters transitioned to the teams from management.

In LeSS, Scrum Masters do both. In fact, good Scrum Masters dial up and down their areas of responsibility (see Figure 5-8). They dial up more authority when the team needs direction and then dial it down when the team is ready to self-manage.

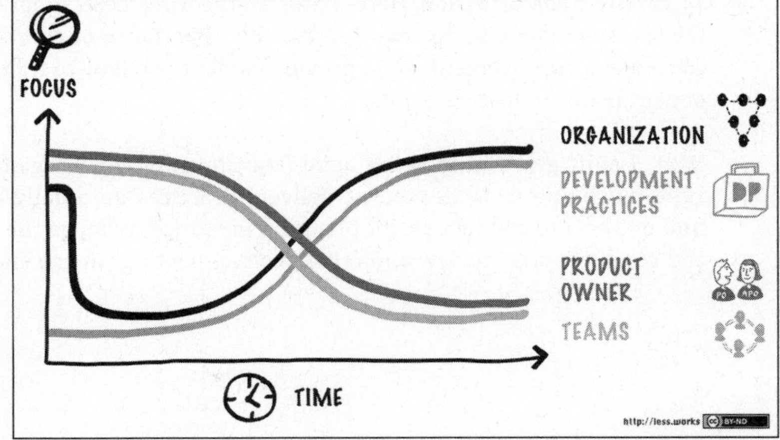

FIGURE 5-8: The Scrum Master's focus over time.

Good Scrum Masters are hard to come by, because they require knowledge and skills that are incredibly diverse. Scrum Masters must be skilled at management, training, and analysis. They need to be quick learners. And they must be able to step back and let the teams manage themselves. It's a little like being a good parent. Some of these skill sets aren't always compatible with traditional roles; for example, strong managers are often reluctant to let go of the reins.

TIP

If you can't find a Jack or Jill of all trades, consider creating a small Scrum Master community of practice populated with those in your organization who represent the breadth of skills needed to be a good Scrum Master. Each Scrum Master can be responsible for her own teams, but seek support and guidance from others when her skill set is a poor match for a certain challenge. Consider adding people to your pool who have the following skills:

- Training or coaching
- Management
- Systems thinking
- Development practices

Moving Up to Scrum at Scale: Adoption

Now that you know what LeSS is all about, the question is how do you do it? In this chapter, I provide the guidance you need to get up and running with the LeSS framework. First, I explain how to lay the foundation for a smoother and more successful transformation. Here, I present the three LeSS adoption principles and the six-step adoption process. I stress the importance of embracing a culture of continuous improvement, and I provide guidance on how to transition from component teams to feature teams.

Next, I shift gears from being agile (transforming your organization) to doing agile (engaging in LeSS product delivery practices on a daily basis). Here, you find out how to conduct sprint planning meetings, manage the product backlog, and conduct sprint review and retrospective meetings at the end of each sprint.

AVOIDING COMMON ADOPTION TRAPS: LARMAN'S LAWS

The LeSS creators base their design on their experience helping organizations transform into agile enterprises, so they know the challenges first hand. One of the creators of the framework, Craig Larman, highlighted the types of friction many organizations encounter when making the transition. These have become known as "Larman's Laws of Organizational Behavior":

1. **Organizations are implicitly optimized to avoid changing the status quo middle- and first-level manager and single-specialist positions and power structures.** In other words, the people who have power and authority want to preserve it. Project managers will become Scrum Masters and business analysts will become product owners. Then everyone just goes back to doing what he or she was doing before.
2. **As a corollary to (1), any change initiative will be reduced to redefining or overloading the new terminology to mean basically the same as status quo.** Organizations adopt the language, but don't make any underlying changes.
3. **As a corollary to (1), any change initiative will be derided as "purist," "theoretical," and "needing pragmatic customization for local concerns" — which deflects from addressing weaknesses and manager/specialist status quo.** Organizations change the framework, so that it fits their organization. For example, the Scrum Masters may direct the team to use milestones so that managers can see what they're doing — the opposite of what self-organized cross-functional teams should be doing. The managers will claim that such a customization is needed to better fit their needs, but in reality, it merely enables the organization to continue operating as it did before.
4. **Culture follows structure.** Organizations try to put a structure in place before changing the organization's culture or mindset in the hopes that people's mindsets will change to conform to the new structure. Such an approach rarely works, which is why the LeSS creators emphasize the importance of discussion, education, and coaching first, followed by implementing the structure on a single product line first.

What these laws are getting at is that most organizations are optimized to maintain the status quo. Be aware that you will face the same challenges. However, by changing the culture first or in tandem with changing the organization's structure, you have a better chance of overcoming these obstacles.

Getting started: Laying the foundation

After deciding to adopt the LeSS framework, you can expect to encounter two major challenges:

- LeSS is for large organizations, so you have to deal with many people who have different ideas about how the organization should be structured and should operate and about the best ways to develop products. You're likely to encounter considerable resistance and plenty of office politics.
- In many organizations, any transformation is a major ordeal, and it's usually handled with a traditional top-down management approach — a change vision with a change initiative, and many change projects, change managers, and change groups. In LeSS adoptions, all of that's unnecessary because your organization is changing to an organization that operates on the basis of change itself — continuous improvement toward perfection. However, even though the top-down management approach is unnecessary, management is still prone to taking that approach.

The LeSS Company, which manages the LeSS framework, provides some direction on how to overcome these and other challenges, as I explain next.

Sticking with the three adoption principles

Embrace the following three principles when adopting LeSS:

- **Deep and narrow over broad and shallow:** Try LeSS on one product line and get it right before rolling it out across your entire organization.
- **Top down and bottom up:** Management should provide support, mostly in the form of training and coaching, to help product owners, Scrum Masters, and teams make the transition. *The focus should be on support, not control.* Everyone in the organization, from the bottom up, needs to embrace LeSS and develop a deeper understanding of its principles and practices.
- **Use volunteering:** Encourage volunteering, through education and discussion, to get the process rolling. Volunteers can help with the formation of teams and communities of practice.

Stepping through the LeSS adoption process

The LeSS Company recommends starting with one product line prior to gradually rolling out LeSS to the entire organization. To transition a product line to LeSS, the LeSS Company recommends the following six steps:

1. Educate everyone.
2. Define "product."
3. Define "done."
4. Have appropriately structured teams.
5. Make sure only the product owner gives work to the teams.
6. Keep project managers away from the teams.

STEP 1: EDUCATE EVERYONE

Transforming an organization to LeSS is less about restructuring the organization and more about educating everyone in the organization and engaging them in discussions about the LeSS approach to product development. Consider hiring a coach to work with your organization to improve product development. You can set up an internal coaching network yourself, but for various reasons, having an outsider with experience in LeSS tends to be much more effective. Most organizations need three levels of coaching:

- **Organizational:** To transition the organizational overall.
- **Team:** To work with one or more teams to improve their ability to work as a team and adopt LeSS principles and practices. Early on, a coach may work as a Scrum Master.
- **Technical practices:** To improve technical practices and development techniques.

REMEMBER

Training may involve more than simply bringing in outside trainers and coaches. You may conduct your own seminars or workshops, encourage employees to form communities of practice, and find other ways to get people thinking about and talking about agile product development. The idea is to get people throughout your organization to start discussing agile, which will strengthen your efforts to nurture a more agile culture.

STEP 2: DEFINE "PRODUCT"

Spend some time defining the product your teams will be developing, but keep your definition relatively broad. For example, instead of defining what the product needs to do and how it needs to do it, you may define the product in terms of the problem it needs to solve. By keeping the product's scope fairly broad, you give the teams more room to innovate and you provide them with a better overview of the value that the product will bring to the customer.

STEP 3: DEFINE "DONE"

All Scrum teams working on a project must agree on a *definition of "done" (DoD)* — a set of acceptance criteria that's consistent across all user stories. (*Acceptance criteria* are conditions that a product must meet to satisfy the stakeholders. A *user story* is a feature described from a user's perspective, as explained in Chapter 1.) For example, the DoD may be that at the end of every sprint, all the code has been tested and works with the rest of the application.

Each function or feature may have its own acceptance criteria, but they all have the same DoD. For example, suppose you're on a Scrum team that's creating a smartphone app to search for local restaurants. Your team is in charge of creating a feature that allows you to search for a menu item across several different restaurants. The acceptance criteria for that feature may include the need for a box into which the user can type keywords, autocomplete based on common menu items, and the ability to limit search results to a certain radius from where the user is located. The feature won't be satisfactory until it meets all of those acceptance criteria.

Another team is working on a feature that enables the user to get directions to whichever restaurant is selected. If the user clicks on a restaurant, the resulting page has a button labeled "Get Me There" that accesses the user's Maps app, inserts the restaurant's address, and triggers the Maps app to conduct the search. These acceptance criteria differ entirely from those of the previously described feature.

Both teams meet with the product owner, who tells them that the features must run on iOS and Android and be unit tested and integrated into the app. These acceptance criteria comprise the DoD, because they apply to both features.

In LeSS, all your teams need to be working off of a common definition of "done" to increase transparency, avoid delays, and increase flexibility. Without a clear idea of what constitutes "done," teams may develop an end product that may or may not be ready to ship, as shown in Figure 5-9. As the figure shows, after releases 21-40 and releases 41-60, the teams are unsure whether the product is done or not done, which leaves the product owner wondering at any given point after that, "Is the product done or not?" Remember that work from all the teams must come together in the end, and they can't do that without a shared definition of "done."

STEP 4: HAVE APPROPRIATELY STRUCTURED TEAMS

"Appropriately structured teams" means feature teams. A *feature team* is a cross-functional, cross-component, and customer-centric group of individuals who can grab a work item from the product backlog and take it all the way through the development process from clarifying the feature to creating, testing, and delivering it.

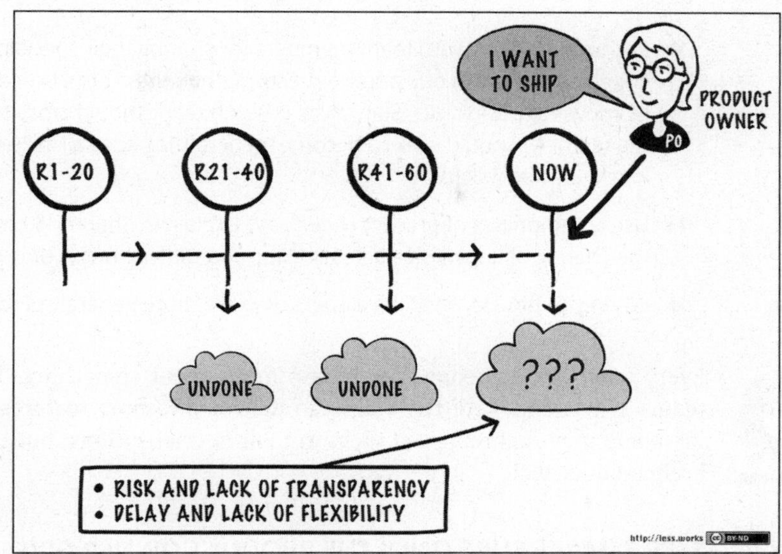

FIGURE 5-9: Without a shared definition of "done," nobody's sure when the product is ready.

Copyright © 2014–2017 The LeSS Company B.V. (`https://less.works`). Reprinted with permission.

If the product teams in your organization are currently formed around components (such as code, design, architecture, analysis, and test), and the teams need to collaborate to deliver product increments, you need to convert or transform your component teams into feature teams.

Such a transformation process may require several months or years to restructure teams and ensure that each team has the knowledge and skills to do all the work required to develop, test, and deliver a feature in a fully functional product increment.

Here are a few suggestions on how to transition component teams into feature teams:

- Reorganize your teams, so each team has a greater mix of knowledge and skills. For example, you may need to distribute your product testers among various teams.
- Keep the members of each team in close proximity to one another — preferably in the same work area or at least on the same floor of the building. Many organizations seat all team members close enough together so they can view each other's screens.
- Keep teams stable (long-lived), so members of each team form personal and professional bonds and develop a strong pool of knowledge and skills as a unit.

- Encourage and reward team members for sharing their specialized knowledge and skills with one another to strengthen the team's breadth and depth of knowledge and skills. Specialists on each team should cross-train others on the team. All should seek to become "generalizing specialists" with broad knowledge and skills.
- Use communities of practice (CoPs), as I explain in Chapter 4, to encourage the sharing of knowledge across teams and throughout your organization.
- When you hire, look for developers who are more generalists than specialists.

REMEMBER

Every team has someone who knows more about something. The goal of these teams is to make sure the team can deliver awesome features as a unit. Team members may maintain and grow in their specializations, but they should try to branch out as well.

STEP 5: MAKE SURE ONLY THE PRODUCT OWNER GIVES WORK TO THE TEAMS

This step in the process is more "what not to do" than "what to do." The only person assigning work to the teams should be the product owner. The purpose of this approach is to ensure a smooth and efficient workflow and prevent line managers, sales, the CEO, or human resources from adding to the team's workload or drawing its focus off product delivery.

STEP 6: KEEP PROJECT MANAGERS AWAY FROM THE TEAMS

Step 6 is an extension of Step 5 — the only person assigning work to teams should be the product owner. However, the LeSS developers are aware that during the transition to LeSS, project managers may be needed to coordinate work when the definition of "done" is still being clarified and program managers and teams need to coordinate their efforts across certain cross-product boundaries.

Ideally, you want to do away with the project manager role. The product owner and teams should be able to deliver a product without additional oversight. If you can't eliminate the project manager role immediately, try to phase it out over time as the product owner and teams become better able to function effectively without a project manager.

Committing to delivery in sprint planning

As I explain earlier in this chapter, LeSS calls for two sprint planning meetings referred to as Sprint Planning 1 and Sprint Planning 2 (see Figure 5-10) that are both held prior to the product development process (the actual sprint). In this section, I provide guidance on how to conduct these two meetings.

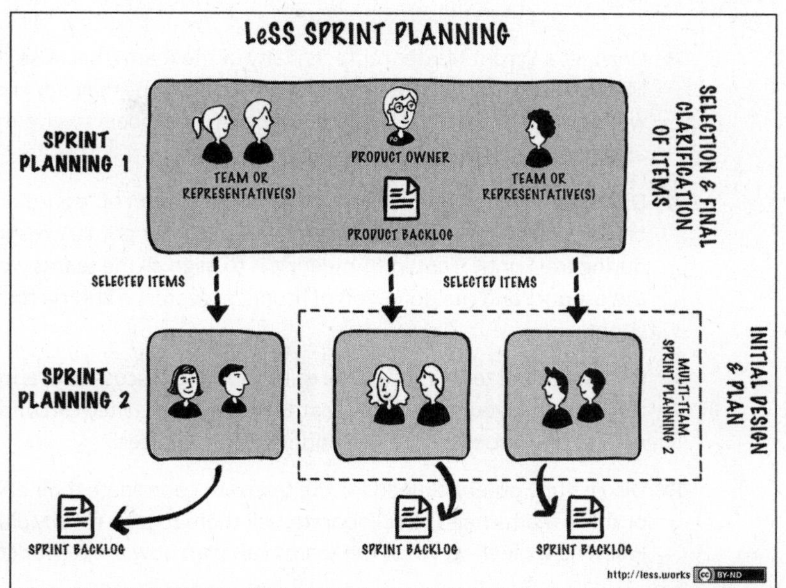

FIGURE 5-10: The two sprint planning meetings.

Copyright © 2014–2017 The LeSS Company B.V. (`https://less.works`). Reprinted with permission.

REMEMBER

Scrum has a single sprint planning meeting that's usually divided into two parts — deciding which work needs to be done and then figuring out how to do it. LeSS simply splits the two-part meeting into two separate meetings.

Conducting a Sprint Planning 1 meeting

In the Sprint Planning 1 meeting, the product owner and all teams meet together to look at the product backlog and determine which teams will work on which items. This meeting is typically short, especially when the product owner and teams are experienced and have been working together for some time. Experienced teams usually know which teams are best at handling different types of work.

If you're the product owner, you conduct the meeting, but your job is pretty simple; you present the highest priority items in your product backlog to the teams and give the teams some time to distribute the work among themselves. You may need to field some questions from the teams to clarify items in the product backlog.

Here are a few tips for conducting an effective and efficient Sprint Planning 1 meeting:

- Limit the number of participants, especially if you have more than two teams. Each team can have one or two representatives who know the team's capabilities.

- Don't let a Scrum Master represent any of the teams, because the Scrum Masters aren't actually members of any team. They may not know the team well enough or have the trust of other team members to give them the authority to select work items.
- Discuss the definition of product and the definition of "done," so all teams are on the same page. As product owner, one of your primary responsibilities during the Sprint Planning 1 meeting is to align all the teams with a vision of the product and the definition of "done" acceptance criteria for the end of the sprint.
- Encourage the team reps to ask questions and discuss concerns. This may be the only time you have all the teams in one room. They can often help to resolve any issues before development commences.
- Discuss any potential need for the teams to coordinate their efforts and, if two or more teams need to collaborate, ask them to plan for a Multi-Team Sprint Planning 2 meeting, when the teams can plan how they'll work together.

Conducting a Sprint Planning 2 meeting

In the Sprint Planning 2 meeting, each team meets to figure out how the team will complete the work it agreed to perform during the Sprint Planning 1 meeting. If two or more teams need to collaborate during the sprint, they meet together, and the Sprint Planning 2 meeting is referred to as a Multi-Team Sprint Planning 2 meeting.

The goal of either meeting is for each team to walk out with a *sprint backlog* — a prioritized list of work items the team must complete by the end of the sprint. Each team may create a sprint task board or just a list of work items.

If you're doing a Multi-Team Sprint Planning 2 meeting, have all the teams involved meet in the same location at the same time with each team conducting its own Sprint Planning 2 session. This gives the teams the opportunity to discuss any shared design, coordinate their shared work, identify opportunities for collaboration and cross-training or knowledge-sharing, and deal with any foreseeable issues.

Coordinating efforts through communication

Outside of the product owner, area product owners, and sprint planning meetings, LeSS offers little formal direction for coordinating team efforts or coordinating individual efforts among team members. That's left up to the teams themselves.

Many large organizations ensure alignment with business analysts and project managers. They're like the coxswain on a crew team. They steer the boat and yell through a megaphone to keep everyone on pace. However, LeSS is Scrum, so it works on the notion that teams will self-organize both within and across teams. Their work is too complicated to have any one person take responsibility for steering the boat.

To ensure alignment within and across teams, LeSS has several practices to encourage and facilitate communication, as explained in the following sections.

Communication and collaboration must be team-driven. You want LeSS to have the minimum processes and practices required to deliver value to the customer and the organization. Don't force teams to conduct meetings that offer little to no value. Allow them to experiment to see what works best for them and for your organization as a whole.

Keeping teams chatty

LeSS encourages teams to be chatty. You don't want any team stuck in formal meetings. Instead you want all teams' members to be able to get what they need by grabbing a neighbor for a quick chat or hollering across the room to a member from another team.

Most formal meetings waste time, dilute focus, and demotivate. Think about the last time you were in a formal meeting with ten or more people sitting around the table. Most of what you hear isn't relevant to your work, so you spend a lot of time just sitting and answering email, thinking about ways you could spend your time more productively, or praying for someone to end the meeting soon.

By encouraging informal communication, LeSS enables teams to work more and spend less time in pointless, unproductive meetings. You get up, grab the person who has the information you need, have a brief chat, and get back to work. You meet on a need-to-know basis.

Coordinating with Daily Scrums

LeSS encourages teams to have Daily Scrum meetings lasting 15 minutes or less, usually at the beginning of the day. In a Daily Scrum meeting, team members stand around in a circle and take turns delivering a brief update on the following three items:

- What they accomplished since the last meeting
- What they'll accomplish before the next meeting
- Any obstacles standing in their way

During the Daily Scrum meeting, don't spend a lot of time in discussion. If more discussion is needed, arrange a follow-up meeting, perhaps with the Scrum Master, to figure out how to remove any obstacles or to deal with other issues.

If your team is collaborating with another team, considering sending a representative from your team to the other team's Scrum meeting to listen in. This is a great way to enhance communication across teams.

Communicating in code

Some teams choose to work with a continuous integration server to "communicate in code." This type of server is usually a central code repository, sort of like Google Docs for programmers. Instead of emailing everyone about a change you made or are thinking of making, you just do the work and add comments about the change. When members of your team or another team check out the code, they can easily spot the change or proposed change.

Creating communities of practice

Like SAFe, LeSS encourages the formation of communities of practice (CoPs) — people across the organization who share a common interest or specialty and often work on developing best practices.

For example, suppose each of your feature teams has a developer who works well as a database engineer. That developer may want to work with other developers and different teams to create a set of common practices. They work together almost like an internal meetup group. They share their thoughts on engineering practices and the best development techniques, and they may even cross-train members of other teams who are interested in database engineering but know little or nothing about it. (See Chapter 4 for more about CoPs.)

Refining the product backlog

LeSS recommends teams allocate five to ten percent of their sprint time to refine the product backlog for *future* sprints. Backlog refinement involves splitting big items into smaller items, analyzing items, reestimating, and reprioritizing, often in collaboration with the product owner, users, and other stakeholders. One or more Scrum Masters attend the initial refinement meetings to coach the group, but their attendance may not be mandatory in later sessions.

The creators of LeSS split backlog refinement into two levels (see Figure 5-11):

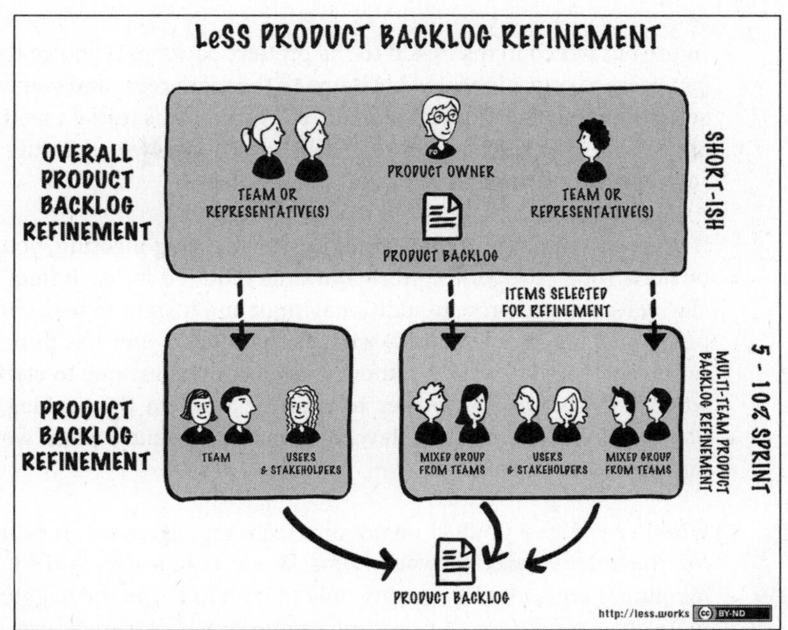

FIGURE 5-11: Refining the product backlog.

- Overall product backlog refinement
- Product backlog refinement
  - Single team
  - Multi-team

Think of these levels as an old-style coffee grinder. You throw the coffee beans in the top in the overall meeting and then as you turn the crank, fine powder comes out the bottom in the form of a product backlog for future sprints. The closer you are to the top, the more likely you'll run into whole beans. As you get close to the bottom, you're grinding the coffee down into smaller and smaller grains.

REMEMBER

Even though LeSS calls for three separate meetings, teams are still encouraged to limit backlog refinement to no more than ten percent of each sprint; for example, during a two-week sprint, a team should spend no more than one day refining the product backlog, typically in the middle or near the end of a sprint to avoid interrupting work during the sprint.

Engaging in an overall product backlog meeting

During the overall product backlog meeting, the shorter of the two stages in the refinement process, teams or team reps work closely with the product owner to figure out which items to add to the product backlog. If you're the product owner, you present your highest value items to the team reps, and you work with them to select items for further refinement. The goal of this initial meeting is to create an aggressive product backlog that'll be whittled down in future product backlog refinement meetings.

If you're a team rep in the overall product backlog meeting, you give the product owner a rough idea of the work and time required for each item, ask questions to clarify items, and provide additional input and insight to help with the refinement process. Make sure you know what the product owner has in mind for each item in the backlog; if you don't know, keep asking questions to clarify. You may also work with the product owner to connect items in the backlog; for example, to identify items that may be developed more efficiently when worked on together during a future sprint.

TIP

Whether you're a product owner or a team rep, agree on an estimation technique for the relative size of work items. Some teams use T-shirt sizing — Small, Medium, Large, and XL. Having only four sizes keeps the haggling over size estimates to a minimum. If you need a more precise estimate, consider using planning poker, as I describe in Chapter 1.

At the end of the meeting, you should have a collection of high-level items ready for individual or multiple teams to refine further.

Refining the product backlog at the team level

After the overall product backlog refinement meeting, the teams or team reps take their portion of the product backlog back to their teams for further refinement. Some items selected during the overall meeting may go to individual teams, while others go to two or more teams (multi-teams) for further refinement:

- **Team refinement:** The team works with users and other stakeholders to refine its portion of the product backlog.
- **Multi-team refinement:** Two or more teams or the representatives of these teams collaborate with users and stakeholders to refine their portion of the product backlog. Multiple teams need to work together on refining the backlog if any items they'll be working on have dependencies that require their coordinated work to complete.

In either case, during the product backlog refinement meeting, team members collaborate with users and other stakeholders to clarify items in the backlog, split big items into smaller items, analyze items, reestimate, and reprioritize. Here are a few suggestions for improving the outcomes of these product backlog refinement meetings, whether they involve one team or more:

1. **Clarify what needs to be done in your team's portion of the product backlog.**

   Consult the product owner if further clarification is needed.

2. **Break down any items that can be broken down into smaller work items.**
3. **Use an estimation technique, such as planning poker (see Chapter 1), to get some idea of the work and time required to complete each item.**
4. **Reprioritize the items on your list.**

At each step, try to give everyone a voice and avoid *groupthink* — a tendency for people to go along with the group or agree with a more charismatic member of the group instead of thinking creatively and expressing their own ideas and opinions.

Multi-team refinement meetings can be nightmarish if not run correctly. Getting five to nine people on a team to agree on anything is difficult enough. Imagine trying to get additional teams to agree on what needs to be done, how to get it done, and how to work together. You may have 15 people or more trying to estimate how long it will take each team to deliver its chunk of the product.

Involve team members in the product backlog refinement process. Don't leave it up to Scrum Masters to make these decisions. Team members have a clearer idea of what needs to be done, how to do it, and how much work each item is likely to require. Work always seems easier when you're not the person who's going to be doing it.

Learning from achievements and mistakes: Continuous improvement

At the end of every sprint, the product owner and teams engage in three meetings to review what they've learned over the course of the sprint and to discuss possible changes to the product and to the process for creating it (see Figure 5-12):

- Sprint review
- Team retrospective
- Overall retrospective

In this section, I bring you up to speed on these three post-sprint meetings.

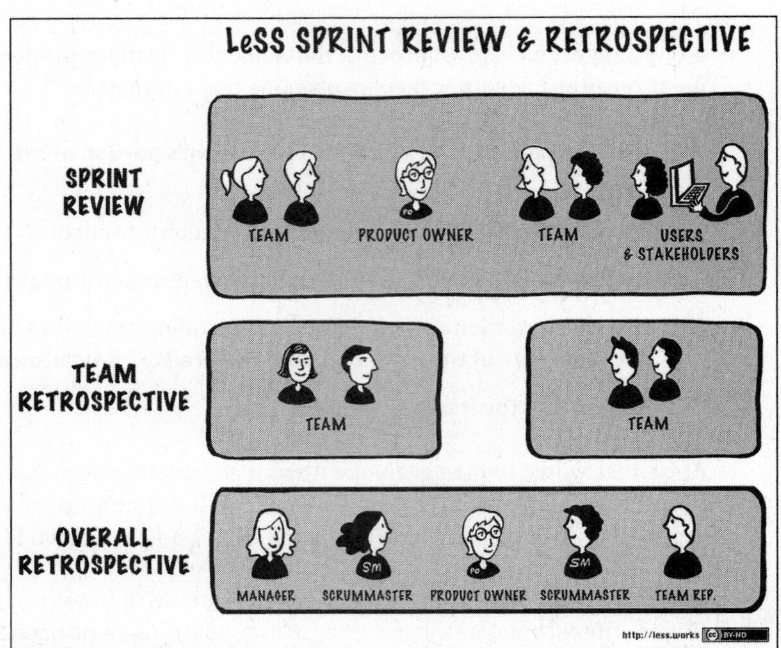

FIGURE 5-12: Required post-sprint meetings.

Copyright © 2014–2017 The LeSS Company B.V. (`https://less.works`). Reprinted with permission.

Conducting sprint reviews

At the end of each sprint, the teams, product owner, customers, users, experts, executives, and anyone else who's interested gather to review the product built during the sprint and discuss changes and new ideas to formulate the future direction of the product and to improve the process for building it. The maximum length of a sprint review is one hour per week of sprint; for example, two hours for a two-week sprint.

REMEMBER

The purpose of the sprint review is to inspect and adapt, *not* inspect and accept. Teams shouldn't just showcase their work in an attempt to impress customers, company executives, and other stakeholders. The product owner and team should come to the meeting with an eagerness to learn from the review, and the users and other stakeholders should be prepared to be approach the process with a critical mind. Maintain focus on *empirical process control* — making data-driven decisions to improve product and process. Shut down any attempts to blame anyone or any team for mistakes, because doing so discourages innovation.

Although a sprint review has no set agenda, it usually goes like this:

1. **The users and the product owner inspect the product (preferably by actually using it).**

For example, you may have a review room with several computers running the program that was developed during the sprint. Users and other stakeholders attending the meeting can take the product for a spin.

2. **All participants engage in a discussion of the product to determine what can be improved.**

3. **The teams, Scrum Masters, and product owner engage in an in-depth discussion of what they need to do moving forward to improve both the product and the process for building it.**

TIP

The LeSS developers recommend a diverge-converge approach to the sprint review:

» **Diverge:** Conduct this stage of the sprint review as a bazaar or science fair. Meet in a large room with multiple "stations" staffed by team reps, where product owners, users, and other stakeholders can try the features each team developed and engage with the team reps in discussions about the product. Stakeholders visit any of the "stations" that interest them.

» **Converge:** Gather as a group and have the stakeholders summarize the insights and opinions they developed during the bazaar. At this time, you may also want to present a subset of items developed during the sprint and inspect the items as a group.

REMEMBER

You may have two or more diverge-converge cycles, culminating with a meeting between team reps and the product owner to clarify the future direction of the product and discuss ways to improve the process for building it.

Try the bazaar/science-fair approach as a first step, but remain open to other options. What works well for one organization or a certain product may not work well for another. Be open an honest about what's working and what's not and look for ways to improve your sprint review process.

Looking back with retrospectives

After the sprint review, each team conducts a team retrospective to discuss process improvements. This is the same as the one-team retrospective in Scrum. During the retrospective, team members discuss the obstacles impeding their work and possibly the work of other teams and add these obstacles to an organizational improvement backlog.

WARNING

Avoid the common mistake of conducting retrospectives as gripe sessions. Keep the focus on improving the process for creating the product. Discourage any attempts to point blame at certain individuals, teams, or others within the organization.

Going deep with an overall retrospective

Unlike Scrum, LeSS adds a meeting after the team retrospectives called an "overall retrospective," which is typically conducted just before the beginning of the next Sprint Planning 1 meeting. In the overall retrospective meeting, the product owner, Scrum Masters, team reps, and any managers gather to discuss cross-team, organizational, and systemic challenges that may be impeding workflow and compromising quality.

Here are some common topics you may want participants to discuss during the overall retrospective:

- Whether teams have close contact with customers and other stakeholders
- Whether cross-team communication and coordination can be improved and, if so, how
- How well the teams are working together
- Whether communities of practice are forming, are active, and are supporting the organization's success
- Anything that happened during the sprint that a team should share with other teams
- Whether teams are engaging in continual learning and are learning from each other
- How well the product owner is maintaining all five of the relationships she's responsible for
- Any organizational issues that are standing in the way of progress or preventing teams from excelling

A key LeSS principle is to use systems thinking. During the overall retrospective, don't focus on what's going on within each team, but what's going on across teams and across the entire organization that may be affecting team performance. The overall retrospective is an exercise in improving the system.

Avoiding common LeSS pitfalls

Organizations that try to transform into agile enterprises using any of the frameworks I describe in Chapters 4 through 8, often fail for a variety of reasons. Some organizations have trouble with feature teams. Teams may have trouble with collective code ownership. Many organizations have Scrum Masters who act more like managers. Still others have product owners who don't spend enough time with their teams.

CASE STUDY

FINDING THE BEST SELF-IMPROVEMENT IDEAS

I once worked for an organization that had a tough time getting value from its overall retrospectives. It was doing a great job identifying systems-level problems but a poor job of solving those problems.

To improve the outcomes, it changed the purpose of its overall retrospectives. Instead of using these meetings to identify system-level problems, it decided to let the teams do that during their team retrospectives. During the overall retrospective, they pulled system-level problems from the various teams and discussed ways to work together to solve those problems. Their approach enabled teams to continue to self-manage while everyone in the organization worked together to eliminate obstacles that were hampering the teams' performance.

This approach to the overall retrospective meeting may or may not work for your organization. The point here is that you need to question whether the overall retrospective is producing real improvement in the system or is just wasting time. If it's wasting time, you need to find a way to change the way you conduct these meetings, so you achieve the desired outcome.

Find out who's best at identifying problems in the system — the product owner, Scrum Masters, or teams — and give them a voice in the process. Then, rally everyone in the organization to solve the problem or remove the obstacle.

Overall retrospectives are crucial for systems-level process improvement. Over time, they improve both process efficiency and product quality.

In the case of LeSS, organizations often fail in their adoption efforts for two reasons: They underestimate the power of their existing culture to undermine their efforts, or they try to go too big too soon. In this section, I address these two common causes of failure to adopt LeSS and provide suggestions on how to avoid them.

Questioning the claim that culture follows structure

LeSS is built on the notion that "culture follows structure," which is the fourth of Larman's four laws (see the earlier sidebar "Avoiding common adoption traps: Larman's Laws"). Others believe that structure follows culture. This debate is similar to that between behaviorists who believe that animal behavior can be conditioned through outside stimuli and cognitive scientists who believe you can control someone's behavior by changing the way the person thinks.

Both debates represent either/or fallacies that are often disproven by others who take a "both, and" approach. In other words, instead of embracing Larman's claim that "culture follows structure" *or* the opposite claim that "structure follows culture," accept that both structure and culture play important roles in a successful transformation and work toward changing both.

REMEMBER

The funny thing is that Larman's fourth law, "Culture follows structure," totally contradicts Step 1 in the six-step LeSS adoption process: "Educate everyone." An attempt to educate everyone is an attempt to change people's mindsets and the organization's culture as a whole. So avoid taking Larman's fourth law too seriously and try to size up your organization first:

- If your organization is highly resistant to big change, you may need to focus on changing minds and culture first. Otherwise, people are likely to reject any new structure you try to implement.

TIP

  If your organization is highly resistant to change, consider introducing big change gradually. You may want to start with one or two Scrum teams and, when they achieve success, expand from there. When people start to see the benefits, they'll be more receptive to accepting the new approach.

- If your organization has a culture that readily embraces change, people will probably embrace any new structure you introduce, whether it's the LeSS framework or something else. If this description fits your organization, you may be able to introduce the LeSS framework without concerning yourself too much about changing your organization's culture.

DOES CULTURE REALLY FOLLOW STRUCTURE?

CASE STUDY

I once worked for an organization that tried a rigorous agile transformation, involving weeks of training and months of planning. Everyone knew the agile roles, meetings, and practices. Yet, people didn't get that much benefit from being agile because it never seeped into their organizational culture.

Most of the people in the organization just stumbled through stand-up meetings and put little effort into their user stories. They just weren't ready to accept an agile mindset.

In this case, the culture-follows-structure approach didn't work. The organization could've done more to force the agile structure, but something deep in the organization's culture wouldn't allow its people to accept the change.

Watching out for over-scaling

One of the most common and serious problems that undermines attempts to adopt LeSS is related to over-scaling in one or both of the following ways:

- Making too many changes too quickly for the organization to adjust
- Choosing big solutions to small challenges

In this section, I suggest ways to avoid these two common pitfalls.

IMPLEMENT CHANGES GRADUALLY

As explained in Chapter 10, organizations change slowly. The larger the organization, the slower it will be to respond to change. You can take a left turn on a jet ski much more quickly than you can make the same turn with a cruise ship. If you try to push through changes too quickly, you're likely to capsize. To increase your chances of success, follow these suggestions:

- **Be patient.** If you expect overnight success and push too hard, you're likely to increase resistance and make little, if any, progress.
- **Manage expectations.** While you want to sell people on the benefits of LeSS, also make them aware that the change is likely to take a long time, present them with a steep learning curve, and require time and effort. Don't make it seem easy.
- **Make incremental changes.** Introduce change slowly, perhaps by starting with one or two Scrum teams. As these teams begin to reap the benefits of agile, team members will become advocates, helping to change the organization's collective mindset and culture. If you feel the winds of change rushing through your hair, you're probably moving too fast.
- **Recruit and educate.** Approach your LeSS transformation as a grass-roots movement. Recruit influential people throughout the organization and try to convince them of the benefits of an agile transformation and of LeSS specifically. The more people you recruit the more likely you are to create a lasting environment for change.

WARNING

Don't ignore the skeptics. If you do, they'll make any setback seem like a disaster.

START SMALL

When large organizations scale anything, they often try to go too big too quickly. They choose an organization-wide solution and try to implement it all at once, as reflected in the sidebar "Big companies love big solutions." Here are a few solutions to avoid this over-scaling trap:

- Approach scaling as a strategy for creating high-quality products in spite of your organization's size, not as a celebration of how big it is.
- Implement changes gradually.
- Look for the easiest, quickest solution. You don't always need a big solution for a big challenge.

CASE STUDY

BIG COMPANIES LOVE BIG SOLUTIONS

I once worked for an organization that was in the middle of an enterprise agile transformation. It had Scrum teams scattered across the organization, some in the United States and some in other countries.

One challenge it faced was that it had teams working in vastly different time zones. As the members of some teams were arriving for work, the members of other teams were tucking themselves into bed. As the Scrum Masters and directors of the various teams discussed options, one of them mentioned that his company had invested in telepresence stations. He said, "I don't know why we bought all the stuff if we're not going to use it."

The other teams didn't have the technology to connect with the teleconferencing bridge, so they worked on that problem and finally came up with a solution. Unfortunately, the telepresence solution failed to address the problem with the vastly different time zones. Once the system was up and running, developers from one team had to stay at work until 9 p.m. to chat with members of the other team as they arrived for work at 9 a.m.

This back-and-forth continued for a few months until the teams realized they were spending more time coordinating than developing. They eventually went with a much simpler solution of creating a different code branch with a few notes to communicate the changes they were making.

The moral of this story is that you don't have to use all the resources your big company has available to solve a problem. Look for the simplest possible solution.

IN THIS CHAPTER

» Looking at the DAD delivery lifecycles

» Reviewing common DAD roles

» Evaluating whether DAD is a good fit for your organization

Chapter 6

Making Process Decisions with Disciplined Agile Delivery

Disciplined Agile Delivery (DAD) is the product delivery process of a larger framework called Disciplined Agile (DA). DA is a *process decision framework*, meaning it encourages you to make certain choices at different points in your product delivery, but does not prescribe any specific process to follow to make your organization agile. Instead of prescribing a process, DA offers guidance in the following ways:

- It describes how various activities of product delivery such as analysis, design, testing, architecture, management, and programming work together as a whole.
- It stipulates what each of these activities should address.
- It offers options for conducting each activity and describes the pros and cons of each option.

For example, DA may look at a certain activity and say, "Here are the goals for that activity, and here are a few approaches for meeting each of those goals."

Then it explains the pros and cons of each approach so you can make a well-informed choice of which is the best approach for achieving a particular goal (or you can choose a different approach or create your own).

In this chapter, I explain how to deliver a product using the DA delivery process (DAD), so you can decide whether it's a suitable agile framework for your organization, and, if you decide it is, you can start taking steps toward transitioning your organization to DAD.

Understanding What Makes DA Tick

Disciplined Agile (DA) is the most complicated of the enterprise agile frameworks because it doesn't present a one-size-fits-all approach with a defined structure, established roles, and a set of practices. It's not a suit off the rack. The solution must be tailored to the organization.

DA considers itself the pragmatic approach to enterprise agility. From DA's perspective, most organizations have a management structure in place, and it's a pipe dream to think the entire organization will become a pure agile enterprise. The DA creators point out that most organizations fumble with agile because it conflicts with the way they're used to working. It's better to be practical and fit agile into existing enterprise practices.

REMEMBER

Agile software development started as a reaction to top-down project delivery, which is why proponents of agile started by releasing the Agile Manifesto. The Manifesto is a battle cry for big change. It challenges traditional organizational hierarchies.

Proponents of DA say, "Hold on. Let's not throw the baby out with the bathwater. There's value in the organizational hierarchy." They want agile developers to put down their pitchforks and instead put on a white shirt and tie. That's one of the big challenges with DA. How do you assimilate the agile movement into a system the movement rejects? You can see hints of the struggle throughout DA's roles and practices (not new roles, but roles that already exist in the traditional organizational structure).

In this section, I describe the highlights of what makes DA unique. By understanding the philosophy that drives it, you'll have the right mindset to begin putting it into practice.

TECHNICAL STUFF

TRACING DA TO ITS ROOTS

Disciplined Agile began as Disciplined Agile Delivery (DAD), an agile framework developed by Scott Ambler while he was working at IBM. Later he co-authored a book with Mark Lines titled *Disciplined Agile Delivery: A Practitioner's Guide to Agile Software Delivery in the Enterprise.*

DAD is rooted in Agile Modeling and the Agile Unified Process (AUP). Agile Modeling came out soon after the Agile Manifesto in 2002. (See Chapter 1 for more about the Agile Manifesto.) The AUP came out a few years later as a mix of IBM's Rational Unified Process (RUP) and early agile ideas.

In their book, Ambler and Lines describe the DAD process decision framework as "a people-first, learning-oriented, hybrid agile approach to IT solution delivery. It has a risk-value delivery lifecycle, is goal-driven, enterprise aware, and scalable."

It is also complicated. If yours is a large organization accustomed to using RUP, then transitioning to DA may be relatively easy. However, if you've never heard of RUP, expect a steep learning curve.

Brushing up on the principles of effective process frameworks

Like many enterprise agile frameworks, DA has its own set of guiding principles that are closely locked together (see Figure 6-1). These principles give you a high-level overview of what to expect when looking at the different process frameworks. Some these principles have a direct effect on each of the processes, while others are more high-level and aspirational:

- **Delight customers:** Successful organizations find new and better ways to delight their customers. Remember that customers are not as interested in your internal processes as they are in making sure their products are easier to use and add real value.
- **Be awesome:** Happy and well-functioning teams produce better products. Remember that part of the Agile Manifesto is "individuals and interactions over processes and tools." Your organization should focus on improving the process by improving how people interact.
- **Embrace pragmatism:** DA sees itself as a pragmatic approach to enterprise agility. It discourages "agile purism." Instead it encourages teams to make as many positive changes as practical within the organization. Teams shouldn't

focus on agile best practices, but look at the organization as a whole and see if it could benefit from a more agile mindset.

- **Context counts:** Organizations are unique; that's why it's difficult to have one set of prescriptive practices that will work in every enterprise. The DA framework tries to give you lots of different buttons and dials to press and twist to create a customized approach for your organization. That way you can adapt the approach to your context instead of relying on one standard set of practices.
- **Choice is good, and making informed choices is better:** Every organization, team, individual, and situation is unique, so DA supports several delivery frameworks and a number of agile and non-agile practices. That's the "choice is good" part. The DA framework also provides insight to help you make the right choices for your organization and teams. That's the "making informed choices is better" part.
- **Optimize flow:** Like most enterprise agile frameworks, DA emphasizes the importance of continuous improvement. You always want to look for ways to improve how work "flows" through the system, for example:
  - *Deliver continuously at a sustainable pace:* The team should be comfortable continuously delivering potentially shippable solutions instead of focusing on releases.
  - *Optimize the whole:* All individuals on an agile team should be aware that they're working in a larger organization. That means that no matter how streamlined a team becomes, team members still need to think of how their work impacts other teams in the larger enterprise.
  - *Make work flow:* DA teams lean heavily on Kanban (see Chapter 8) as a way to manage their work in progress (WIP) and look for potential bottlenecks.
  - *Eliminate waste:* One of the best ways to improve is to eliminate waste in your process. (*Waste* is anything that doesn't deliver value to the customer, including inefficiencies in processes.) When you simplify a process, it's much easier to manage flow and find areas for improvement.
  - *Improve continuously:* A DA team should always look for ways to improve the process. This means taking time to learn from the team's mistakes and being open about ways to improve.
  - *Experiment to learn:* This idea was popularized with Lean Startup. It's also one of the core ideas behind Scrum's empirical approach to delivering a product. Your team should have a scientific mindset, which encourages the team to run small process experiments. Don't be afraid to make small changes and be transparent about the results.

* *Measure what counts:* Establish early on what metrics you want to use to look for ways to improve. You may want to focus on on-time delivery, customer satisfaction, or the happiness of the team. Look for specific things to measure as the first step to improving your delivery.
* *Prefer long-lived stable teams:* In most organizations it's common to have temporary teams that are quickly assembled for one-off projects. A DA team is always working to become better optimized. The longer teams stay together, the more waste they'll eliminate from their own process.

» **Be enterprise aware:** A well-run agile team can quickly deliver a high-value product. Yet these team efficiencies don't necessarily scale to the rest of the enterprise. DA teams look for ways to improve the whole system. DA teams know that tuning your own race car doesn't make the rest of the traffic run any smoother.

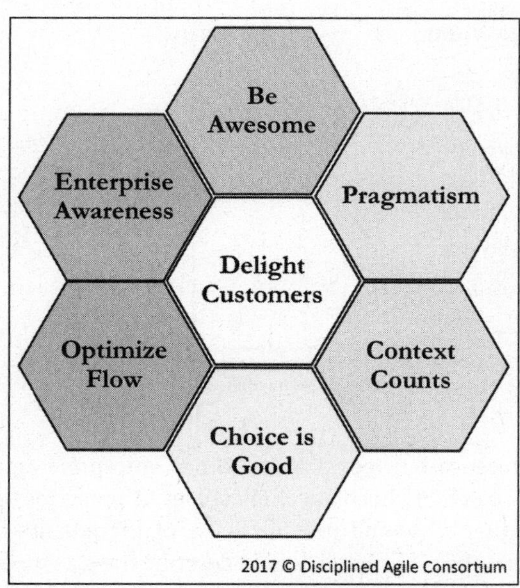

FIGURE 6-1: The Disciplined Agile principles.

2017 © Disciplined Agile Consortium. Reproduced with permission.

Exploring the DA process decision framework

REMEMBER

DA is based on the premise that every organization, team, and individual is unique, so frameworks should offer choices, not prescribe solutions. It helps organizations ask the right questions, and for each question it provides a set of answers (solutions) from which to choose.

That's much different from more prescriptive enterprise agile frameworks with clearly define processes, meetings, and roles. For example, the Scaled Agile Framework® (SAFe®) introduces the idea of the agile release train (ART), as explained in Chapter 4, and Large-Scale Scrum (LeSS) creates several new meanings for planning and conducting retrospectives (see Chapter 5). Disciplined Agile Delivery (DAD), on the other hand, doesn't require specific meetings, and the roles involved are probably already in your organization.

REMEMBER

DAD represents all the practices centered around enterprise agile product delivery, whereas DA casts a much wider net and is more attuned to business agility (see Figure 6-2). In addition to product delivery, DA covers marketing, sales, governance, legal, and human resources (HR). In this chapter, I discuss DAD, which focuses more narrowly on delivering enterprise products.

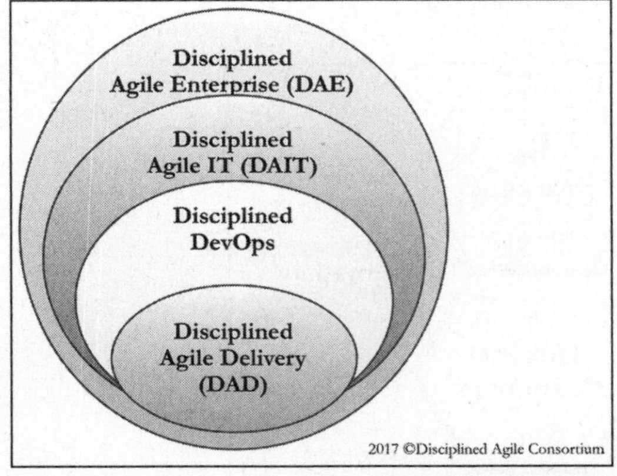

FIGURE 6-2: The Disciplined Agile framework goes beyond product delivery.

2017 © Disciplined Agile Consortium. Reproduced with permission.

Think of the difference between DA and other enterprise agile frameworks in terms of baking a batch of chocolate chip cookies. A prescriptive framework such as SAFe (see Chapter 4) would provide a list of ingredients and step-by-step instructions. DA, on the other hand, would describe the size, texture, and flavor of the cookies and offer some general guidance, such as "all ingredients must be mixed in the right proportions, and the mixture divided and heated." The pastry chef would then be free to choose the ingredients and quantities, decide how to mix them and how to divide the mixture, and figure out how to heat it to produce the desired final product.

Small- to medium-sized organizations may find the DA approach unsatisfying, but it may be the perfect fit for large organizations, where many different teams are trying out different agile ideas. Instead of telling people how to do their jobs, you set common goals and leave it up to the teams to decide how to meet them. You specify the *what* and let your agile teams address the *how*.

Unfortunately, giving people so many choices and then trying to educate them on how to make the best choices is often much more challenging than simply giving them a uniform process to follow. The sheer number of choices can boggle the mind.

TIP

DA can become agile quicksand in that the more you struggle, the deeper you get sucked into the framework. When starting with DA, take a very high-level view. Steer clear of the goals and milestones and focus on the higher-level processes — the DAD principles, primary roles, secondary roles, and the three-phase delivery lifecycle (see the later section, "Delivering in Lifecycles").

Seeing DAD as a goal-driven, hybrid approach

DAD isn't for micromanagers. It encourages you to identify the goals for a certain activity and then allow your teams to choose the best approach(es) for achieving each of those goals. In other words, it is a goal-driven, hybrid approach to enterprise agile:

- **Goal driven:** DAD lays out certain goals for you to meet to get value from any given process. For example, suppose you're planning your project in *inception phase* (one of the three phases of the delivery lifecycle). You may have goals such as secure funding, form initial team, and explore the scope. DAD doesn't tell you how to do these things; it just points out that they must be done.
- **Hybrid:** DAD is a hybrid approach in that it allows teams to choose various methods to achieve their goals. For example, a team can choose Scrum, Lean, Kanban, or some other approach or it can mix-and-match or develop a system of its own. As Ambler and Lines, the originators of the DA process decision framework, explain it, "methods such as Scrum, Extreme Programming (XP), Kanban, and Agile Modeling (AM) provide the process bricks and DA the mortar to fit the bricks together effectively."

Looking at DAD as a group of process blades

A *blade server* is a stripped-down version of a server computer with a modular design. The chassis of a blade server is an enclosure that provides physical space, along with services, such as power, cooling, and networking capabilities, that can be shared among the blades. Each blade is a server unto itself, complete with a processor, memory, storage, and so on that plugs into a slot in the chassis. Each blade has a specialized capability, such as file sharing, serving up web pages, or streaming audio and video content.

DA follows the blade server model through its use of process blades (see Figure 6-3). A *process blade* is a set of practices and strategies focused on a certain capability.

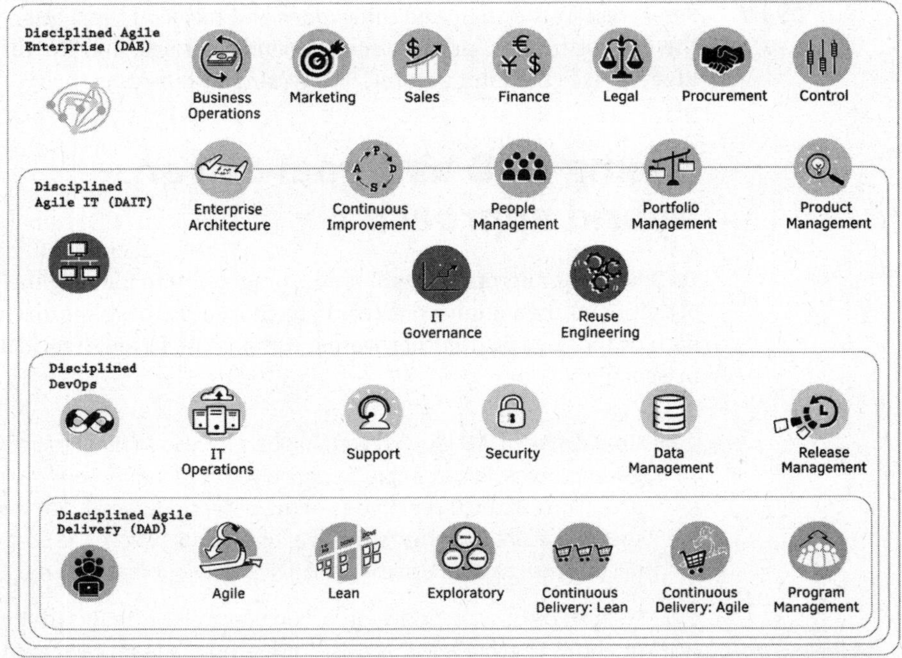

FIGURE 6-3: The Disciplined Agile process blade groups.

2017 © Disciplined Agile Consortium. Reproduced with permission.

The latest version of DA has four groups of process blades:

- **Disciplined Agile Delivery (DAD):** The area that focuses on product delivery.

  Earlier versions of DA called the entire framework "Disciplined Agile Delivery (DAD)." The current version makes DAD a group within the larger framework called DA. That being said, most of the good stuff is still focused on delivery.

- **Disciplined Agile DevOps:** The area of intersection between development, operations, and quality assurance. This process blade group contains:
  - Release management
  - Operations, support
  - Data management

» **Disciplined Agile IT (DAIT):** The area that involves the application of agile and Lean strategies to all aspects of information technology (IT) practices, including IT operations, support, data management, reuse engineering, and other capabilities. This process blade group looks like a standard IT department process map:

- Product management
- Portfolio management
- Enterprise architecture
- IT governance

» **Disciplined Agile Enterprise (DAE):** The area where DA starts to bleed into business agility. It's about taking the agile mindset and applying it to all the other areas in the organization (see Figure 6-4):

- People must be agile
- Optimize your value streams
- Don't focus solely on practices
- Sense, respond, learn, and adapt

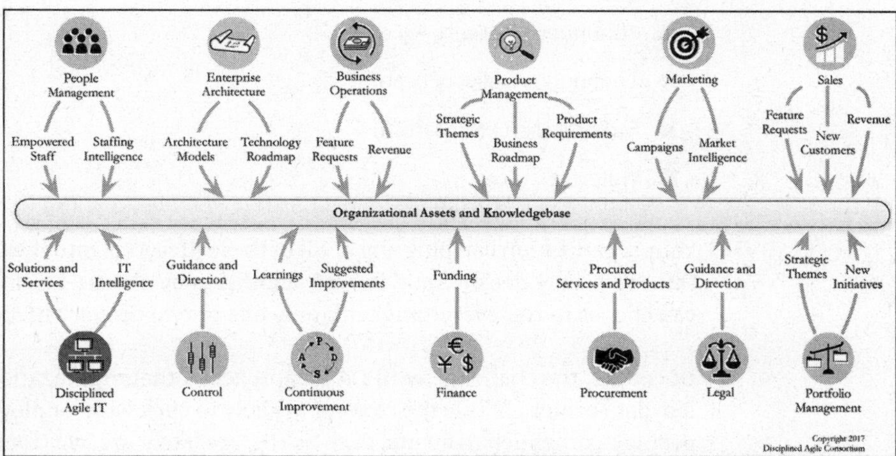

FIGURE 6-4: The Disciplined Agile Enterprise process blades.

Each of these four process blade groups contains a set of "blade" processes. Confusingly, you can have processing blade groups within other process blade groups. Notice that the Disciplined Agile IT (DAIT) process blade group is within the Discipline Agile Enterprise (DAE) process blade group.

DA doesn't try to reinvent the wheel. In terms of DAD, the emphasis is on making your solution delivery teams more enterprise aware, so the enterprise functions as a well-oiled machine (or a highly efficient blade server). DA is less about organizational change and more about teams building on and adding value to what's already there.

DA gives you the option of fitting agile into your organization without making lasting changes, using the framework to effect radical change across the organization, or, when agile doesn't fit, sticking with what you have.

REMEMBER

Consider your organization's existing culture (see Chapter 9). If your organization has a difficult time accepting even modest changes, then DA may be the best way to gain some benefits of an agile mindset. If your organization is more flexible, then don't worry so much about "enterprise awareness" and instead spend more time driving widespread organizational change using some other agile framework.

Because the focus of this chapter is on DAD, consider how this works in DAD. You have a process blade called DAD that can hold several delivery lifecycles:

- Agile/Basic
- Lean/Advanced
- Continuous Delivery Agile
- Continuous Delivery Lean
- Exploratory (Lean Startup)
- Waterfall

Your organization can plug any or all of these lifecycles into the DAD process blade. One team may decide Agile is best, another may choose Lean. Your organization can choose to run everything with only one or two delivery lifecycles or use all six.

Of course, the challenge with DA's approach is that organizations rarely function like data centers. While the concept is likely to click with employees in technology, people in other departments, such as HR, are likely to have trouble wrapping their brains around the concept of a Disciplined Agile Enterprise (DAE) process blade group. I can't imagine an HR manager describing her department as a "people management process between the DAIT and the DAE process blade group."

SCRAPPING SCRUM'S SOUL

In many ways, it seems like the DA developers went out of their way to take Scrum out of the Agile lifecycle. They retain the Scrum product delivery framework, but scrap Scrum terminology and ideology. DA has no Scrum Masters, product backlogs, sprints, or stand-up meetings. Instead DA calls for team leads, iteration backlogs, iterations, and daily coordination meetings.

Even worse for Scrum aficionados, DA keeps the body of Scrum — everything relevant to product delivery — and scraps its soul — the principles of self-management and experimentation. In fact, DAD Scrum is so different from original Scrum that the two probably don't even belong in the same sentence.

If your organization has blade-server data centers and is already using RUP, then DA makes sense. No doubt this is one of the big selling points for many large organizations. However, if the people in your organization aren't familiar with the concept of blade servers and RUP and the language surrounding these concepts (primarily from IBM), the transition can take quite a bit of time and generate a great deal of confusion.

Delivering in Lifecycles

In DAD, agile product delivery systems, such as Scrum and Lean, play a small role in a larger *delivery lifecycle* — a process for delivering product that consists of the following three phases. The delivery lifecycle (see Figure 6-5) is a subset of the larger six-phase system lifecycle:

- **Inception:** The team plans all *iterations* (versions of the product), detailing the work that must be done and setting milestones. The inception phase typically takes at least one week and sometimes up to a month.
- **Construction:** The team does the work. Team members may create work items for their to-do board or react to change requests. The team may have a daily coordination meeting and an iteration review for key stakeholders. It typically uses an agile team or enterprise agile framework, such as Scrum, Lean, XP, SAFe, or LeSS.
- **Transition:** The team releases its work to the rest of the organization. Over time, this phase should shrink to the point at which the teams are releasing the product shortly after the construction phase to more closely align with an agile team's emphasis on frequent delivery.

For more about this three-phase lifecycle, see the later section, "Navigating the three-phase delivery lifecycle."

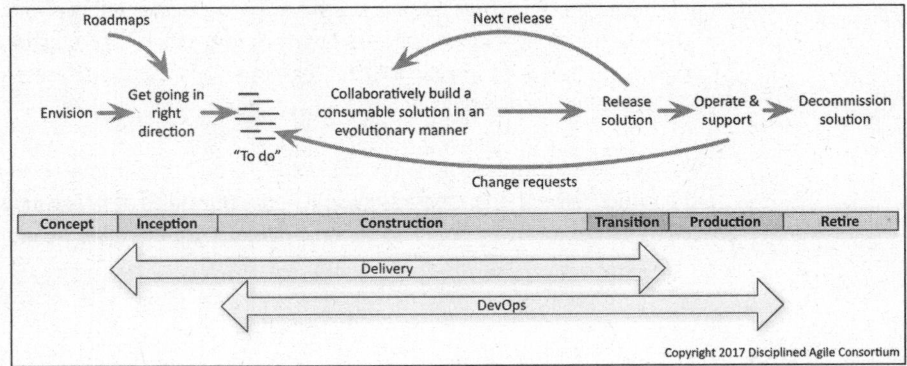

FIGURE 6-5: The Disciplined Agile delivery lifecycle.

2017 © Disciplined Agile Consortium. Reproduced with permission.

REMEMBER

In its spirit of giving you options from which to choose, DAD actually has a number of delivery lifecycles, including Agile/Basic, Lean/Advanced, Continuous Delivery: Agile, Continuous Delivery: Lean, and Exploratory (Lean Startup). (The list of options continues to grow over time.) All of these options conform to the three-phase delivery lifecycle.

A PROCESS-HEAVY APPROACH

DAD's delivery lifecycle is a classic process-heavy approach where each phase represents a subset of the larger process. The DA creators call this the "full agile delivery lifecycle," with "full" implying that delivery extends beyond what a typical agile team does (construction).

These phases are similar to the classic waterfall approach, except that some phases may overlap a little. This approach seems to contradict agile ideology. Remember that agile favors experimentation over planning. Teams experiment, test, learn, and adapt. Product development doesn't involve a lot of up-front planning, and it isn't linear; it's cyclical.

The three-phase delivery lifecycle seems to encourage you to do considerable planning at the beginning, some work in the middle, and a big bang release at the end.

IS THIS *REALLY* AGILE?

This team agile lifecycle is a strange mishmash of agile and phased delivery. The three phases are similar to the traditional waterfall model — *plan the work, and then work the plan*. On the other hand, DAD does allow for iterative delivery and continuous incremental improvement.

The real question is whether DAD delivers the full benefits of a purely agile approach. Typically, organizations embrace agile when they don't have clear requirements. Instead they have a set of high-value features that can change based on what the team learns.

DAD's agile approach can tie down a lot of that work in the inception phase. If it's all planned out, then what's the point of having agile teams? If little is planned out, then why have an inception phase?

In this section, I focus primarily on the three phases and less on the distinctions between the different delivery lifecycles, because the different lifecycles are merely variations of the three-phase delivery lifecycle. I introduce you to the key and supporting players who drive the delivery lifecycle, and I lead you through the process of using the delivery lifecycle as your enterprise agile framework.

WARNING

Tread carefully in the inception phase. Defining a rigid concept up front is a waterfall approach that can lead to inflexibility during development or result in a total waste of time in the inception phase if the development process takes the product in a different direction.

Navigating the three-phase delivery lifecycle

With basic understanding of the three-phase delivery lifecycle and the various roles involved, you're better prepared to understand how the delivery lifecycle works. You're also better prepared to start adopting DAD in your organization.

In this section, I lead you through the three-phase delivery process from inception to transition.

Planning ahead with the inception phase

The main purpose of the inception phase is to ensure that your teams create a high-quality product that hits the bull's-eye in terms of customer requirements and the needs of the organization. This is in line with the DAD principle "Optimize the whole" and its emphasis on the risk-value lifecycle (see the later section "Striving to become enterprise aware and to consider the risk-value lifecycle.") Effective planning reduces risks, such as unaligned stakeholders, inappropriate architecture, building the wrong thing, and insufficient functionality.

To lay the groundwork for the construction phase, you must meet the following goals in the inception phase:

- Form your initial team.
- Develop a common vision.
- Align with the enterprise direction.
- Explore the initial scope of the product.
- Identify the initial technical strategy.
- Develop an initial release plan.
- Secure funding.
- Form a work environment.
- Identify risks.
- Develop an initial testing strategy.

WARNING

Organizations that adopt DAD often take the inception phase to the opposite extreme — overplanning. Using words such as "goals," "milestones," and "phases" leads the people involved in inception to start thinking in terms of heavy top-down planning. If your organization has a lot of planners involved, such as project managers, business analysts, and database developers, they tend to magnify the problem. They want to push the team to create detailed plans, because that's what they do.

TIP

To achieve a healthy balance between a detailed plan and agile team flexibility, do the following:

- **Avoid narrowing the scope of the work too much.** Allow the vision to be somewhat broad and "open to interpretation" to give your agile teams license to innovate.
- **Skip the details.** Set the goal and let your agile teams figure out how to achieve it.
- **Attend to logistics.** Set up a workspace, agree on common coding practices, and even go through user-story training. Spend your planning time working out the logistics and making sure your teams have what they need to do their work.

- **Squeeze your inception phase.** If you're spending more time in inception than in construction, you're wasting time and not gaining the full benefit of having agile teams. Allocate less time to the inception phase to discourage overplanning.

DAD is so enamored of planning that its creators point out that most agile teams have several *sprint zeros* — often three two-week planning sessions. In comparison, LeSS (see Chapter 5) starts with a Sprint 1 to figure out what each team needs to do and then conducts a Sprint 2 during which each team figures out how it will complete its work. LeSS has no Sprint 0.

WARNING

I'm not suggesting that having an inception phase is necessarily a bad idea. Setting a goal, working out the logistics, and getting everyone on the same page is always a good idea before starting a project. However, you need to be careful in two areas:

- **Time:** You can waste a lot of time planning a product if your agile team determines later that it needs to change the product design, which is what agile is all about. In addition, the more time you spend in planning meetings, the less time your agile teams may have to do their work. If you spend half your time planning, you're probably not getting much benefit from having agile teams.
- **Flexibility:** If you emerge from your sprint zero meetings with a rigid plan in place that your agile teams must follow, you're losing out on the biggest benefit of agile — highly skilled teams that can make decisions on the fly to create superior products.

Building it out in the construction phase

In the inception phase, you plan the work. In the construction phase, you work the plan. The purpose of the construction phase is to build or configure a consumable product that has the functionality required to meet the needs of the product's stakeholders (your customer and your organization). To achieve that mission, your teams must meet the following construction goals:

- Produce a potentially consumable solution.
- Address changing stakeholder needs.
- Move closer to a deployable release.
- Improve quality.
- Prove architecture early.

CASE STUDY

SPRINT ZERO

I once worked for an organization that had something very similar to the inception phase. It created three sprint zeroes, each of which was two weeks long. It set aside six weeks to create high-level goals and organize the project.

This organization had trouble figuring out where waterfall ended and agile started. There was a project manager in the meeting who quickly jumped to the white board and started creating the scope and milestones. To the project manager, this made a lot of sense. He was used to planning out these projects before the work began.

At the end of the meeting, everyone was confused about what would happen next. The Scrum Masters said that the milestones didn't really matter; the team could get new information from the product owner and quickly change direction. They pointed out that you can't plan out the work while at the same time giving the product owner the flexibility to make real-time changes.

The project manager was also confused. Why did they just spend several hours planning out the work if the team was going to ignore the project's scope and deadlines? They had waterfall and agile, and they were making a mess of both.

The moral of this story is this: Don't waste time planning if your agile teams are going to ignore the plan, and don't develop a plan that's so rigid it prevents your agile teams from being agile.

In the construction phase, each team chooses the agile approach that works best for it — Scrum, XP, SAFe, Kanban, Lean, LeSS, whatever. Remember DAD's principle "Choice is good" — the emphasis is on seeing all the options.

Disciplined agile even encourages you to mix and match these approaches. You can have some Scrum roles and then use XP's engineering practices. Maybe your teams want to use Kanban and parts of SAFe. DAD sees these agile approaches as a cafeteria of different ideas. You can pick and choose, mix and match, or build your own.

WARNING

Be careful mixing and matching various agile approaches, because many of them are already a mix of different agile methodologies. For example, Scrum already includes a lot of Kanban, and Kanban is heavily influenced by Lean Software Development. Each approach has its own strengths and weaknesses, but one approach's strengths may not cover another one's weaknesses. In the end, your hybrid approach may be more confusing and less effective than one of the prepackaged team agile solutions.

Deploying your product in the transition phase

The transition phase is, by far, the shortest of the three phases in the delivery lifecycle. In fact, if your team is following the continuous delivery lifecycle, the transition phase may be completed in a matter of minutes or hours instead of days or weeks. You get some idea of just how short this phase can be by glancing at the two goals for the transition phase:

- Ensure the solution is consumable.
- Deploy the solution.

Having a "consumable" solution at the end of the construction phase is nothing new. In LeSS, the goal of each sprint is to have a "potentially shippable product increment." SAFe has a "continuous delivery pipeline" with "release on demand," which essentially means the same thing as having a consumable product at the end of every iteration that's ready whenever the customer demands it and the organization decides to release it.

The big difference in DAD, when compared to other agile and enterprise agile frameworks, is that DAD tends to discourage deployment until the product is deemed ready in accordance with the vision agreed upon during the inception phase. In other words, teams are free to develop a consumable solution or a potentially shippable product increment at the end of each sprint, but they can't deploy it until the product is "done" as defined in the inception phase.

The trouble with this approach is that it tends to discourage agile teams from making changes during the construction phase — changes that are commonly initiated by the evolving needs of the customer and by agile team innovation. Even more troubling is the lack of opportunities for earlier feedback and learning based on incremental releases. Nor does it provide much support for a continuous delivery cycle in which customer demand determines when a product is "done" or ready for deployment.

Think of it this way: If you're working on an agile team, your iterations release a potentially shippable product at the end of each sprint. If you're building a car, your first iteration may be roller skates. Your second iteration may be a bicycle; your third, a motorcycle; and your fourth, a car. At the end of every iteration, the customer can decide, "It's good enough for now, give me what you have." Or, after seeing the bicycle, she can decide, "I really don't want a car, I want spaceship," at which point your team scraps the car idea and starts working on iterations that bring the team closer to building a spaceship, perhaps developing an airplane first.

DAD makes these decisions and changes in direction more difficult because "done" has been defined as a fully operable car during the inception phase. Iterations continue and deployment doesn't happen until your team produces that car. The missed opportunities for early feedback have the potential to accrue toward a much larger, later-stage potential for waste.

To be fair, DAD does allow for changes during the construction phase. If you look back at the goals in the inception phase (in the earlier section "Planning ahead with the inception phase"), you see the word "initial" repeated several times. At the end of the inception phase, you have an *initial* team, *initial* scope, *initial* technical strategy, and *initial* release plan. The implication is that plans can change during the construction phase. In addition, DAD offers an optional "product viability" milestone that enables stakeholders to check in with the agile teams to check status and discuss changes (see the later section "Governing the lifecycle with milestones").

In practice, however, after the stakeholders develop a "common vision" in the inception phase, redirection becomes difficult.

Choosing a DAD delivery lifecycle

DAD has a number of delivery lifecycles, and the list continues to grow. At last count, the number was up to six. All of these alternative lifecycles have three phases, and they have similar goals and milestones. The big difference is how much time they spend in each one of these phases. Here are the six current delivery lifecycles:

- **Agile/Basic:** The Agile/Basic lifecycle is an extension of Scrum's construction lifecycle, and it's a good one to start with because it's the most prescriptive of the bunch and facilitates the transition from Scrum or RUP to DAD. It may also be the best lifecycle to start with if your teams are new to agile. Agile/Basic
  - Is more detailed than Scrum, XP, and Kanban.
  - Is iteration based.
  - Uses non-Scrum terminology (Scrum rebranded).
  - Includes inputs from outside the delivery lifecycle.
  - Uses a work item list as opposed to a product backlog.
  - Includes more specific milestones than Scrum, XP, and Kanban.
- **Lean/Advanced:** This lifecycle embraces Lean principles, including maximizing workflow, reducing bottlenecks, and minimizing waste. Work is pulled through the process when teams have the capacity to do it. It's a good choice

if you need to get your product to market fast and your teams are highly skilled and disciplined. It's also a good choice when you're working on projects that have quickly evolving requirements. The Lean/Advanced lifecycle

- Supports continuous flow.
- Enables teams to work at their own pace.
- Uses a work item pool instead of a backlog.

» **Continuous Delivery Agile:** Agile/Basic is intended to evolve toward this Continuous Delivery Agile lifecycle, which results in a consumable product at the end of each iteration rather than after a set of iterations. The inception phase is nonexistent, the construction phase is long, and the transition phase is significantly compressed. In other words, it's more like the agile we know and love. This lifecycle is a good choice if you need to get your product to market fast and you have highly skilled teams that have been working together for some time. It requires automated testing, integration, and deployment.

» **Continuous Delivery Lean:** Like Continuous Delivery Agile, Continuous Delivery Lean is meant for teams that have developed a mature set of practices around continuous integration and deployment. Its focus is on maximizing workflow, reducing bottlenecks, and minimizing waste. It has no inception phase, an expanded construction phase, and a compressed transition phase. This lifecycle is a good choice if you need to get your product to market quickly and you have highly skilled teams that have been working together for some time. It requires automated testing, integration, and deployment.

» **Exploratory (Lean Startup):** The Exploratory (Lean Startup) lifecycle is ideal for nailing down what a customer needs by conducting quick learning experiments. You can use this lifecycle to enhance or replace the inception phase or within the construction phase to clarify a feature or capability. With this lifecycle, a team engages in a continuous cycle of envision, build a little, deploy, and test until the team is satisfied with the result.

» **Waterfall:** This lifecycle is suitable for experienced IT professionals who aren't yet comfortable with the agile approach. It's slow and tends to carry a high risk due to long feedback cycles and delivery at the end of the lifecycle. Use it only in low-risk situations in which the vision is clear, the requirements are stable, and you don't need to deliver a solution quickly. The Waterfall lifecycle is a linear eight-step process divided into two stages:

Decomposition and Definition

1. Requirements
2. Architecture

3. Design
4. Construction

Integration and Validation

5. Unit test
6. Function test
7. Integration test
8. Acceptance test

Striving to become enterprise aware and to consider the risk-value lifecycle

DA emphasizes the importance of being *enterprise aware,* which aligns with the principle of "Optimize the whole." In some ways, the emphasis on enterprise awareness is an implied criticism of how agile teams tend to function in a large organization. DAD sees these teams as trying to create their own set of processes without considering the teams' responsibilities to the larger enterprise. From DAD's perspective, it's fine if your agile teams deliver every two weeks, but that doesn't offer much value to the enterprise if it's not how the rest of the organization deploys its products.

Another implied criticism of many agile frameworks is DAD's shift from the value lifecycle to the risk-value lifecycle. Instead of simply adding work items to a backlog and relying on iterative development to work out the imperfections, DAD insists on planning ahead to reduce the risks, such as unaligned stakeholders, inappropriate architecture, building the wrong thing, and insufficient functionality. The idea is that by identifying risks early on, you're more likely to reduce delays and to deliver higher quality products.

Governing the lifecycle with milestones

While most agile methods deplore any hint of management planning and oversight and encourage teams to self-govern, DAD introduces a light amount of governance in the form of milestones that serve more like checkpoints to ensure that everyone involved stays on track. Milestones are placed at various points along the delivery lifecycle. DAD uses the following milestones:

- **Stakeholder vision:** At the end of the inception phase, you should have a vision statement that describes the agreed upon stakeholder vision for the product.

* **Proven architecture:** Having a proven architecture early in the construction phase helps to mitigate risk. The team's architecture owner (described in the next section) is encouraged to identify risks in the inception phase and make sure these risks have been reduced or eliminated by implementing related functionality between one and three iterations into the construction phase.
* **Project viability:** Project viability milestones give stakeholders an opportunity to check progress during the construction phase, ensure that the project's progression aligns with the stakeholder vision agreed to in the inception phase, and discuss possible changes with the agile teams. Project viability milestones are optional.
* **Sufficient functionality:** Sufficient functionality means that the product has the minimum feature set to satisfy the stakeholder needs. This milestone comes at the end of the construction phase. It is similar to what Scrum refers to as a "potentially shippable product increment," but is more like what some agile teams refer to as a minimum viable product (MVP).

  REMEMBER

  This milestone is reached only when functionality is sufficient to meet the cost of transitioning the release to stakeholders. So, while a product may be viable after a two-week iteration, it may not have sufficient functionality to justify the cost of deploying it in a high-compliance environment.
* **Production ready:** During the construction phase, other activities must be conducted and completed as part of the final preparation to deliver the solution to stakeholders, such as final acceptance testing, data conversions, and documentation. Near the end of the transition phase, everything required for the solution to be delivered to stakeholders must come together to make the solution production-ready.
* **Delighted stakeholders:** The delivery cycle extends beyond the transition phase before a project can be considered completed and the team can begin on another release. These post-transition phase activities include training, deployment tuning, support, reviews, and warranty periods. The project isn't considered complete until stakeholders feel delighted.

Getting to Know the Cast: Roles

All the various delivery lifecycles share a common set of roles. They divide these roles into two categories (see Figure 6-6):

* **Primary roles:** Those roles that every organization has (or should have) and who are always involved in the delivery lifecycle.

» **Secondary roles:** Those roles that may be required if teams don't have someone in a primary role with the skills or expertise it needs to complete its work.

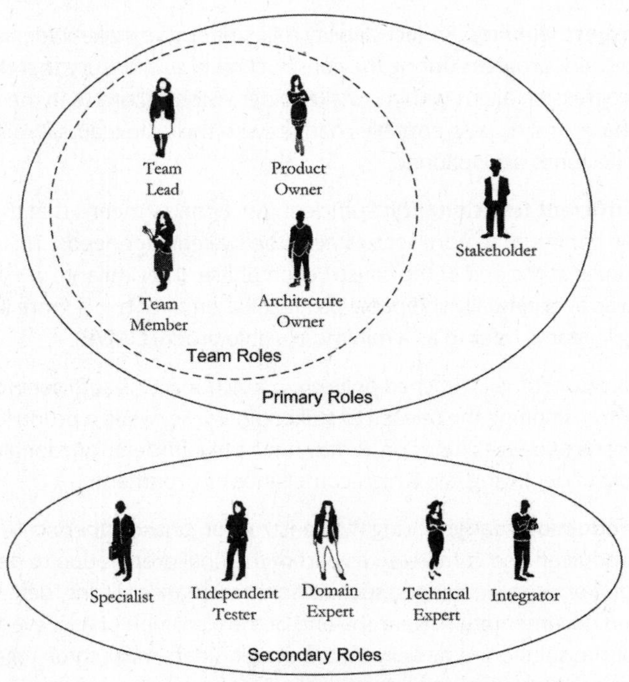

FIGURE 6-6: Disciplined Agile Delivery roles.

2017 © Disciplined Agile Consortium. Reproduced with permission.

Each category has several roles, and many of these roles can be filled with people who have different job titles. For example, one of the secondary roles is "specialist," who may be a database engineer, a senior developer, or a project manager. A "domain expert" may be a marketing specialist, sales director, or even a lawyer. As you may imagine, having people with different titles and role designations can become very confusing.

Meeting the lead actors: Primary roles

Five roles play a part in the delivery lifecycle: stakeholder, product owner, team members, team lead, and architecture owner. Here, I introduce you to these key players.

REMEMBER

The team lead, team members, and architecture owner form the core of your agile team. When assembling a team, make sure each person has the qualifications required for the given role and that all members of the team are a good fit.

Many of the primary roles are influenced by both agile and traditional project management. For example, having a team lead aligns with traditional project management practices, but the team lead in DAD doesn't exactly serve a traditional management role; the team lead doesn't assign or supervise the work. Instead, this individual sets the direction and motivates and supports the team, serving a role that pure agile advocates may find more acceptable.

STAKEHOLDER

Stakeholders are those who are materially impacted by the outcome of a solution, such as end users, sponsors (DAD calls these "gold owners"), partners, and insiders who work on the project or provide technical or business services in support of the project.

PRODUCT OWNER

The product owner, primarily a resource for the development team, focuses on the functional requirements of the product (its features). Product owners answer questions about requirements and represent the team to the rest of the organization. Someone who's part business analyst and part project manager is typically a good fit for this role.

REMEMBER

In DAD, a product owner doesn't own the product in the same sense as does a product owner for a Scrum team. Instead, a DAD product owner helps the team understand the requirements and communicate the project's status to key stakeholders.

TEAM MEMBER

In DAD, the team member role is influenced by both agile and traditional project management. Like agile, DAD encourages teams to self-organize. In keeping with traditional project management, DAD does not emphasize the need for team members to be cross-functional (have a variety of skill sets). Team members can stick closely to their traditional roles, such as user-experience/user-interface (UX/UI) designers or even testers.

TEAM LEAD

Team lead is part Scrum Master and part lead developer. DAD distinguishes leadership from management. Unlike a manager, a team lead doesn't assign work to team members and supervise their work. Instead, he sets direction, motivates the team, and serves as a resource person. A team lead is like an administrator who fights for the team's shared workspace and orders pizza for planning meetings.

WARNING

Don't position your team lead as a project manager. The team lead is not responsible for the work and shouldn't push the team to deliver.

Having a team lead is another area where DAD diverges from agile. Most agile teams shy away from having any team-member with a leadership title. Most managers think of themselves as leaders, and many leaders think of themselves as managers, so the "Team lead" title may encourage the person serving this role to overstep his boundaries. A team lead must guide the team without managing any of its work, and that's a tall order.

ARCHITECTURE OWNER

Think of the architecture owner as a developer who knows more about many of the architectural issues in your organization. Any authority he has on the team comes from his expertise. He can overrule other team members on technical matters but doesn't assign work or supervise.

REMEMBER

While the product owner focuses on a product's functional requirements, the architecture owner focuses on its nonfunctional requirements to ensure, for example, that the product integrates with the enterprise database, the commonly used software, and even the testing platform.

Stepping behind the scenes with the supporting cast: Secondary roles

Secondary roles come into play on an as-needed basis; for example, if a team needs expertise in a certain area that nobody on the team has, the team calls in a specialist. If the team is required to build a product that meets a certain compliance requirement that it doesn't have the testing expertise to validate, it calls in an independent tester who's capable of providing that service.

At the team level, these are temporary roles. A person pops in to do a specific type of work or to offer specialized knowledge or insight and then leaves the team. Because they're temporary, they're referred to as "secondary."

REMEMBER

Don't think of these secondary roles as job titles. Think of them more as consultants or service providers. When they're not serving a secondary role, they may work on another team or outside of the teams. They jump in when needed to provide a service and then go back to their usual jobs.

TIP

Try your best to reduce the need for secondary roles over time by having these specialized personnel educate and train your teams. Otherwise, the organization will end up doing what it has been doing and how it has been doing it all along only perhaps less efficiently.

Specialist

DAD distinguishes between *specialists* and *generalizing specialists.* A specialist has specific skills and expertise in one area, whereas a generalizing specialist has a broad range of skills and expertise. Agile teams are typically composed of generalizing specialists, because team members are expected to be cross-functional — they need to be competent in several disciplines that the team requires.

DAD uses specialists primarily to help teams function and scale as a temporary measure until team members develop skills and expertise in the required disciplines. For example, agile business analysts may join a team temporarily to explore requirements for what the team is building, or a program manager may step in to work with team leads to coordinate the various teams' efforts. However, team members should acquire the requisite knowledge and skills over time.

When your organization is getting started with agile, your teams may have several specialists as team members. The idea is that over time, these specialists will broaden their base of skills and expertise to become generalizing specialists. Until then, you may need to pull a specialist from one team temporarily to serve as a specialist on another team that lacks someone with that specialized knowledge and skill set.

TIP

Look across teams and across your entire organization to find specialists. A specialist may be a manager who comes in to explain organizational policies or a developer who specializes in a certain programming language.

Independent tester

Although teams are responsible for testing their products themselves, independent testers may be called in to test the product on different platforms or test it for security or compliance issues or provide other specialized testing.

Domain expert

Domain experts are internal consultants who offer teams insight into the expert's sphere of activity or knowledge. For example, your organization may have an expert handling compliance issues. You probably have sales and marketing staff who have a better understanding of the customer's needs. Teams can call on these domain experts, and others, when they need their special knowledge and insight.

PURE VERSUS IMPURE AGILITY

As I mention earlier in this chapter, DA positions itself as a more "pragmatic" approach to agile. It's pitched as an alternative to agile purists, almost as if the purists demand that every organization bathe in the crystal waters of Lake Agile.

But many large organizations that operate with an agile mindset are not pure or idealized. They experiment, fail, inspect, and adapt. It's a rough and impure process through which they get better by learning from their mistakes. Recognizing agility as a mindset rather than an end state, a true agile team works in the mud grinding out improvements and delivering valuable products.

REMEMBER

Domain experts don't do the work or train the team how to do it. Instead, they offer information and insight that helps the team build a better product.

Technical expert

A technical expert is someone who has specialized skills and expertise that a team doesn't generally need on a daily basis. For example, a team may need a UX/UI designer to design an interface for the product it's working on or a build master to set up its build scripts. The technical expert steps in, provides the service, and then leaves the team. Technical experts can be members on loan from other teams.

Integrator

On a large team organized into sub-teams, an integrator builds the entire system from the various subsystems contributed by the sub-teams. On smaller teams, the architecture owner serves in this role, but larger teams need an integrator. The integrator may work closely with the independent testing team to ensure that the entire system works as a whole.

Deciding whether DA is worth the trouble

If your organization is already following RUP, you will have an easier time transitioning to DA. For organizations unfamiliar with RUP, DA might not add enough value to justify the learning and aggravation that will, with great certainty, accompany the transition. By starting with DA from scratch, you would encounter a learning curve so steep and ideas so abstract that all individuals in your organization would spend most of their time scribbling notes in training sessions and then scratching their heads later, trying to make actionable sense of it all.

There's an old joke about a writer who sent a letter to a friend that ended, "Sorry this letter is so long. I didn't have time to make it shorter." I get the same feeling when I write about DA. I keep thinking, "If only they had taken the time to strip down this framework, it could have been more useful." Including a milestone that's useful for only about 5 percent of adopters and irrelevant to the other 95 percent strikes me as undisciplined and impractical. Sometimes, it feels that the developers were just throwing agile processes in their cart like happy gift-card holders at a shopping mall.

Appreciating the value in simplicity

> Learning to choose is hard. Learning to choose well is harder. And learning to choose well in a world of unlimited possibilities is harder still, perhaps too hard.
>
> —Barry Schwartz, *The Paradox of Choice: Why More Is Less*

The developers of DA argue that enterprise agile is complicated so the decision framework needs to be complicated as well. That to be an effective process decision framework you have to see all your options. However, such a perspective discounts the value in simplicity. It's a little like that old Albert Einstein quote: "If you can't explain it simply, you don't understand it well enough." Enterprise products are complicated, but it's not theoretical physics. A large organization should look to an enterprise agile framework to help identify the best ideas and methods and not just provide an endless supply of options.

The very first language around the Agile Manifesto was about creating a "lightweight" framework for product delivery. The developers of DA would argue that "lightweight" doesn't scale well for enterprise products. That may be true, but then you have to question whether the DA framework still fits the common interpretation of agile software development.

DA presents a number of interesting ideas, and it may be a great framework for delivering enterprise products, but whether it encourages an enterprise agile mindset is open for debate.

I have little doubt that many organizations are trying something similar to DA. They may not call it DA, but their transition from a top-down approach to agile probably mirrors the DA framework. DA would be far more valuable if it helped these large organizations pare down their choices instead of providing them with more.

- Getting friendly with failure
- Considering two approaches to product development
- Figuring out whether the Spotify approach is best for you

Chapter 7

Working in Tribes with the Spotify Engineering Culture

Spotify is a digital streaming service that gives its subscribers access to a huge selection of music, podcasts, and videos via their smartphones and other electronic devices. The company developed its own approach to enterprise agility that borrows from numerous agile methodologies and practices, including Agile, Scrum, Lean Software Development, and Kanban. Spotify refers to its approach as the "Spotify Engineering Culture."

Like other enterprise agile frameworks, Spotify's approach is centered on self-organizing, cross-functional teams (called *squads*) collaborating to deliver value to customers. However, it's less structured than most frameworks, such as Scaled Agile Framework® (SAFe®), Large-Scale Scrum (LeSS), and Disciplined Agile Delivery (DAD). In fact, it's kind of messy. It may just be the most adaptive of all the enterprise agile frameworks.

In this chapter, I bring you up to speed on the Spotify Engineering Culture so you can determine whether it is the framework you want to use in your organization.

If it is, you'll gather enough information and insight along the way to start moving your organization in that direction.

REMEMBER

Spotify is not in the business of creating enterprise agile frameworks; it is in the business of creating an awesome digital streaming service. As such, it presents its approach to enterprise agility (check out its video on the Spotify website at `https://labs.spotify.com`), but it doesn't recommend it or support it. Instead, Spotify basically says, "Here's what we're doing. You may find it helpful. Feel free to customize it."

Building Your Spotify Community

In the Spotify Engineering Culture, employees organize into four different group types, as shown in Figure 7-1:

- **Squad:** A self-governing, cross-functional group, typically fewer than eight people, that's responsible for one or more features. The squad's focus is on product delivery and quality. According to Spotify, each squad should focus on how to "Think it, build it, ship it, and tweak it," which is in line with the Lean Software Development approach.
- **Tribe:** A group of squads that work on a related area of the product, such as search.
- **Chapter:** A group that cuts across squads and is composed of employees who share a certain competency, such as database administration, web development, or testing. The chapter lead serves as a sort of line manager for everyone in that chapter, providing coaching and mentoring. With this approach, you can switch squads without a change in manager.
- **Guild:** An informal group of people throughout the organization that forms around a shared interest, such as user-experience/user-interface (UX/UI) design, Java programming, or even photography.

REMEMBER

The focus here is on building community and culture, not on organizational structure. The intent is to remove any speed bumps that impede product release, so releases can be smaller and occur faster and more frequently. As Spotify puts it, "release should be routine, not drama."

In the following sections, I describe all of these groups and their purpose and function in greater detail, and I offer guidance on how to get the most out of each.

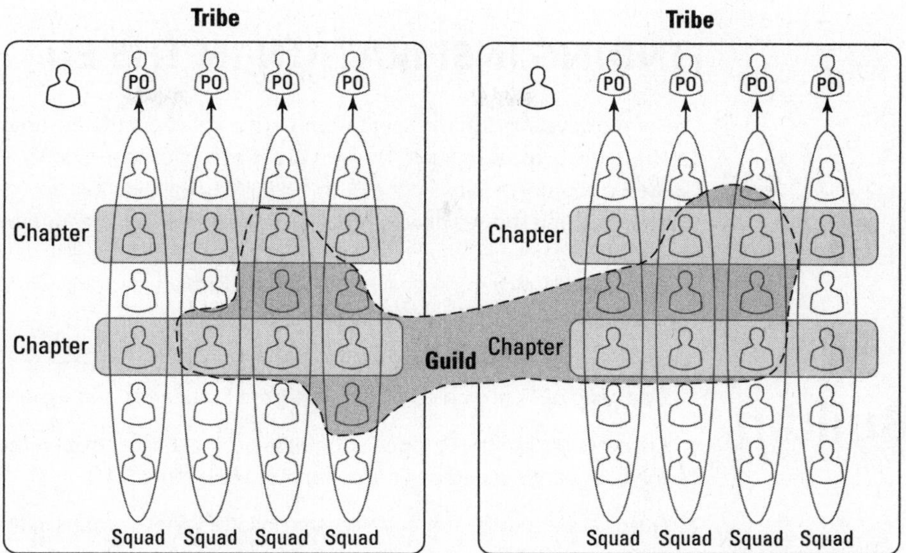

FIGURE 7-1: Employees are grouped into squads, tribes, chapters, and guilds.

REMEMBER

Spotify started as a small company that followed the Scrum approach. As it grew, it found that certain Scrum practices, such as the sprint planning meeting, task breakdown, and estimation, were getting in its way, so it made these practices optional. The idea is to start with a framework and rules, but then "screw the rules," when it makes sense to do so.

Starting with a squad

In Spotify, the smallest functioning unit is a *squad*, which has the following characteristics:

- **Autonomous:** Each team defines what to build, how to build it, and how to work together (and, if necessary, with other squads) to build it.
- **Close proximity:** Team members sit in close proximity to one another to facilitate communication and collaboration.
- **End-to-end responsibility:** Each team is responsible for one or more features from beginning to end — design, commit, test, deploy, maintain, and anything else that may be required.
- **Long-term mission:** Every team has a long-term mission, such as to make Spotify the best place to get music or to build infrastructure for *A/B testing* — comparing two versions of a feature or product to determine which is better at producing the desired outcome.

FINDING INSPIRATION IN THE EU

One of the developers of the Spotify approach pointed out that he drew a lot of inspiration from the European Union. This was pre-Brexit, of course. (Spotify was founded in Sweden, a country that joined the EU in 1995.) Although Spotify's approach frowns on bureaucracy, you can see how the EU's structure influenced the framework:

- Each squad functions like each country's parliament, deciding what's best for its people. Each country is autonomous in this respect.
- Tribes are like the national governments (countries), each of which is represented by a head of state who collectively form the European Commission.
- Chapters are like the European Commission, creating legislation that cuts across the boundaries separating the national governments.
- Guilds are institutions or practices that involve various groups in the different countries, such as the shared currency, access to common universities, and the ability to cross borders without a passport.

Like the European Union, the Spotify approach struggles to find the right balance between autonomy and unity. That's why the EU is sometimes called "the great experiment." It has no blueprint or clear formula on how to achieve this balance. It's hard work that involves a lot of conflict and compromise and relies on mutual respect and trust.

REMEMBER

One of the key benefits of having small, autonomous squads is speed. Squads make decisions locally and are given the freedom to fail, so they're not wasting time seeking permission or approval. It also minimizes *handoffs* (passing a task to another team to complete the work), waiting, and time spent coordinating efforts.

Spotify doesn't endorse any one type of agile team, nor does it prescribe a methodology. Squads are similar to feature teams in LeSS, in that they focus on a feature in a product. (See Chapter 5 for more about LeSS.) The differences are that Spotify teams are generally smaller, and they're not required to use Scrum. Squads can use Scrum, Kanban, Lean Software Development, Extreme programming, or any other approach, or they can mix and match agile team models or create their own model. Whatever works.

The only limits on teams is that they align their activities with the squad's mission, the company's product strategy, and the squad's short-term goals, which are reviewed monthly.

Not all squads work on product delivery. Squads may work in operations, on infrastructure, or in other functional areas of the company. Whatever the squad's mission, it is expected to communicate and collaborate with other squads as needed. Spotify encourages a "we're all in this together" culture. Although squads are generally self-sufficient, they're not silos.

Maintaining autonomy and alignment

Although squads are autonomous, you don't want every squad going off in its own direction. Spotify prevents the fall into chaos by requiring that teams be aligned with product strategy, company priorities, and other squads. As Spotify puts it, each squad is expected to "be a good citizen in the Spotify ecosystem." The company's mission is more important than that of any of the squads. Ideally, squads are autonomous but aligned.

Spotify sees autonomy and alignment as two different dimensions (see Figure 7-2). It charts the two with autonomy along the x-axis and alignment along the y-axis to create the following four quadrants:

- **Low-alignment, low autonomy:** A high-control culture in which teams do what they're told.
- **High alignment, low autonomy:** Leadership defines the problem and prescribes the solution. Teams execute the solution.
- **Low alignment, high autonomy:** Teams do whatever they want, wandering off in different directions, which leads to chaos.
- **High alignment, high autonomy:** Leadership defines the problem and leaves it up to the teams to figure out how to solve it. Spotify tries to stay in this upper-right quadrant.

At the squad level, alignment is primarily the responsibility of the system owner who keeps the squad aligned with its mission and creates and maintains a prioritized list of work items to help the team prioritize its work. She also communicates with other system owners in different squads to help coordinate the work and even manage any dependencies. (For more about the system owner role, see the later section "Having a system owner.")

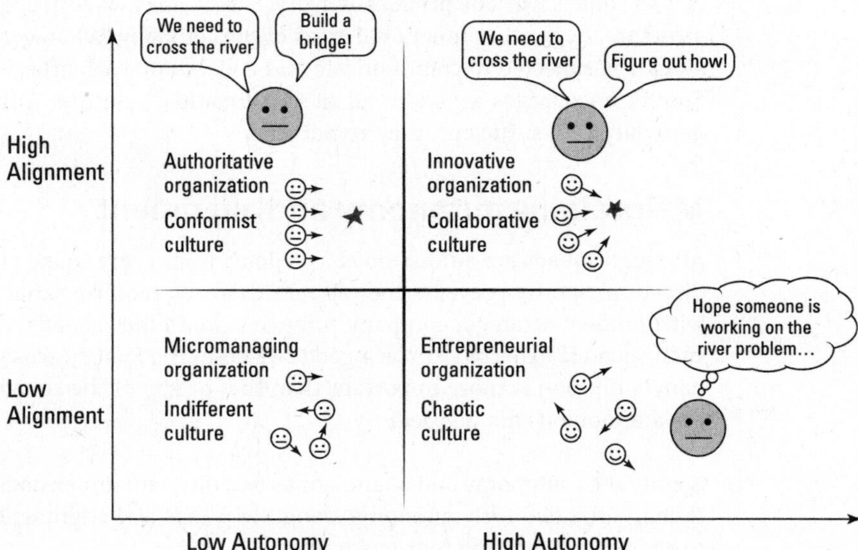

FIGURE 7-2: Striving for high alignment, high autonomy.

Balancing flexibility and consistency through cross-pollination

Instead of mandating that squads adopt certain processes and practices, Spotify gives squads freedom to use whatever processes and practices work best for them. Instead of setting standards, it relies on squads to cross-pollinate by learning from one another. When enough squads are following a certain process or engaging in a certain practice and having great success with it, word spreads through the community. Squads start supporting the tool and helping one another use it. Over time, it may become a de facto standard. Cross-pollination gives squads flexibility, but it also promotes consistency across squads.

Decoupling systems and squads

One way Spotify supported squad autonomy as it was scaling Scrum is that it changed its architecture to decouple its systems. Its product consists of over 100 interacting systems, with each system dedicated to one specific need, such as playlist management or search. Each squad "owns" one or more of these systems, so each squad can work on its system(s) independently. Spotify's software development model is open source, which promotes squad innovation and sharing among squads.

Prior to changing its architecture, Spotify was a single application. The company noticed that teams were spending a lot of time and effort synchronizing for each new release. Instead of creating numerous processes and rules to govern synchronization, Spotify changed the architecture to create a product that functions more like a website with different frames. Each squad can update its frame with little or no effect on the other frames.

If a squad needs something done to a system it doesn't own, it asks the squad that owns it to do the work. If that squad is too busy to do it, however, the squad that needs it done is free to edit that system. The squad that owns the system must then review the changes. This approach reduces wait times, increases quality, and spreads knowledge. Minimal standards are in place to improve efficiency (reduce friction).

Nurturing trust and mutual respect

For the squad concept to work well, you must nurture a culture of trust and mutual respect. Keeping the focus on the product is a great start. When your people are focused on making a great product, ego, authority, and politics take a back seat behind product quality. People are more willing to share knowledge, ask for help, and give in and collaborate with one another. People are more likely to give credit to others than to seek it for themselves.

Keeping the squads sticky

Much like Disciplined Agile Delivery (DAD) teams (see Chapter 6), squads like to be "sticky." They stick together and they stick with one or more features throughout the life of those features. This stickiness makes squads different from typical Scrum or LeSS teams, where team members work where they're needed most.

One of the downsides of using sticky teams is that you may have trouble divvying up the workload. Spotify's approach to decoupling the systems that make up its product works for Spotify, but it may not work as well for you, especially if teams are required to work on different products or when they need specialized expertise. If you have one squad working on the most important features of a product, you can end up with a lot of dependencies and, as a result, bottlenecks and roadblocks.

You don't want to create a squad that could be a potential bottleneck. A lot of software development organizations have a separate team for testing. If you created a squad that focused solely on testing, then you may create a backup if several other squads finish their development at the same time. This team would go from being overworked at certain times to being underworked at other times.

Spotify addresses this problem through *validated learning*, a common term used in Lean Startup — it tests, measures, and adjusts. In this testing scenario, the squad would quickly realize that it's creating a bottleneck for the rest the organization.

It would probably break up the squad and distribute testers to different squads. Then they would test this out and see if there's an improvement and how work flows through the system.

Conducting retrospectives

Each squad meets regularly (every few weeks at Spotify) to discuss what's working well and what it needs to improve. These informal meetings, referred to as "retrospectives," are less about planning and more about improving the product and the process and learning from failure.

Forming tribes of squads

For large products, such as Spotify, squads are grouped into tribes (see Figure 7-3), with each tribe focusing on a specific area in product development. For example, Spotify has three tribes:

- **Client app tribe:** Each squad in this tribe facilitates the release of features on one specific platform, such as iOS or Android.
- **Feature tribe:** Each squad in this tribe focuses on a specific feature area, such as search or playlist management. The squad builds, ships, and maintains features in that area for all platforms.

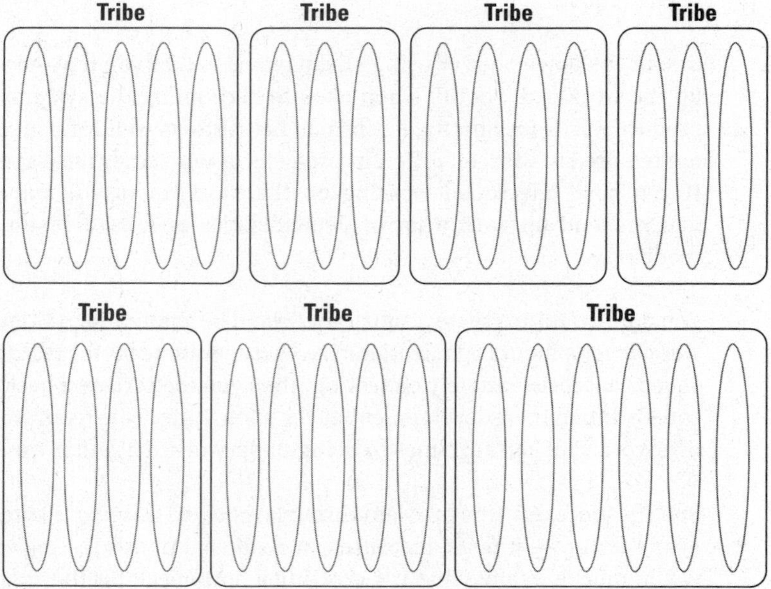

FIGURE 7-3: Organizing into different tribes.

- **Infrastructure tribe:** The squads in this group focus on making other squads more effective by providing tools and routines for operations, monitoring, testing, and so forth.

The tribes are built on a self-service model. Tribes don't push what they have on other tribes; they simply make it available to the tribes to use the services when needed. The client app tribe enables and supports the feature tribe, and the infrastructure tribe enables and supports both the client app and feature tribes.

Following some tribe-formation guidelines

When forming tribes, consider the following (very loose) guidelines:

- Try to keep the squads that form the tribe in close physical proximity — the same floor and the same room or work area.
- Limit the population of a tribe to no more than about a hundred people total. If each squad has six or seven members, then you should have no more than about 14 to 16 squads in a tribe.

COMPARING SPOTIFY TO SAFe AND LeSS

Spotify's squads and tribes are like SAFe's teams and agile release trains (ARTs). Like ARTs, tribes group teams to create a virtual organization. Similar to LeSS, which has sprint planning and review meetings where the various teams gather to discuss the product, the squads in a tribe gather regularly to discuss the product, share knowledge, and ask questions.

Tribes differ from teams and ARTs in that they are "sticky" like squads. Squads don't move in and out of different tribes. Instead the tribe functions as a small business or organization that serves the community.

Tribes also have a much less formal meeting structure than that of other enterprise agile frameworks. SAFe has program increment planning meetings in which the Release Train Engineer coordinates the work of the different teams in the ART. LeSS has science-fair style sprint reviews in which teams give presentations to one another about their piece of the larger product. When squads meet as a tribe, they may share knowledge, ask questions, and celebrate their accomplishments and what they've learned from their failures.

Syncing squads with release trains and feature toggles

To keep squads in sync and maintain flow, Spotify uses release trains and feature toggles:

- **Release train:** The release train is a scheduled release for each client app that includes features from all the squads working on that client app. Features are loaded onto the train whether they're done or not to prevent delays. Undone work is flagged to help the squads identify integration problems. At Spotify, the train leaves the station every week or every three weeks.
- **Feature toggles:** Features that aren't done are toggled off (hidden) in testing and production. The record of features that are toggled on and off helps the squads A/B test their products and roll out new features.

Setting up chapters

Within each tribe are chapters that cut across the squads (see Figure 7-4). Each chapter has a chapter lead and is composed of people with a shared competency, such as software development, web development, data management, or testing. The chapter lead acts as line manager, but without some of the traditional management responsibilities. The chapter lead is more of a service position, coaching and mentoring the chapter members. She doesn't assign work or supervise employees, but she may set salaries, schedule vacations, or help squad members obtain additional training.

One of the key benefits to having chapters is that people can move from one squad to another without losing their chapter lead. In that way, a chapter is more like a traditional department, although Spotify would never think of calling it that.

Sharing interests and knowledge in guilds

To encourage knowledge sharing, promote professional development, and support the wider community (beyond squads and tribes), the Spotify approach uses *guilds* — informal groups that form around a shared interest. A guild is basically a community of practice (CoP) (see Figure 7-5), which is common in other enterprise agile frameworks, such as SAFe and LeSS.

Each guild has its own coordinator, who sets the time and location of meetings and may create a loose agenda based on the guild members' needs. These meetings, often referred to as "unconferences," are a time for different parts of the organization to get together and share ideas in an informal setting.

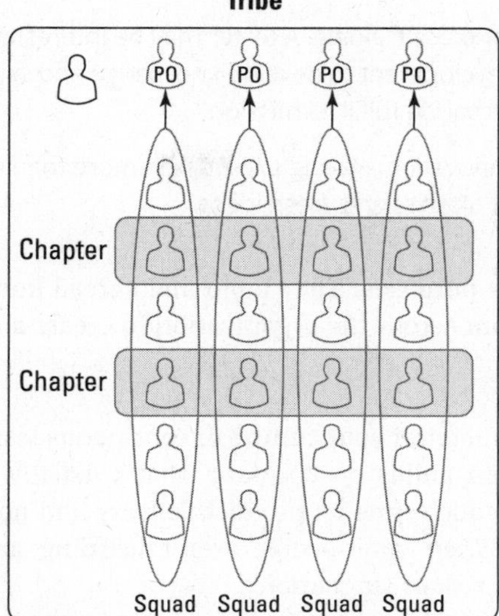

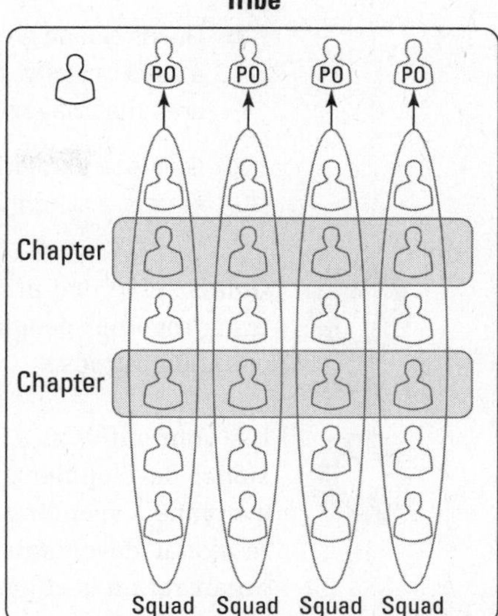

FIGURE 7-4: Chapters cutting across squads.

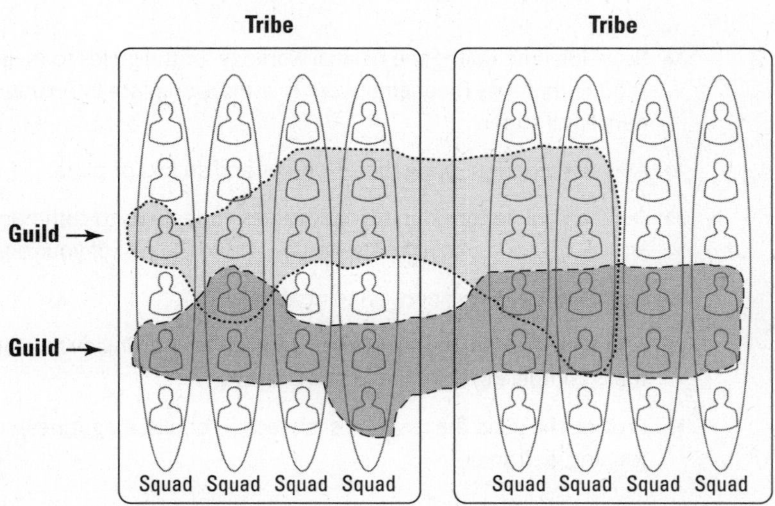

FIGURE 7-5: Establishing interest guilds.

Guilds offer numerous benefits beyond knowledge sharing among a group of people with shared interests, including the following:

» Guilds can be a great tool for improving understanding across squads and across chapters. For example, a frontend web developer may join a guild on backend development practices to gain a better understanding of the challenges involved in backend development.

- Guilds can be great for cross-training. A tester may be interested in attending a guild on software development to develop knowledge and skills in another area that may help his squad fulfill its mission.
- Guilds tend to drive innovation. Having expertise in more than one area creates a synergy that often sparks fresh ideas.

Guilds serve two primary purposes: They build and spread knowledge, and they bring together people from across the organization to create a greater sense of a common purpose.

Use your guilds as a barometer of your culture of continuous learning and professional development. When guilds go dormant, that's usually a good sign that everyone's spending too much time on product delivery and not enough on professional development. When your people aren't learning and growing, your organization is at greater risk of stagnation.

To keep your guilds thriving, make them a priority by doing the following:

- Set aside time during the normal workday for the guilds to meet. If you require that they meet after work to avoid workplace interruptions, attendance will suffer.
- Add some perks. Spring for beverages and snacks or pizza.
- Build an online community that enables your guilds to communicate, share knowledge, and make themselves known to the rest of your organization.
- Keep the meetings short, an hour at most.
- Make attendance optional, but provide an agenda in advance of the meetings that's compelling enough to draw a crowd.
- Provide the guild the resources it needs — books, magazines, subscriptions, training, and so on.

The vitality of a guild depends a great deal on its coordinator. Generally, the person or people who form the guild are the most passionate about their shared interest, but someone else in the organization may be better suited for that role. You want someone with passion, knowledge, and charisma. Encourage your guilds to choose the best person for the role and look past ego and politics. The best coordinator is the best for everyone in the guild.

Discourage guild coordinators from trying to set standards. It's easy for a guild to devolve into a sort of political action group that tries to set standards or rules for the entire organization.

DON'T LET YOUR GUILDS FADE AWAY

I worked for an organization that had a number of active guilds at the very beginning of its enterprise agile transformation. However, as soon as the workloads increased, most teams were so busy just keeping up with their work that few people attended the meetings. Over time, people who routinely attended the meetings fell into a routine of not attending the meetings.

Don't let your guilds fall into this pattern. Make them a priority. The long-term health of your organization depends on it.

Embracing a Creative, Failure-Friendly Culture

If you choose the Spotify model for your enterprise agile framework, you're committing your organization to a culture of creativity that's failure-friendly. As Spotify founder Daniel Ek said about his company, "We aim to make mistakes faster than anyone else." Spotify sees failure as a learning opportunity. Squads release new features quickly and frequently, test those features, conduct retrospectives to discuss their success and failures, and then tweak the product and the process in the spirit of continuous improvement. Perhaps most important, when they discuss failure, they don't try to figure out whose fault it was; they're more concerned with finding out what happened and why and then using that insight to make changes.

This experiment-fail-learn-improve approach is reflected in how the company handles incident reports. Instead of closing an incident after it's been resolved, the company closes it only after the squads have captured the learning via a post-mortem. Making mistakes is fine; repeating them isn't.

In this section, I discuss other ways you can nurture a creative, failure-friendly culture by following Spotify's lead.

Driving agility and innovation through culture and values

Agile frameworks tend to communicate culture through manifestos and principles more than anything else. Although Spotify doesn't exactly list its principles, the creators of its approach highlight what the organization values in terms of inequalities. As you read through this list of Spotify's "values," note how nearly every one of them supports squad autonomy and innovation over methodologies and practices:

- **Agile > Scrum:** Being agile is more important than adhering to any agile framework, such as Scrum, Kanban, or Lean Software Development.
- **Chaos > Bureaucracy:** Although Spotify doesn't exactly yearn for chaos, it strives to have the least amount of structure and process (bureaucracy) to avoid total chaos. It relies on its foundation of community and culture to keep from tipping into chaos.
- **Community > Structure:** A thriving community drives innovation, whereas a highly structured organization tends to stifle it. As Spotify puts it, "If you always need to know exactly who is making decisions, you're in the wrong place."
- **Cross pollination > Standardization:** Allowing practices to spread from squad to squad leads to a healthier balance of consistency and flexibility than does requiring that all squads adopt a specific set of practices.
- **Enable > Serve:** Facilitating other people's work is more effective than doing it for them.
- **Failure recovery > Failure avoidance:** The Spotify approach doesn't punish failure. Learning from failure and using the lessons learned to improve the product and process is what matters most.
- **Impact > Velocity:** A feature isn't done by a certain deadline or at the end of a given sprint but when the product achieves the desired impact — when it produces the desired results.
- **Innovation > Predictability:** Spotify sees innovation and predictability as opposite ends of a spectrum. It wants some predictability but prefers to be more innovative than predictable. The focus is on delivering value, not on meeting deadlines.

  REMEMBER

  When higher predictability is needed (for example, to coordinate a release with a planned marketing activity), Spotify may slide closer to the predictability end of the spectrum and use standard agile planning techniques, such as epics and user stories.
- **People > *:** An organization's people are its most valuable asset. Mutual respect is essential.
- **Principles > Practices:** Guiding principles promote agility, whereas established practices may just get in the way.

» **Servant > Master:** Servant leaders are more empowering than process masters. In line with this value, Spotify changed the name Scrum Master to Agile Coach.

» **Trust > Control:** Trust gives people the freedom and confidence to try new things and take initiative. Control hinders agility and stifles innovation by creating a culture of politics and fear.

Reducing the negative consequences of failure

To prevent experimentation and failure from negatively impacting customers (or to minimize that impact), Spotify introduced the concept of having a "limited blast radius." That is, if failure occurs, it negatively impacts only one feature or feature set and very few customers. Spotify limits its blast radius in two ways:

» **Decoupled architecture:** The decoupled architecture (see the earlier section "Decoupling systems and squads") enables each squad or tribe to work on an isolated system within the product, so any mistakes affect only that system.

» **Gradual rollout:** When the squad or tribe deems a feature good enough to roll out, it makes the feature available to very few users. It then monitors how users respond to the change to determine whether it had the desired impact; for example, whether users are logging on more often or sharing more music. If the feature functions well and has the desired results, it's gradually rolled out to more and more users.

REMEMBER

Having a limited blast radius reduces the squad's fear of making mistakes. As a result, it's a great way to encourage your squads to take chances.

Encouraging innovation

Throughout the year, Spotify encourages squads to spend ten percent of their time to invent and build whatever they want with whomever they want. The squads set aside one of every ten days as a *hack day* — innovative play time. Twice a year, the entire company joins in a hack week at the end of which the company has a party and reveals the inventions developed over the course of the week.

The hack day is nothing new. Several companies, including Sun Microsystems, allocate play time to give programmers the opportunity to engage in exploratory programming and explore ways to improve the product. They could rework the code or even research new ideas. At Spotify, squads are encouraged to create anything they like — the idea is to get the creative juices flowing.

Developing an aversion to waste

One way Spotify promotes creativity while improving efficiency is by eliminating *waste* — anything that doesn't add value to the product, such as time reports, handoffs, separate test teams, task estimates, useless meetings, and corporate nonsense.

TIP

To develop an aversion to waste, simply give your squads license to stop doing whatever doesn't help them or whatever doesn't contribute value to the product. People naturally stop using tools that don't make their jobs easier; they just need permission to do so.

Engaging in continuous improvement

Like all other enterprise agile frameworks, Spotify's approach stresses the need for continuous improvement. The company drives continuous improvement in the following ways:

- **Conducting retrospectives:** Squads and tribes meet regularly to discuss what's working, what's not working, what's getting in their way, and what they need to do about it.
- **Experimenting and capturing the learning:** Squads and tribes experiment and then analyze the results to figure out ways to improve both the product and the process for creating it. By measuring and collecting data, squads are able to make data-driven decisions instead of having their decisions driven by ego, authority, or opinion.
- **Using improvement boards:** Improvement boards, such as the kata board, shown in Figure 7-6, help the squads move from problem to solution. The improvement board Spotify uses has four quadrants:
  - *Top left:* A description of the current situation — the problem.
  - *Bottom left:* The definition of awesome — a description of what the situation will look like when the problem is gone.
  - *Top right:* A realistic target that brings the situation closer to awesome.
  - *Bottom right:* Three concrete steps the squad can take to achieve the realistic target. (After taking these steps, the squad reassesses the situation and sets more steps to reach the realistic target or, if it has already hit that target, it sets another realistic target that brings them even closer to awesome.)

REMEMBER

Continuous improvement must be driven from below and supported from above.

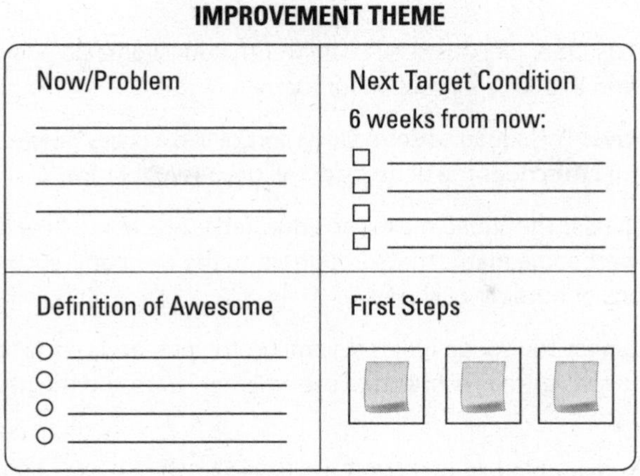

IMPROVEMENT THEME

Now/Problem	Next Target Condition 6 weeks from now:
Definition of Awesome	First Steps

FIGURE 7-6: A typical kata improvement board.

Strengthening community and culture overall

The very foundation of the Spotify approach is community and culture. According to the creators of this approach, "Healthy culture heals broken process." Spotify nurtures community and culture with the following:

- People operations dedicated to supporting the needs of community members
- About 30 Agile Coaches that spread across all squads
- Boot camps for new hires, during which new hires form a temporary squad and work together to solve a problem while learning the Spotify approach to enterprise agility
- Storytelling, which spreads the culture throughout the organization via blogs, post-mortems, retrospectives, demonstrations, or even conversations over lunch

Understanding Spotify's Approach to Product Development/Planning

Spotify's approach to product development/planning is deeply rooted in the Lean Startup approach of "Think it, build it, ship it, tweak it." Here's how it works at Spotify:

- **Idea/Problem:** Somebody in the company has an idea for a feature. Research is conducted to determine whether the idea is likely to deliver value to the customer. Squads seek to answer the questions: Do people really want this? Does this solve a problem for them?

- **Narrative:** The squad writes a story, sort of like a press release or elevator pitch, that describes the benefits of the proposed feature.
- **Hypothesis:** The squad makes an educated guess about how the new feature will impact some metric that's important to the company, such as frequency of logons or number of shares.
- **Prototypes:** The squad builds several prototypes, and various people test them to see which is best and to see whether users find the new feature valuable.
- **Minimum viable product (MVP):** If, based on the results of the prototype testing, the feature is deemed worthy to build, the squad builds an MVP.
- **Gradual rollout and tweaking to perfection:** The squad rolls out the MVP to a tiny percentage of uses, measures its impact, and tweaks the feature. It repeats this process until the product is "done" — it has the desired impact.

Changing the game plan for larger products

While Spotify's usual approach works for small products, such as a feature, it's less successful for large, complex products. Spotify tries its best to steer clear of larger products by breaking the product down into smaller products, so it can use the "Think it, build it, ship it, tweak it" approach described in the previous section. However, if that's not an option, it takes a more traditional approach to product development.

For big products, Spotify adds a small, tightly knit leadership group, which typically includes a tech lead, product lead, and (sometimes) a design lead. The leadership group isn't exactly management. They don't assign and supervise work. Their function is to communicate the vision and maintain alignment among the squads and tribes.

The squads track progress visually using a Kanban board. They conduct daily syncs to facilitate coordination and collaboration and ensure alignment. And they produce a weekly demo to check how the product is coming along. The idea is increase collaboration and reduce risks by keeping the feedback loops as short as possible.

REMEMBER

Spotify sees big products as a major source of risk, the biggest risk being building the wrong thing.

Having a system owner

For large enterprises and large products, Spotify recommends adding a role called a "system owner." Even though "system owner" sounds like one person, it's actually the role of two people — a developer and an operations expert, each of whom works in her own squad. Every so often (on "system owner day"), they get together to make system-level decisions.

The system owner role is based heavily on the DevOps (development and operations) role, which is an attempt to combine two roles that may seem incompatible at first glance:

- **Development:** Development is more in the sphere of agile, relying on innovation and experimentation through frequent iterations to achieve continuous incremental improvement.
- **Operations:** Operations relies on planning ahead to make sure all components or systems of a product work seamlessly together.

Having a systems owner is an attempt to strike a healthy balance between predictability and innovation on large products. The system owner should always be pushing to achieve a healthy balance between frequent changes and the stability of the whole.

Deciding Whether the Spotify Approach Is Right for You

On its surface, Spotify's approach to enterprise agility is attractive, but it may be more like a utopian dream for larger enterprises. Its success relies on entirely on the ability of people to bond and to respect and trust one another. While that often works on a small scale, it's often less effective on a larger scale. Just as smaller countries can typically function well with less bureaucracy, and larger countries crumble when they don't have enough central control, a small business may thrive with less management, while a large enterprise can fall into chaos without a more structured framework.

To decide whether the Spotify approach is best for your organization, ask yourself and your organization's leadership the following questions:

- **Does our organization have a strong sense of community? Do people trust and respect one another? If not, can we create a culture of mutual respect and trust?** If your answers to any of these questions is "no," then

I don't recommend the Spotify approach. Without a strong collaboration culture, such an organization is likely to fall into chaos.

- **Is our organization comfortable with experimentation, failure, and compromise?** Your answer needs to be "yes" to this question if you plan on adopting the Spotify approach. The level of autonomy is much higher at Spotify than at most large organizations. If this isn't how your organization currently operates, leadership will need to completely reimagine its corporate vision. This isn't entirely a bad thing. If your organization truly wants to be agile, a change in vision is required regardless of the enterprise agile framework you choose.
- **Are we a heavy top-down, process-oriented organization?** If you answer "yes" to this question, then you may want to draw inspiration from the Spotify model without completely adopting it. If you're a smaller, more nimble, community-focused organization, this approach can give you a lot of guidance.
- **Are we comfortable adopting a relatively unproven approach?** If you answer "yes," the Spotify approach may be worth trying. However, while it has proven effective in scaling one organization up to a medium-sized company, the jury is still out on whether it can work for a large enterprise. If you're a large enterprise with thousands of developers, then you may test the limits of this approach.

Other enterprise frameworks, including SAFe, LeSS, and DAD, are all currently being used in very large companies. As of this writing, there haven't been any public demonstrations of really large organizations using the Spotify approach.

WARNING

Don't think of Spotify's approach as a separate solution or a clear roadmap. Approach it as a case study of how a very novel organization decided to scale agile to an enterprise level. It may give you some good ideas for making your organization more agile, and it may provide the inspiration to do so, but it's not a prepackaged solution.

The good news is that if you follow the Spotify approach, you're likely to end up with an agile framework that's tailored to your organization. You will adopt what works, toss what doesn't, adopt elements of other agile frameworks, and create your own principles, processes, and practices. As a result, your organization would probably be much more agile than if you had chosen a more substantive framework, such as SAFe, LeSS, or DAD.

In some ways the Spotify approach is like flipping through a weightlifting magazine. Some organizations may find it inspirational, while others look at the shiny mounds of muscle and think to themselves that there's no way they could (or would even want to) do that to themselves!

» Understanding and adopting Lean principles

» Putting Kanban and Lean into practice

» Deciding whether Kanban and Lean are the best solutions for your organization

Chapter 8

Improving Workflow and Eliminating Waste with Kanban and Lean

Kanban and Lean started out as a Japanese manufacturing processes developed in the mid-twentieth century to optimize efficiency and reduce waste:

- *Kanban* is a system for pulling just enough product through a process to meet demand. Kanban (signal) cards are used to indicate when supply is running low. The emphasis is on maintaining smooth and continuous flow.
- *Lean* is a system for reducing waste in products and processes by eliminating anything that's unnecessary, including excessive steps in a process and functionality that doesn't bring value to a customer in a product. The focus is on minimizing waste and maximizing value.

These manufacturing systems have since been adapted for use in a wide range of industries and even in personal time management systems to ensure continuous workflow and improve productivity. In this chapter, I bring you up to speed on

Kanban and Lean basics, offer guidance on how to implement them, and reveal some of their limitations in terms of using them to make an organization agile.

The purpose of Kanban is to improve efficiency and flow in any system. The purpose of Lean is to eliminate waste.

Grasping Kanban Principles and Practices

Kanban employs visualization methods to increase visibility into a process, eliminate bottlenecks, and facilitate collaboration. At its core are several principles and properties that govern its use. In this section, I introduce you to these principles and properties.

EXPLORING KANBAN'S ROOTS

For most of the twentieth century, manufacturers in the United States used a large-inventory model to manufacture and deliver products because they had plenty of land and resources to build and maintain warehouses. For example, suppliers in the auto industry created and shipped large quantities of parts to manufacturers that stored them in warehouses or on the manufacturing floor until they needed them. Auto manufacturers built thousands of cars and shipped them to dealers where they were stored in warehouses or on large lots until customers purchased them.

In the small island nation of Japan, that model didn't work so well, because Japan has less land and limited natural resources. Warehouses added significantly to the cost of products, both in the building and maintenance of warehouses and in *carrying costs* — automobile manufacturers would build thousands of cars and then have to wait months to recoup their investment.

To address this problem, Toyota's Taichi Ohno developed *just-in-time manufacturing* — building cars in smaller batches as driven by dealership demand, no warehouse needed. His inspiration came from grocery stores he had visited in the United States. He noticed that grocery store inventory was not based on what suppliers pushed to the store, but on what customers pulled off the shelves. He was impressed that stores were never overstocked and always had sufficient quantities to meet customer demand.

In Toyota's manufacturing plants, Ohno introduced the practice of using Kanban (signal) cards to indicate when part inventory was running low. When managers saw a Kanban card for a certain part, they knew they needed to reorder it. This card approach has since been adapted for use in project management to indicate the status of work items as those items flow through a process.

Brushing up on Kanban principles

The following four Kanban principles are intended to help an organization develop the right mindset for implementing Kanban. The principles are more about *how* people think than *what* they do.

REMEMBER

Kanban principles and properties are not written in stone. You are likely to see Kanban books and presentations that list additional principles and properties than those presented in this section.

Start with what you do

Unlike the Scaled Agile Framework® (SAFe®) and Large-Scale Scrum (LeSS), Kanban requires no major overhaul to an organization's structure and adds no new roles. Instead, it encourages you to start with what you already have in place and work toward improving it, which makes Kanban much easier than other frameworks to start with.

Pursue incremental, evolutionary change

Kanban improves visibility into systems and encourages everyone in the organization, from the top down, to suggest ways to improve the system. The emphasis is on incremental change, which minimizes resistance to change.

Respect current processes, roles, responsibilities, and titles

Kanban doesn't necessarily eliminate positions within an organization or add a bunch of new roles, and it doesn't force you to restructure your organization. You keep what works and, over time, fix, replace, or eliminate what doesn't work well.

Encourage acts of leadership at all levels

With Kanban, everyone in the organization plays a role in its continuous improvement *(kaizen)*. Everyone is involved in looking for ways to improve systems and practices.

Embracing Kanban properties

Kanban is all about looking at how your organization does what it does and figuring out ways to do it better. Unlike the principles that focus on *how to think*, the properties tell you *what to do* to ensure smooth and continuous workflow in your organization.

Visualize the workflow

Visualizing the workflow is based on the premise that you can't fix what you don't see. By mapping the current workflow, inefficiencies become more obvious. To visualize workflow and to schedule and manage work, you use a *Kanban board* that typically breaks a process into steps with a queue for each step, such as Input Queue, Analysis, Development, Test, Stage, and Production. The Kanban board provides an easy way to view and communicate the status of work, and it exposes workflow issues that need to be addressed.

Figure 8-1 shows a basic Kanban board that reflects six stages of a process — Input Queue, Analysis, Development, Test, Stage, and Production. For more about Kanban boards, see the later section, "Creating Kanban boards."

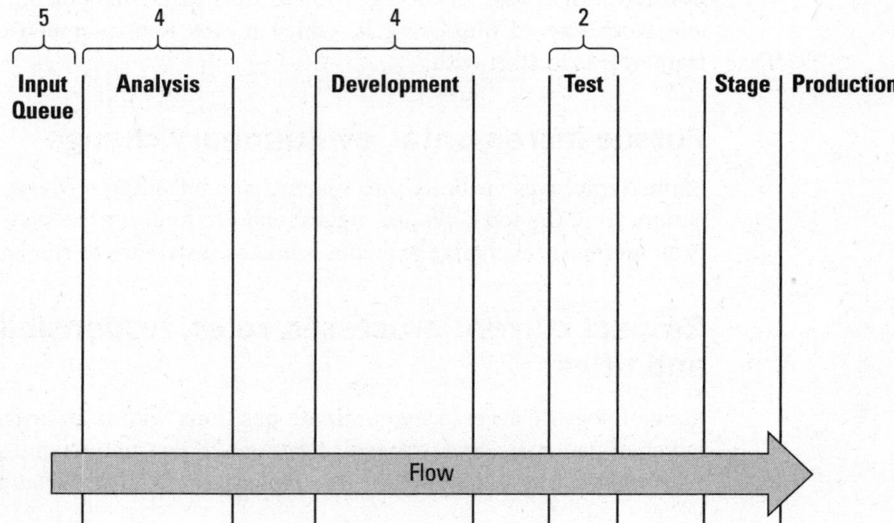

FIGURE 8-1: A simple Kanban board.

REMEMBER

Kanban is about much more than creating and using Kanban boards. It emphasizes continuous improvement through transparency and collaboration.

Limit work in progress

Kanban sets limits for work in progress (WIP) at each stage in a process, as shown in Figure 8-1. At the top of each queue is a number that represents the number of work items that can be in that queue (at that stage in the process) at any one time. In Figure 8-1, only five work items can be in the Input Queue at any one time, so if that queue already contains five items, the team can't add more until one of the items is moved to the In Analysis queue.

A *WIP limit* is the maximum amount of work that can exist at a certain stage of a process; it represents a team's capacity for completing work. Think of WIP limits as water valves that ensure a steady flow so that the team can deliver a consistent stream of work to the next stage of the process.

You can adjust WIP limits to improve workflow. See the later section, "Improving workflow," for details.

Manage flow

The goal of smooth and continuous flow involves identifying and removing bottlenecks in the system and exploring other ways to optimize processes. While "managing" flow may appear to suggest that this is management's job, all employees should be involved in identifying and addressing inefficiencies in the system.

Make process policies explicit

To make well-informed workflow decisions, process policies must be defined, documented, and discussed. For example, organizations must document each step in a process and provide specific criteria to determine when that step or what it produces is considered done.

Improve collaboratively

With Kanban, individuals and groups throughout the organization work collaboratively to solve problems and address issues that may be impeding the flow of value to the customer or, on a more local level, the workflow. Everyone is expected to develop a shared understanding of theories and models of workflow, process, and risk to inform discussion.

Pulling rather than pushing work

Traditionally, software development has been a push process, with managers pushing features and other requirements to the development team and requiring them to keep up with the demand. Kanban is a pull process, in which a product owner develops a prioritized list of work items, and developers pull from the list according to their capacity to work on those items.

A Kanban board, an example of which is shown in Figure 8-1, is key to managing this process. The team creates a backlog (a prioritized list of work items) and then moves items from the Input Queue to the Analysis queue when they're ready to be worked on. When the team is ready to work on an item, it moves the item from the Analysis queue to the Development queue. When the team is done with the work, it moves the item to the Test queue and then moves the next item from the Input Queue to the Analysis queue. As the team pulls items from the Input Queue, the team moves the next item from the Backlog queue to the Input Queue.

The Kanban board provides full visibility of progress, as work items move through the process from the Input Queue to the Production queue.

Why pull instead of push? The pull system enables teams to work at their own pace and focus on a limited number of work items at a time, which results in the following benefits:

- Less stress
- Higher quality
- Greater efficiency — less rework, less task-shifting
- Greater productivity
- Fewer crises
- Reduced turnover

The pull approach discourages managers from overloading teams with work to the point of dysfunction. Teams can focus on quality and on improving their skills. With less stress and turnover, teams maintain continuity and focus, which boosts productivity.

Working in small batches

While the traditional method of manufacturing relies on maintaining large inventories to meet customer demand, Kanban relies on flow — keeping small batches continuously moving through the system. You can see this approach in action at many fast-food restaurants, where they prepare food continuously to meet fluctuations in customer demand while ensuring the food is fresh (and hot when necessary). The grill cook, for example, may prepare six Big Macs whenever only two are remaining. Whenever the french fry supply dwindles, the fry cook lowers another basket of frozen fries into the grease.

Part of what maintains a smooth flow in the system is that the workers deal with small batches — a basket or two of french fries, a half dozen Big Macs, and so on. If they had to prepare everything all at once, they would quickly be overwhelmed, and gridlock would ensue. If they had to cook everything to order, the process would slow to a crawl.

CASE STUDY

KANBAN FOR A COMMUNITY SWIMMING POOL

When I was younger, I lived in a large subdivision with a swimming pool that had a maximum capacity of 120 swimmers. Kids had to be a certain height to get in. The managers of the pool had painted a red line on the chain link fence outside the pool to indicate how tall you had to be to get in. In the summer, kids flocked to the pool. The crowds easily exceeded capacity.

The maximum capacity and the required height to get in were fixed, but the managers also had to deal with variability. A rainy day could easily turn sunny and then the pool would fill up in less than an hour. Some kids would stay all day, while others only came in for a quick dip.

The managers could have developed all sorts of complicated systems to adhere to the capacity limit, such as alternating days for different groups of residents or restricting the amount of time swimmers could stay. Instead, they introduced a simple, elegant Kanban solution. Kids who met the height requirement were given a red elastic bracelet to put on their left wrist. When the bracelets ran out, kids without bracelets had to wait outside the pool for someone to leave.

Instead of preventing kids from pushing their way into the pool, the managers created a system that pulled swimmers in based on the pool's capacity. Very little management oversight was necessary, because the system was mostly self-regulating.

Kanban in manufacturing and product development works the same way. Teams break down each work order into smaller tasks called "work items," and each team focuses its efforts on only a small batch of work items at a time. As a team completes a work item, the next team in the process can pull it from the queue when that team is ready to work on it. This approach reduces the need for multi-tasking and task-switching, which enables teams to complete each work item faster.

Making Systems Lean

As I mention at the beginning of this chapter, *Lean* focuses on minimizing waste (*muda* in Japanese) and maximizing value to the customer — delivering more value with fewer resources. When you engage in Lean practices, you're trimming the fat. Like Kanban, Lean was developed to make manufacturing processes more efficient, but has since been applied to a variety of industries. However, using Lean in contexts other than manufacturing often requires some modification.

In this section, I introduce you to the Lean principles and explain how Lean has been modified over the years to become an effective tool for making large systems more efficient and adaptive.

Getting up to speed on Lean's core values

Lean Manufacturing is based on several principles to improve productivity, quality, and lead time, and eliminate waste. The principles reflect the following core values:

- **Built-in quality:** With Lean, quality pertains to all steps in a process, not only in the final product, which reduces defects and time-consuming review and revision.
- **Continuous improvement *(kaizen)*:** Everyone in the organization must seek ways to continuously improve products and processes.
- **Just-in-time (JIT) production:** Like Kanban, Lean is a pull system; demand, not supply, drives production.
- **Leveled production:** The goal is to maintain stable production levels to avoid overproduction, workplace stress, and defects.
- **Respect for humanity:** The most important part of any business is people — customers and employees. Employees need to feel respected, and the organization must attend to their needs and listen to their ideas. Likewise, customers are treated as members of the team who often drive innovation.
- **Waste elimination:** *Waste* is anything that doesn't deliver value to the customer, including overproduction, excess inventory, defects, wait times, overprocessing, unnecessary steps in a process, and other inefficiencies.

REMEMBER

Lean and Kanban principles overlap quite a bit. Just remember that Kanban is more about optimizing workflow, and Lean is more about eliminating waste. The two work well together to improve productivity.

Connecting Lean manufacturing to software development

In manufacturing processes, wastes are easy to identify and monitor, including transportation delays, excess inventory, unnecessary activity, overprocessing, overproduction, task-switching, and defects. In software development and other industries, waste can be more difficult to identify. Here are a few examples of waste in areas outside of manufacturing:

- Systems or processes that don't deliver value to the customer
- Excess or sloppy programming code
- Overcomplicated systems, processes, or solutions
- Delays from failing to address defects early in a process (such as software bugs)
- Waiting to pass along a work item to the next stage in a process
- Delays in information being communicated to the people who need it

To become Lean, organizations must first map out everything they do and eliminate anything that's not a value stream — processes they engage in that do not deliver value to the customer. Then, they must look at ways to optimize those value streams, primarily by streamlining them.

On a smaller level, teams can use Lean Manufacturing principles to develop products in shorter cycles that drive continuous, incremental improvement. Shorter cycles (iterations) improve early error detection, often reducing the time and effort required to deal with issues. Lean Software Development embraces the following principles, many of which are nearly identical to Lean Manufacturing principles:

- **Build in quality.** Develop in a way to minimize defects in the first place and in short cycles that enable you to work, test, and fix problems during development instead of queuing up problems or waiting to fix them later.
- **Create knowledge.** For teams to improve their products and processes, they need to communicate more closely with stakeholders and among themselves. Lean is big on continuous learning.
- **Delay commitment.** To allow for changes during the development process, develop flexible architectures and wait until the last possible moment to make irreversible decisions.
- **Deliver quickly.** Produce potentially shippable products quickly by limiting workloads to a team's capacity and by having teams self-organize and determine what they can accomplish.
- **Eliminate waste.** In software development, the biggest sources of waste are unnecessary features or capabilities, excessive or sloppy code, requirements

churn (changing requirements rapidly or late in the process), and the crossing of organizational boundaries.

- **Optimize the whole.** Deliver complete solutions that provide value not only to customers but to the organization as well.
- **Respect people.** Enable teams instead of controlling them. Allow teams to self-organize and self-direct.

REMEMBER

One of the big themes in enterprise agility is that software differs significantly from manufacturing. In fact, many agile developers argue that using traditional manufacturing processes leads to failed software projects. They argue that software development is much more dynamic and can't conform to a step-by-step process. You can't really predict what open-source project will take off or what technologies will fall out of favor. Customers may change their minds, and developers may discover solutions that are better at meeting a customer's needs.

Combining Kanban and Lean is way to resolve this dilemma. These two approaches provide teams with the principles and tools (such as the Kanban board) they need to develop software in short cycles that drive built-in quality and continuous improvement while facilitating communication and close collaboration. In addition, they allow for teams to self-manage and provide management greater visibility of work status, so that management feels less need to get involved — another factor that often causes delay.

LIKE THE STOCK MARKET

One of the unspoken rules of Kanban and Lean is that complex, adaptive systems don't need a lot of rules and regulations. Given a few guidelines, organizations can create their own complex and adaptive systems.

Think about a stock market. It has a few simple rules. You can buy stocks and sell stocks. However, these two rules are very accommodating, allowing for the creation of a complex adaptive system that can handle huge trade volumes and a variety of investment strategies.

You probably can't predict what will happen to the stock market each day. Total market value can fluctuate, but over the long haul, value rises according to a fairly predictable pattern.

In the same way, Kanban and Lean provide some guidance and then step out of the way to let organizations take it from there.

Implementing Kanban and Lean

Knowing principles, properties, and practices is only the first step in the process of adopting Lean and Kanban to make your organization agile. The second, bigger step is to start applying what you know. Fortunately, you don't need to overhaul your organizational chart and add a bunch of new roles. You can start with what's already in place.

In this section, I lead you through the process of implementing Lean and Kanban to minimize waste and optimize workflow.

Mapping your value stream

REMEMBER

Kanban and Lean are much different from the leading enterprise agile frameworks. Most of those frameworks call for big changes that involve new roles, new workflows, lots of new terminology, and even a new way to deliver product. Kanban and Lean take a softer approach. They don't try to rewire your organization — at least not all at once. Instead they start by looking at what's in place and identifying areas that could be improved or eliminated.

Start by mapping your value stream — all processes your organization does to deliver value to the customer. Find the biggest whiteboard or wall, and start taping 3-x-5 index cards or sticky notes to it, typically from left to right, to map the stream. Moveable notes make it easier to edit your maps. If yours is a large organization, you may want to divvy up the work among various departments or teams. Depending on the complexity of your value stream and the number of dependencies, this step can take a day to several weeks.

REMEMBER

Kanban is designed to optimize your process. Your Kanban value stream will be about eliminating the waste in your *process*. Other enterprise agile frameworks, such as the Scaled Agile Framework, are designed to deliver an enterprise-level product. They use value streams as a way to determine what steps your team takes to deliver a *product*. Even though they're using value streams in slightly different ways, they both focus on optimizing your stream into the fewest possible steps.

For example, suppose your organization develops software. You may have ten 3-x-5 cards that represent sequential processes in the stream (see Figure 8-2):

1. The customer describes a challenge and requests a solution.
2. The business owner and customer discuss the challenge and possible solutions.

3. A business analyst and the development team meet to discuss the solutions, choose the best one, and agree to add a new feature to the software.
4. The development team commits to a delivery date.
5. The development team develops the feature.
6. The quality assurance team tests the new feature.
7. The development team integrates the new feature into the existing software.
8. The business analyst works with the customer to conduct user acceptance testing.
9. The business analyst meets with the development team to deliver any feedback.
10. The development team incorporates the changes and fixes and releases the upgrade for delivery to the customer.

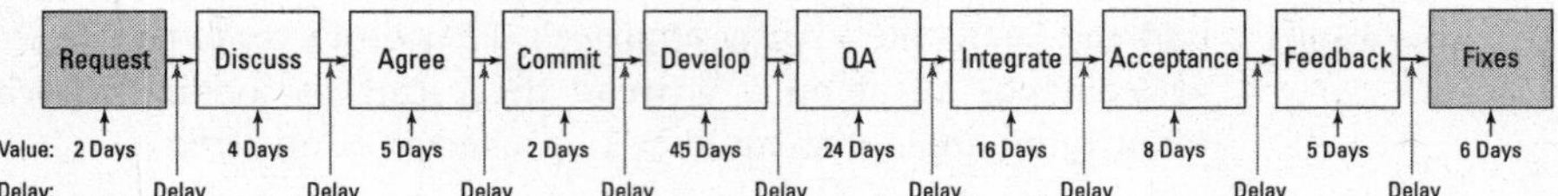

FIGURE 8-2: A sample value stream.

As you map your value stream, think about and record the rationale behind every process that contributes to the stream. You can write notes on the 3-x-5 cards or use sticky notes. Why does your organization do it? How does it contribute to the value stream? What value does it add? If it were eliminated, would the value stream suffer? Would the customer even notice? These are all questions that get you thinking about how processes contribute to your organization's value stream.

WARNING

Map your value stream as it is, not as you think it should be. As soon as you start mapping, you will begin to notice inefficiencies that you may feel too embarrassed to admit or disclose, but admit and disclose you must. Kanban and Lean both emphasize transparency to provide visibility into work processes.

In large organizations, mapping the value stream is a very difficult task. Most processes are created with little thought or planning; they just evolve over time. Often they're based on assumptions, and one of the big false assumptions is that a lot of thought went into process design. Many processes evolve to solve an immediate problem, so when adding the process, the organization doesn't consider the cost or how the process will impact the overall system. Over time your business processes can start to feel like office furniture. Everyone takes it for granted, and no one thinks about how it looks.

CASE STUDY

YOU CAN'T FIX WHAT YOU DON'T SEE

I once worked for an organization that was trying to map its value stream. It was a financial company, so it had many regulatory hurdles to overcome. The teams accepted many of the processes even though they seemed strange and inefficient. When asked about a process, team members often replied that somebody in legal had told them it was necessary.

At first, the organization struggled; it wanted to map the way things should be instead of the way things were. Team members knew their process was inefficient, but they didn't feel like broadcasting that to the rest of the organization. After some convincing, they agreed that they needed to map their value stream in its current state before they could improve it.

The organization took weeks to fully deconstruct its own value stream. Team members taped dozens of 3-x-5 cards to a whiteboard. Then they put little yellow sticky notes that branched out from the larger cards to illustrate different sub processes and their justifications.

When the team was close to finished, its members were shocked by what they saw. Their process map looked like a gnarled branch. It twisted and turned and went backward. Sometimes it would branch off in other directions. The inefficiencies became clear. Everyone could see why delivering a product was often frustrating. One wrong turn, and you'd be heading down a branch with many more work items and sub-processes.

The next step was to try to get all the players in the organization to sit in the room and figure out how to optimize the value stream. The team identified the part of the process that added the most value to the customer and drew a long blue line on the whiteboard that showed the clearest path from beginning to end. All the work items outside of that value stream might be necessary, but they didn't always add value.

The team highlighted three levels of quality testing that may have been improving the product but weren't explicitly adding value to the customer. Then the team gathered people from legal, marketing, and other departments to discuss possible solutions. Now that all of them could see the process, they thought of many new ideas to improve it.

They spent several weeks choosing areas to address and discussing them. Over time, the value stream became more linear and logical as inefficiencies were addressed and corrected.

The exercise taught them a key lesson — you can't fix what you don't see.

Eliminating waste

With value stream map in hand, it's time to trim the fat (waste) — the extra steps in your process that don't deliver value to the customer. Waste can be any steps from when the customer makes a request to when you deliver value to the customer or steps related (or unrelated) to that flow.

For example, if you have your business analyst discussing a solution with a customer and then relaying that information to development, that may be an inefficiency. It may make more sense to have the business analyst and a member of the development team meet together with the customer or for the customer to deal directly with the development team. You may be able to eliminate a few meetings or reduce the potential for miscommunication by having the customer talk directly to the team.

You may also want to dig deeper into certain processes, such as quality assurance testing. For example, you may find that waiting to test after a new feature is fully developed often results in delays, and that your development team could be more efficient by testing iterations throughout the process.

Identifying potential bottlenecks

One of the major sources of waste in any organization, especially a large organization, is in the form of delays. One department gets bogged down, and everyone has to wait, upstream and downstream, for that department to clear the logjam. A detailed map of your value stream improves visibility into your system, so you can pinpoint the location of each bottleneck and boost workload capacity at that point in your organization. A certain department may be understaffed, it may need to review and change its operations, or it may need other resources to improve productivity.

In addition to the map, work on developing a better understanding of dependencies and how workloads fluctuate and change over time, specifically in your organization. For example, some organizations require a lot of regulatory work at the beginning of a project. Other organizations may get a big bunch of change requests during certain months of the year. Your organization needs to figure out ways to deal with changing workloads.

Teams must analyze demand patterns and use the results of that analysis to predict future demand to ensure they have the capacity to meet that demand. Conducting demand analysis isn't easy. Your team must understand how work items bounce through the organization. To get started with demand analysis, answer the following questions:

- Do some departments take longer than others?
- Do others have long periods of silence that end with a sudden stack of requests?

For some ideas on how to monitor and improve workflow, see the later section, "Improving workflow."

Demands on your team may fluctuate over the short term and change over time. One of the biggest mistakes organizations make is to assume that the way things are is the way they'll always be.

Creating Kanban boards

After trimming the fat from your value stream, create a Kanban board for each process in that stream. (As discussed in the earlier section, "Embracing Kanban properties," a Kanban board consists of several queues that represent the different stages in a process, as shown earlier in Figure 8-1.) Delegate the responsibility for creating Kanban boards to the team or teams involved in each process.

You can use any of several methods to create a Kanban board, including the following:

- Use a whiteboard (or a wall near your team), a roll of colored masking tape, and a marker to create and label the queues.
- Use a spreadsheet program or create a table using a word processor, such as Microsoft Word.
- Use a graphics program.
- Use team-management software, such as Trello, to create your Kanban board. Every project-management software package includes a Kanban feature for creating and sharing the board with team members.

Create a separate queue for each step in the value stream and add a label at the top of each queue that describes that step. For example, software development teams typically create five queues:

- Input
- Analysis
- Development
- Test
- Release

You now have a Kanban board. However, you may want to make a couple modifications, such as splitting queues and adding work in progress (WIP) limits, as discussed next.

Splitting queues

To break down stages of a process further, consider splitting one or more queues. Software development teams often split Analysis and Development into two subprocesses: "In Progress" and "Done." (You'll probably need to widen a queue before splitting it.) Then, they split the queues using a different colored line to separate the two (see Figure 8-3).

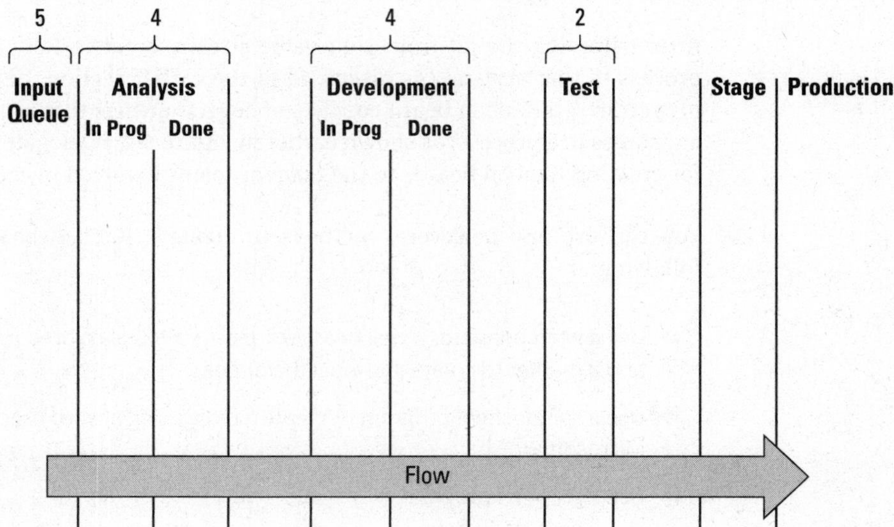

FIGURE 8-3: A sample Kanban board with split queues.

Some teams prefer to create buffer queues. For example, they may add a queue to the right of "Analysis" labeled "Dev Ready," to the right of "Development" labeled "Build Ready," and to the right of "Test" labeled "Release Ready." (See Figure 8-4.) The buffer queue enables them to move items out of their queue without "pushing" those items to the next team before the next team is ready for them.

Although many experts discourage teams from splitting queues, because it leads to a more cluttered Kanban board, the buffer queues may make it easier for your team to pinpoint bottlenecks. For example, if a lot of work items are stuck in "Build Ready," the problem that needs to be addressed is probably in the next step (testing) and not in development. Without that buffer queue, everything would be stuck in development, making it less clear whether the problem is related to a slowdown in development or testing. In other words, if something is stuck in the buffer, it's much more likely the backup is related to where the work item is going than where it came from.

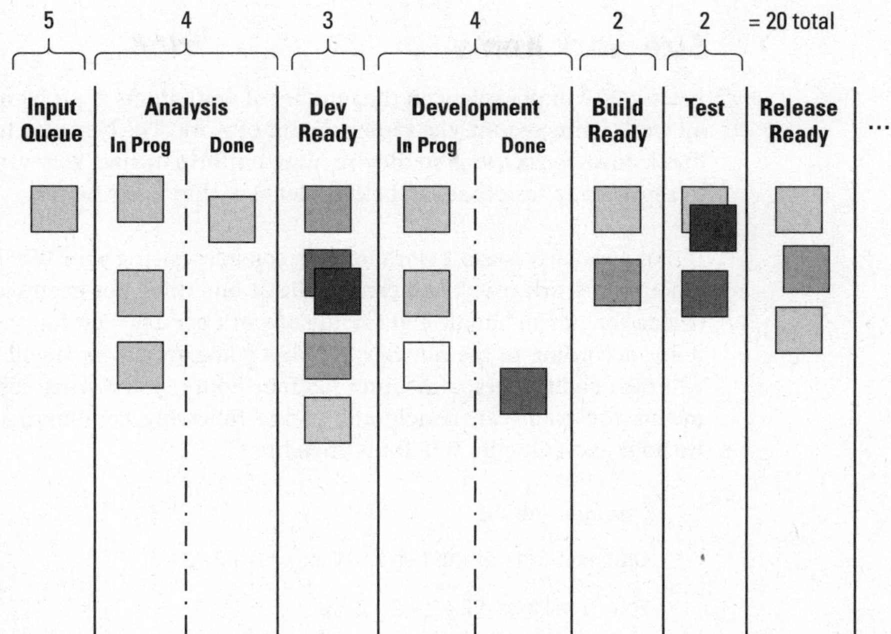

FIGURE 8-4: A sample Kanban board with buffer queues.

REMEMBER

When your team is creating its Kanban board, strive to create a healthy balance between simplicity and detail. Do you want a board that has more information but is a little bit more difficult to read? Or do you want a simpler board with less information that gives you a clearer high-level view of the process? More information increases visibility, whereas less information improves readability.

Adding work-in-progress limits

Near the top of each queue heading, write the number that reflects the team's WIP limit. This is typically the number of work items a team can handle at one time — its work capacity. For example, if a team thinks it can handle five jobs at a time, its WIP limit is 5. Have each team make its best guess. You can adjust WIP limits up or down later.

TIP

Some experts suggest that ideally, the WIP limit should be equal to the number of people on a team, because each person should be able to take responsibility for one work item in the queue.

WIP limits are somewhat arbitrary, and they don't account for fluctuations and changes in workloads over time, so you may need to adjust them later. Demands fluctuate and, at times, may exceed the capacity of a team to meet those demands. With a Kanban board, a team can tell the organization, "Enough is enough! Here's how much work we can handle at one time. We won't accept any more than that," and the team sets a WIP limit to reflect that.

Size work items

Basing WIP limits solely on the number of work items is problematic, because not all work items require the same amount of work. The best way to handle this is to break down work items so they're more uniform in size. You want each work item to represent a task that can be completed within a few hours.

If that approach doesn't work for you, consider basing your WIP limits on the total amount of work your team can handle at one time. For example, your team may decide that it can handle eight hours of work per day. You can then size your work items according to the number of hours you estimate each will require. A big job will take eight hours, a medium job four hours, and a small job two hours. That means the team can handle any of the following combinations of work items without exceeding its WIP limit of eight:

One large job = 8

One medium job and two small jobs = 4 + 2+ 2 = 8

Four small jobs = 2 + 2 + 2 + 2 = 8

More important, you can see how this would affect the number of cards a team could have in its queue — only one card for a large job, three cards for a medium job and two small jobs, or four cards for four small jobs. For more about estimating work items sizes and WIP limits, see the later section, "Making high-level estimates . . . or not."

Imagine workflow in terms of traffic crossing a bridge. You have motorcycles, cars, and trucks crossing the bridge, but the bridge has a weight capacity, so it can carry a lot of motorcycles at a time, several cars at a time, or a few trucks at a time. It can also carry a mixture of motorcycles, cars, and trucks, as long as their combined weight doesn't exceed the bridge's capacity.

Using swim lanes to group work items

You can enhance your Kanban board by adding *swim lanes* — rows that cut across the queues and enable you to categorize related work items. For example, you can create three swim lanes to set the priority of work items or service-level classes, such as "Changes," "Maintenance," and "Defects"; to group them by deadline; to set off blocked work items from those that are currently in process; or to track supporting work that runs parallel to development but is not part of the actual product. (See Figure 8-5.)

Consider using a swim lane to move high-priority work items faster through the process. Think of such a swim lane as the commuter lane in rush-hour traffic. It allows certain work items to bypass items that move more slowly through the process.

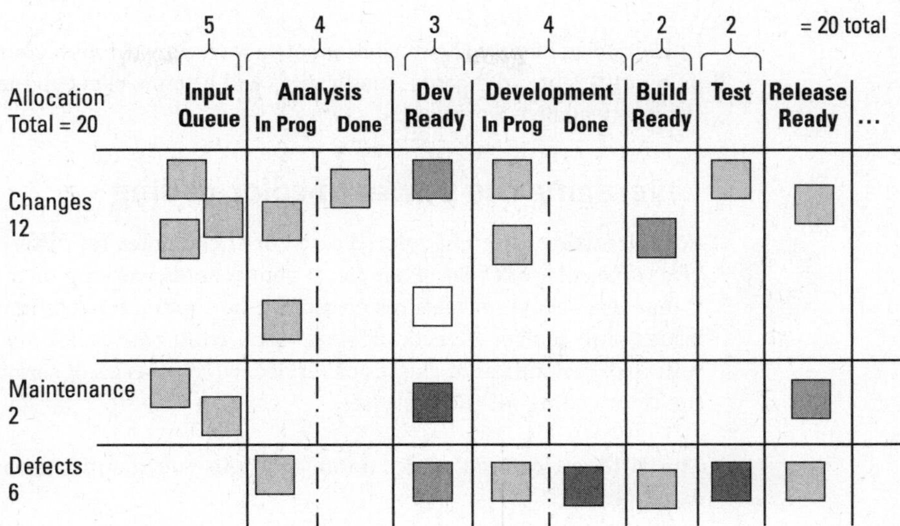

FIGURE 8-5: Use swim lanes to group related work items.

You can also assign a WIP limit to a swim lane to indicate the maximum number of work items that can be in that swim lane at one time. Just write the WIP limit near the label that describes that swim lane.

Creating Kanban cards

You use Kanban cards to track the status of work items through the process. As a team completes a work item, it moves the related Kanban card to the next stage in the process. Sounds simple, right? Well, it is, but you can introduce a great deal of variation in Kanban cards to convey more information to team members. In this section, I explain your options.

REMEMBER

You can use various media to create Kanban boards and cards — a whiteboard or wall with index cards or sticky notes, a spreadsheet or table, a graphics program, or project-management software. When I discuss Kanban "boards" and "cards," I am referring to physical boards and cards, but this can all be done virtually using project-management software.

Right-sizing your cards

If you're using index cards or sticky notes, use a consistent size for each work item, regardless of how big the work item is or the amount of time it requires. Whether a work item will take two hours or a day, use the same sized card or sticky note. (You may use color-coded cards or notes or write on the cards or notes to indicate the relative size of the job.)

Uniform size helps you get a better sense workflow through your system. If you're using different sized cards, the "rows" will become skewed, making it more difficult to visualize workflow.

Leveraging the power of color-coding

TIP

Consider using different colored cards or sticky notes for different classes of service (types of work). For example, if your team is working on a software product, it may use yellow for features or user stories, green for maintenance or technical issues, and red for defects or bugs. Each team can decide for itself whether it wants to track different classes of service, which classes of service it provides, and the color coding for those classes.

The different colored sticky notes can help you identify areas of concern; for example:

- Too many green notes may indicate that you're spending too much time on operational issues and too little time enhancing your value stream. In a sense, you're spending too much time setting the table and not enough time delivering the meal.
- Too many red notes might indicate quality control issues. Maybe the development team is moving too quickly, or the testing team is overloaded.
- Too many yellow notes may show that the team is taking on too many new features. It's trying to add bells and whistles to the software without taking into account quality or operational stability.

Using a variety of colors can also bring a fairly drab Kanban board to life, but avoid using color merely as eye candy. The different colors should serve a useful function; otherwise, they may just cause confusion.

Adding information to your cards

Kanban cards typically include information about the work to be done, who's supposed to do it, when it needs to be done, and so on. You can add notes to the back of the card, as well, to indicate how difficult the work was, ideas for making the task easier next time, and so on. On the front of your Kanban cards, consider adding the following information:

- Work item name and description
- Estimate of the amount of time required to complete the work or some other metric for estimating the amount of work required
- The deadline, if any

- The priority of the work item (or simply whether a work item is a high priority)
- The name or other indicator of the person or people who will do the work
- Class of service (unless you choose to communicate this through color-coding)

On the back of the card, consider including information that may help identify and address process issues that can be addressed later, such as the following:

- Start date
- Blocked days (the number of days the item couldn't be worked on due to the team's need for further clarification or some other external dependency)
- Blocked location (the team or individual responsible for preventing the work from moving forward)
- Blocked reason (the reason for preventing the work from moving forward)
- Completed date
- Lead time

ANOTHER FUNCTIONAL USE OF COLOR-CODING

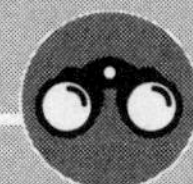

CASE STUDY

I once worked for an organization that was using Kanban to try to improve its help desk. It created classes of service around the priority of each ticket. It used a red sticky note to indicate when the entire team was working to resolve an issue, a yellow note when the issue required the attention of only one person, and a green note to flag a question or a training issue.

These different classes of service not only improved workflow for the team, but also communicated the status of service requests to the entire organization. If someone was wondering why a particular issue hadn't been resolved yet, that person could just visit the Kanban wall to see the position of the issue in the queue. If he saw a bunch of red sticky notes ahead of his, he understood why he might be forced to wait.

The different classes of service also showed that the help desk was spending much more time putting out fires than preventing them (through training). It also showed how critical issues were often related to one another; when a bunch of red Kanban notes appeared, they could often be removed by addressing a single issue.

REMEMBER

Handwriting counts! If you're handwriting notes on your Kanban cards, be sure they're legible and your notes are worded in a way that makes them easy for others to understand.

TIP

You can find plenty of free templates and programs for creating Kanban cards. On many sites, you can even color-code your cards. You can then print them out and laminate them for future use.

Overcoming the challenge of feature cards

Many new teams find that feature cards are the most difficult to create, which makes sense because these Kanban cards represent something new. Describing a bug or a maintenance issue is usually straightforward, but describing a new feature in a way that makes it clear to everyone on the team can be quite a challenge.

For one, you need to have a clear understanding of what the customer thinks is valuable. Then you have to translate that into something that can be delivered. Customers can usually describe what they want, but it's up to the team to describe how it gets done.

Many teams employ a *user story* (see Chapter 1) — a sentence or brief paragraph that describes the user, what she wants, and why she wants it; for example, "As a mobile application user, I want to see ratings data so that I can pick a good restaurant." If you decide to describe features with user stories, consider following this format:

> As <user title or description>, I want to be able to <task description>, so that <reason or purpose>.

WARNING

User stories are a good place to start, but don't include them on your Kanban cards. Instead, break down the story into a number of smaller tasks that must be completed to deliver the feature. For example, if the user story is "As a mobile application user, I want to see ratings data so that I can pick a good restaurant," break it down into tasks, such as the following:

- Create restaurant search screen
- Create database view that retrieves restaurant ratings
- Display rating next to each restaurant in the search results

REMEMBER

You may need to meet with the customer to find out more precisely what she wants and how she expects the feature to behave, so you have all the details you need to "task out" the story.

Agile teams often talk about the difference between the "what" and the "how." User stories tell the team what the users want, but it's up to the designers and developers to describe how that feature behaves and how they'll get the work done. When a team places user stories on its Kanban cards, it's including the "what" but not the "how." A team member can't just pull a card to find out what to do.

TIP

Make your Kanban cards task-specific. Ideally, each card represents a task that a team member can complete in a few hours or a day. If the task takes longer than that, look for ways to break it down even further. A team member should be able to pull the card off the board and start working on the feature. Team members shouldn't have to go back and meet with the customer or product owner for clarification.

Feature cards are much more likely to have extra information on them, such as the following:

- Date stamps to track how long it a work item took to complete
- Emoticons to show how much fun the employee is having doing the work or how frustrated she is
- Estimates to indicate the expected amount of time or effort a work item is likely to require
- Red stickers to indicate *blockers* — impediments (problems) or dependencies, such as having to wait for clarification from another team

REMEMBER

Keep it simple and lean. More information may be helpful, but don't overdo it. That's one reason why Kanban uses cards and sticky notes instead of 8.5-x-11 inch paper. The more information you add, the harder it is to read the Kanban board. Virtual Kanban cards typically do not have this drawback, because you can add notes that stay in the background until you choose to view them.

Making high-level estimates . . . or not

Agile teams commonly include high-level estimates on their Kanban cards. "High-level estimate" is a fancy term for ballpark figure. You look at a work item and guess how big it is, how much work it will require, or how much time it will take to complete. These estimates are often helpful for prioritizing features with customers. When customers want everything under the sun, and they see that your organization has the capacity to deliver only everything under the moon, customers can start figuring out what they really need right now and what can be held back for future development.

Based on the number of cards in a team's queue and the high-level estimates on those cards, anyone looking at the board can easily determine whether the work items exceed the team's capacity to complete them.

However, high-level estimates aren't always necessary. For example, if you're running a help desk and using a Kanban board to track tickets, estimating the time to resolve issues doesn't make sense. When a red note appears on the board, the team addresses that issue regardless of how long it takes. When you're developing a product, such as a software release, high-level estimates can improve workflow. You need to decide whether they make sense for your particular workflow.

If you decide that high-level estimates would be helpful, you can use various estimation techniques. Following are two techniques commonly used in software development that are based on *story points*, the relative effort required to complete a task (see Chapter 2):

- **A Fibonacci sequence, such as 1, 2, 3, 5, 8:** (A *Fibonacci sequence* is a series of numbers in which each number is the sum of the preceding two numbers.) These numbers represent level of effort, not hours or days. A two is roughly twice as difficult as a one. And eight is roughly four times as difficult as a two.
- **Planning poker:** Each team member has a stack of cards with numbers on them that represent the amount of time or effort a task will take. Each team member chooses a card, and then when the team receives the signal, they all flip their cards over at the same time, indicating their idea of how long a task will take.

Agile teams commonly use the results to rough out a delivery schedule. Scrum teams use the results to gauge their *velocity* — a rough estimate of how quickly the team can complete a *sprint* — a brief development cycle, typically about two weeks. Extreme Programming teams may use story points to see how much effort to put into their weekly or monthly iterations.

REMEMBER

Not all Kanban teams operate the same way. Some may benefit from high-level estimates, while others may not. Include estimates on your Kanban cards only if doing so makes sense for your team.

Using Kanban boards to track workflow

When you have your Kanban board and cards ready, you can use them to start tracking and managing workflow. To start tracking workflow, take the following steps:

1. **Place the Kanban cards in the leftmost queue to create a prioritized list of tasks that must be completed.**

   This queue is typically labeled "Backlog."

2. **Have teams draw cards from the top of the queue to the left of theirs and add the cards to the bottom of their queue as their WIP limits allow.**

REMEMBER

Always move items from the top of the previous queue to the bottom of your team's queue, so the highest priority item is always at the top of the queue. For example, if I have the first three items in my queue and I draw another item from the top of the previous queue, I push the existing three items to the top of my queue and add the fourth item below those three.

This is a *pull* system. Teams don't push items to the next team; they pull items from the previous team when the previous team has completed its work.

3. **Repeat Step 2 to continue moving items from the Backlog through the process, until all items that were in the Backlog are completed.**

While these steps make the process appear linear, more can be going on. Teams may be adding notes to the Kanban cards, adding blockers to indicate when progress on a work item comes to a standstill, communicating with one another to coordinate their efforts, and so on. Although you can certainly run a Kanban board like an assembly line, it's most valuable when it's used as a communication and collaboration tool as well.

Improving workflow

In addition to tracking workflow, your Kanban board is a valuable tool for managing workflow and identifying workflow issues and areas needing improvement. Ideally, you want your work to flow through your system like a leaf on a lazy river. You don't want work to get stuck in little corners or swirl endlessly in eddies of organizational processes. A good flow should be steady and predictable from start to finish.

To maintain flow and improve it, start by tracking the following Lean metrics:

- **Blockers:** A *blocker* is an indication that work is stopped, typically due to an external dependency or a failure in the system. Measuring the total blockers and the time work items remain blocked provides a fairly good indication of areas that need to be addressed to improve workflow.
- **Cycle time:** *Cycle time* is how long it takes a work item to get from one point to another in a process. By tracking cycle times over time, you gain insight into workflow within a step and across steps in a process. As with lead time, cycle time enables you to determine whether changes you've implemented have had a positive or negative impact on workflow.

- **Lead time:** *Lead time* is a measure of how long it takes for work to move through the value stream from request to delivery, including process time and delays. Tracking lead times can help you optimize workflow in several ways:
  - You gain insight into whether a change you implemented improved workflow.
  - You can make better informed estimates of the amount of work that can get done in a given amount of time, which helps with estimating job sizes.
  - You can study patterns in lead time to predict future fluctuations in workloads.
- **Queues:** *Queues* represent the amount of work waiting between steps in a process. You can use an efficiency diagram to measure the difference between WIP and the work waiting in queues to see where in a process workflow is stuck or slowing.
- **Throughput:** *Throughput* is the average number of units processed per unit of time, such as Kanban cards per day or per week. By analyzing throughput over time, you can get a general idea of whether workflow is improving or declining.
- **Work in progress (WIP):** Work doesn't add value to the customer until it's completed. By charting WIP over time, you can see whether your WIP is growing, remaining steady, or declining. WIP that's on the rise is a warning sign that workflow is slowing.

One huge benefit of using a virtual Kanban board is that the software tracks these metrics for you. With physical Kanban boards, you need to collect the data, create a spreadsheet, enter the data, and produce graphs. A project-management program can do all of that for you.

In the following sections, I explain various ways to improve workflow with the guidance and insight these metrics provide.

Adjust WIP limits

Little's Law (see Chapter 4) states that the average number of customers in a stable system over a given time period is equal to their average arrival rate multiplied by their average time in the system. In terms of Kanban and Lean, this means that work starts to back up if you put work into the system faster than you take it out. A variation of Little's Law provides a formula that reveals an interesting relationship between cycle time, WIP, and throughput:

$$\text{Cycle Time} = \frac{\text{Work In Progress}}{\text{Throughput}}$$

For example, if a team has 30 cards in progress (total WIP) and a throughput of five cards per day, then it has a cycle time of six days: 30 ÷ 5 = 6. That is, it takes an average of six days for the team to move its WIP to the Done queue. By reducing its WIP to 20 cards and keeping its throughput the same, the team can move its WIP to the Done queue in the span of only four days: 20 ÷ 5 = 4. In other words, decreasing WIP reduces cycle time. (The formula also shows that increasing throughput reduces cycle time, but that's usually more difficult, because it requires the team to work harder or faster or increase its efficiency.)

The fact that decreasing a team's WIP reduces cycle time seems counterintuitive, but it supports the Kanban approach of moving work through a process in small batches. The smaller the batches, the lower the cycle time, and the smoother the workflow.

TIP

You may want to experiment with other methods to reduce WIP without actually lowering the WIP limit:

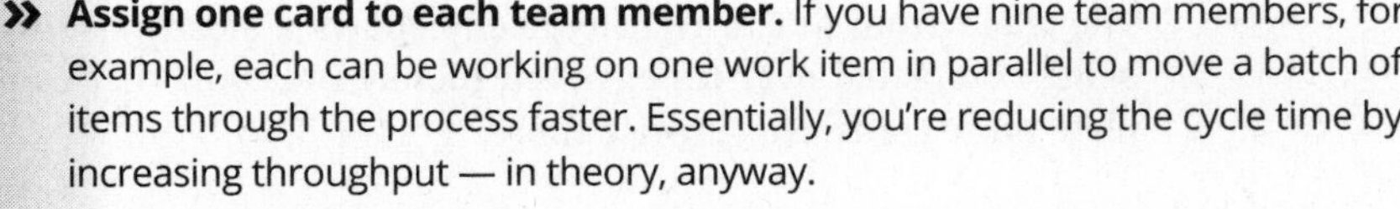

- **Assign one card to each team member.** If you have nine team members, for example, each can be working on one work item in parallel to move a batch of items through the process faster. Essentially, you're reducing the cycle time by increasing throughput — in theory, anyway.

  WARNING

  Having each team member responsible for one card may make it difficult to manage the natural cadence of the team, especially if one of the team members calls in sick or is on vacation.

- **Use a buffer queue.** Adding a buffer queue enables a team to move work items to a buffer queue as it completes those items. It's almost the same way airports put airplanes in a holding pattern when the runways are filled to capacity.

  Keep in mind that a buffer queue can make the Kanban board more difficult to read. In addition, buffer queues are almost like flow regulators — they can help the team achieve a sustainable flow, but they may restrict the team's capacity.

Minimize queue times

Queue times are often an indication of work items being stuck in a process. Identify queues and work toward making them shorter to reduce delays and lower overall cycle time.

Eliminate blockers

Unlike work items in a queue that are waiting to be worked on, a blocker is a work item that's stuck in the process waiting for response from an external dependency or waiting for an issue to be resolved. You can improve workflow by reducing both the number of blockers and the average amount of time work items remain blocked.

Clarify the definition of "done"

Delays in development often arise when individuals or teams don't agree on the definition of "done." As a result, one team may send a work item back to the team in the previous step and say something like, "You consider this done?!" By clarifying and agreeing to the definition of done up front, you can prevent these delays.

Consult a cumulative flow diagram

A *cumulative flow diagram* is a chart that represents changes to WIPs in a process over time. It essentially rotates the Kanban board 90 degrees clockwise and color-codes the queues to create the appearance of a layer cake (see Figure 8-6). The x-axis represents the number of Kanban cards completed, and the y-axis represents time. The work completed makes the horizontal queue fatter or thinner.

The trend from left to right typically shows a steady rise in total Kanban cards being completed over time, which merely indicates that over time, teams complete more cards. No surprise there.

What you want to focus on are the queue widths, which tend to fluctuate over time. For example, if a queue is narrow early in a project and widens toward the end, you can tell that a team's throughput increases toward the end of a project. A bulge in a queue shows a team's increase in throughput at a particular stage in the process. A narrowing of the queue indicates that the team is completing fewer tasks.

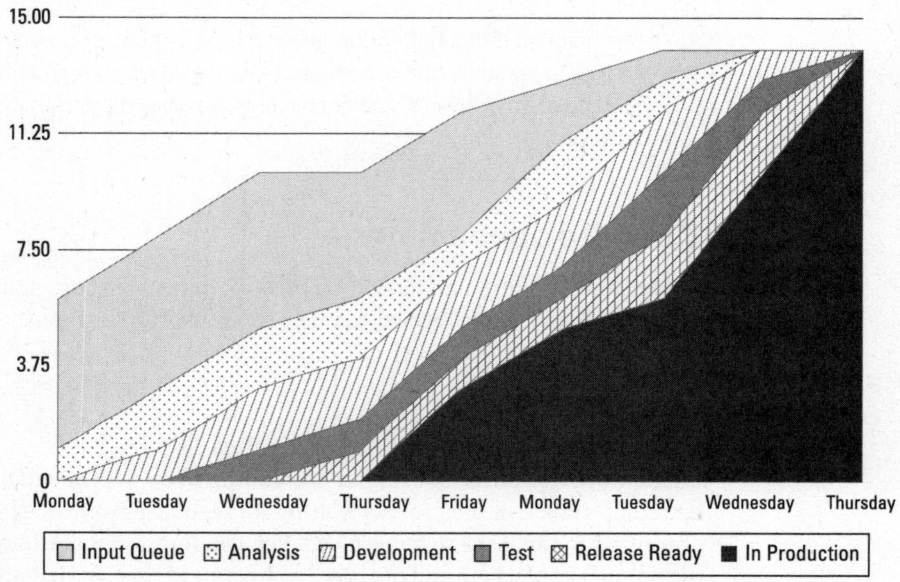

FIGURE 8-6: A cumulative flow diagram.

Ideally, you want to see the relative widths of the queues remain fairly constant over time. If you notice a bulge in one queue width and a narrowing of another at the same point in time, it could be a sign of workflow issue.

For example, if the deployment queue bulges and the testing queue narrows or remains constant, then testing needs to reduce its cycle time (perhaps by reducing its WIP limit) or deployment needs to increase its cycle time (perhaps by increasing its WIP limit).

It's normal to have your cumulative flow diagram book-ended by two opposing work queues, such as an input queue and a production queue. If you think about it, that makes a lot of sense. You should expect that the work you need to do will go down over time. On the other side, you should expect that the amount of work completed will go up over time.

That means that if your team's flow diagram only had these two queues, it would look like one queue was being replaced with the other. Almost like an upward sloping Yin-and-Yang.

Still, even these two queues can give you a better sense of how work is flowing through your system. If you have a big bulge on the far left of your diagram in your input queue, it might show that your team has overcommitted the amount of work it can complete. If you don't see a bulge at the end of the diagram, it might mean your team is not deploying the product to production. When that happens, you might want to look in the testing queue to see if there's a bulge near the end. That might mean your team is spending too much time testing the product and not enough time deploying it to the customer.

Using Kanban to reduce management meddling

One of the most practical ways to apply Kanban is to keep management from pulling people off of their teams to work on other projects. Such scenarios are common in organizations that retain a traditional organizational structure and assemble interdepartmental teams to work on projects. Whenever the manager or a certain department needs something done, he pulls a team member off what he's doing, with the obvious consequence of reducing the team's throughput.

However, that's rarely so obvious to the manager. By using a cumulative flow diagram, you can show the manager the impact of his decision on the team's throughput and how it affected overall workflow. This approach is often sufficient to give managers pause before deciding to pull an employee off of a project.

CASE STUDY

I DID THAT?!

I once worked for an organization that was having trouble maintaining continuity on its Kanban team. The company had a traditional organizational structure, so everyone on the team had an outside manager as well as the team's project manager.

Every time one of the managers had a challenge, he would pull his employee from the team to work on the issue. From the manager's perspective, this was his employee, and he was just loaning the person to the team.

I worked with the team to create a *peel-off board*. The board clearly showed that all of these peel-offs had an impact on the project timeline. But that didn't change the managers' behavior. They were behaving as they always had and the added visibility wasn't an incentive to change.

Still, it's worth a shot.

TIP

Better yet, create a *peel-off board* to more clearly show the impact of "peeling off" a team member from a team. Simply list the employees by name, and next to each name, write the number of Kanban cards that weren't moved when that person was pulled from the team.

Is Lean Kanban a Viable Enterprise Agile Framework?

Lean and Kanban are useful tools for minimizing waste and maximizing workflow, but they may not serve as a suitable replacement for a bona fide enterprise agile framework, such as SAFe or LeSS. Lean and Kanban are easy to implement and may provide a good start for smaller organizations, but they have too many shortcomings, including the following:

- **No guidance for organization change:** Without a change in organization and in leadership's mindset, teams often fight a losing battle against management intrusion.
- **Little guidance for cultural change:** Lean and Kanban principles provide some guidance for cultural change in terms of committing to continuous change, respecting people, building in quality, and embracing acts of

leadership at all levels, but without a more structured framework to support those principles, it doesn't go far enough, especially in large organizations.

- **Little enthusiasm for change:** The idea of making practical incremental improvements may be realistic, but it doesn't have people springing out of bed in the morning. Big, bold changes get people excited. They want the organization to dream big and make huge leaps.
- **Poor support for knowledge work:** The Kanban board is linear, which makes sense, because it came out of manufacturing. As such, it doesn't track well with creative endeavors, such as product development, which is rarely linear. In fact, creatives often find Kanban boards monotonous or even boring. However, Kanban can be a useful tool when combined with other frameworks that are more conducive to creativity.
- **Lack of motivational components:** Very little in Kanban or Lean motivates teams to work faster, improve their skills and knowledge, or collaborate across teams. Both SAFe and LeSS include sprints to increase the pace of development, whereas Kanban leaves it up to the teams to set their own WIPs and work at their own pace.

REMEMBER

Think of Kanban and Lean as tools for improving workflow and reducing waste. Use Lean to trim the fat from your value streams. Use Kanban to help teams manage their workflow, monitor progress, and communicate with one another. But when your goal is to make your organization agile, look for a more robust enterprise agile framework.

Most large organizations need to change from the top down and the bottom up. Employees must be motivated to change the way they work, and managers must buy into fixing the status quo. Lean and Kanban's focus on improving current processes might shortchange the momentum you need to make big changes. Many organizations need a major overhaul, including a radical change in the way they think about work. Small, incremental improvements are rarely enough. As Henry Ford famously said, "If I had asked people what they wanted, they would have said faster horses." No one would've thought that what they really needed was an entirely new form of transportation.

3

Leading a Large-Scale Organizational Change

IN THIS PART . . .

Evaluate your organization's existing culture to gauge its tolerance for change and identify areas in your organization that are likely to be receptive or resistant to change, so you have a clearer idea of how to introduce your organization to enterprise agility.

Develop your game plan based on whether you decide to implement change using a top-down or bottom-up approach.

Explore the differences between the step-by-step, top-down Kotter approach and the bottom-up Fearless Change approach to introducing change.

Discover ways to address pockets of resistance.

Develop a custom approach to enterprise agility by picking and choosing the enterprise agile framework, policies, and practices you want and leaving everything else behind.

- **Grasping the challenges you're likely to face**
- **Getting to know your organization's existing culture**
- **Preparing for a cultural overhaul**

Chapter 9
Sizing Up Your Organization

In many organizations, people think of enterprise agility as a bunch of new roles and practices. They spend most of their time transitioning people to new roles and having them adopt agile practices, such as writing user stories and conducting 15-minute stand-up meetings. Such an approach doesn't really address the biggest hurdle most organizations face. Enterprise agility is a *radical* organizational change. It requires the people in your organization think about their work in an entirely new way and act accordingly. They need to change ingrained behaviors and interact differently. This is a much larger challenge, and it's one your organization should immediately start to tackle.

From the outset, start to think about your organization's culture and its tolerance for big changes. Almost every organization can make big changes, including yours. You just need to know how tall of a mountain you're climbing, what the obstacles are along the way, and how to avoid or overcome these obstacles. This chapter helps you identify your organization's culture to better determine if you are ready for a big change, and then provides you with a starting point for making that change.

Agilebots Transform! Committing to Radical Change

Transformation means dramatic change. *Enterprise agile transformation* involves radical change in how an organization is structured and managed, how its people think and interact, how information flows, and how the organization responds to change and engages in innovation. As with most endeavors that require radical change, the most difficult challenge is to accept and embrace all that's required to make the change. Your entire organization must commit to no less than transformation.

A transformation is not a quick fix; it's a long and hard transition to get your organization where you want it to be. If you're unprepared or don't commit fully, you'll stumble through the transformation and gain only a small fraction of the potential benefit.

One of the biggest mistakes organizations make when trying to improve their enterprise agility is to underestimate the effort required to make lasting changes. To avoid this common pitfall, prepare everyone at the very beginning for a long change process, as I explain in Chapter 10. Encourage everyone in your organization to think about the transition as though he or she is packing for a long trip. If employees start out thinking that the transition will take only a few days or a couple of weeks, you're likely to experience one of the following outcomes:

- They'll short-change the transformation by declaring victory after only a few process improvements.
- They'll become overwhelmed by the change and quickly run out of steam.

Approach your enterprise agile transformation as you would a physical fitness routine. Can you imagine saying, "Of course I'm committed to better fitness, but I'm not ready to give up sweets," or "I'm ready for the change, but I don't have the time to exercise every day"? Achieving an aggressive health and fitness goal involves changing routines, working out, adjusting your diet, giving up bad habits, reducing stress, and so on. If you take only one or two of those steps, you'll get some benefit, but you won't achieve your goal.

Don't try to shoehorn agile into how your organization already operates. For example, I once worked for an organization that started its transformation to enterprise agility by saying, "Of course we want to be agile, but we can't combine our quality assurance team with our developers. They report to different managers." Another organization said, "Yes, we want to give agile a try, but we still need to work with scheduled milestones. That way, there's plenty of time for testing." That's not transformation. Following such an approach, the most you can hope for is a few positive agile-like changes; you won't achieve a true transformation.

CASE STUDY

GET REAL

I once worked for an organization that hired an agile coach to help with its transformation. The coach had come from another organization that was well-known for its success with agile. During the interview, the coach talked about how the agile teams at his organization had worked together to deliver enterprise products. He wowed the managers with stories of close collaboration and frequent product deliveries. The managers were thrilled to hire the coach, and a few weeks later they started their transformation.

However, this organization was quite different from the one the coach had come from. It would take years for them to reach that level of cross-functionality and product delivery. The managers were thinking in terms of months, but they should've been thinking in years. In less than a year, the agile coach moved on, frustrated by the lack of progress.

The story highlights the importance of managing expectations in the lead-up to the transformation. Everyone in your organization must have a realistic expectation of how long the change is likely to take and how much work is involved, especially if you're dealing with a culture that has a strong resistance to change.

Understanding What Culture Is and Why It's So Difficult to Change

Have you ever started working at an organization and been told, "This is how we do things here"? Maybe you made a mistake, and a colleague or supervisor said, "This is not how we work."

Now imagine if you responded, "Well, maybe we should change how we do things." How do you think that would be received by your coworkers? It's a safe bet most people working with you would find that attitude jarring, bordering on hostile.

That's what *culture* is — shared, deeply ingrained assumptions and beliefs that control the thoughts and behaviors of individuals in a group. Culture is at the very core of what makes a particular organization unique. The managers, business analysts, and project managers have all accepted that these practices (often referred to as *success patterns*) are the way to succeed in the organization. Fortunately, although these assumptions, beliefs, and success patterns are deeply ingrained, they're also learned, so they can be unlearned and replaced. But it's not easy.

DEFINING "ORGANIZATIONAL CULTURE"

Former MIT professor Edgar Schein wrote a terrific book on culture called *Organizational Culture and Leadership.* He defined an organization's culture as a "pattern of shared basic *assumptions* that the group learned as it solved its problems that has worked well enough to be considered valid and is *passed on* to new members as the *correct* way to perceive, *think,* and feel in relation to those problems."

One of Schein's key points is that culture is deeply ingrained, so ingrained that it controls how people perceive, think, and feel. Changing culture requires changing thought and behavior patterns, and that is no small feat.

Many organizations start by trying to scratch and claw their way through the agile practices, changing the way a few teams work. All their effort goes into implementing specific agile practices, such as standing up during meetings and creating new user stories (common agile practices described in Chapter 1), but these practices only scratch the surface; they don't change the thinking and behaviors required to stimulate innovation and achieve continuous competitive advantage.

Understanding why culture is so entrenched

In his book *Organizational Culture and Leadership*, Edgar Schein presents culture as three levels of stacked assumptions (see Figure 9-1):

- **Artifacts:** Subtle expressions of values, such as the organization's dress code, workspace, hours, posters, and even its perks, such as flextime or free coffee.
- **Espoused values:** The organization's values, as expressed in its mission statement, vision statement, and goals. These values reflect the way the organization *wants* to be perceived.
- **Underlying beliefs:** The thoughts, feelings, perceptions, and beliefs that employees share without explicitly talking about them. For example, everyone in the organization may value creativity and innovation over predictability or the organization may have an unspoken bias against women in leadership positions.

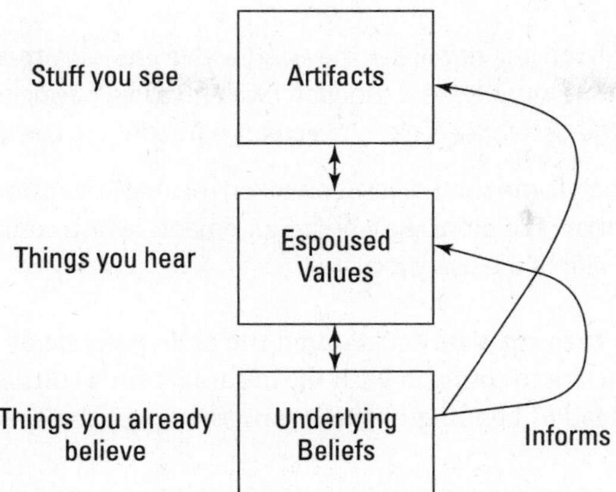

FIGURE 9-1: Three levels of assumptions about organizational culture.

You can usually sense an organization's culture when you first step into its office space. A high-tech business in Silicon Valley has a vastly different feel from that of a top law firm in Chicago. The tech business is likely to have large, shared workspaces. You'll probably see bicycles in the hallways, toys on desks, and people walking around in jeans. At the law firm, on the other hand, you'll likely see orderly desks, people in suits, large windows overlooking the city, and a tone that's more "professional."

Schein groups assumptions into three levels to shed light on why culture is so entrenched and how challenging it can be to change an organization's culture. The most deeply rooted beliefs may be buried under layers of everyday assumptions. An organization can't change its culture simply by revising its mission statement or putting a new organizational framework in place. Changing culture involves changing deeply engrained mindsets.

Avoiding the common mistake of trying to make agile fit your organization

> Do not try and bend the spoon. That's impossible. Instead . . . only try to realize the truth. There is no spoon . . . it is not the spoon that bends, it is only yourself.
>
> —Spoon Boy in *The Matrix*

When large organizations start an agile transformation they often try to bend agile to fit their reality instead of changing their organization to fit agile. Here's an example:

> In many organizations, management defines the product and hands the developers a detailed list of work requirements. The idea is that the more detailed the list of requirements, the more likely the customer will be satisfied with the result. In agile,

on the other hand, the developer may start with a *user story* that describes what the user needs; for example, "As a shopper, I want to avoid having to wait in line to check out." The developer is given the creative freedom to come up with a solution.

However, when some companies embark on their agile transformation, they write user stories that read more like work requirements, which completely eliminates the main benefit of the user story.

In this example, the organization adopted the agile practice of user stories, but it changed that practice to conform with the organization's culture (a need to be told what to do). Instead of bending to the spoon, they bent the spoon.

As you educate and train people in your organization, spend time both on training people what to do and on explaining the reasons why they're being instructed to do things a certain way. When people understand the *why* behind the *what*, they're more likely to "get it." Otherwise, they'll just go through the motions. For example, if people understand that user stories are supposed to give the developer more creative freedom, they're less likely to write user stories that read like requirements.

Identifying Your Organization's Culture Type

One of the first steps in changing anything is to identify what you're changing. You need to know what you have to work with. In the case of transforming corporate culture, you first need to recognize the nature of the existing culture.

Thankfully, William Schneider's book *The Reengineering Alternative* serves as a great resource for identifying organizational culture types. In his book, Schneider presents the following four culture types (see Figure 9-2):

- Control
- Collaboration
- Cultivation
- Competence

In his book, Schneider provides a questionnaire you can pass around your organization to help determine which of the categories best describes your organization.

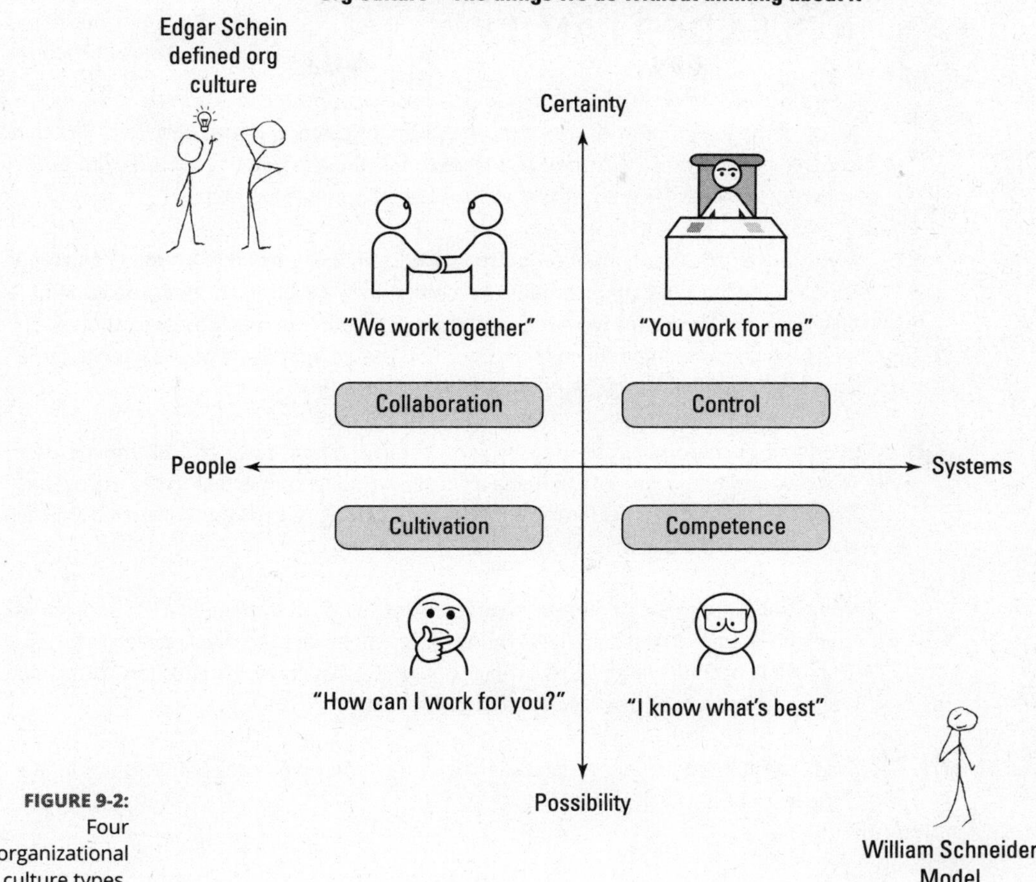

FIGURE 9-2: Four organizational culture types.

In this section, I describe each of the four types, so you can figure out which of the categories best describe your organization's culture. Your organization's culture may fit in more than one category. It may value competence highly, but also value collaboration, for example. Also, different divisions or departments in your organization may fit in different categories; for example, your warehouse may operate in a culture of collaboration, while sales functions more in a culture of control, and the overall organization operates mostly in the spirit of cultivation.

Each one of these cultures has strengths and weaknesses. One culture may readily accept change, while another fights even the most sensible change but is highly efficient. The key is to understand the various cultures at work in your organization, so you can more easily determine the changes required to transform your organization's mindset and anticipate the challenges in making these changes.

CASE STUDY

A BLENDED FAMILY

I once worked for an organization that was closely connected to a branch of the military. Many of the top employees were retired officers or career military specialists. You could see that most of these top managers were comfortable in a strong control culture. They knew who worked for them, and they maintained a simple hierarchy.

If you looked at this organization, you'd immediately assume it had a strong control culture. Yet the founders of the organization made a special effort to stress the value of collaboration. The teams were required to work together to reach consensus on decisions, which made them much more informal. The top managers had worked together for decades and made decisions in weekly lunch meetings.

Even though this organization looked like a control culture, it was actually much closer to a collaboration culture. Each manager had a personal connection to the team. They interacted like friends and family. They created trusting relationships and tried to collaborate closely on decisions.

When they started their enterprise agile transformation, they needed a key sponsor to drive the change. In this case, it was a longtime employee everyone knew and trusted. They didn't need the large system most control cultures crave. Instead, they focused on a few relationships and relied a great deal on trust.

Think carefully about your organization's culture. It may be more complex than what it appears to be.

Running with the wolf pack in a control culture

The control culture has a tendency to be very authoritarian. Think of it as a wolf pack. Alpha managers set the direction for the entire organization with beta managers following closely behind to keep the rest of the organization moving in the same direction.

These companies tend to have a conservative management style and put a lot of emphasis on hierarchy. Everyone knows his place in the pecking order.

Emphasizing compliance

A control culture emphasizes compliance. The role of the individual is to comply with the requirements stipulated by that person's supervisor. The head of the organization communicates a vision and delegates to others who are responsible for bringing that vision to fruition. Some people in the organization, typically project managers and quality assurance people, make sure everyone follows along and that the resulting product conforms to the vision.

A control culture prefers that individuals stay within their functional areas. People don't usually move around much. If you're a project manager, then you're unlikely to ever move into another area, such as marketing or human resources. Roles and titles tend to determine the pecking order. Directors have authority over managers, and managers have authority over supervisors.

Seeking certainty with decisions

With so much emphasis on compliance, decision-making in this culture has a tendency to be very methodical . . . and slow. The highest levels push for certainty and demand accountability. Although the C-suite leaders and directors may not micromanage, they want reports showing that decisions are being made and their directives are being carried out. They want to know that their employees have "signed off" and taken responsibility for their decisions.

Favoring big systems

Organizations with a control culture tend to be conservative. The rhythm of the organization favors order and certainty, and they rely on large management systems that ensure predictable outcomes. Many of them follow variations of the *Rational Unified Process* (RUP) — a software delivery framework that has a predictable lifecycle and many building blocks. (Several of the enterprise agile frameworks come from contributors to RUP.) An agile framework, such as the Scaled Agile Framework® (SAFe®), has a built-in advantage in organizations with a control culture; it plays well with organizations that tend to like large complex frameworks with a lot of roles and clear lines of responsibility. These control cultures also tend to like the top-down alignment you see in SAFe.

TIP

If you're in a strong control culture, try to be aware of how your organization deals with big changes. Fight the urge to go big just because you're a big organization. Remember that agile is not about changing everyone's roles. It's about changing a larger organizational mindset. Looking for another big system maybe not be enough to change how people think about their work.

Effecting change in a control culture

TIP

The best way to make big changes in a control culture is to get someone at a high level to sponsor the change. Think of this sponsor as the driver of change. Without a sponsor, conducting an agile transformation will be very difficult, if not impossible, in a control culture.

CASE STUDY

CULTURAL BIAS WINS OUT

I once worked for an organization with a strong control culture. Its leaders liked the idea of being agile, but they struggled with some of their agile teams. The product owners couldn't work outside of their departments. The developers couldn't self-organize. All too often their managers would pull them off for other projects.

Even though they struggled with team agile, they decided to scale up to an enterprise agile framework. They wanted to try the Scaled Agile Framework (SAFe). They figured they'd substitute their current set of roles and responsibilities for a more agile set of roles and responsibilities.

In the end, they just ended up going back to their old way of working. They merely called the system something new. It was a little like that old rock 'n' roll lyric, "Meet the new boss/same as the old boss."

They would have been far better off if they had tried to understand why their agile teams were struggling before they tried something new. Bigger isn't always better. Whether this organization tried to be agile on a small scale or a large scale, it was bound to fail, because the organization had a strong cultural bias that favored control — a bias that's difficult to overcome when encouraging a more agile mindset. To succeed, it had to give up its cultural bias and relinquish some control.

Unfortunately, control cultures put so much emphasis on certainty that recruiting high-level sponsors becomes a huge challenge. Big changes involve a high level of uncertainty. The most common motivation for control cultures to make big, risky changes is when they have no viable alternative — when their backs are against the wall, sometimes when it's too late.

Rising with your ability in a competence culture

The competence culture, prevalent in software development companies, develops a hierarchy that's based on expertise. In a typical competence culture, a group of software developers creates a tool that becomes popular, and these developers become *de facto* managers. Because they were developers, they invest all their effort into making sure everyone conforms to their views of technical excellence.

The leadership focus in a competence culture is about setting standards and creating tasks. Leaders delegate tasks based on each employee's perceived competence level, resulting in a task-driven approach to management. As a result, people tend to specialize, which leads to the creation of deeply ingrained silos.

Living in the matrix

Organizations with a strong competence culture have a tendency to be set up like a matrix, with each person having two or more managers. For example, an analyst may have a department manager, such as a manager who oversees testing or analysis, and a project manager who's responsible for delivering a certain product. They approach any big change or challenge like engineers, breaking it down into tasks and distributing the tasks to various specialists. In a competence culture, managing the organization is like handling an engineering problem.

Suppose you're a quality assurance developer, and you report to a quality assurance manager and to a software development manager. Like everyone, you're prone to gaming the system. You don't like having two bosses asking you to perform different tasks, so you specialize in one area — quality assurance *or* software development. In other words, the company rewards employees for becoming highly competent specialists (though nobody in a leadership position is probably aware this is happening).

Managers within this culture tend to be professional, and a strong sense of meritocracy drives promotions. You can start as an intern and if you develop a high level of expertise, you'll quickly move your way up through the organization.

Putting in the hours

Organizations with a competence culture have a tendency to operate at a really intense pace. They're not always the easiest places to work.

Effecting change in a competence culture

Competence cultures can have a difficult time embracing an agile mindset, because agile teams favor generalization over specialization. On an agile team, you may have people who know how to both develop and test software. A product owner may also work in sales or marketing. (A *product owner* is a Scrum role responsible for representing the end user to determine what features will be in a product release.) You don't see that kind of fluidity in a competence culture. In addition, agile promotes open communication and knowledge sharing, which contradicts what's rewarded in the competence culture.

TIP

If you have a strong competence culture, you must find ways to encourage organizational learning; for example, you can create communities of practice (CoPs) in which different developers share their knowledge and expertise. These CoPs may meet every week or so to share their work and build up their organizational knowledge. Without some way for knowledge sharing, competence cultures will usually end up with superstar developers who jump from team to team.

A CASE OF CULTURE CONTROLLING BEHAVIOR

CASE STUDY

I once worked for a company, started by two engineers while they were still in grad school, that fostered a strong competence culture. Their organization didn't have as much direct authority as you see in a control culture. The founders had a glass office, and you could see them pacing in their white socks. Anyone could walk into their office with new ideas and suggestions.

Still, the organization struggled with many different managers and areas of control. It was a great example of Conway's Law, which states that a technology company's management structure is often set up the same way as its software: It had a different department for the database, web front end, and testing — each with its own managers.

Even with this strong emphasis on software development, the organization struggled to have a more agile mindset. The best software developers had to be shared across many different teams. They also didn't take the time to teach others their expertise. They knew that if many people shared their level of competence, it would give them less authority. No one on the agile teams knew what the other developers were working on.

The managers wanted their agile teams to share knowledge, but the culture made the developers focus on their own expertise. Since they had this culture without thinking about the consequences, the managers struggled to make changes.

In addition, competence cultures are likely to have some characteristics of a control culture, as well, such as top-down management. If your organization is a blend of competence and control cultures, you'll also need to recruit a sponsor from a high level of leadership to drive your enterprise agile transformation.

Nurturing your interns in a cultivation culture

In a cultivation culture (the rarest of the four culture types), leaders focus on empowering and enabling people to become the best possible employees. The managers like to make sure everyone is happy being part of the organization.

These organizations have a tendency to be set up like an authority wheel with the employee in the center surrounded by managers and resources to support the employee's success. Each manager is a spoke in the wheel.

In a cultivation culture, employees are encouraged to express themselves, so the culture places a lot of emphasis on employee surveys. These surveys enable managers to perform their primary function — employee development and growth. In this culture, managers want to bring someone into the organization, hold them up, and then build them up.

Using your smile, charm, and team-building skills

The leadership in a cultivation culture is typically based on how well you're able to convince people to follow your lead. If you're a charismatic person in a cultivation culture, you can become an authority very quickly — even if you're someone who's just started at the company in a low-level position. Managers focus on cultivating the strengths of other people, and they rise in the organization according to their ability to build teams and harness a team's talent to solve a problem quickly.

Embracing generalists

A cultivation culture is a good culture to belong to if you're a generalist. If someone with a problem knocks on your door, you never want to send him away disappointed. You solve the problem, refer him to someone else who can solve the problem, or assemble a team that's qualified to solve the problem.

Other characteristics of a cultivation culture

In addition to favoring generalists and charismatic individuals, the cultivation culture has several other identifiable characteristics, including the following:

- **The focus is on the people over the system.** People who thrive in large, complex systems (typical of control cultures) and are unable to adapt generally do poorly in a cultivation culture.
- **Departmental divisions are less relevant.** Employees are encouraged to work together to solve problems, even if they have to consult with other departments.
- **Employees are not always required to follow procedures.** If an employee has a better way to achieve the same or a better outcome, he's encouraged to do so.
- **The organization is probably a fun place to work.** Growth and development are encouraged, and employees are free to make mistakes on their paths to success.
- **Decision-making relies on consensus.** Decision-making can be difficult and slow, because it is highly participative and organic. As you can imagine, big groups of people can take a long time to achieve consensus.

REMEMBER

True cultivation cultures are rare. Some organizations may think they have a cultivation culture, but if you look closely, you'll see that they're control cultures with a thin coating of people-focused practices.

Millennials and other people under the age of 30 tend to be successful in cultivation cultures, because they often require more cultivation, and they typically seek consensus when making decisions. Organizations run by young entrepreneurs often operate in a cultivation culture.

Effecting change in a cultivation culture

People in a cultivation culture are more likely than those in other cultures to embrace change and adapt to new ideas, because change is part of the cultivation process. They have participatory meetings during which people talk about change, and after they reach consensus to make a change, they quickly embrace it.

Members of a cultivation culture tend to be more receptive to adopting an agile mindset. In many cases, as soon as the organization decides to transform, employees will self-organize into teams with a focus on learning more about agile. However, due to the slow decision-making process characteristic of the cultivation culture, expect to run into some delays.

TIP

Look to enterprise agile frameworks that focus on development practices and software craftsmanship. Some of these elements are in Large-Scale Scrum (LeSS), Disciplined Agile (DA), and the Spotify Engineering Culture. (See Part 2 for details about several of the more commonly used and useful enterprise agile frameworks.)

Working it out together in a collaboration culture

In a collaboration culture, leaders are team builders and coaches, and generalists are favored over specialists. Management style is democratic, but it's not quite as fluid as in a cultivation culture. And while success in a cultivation culture is measured by how well you work with others, in a collaboration culture, success is often based on how long you've been with the company.

In a collaboration culture, the organization has less need to reach consensus when making decisions. Managers work closely together like a small group of friends to make decisions and to build and lead teams. Small clusters of coworkers are likely to form loose social networks.

Collaboration cultures are almost as scarce as cultivation cultures. You rarely see such a culture in software development organizations; it just doesn't play to that industry's leadership style. You see it more often in schools and professional training organizations.

Honoring the family

The big difference between the collaboration and the cultivation cultures is that the authority in collaborative cultures comes from long-term relationships. Organizations are run almost like a family business. The closer you are to people at the head of the organization, the more authority you have. The top people collaborate closely on the overall direction. Think of it like a classic crime family. You have a few older founders at the top and then their trusted group of friends and family all the way down.

These organizations tend to make decisions via brainstorming meetings and through some experimentation. They're a little more open to change than the control or competence cultures, which helps when the organization is trying to embrace an agile mindset. If you have a collaborative culture, it's usually easy for your organization to accept change.

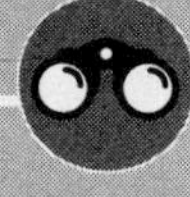
CASE STUDY

THAT'S NO WAY TO DEVELOP SOFTWARE!

I once worked for a group of private preschools that were trying to create an in-house, web-based student management system. They had a strong collaboration culture. The owner founded the schools as a family business. Its top managers had been with the school for decades. They all went to each other's houses for the holidays.

The software project was driven by one of its earliest employees, now a manager. The owner and this manager would go to lunch and plan the software on napkins using crayons. Then the manager would come back and give the napkins to the product owners. When the product owners had questions, the manager had few answers. They could never meet with the owner directly because they weren't comfortable working with the newer employees.

The agile teams ran into the same challenges as they would in a strong control culture. They didn't have the authority to make their own decisions, so they had to rely on the owner and manager (two people outside the team) to design the software, and these people were often unavailable to provide feedback.

However, some key components of an agile mindset may be difficult to adopt. An agile team must have the authority to pursue new ideas and make mistakes. That authority is pushed down to the team level. However, collaboration cultures tend to cluster the authority at a high level. They're more democratic, but only slightly more.

Even with their family appeal and open collaboration, this culture has many of the same challenges as a classic control culture. You still have a concentration of authority that makes embracing an agile mindset more difficult.

Effecting change in a collaboration culture

Although a pure collaboration culture is rare, many organizations have some aspects of it. Typically, what happens is that a company starts as a family business or partnership and grows to become a large company in which that culture can no longer operate, but remnants of the culture still exist near the top.

When transitioning a collaboration culture to enterprise agility, I suggest the following:

- **Look for key aspects of a collaboration culture to adopt.** The collaboration culture has many characteristics that support an agile mindset, including collaborative teams, a preference for generalists over specialists, and a democratic management style. Leverage these characteristics as you move the organization to a more agile mindset.
- **Recruit a sponsor from the top ranks.** This is the same approach I recommend for control cultures. To get anything done in a collaboration culture, you must get leadership's endorsement. They are the only ones with the authority to approve the change, and they need to loosen the reigns to give development teams more freedom to make decisions. More important, they're the only people the rest of the organization will follow.

- **Watch out for family arguments.** When you're transforming an organization with a collaborative culture into an agile enterprise, you may encounter competing visions among the "family members" regarding the end product — the organization's structure and function after the transformation. When visions clash, you're likely to get caught up in family squabbles that can slow and even undermine your efforts and make your job that much more difficult.

You're unlikely to have an organization that's large enough to deliver enterprise software but still runs like a family business. However, parts of your organization may have certain elements of this culture, so be prepared to address the challenges that this culture type presents.

Laying the Groundwork for a Successful Transformation

In general, organizations fail to make real changes for three reasons:

- The organization's leadership doesn't fully understand the purpose of the change or appreciate its value, or they do a poor job of communicating it to others in the organization. As a result, they meet with a lot of resistance. After all, why would you change what you're doing if you don't think the change is necessary or beneficial?
- The organization's leadership doesn't have a clear vision of what the organization will look like after the change has been successfully implemented, or they have the wrong vision. In other words, they have no goal or the wrong goal. An example of a wrong goal in an agile transformation would be trying to maintain a strict top-down organizational structure to micromanage the development teams.
- The organization's leadership doesn't have a plan for implementing the transformation, so they fail to "pack for the long journey." They expect the transformation to occur over days or weeks, when it requires months to years. As a result, they often give up prematurely before they have a chance to capitalize on the many benefits that the big change has to offer.

REMEMBER

Note that none of these challenges references agile practices, such as user stories, 15-minute stand-up meetings, or planning poker (all described in Chapter 1). Adopting these practices is relatively easy. The difficult aspect of any agile transformation is not in changing what people do on a daily basis, but in changing the organization's structure and the way it operates, and in changing how people approach their work and how they work together. Replacing a control culture that has clearly demarcated departmental boundaries with cross-functional, self-managed teams is much more challenging than having your developers play a round of planning poker to estimate their workloads.

In this section, I offer guidance on how to prepare the foundation for a successful enterprise agile transformation by avoiding these common mistakes.

Appreciating the value of an agile organization

People don't change unless they have good reason to do so. I've seen many organizations fail to implement major change initiatives simply because management wasn't fully convinced of their benefits or failed to communicate those benefits to the people in the organization who needed to implement the change. As a result, everyone made half-hearted or symbolic attempts to change, failed, and then concluded that the change was simply a bad idea.

Prior to embarking on your journey to transform your organization into an agile enterprise, make sure the benefits are clear in your own mind and in the minds of everyone in your organization who will be leading the change:

- **Collaborative excellence:** In agile enterprises, everyone, including management, employees, customers, and stakeholders, collaborates to create and deliver value. You don't have just a few people at the top of the organization determining what's best for the customer and the organization.
- **Continuous improvement:** Agile enterprises embrace continuous improvement in both the product and the process for creating it. Over time, the organization evolves, often with little, if any, management oversight.
- **Improved transparency:** Enterprise agility drives a culture of transparency that increases visibility of obstacles and dysfunction in both products and processes. After adopting an agile framework, you may be surprised at the number of problems your organization has. In most cases, the transformation didn't create the problems, it merely exposed them.
- **Increased business value:** With enterprise agility, the entire organization focuses on delivering value to customers and to the organization. The emphasis is on eliminating or at least significantly reducing anything in the organization that doesn't contribute value.
- **Ability to exceed customer expectations:** By involving customers in product development, the organization is better equipped to meet customer needs and exceed their expectations.
- **Enhanced innovation:** Enterprise agility encourages teams to experiment and to learn from success and failure, promoting a spirit of innovation that gives agile enterprises a competitive edge.
- **Ability to adapt quickly to changing conditions:** By localizing decision-making and accountability, teams can adapt more quickly to take advantage of emerging technologies and respond to changes in the marketplace. Enterprise agility essentially gives large organizations the agility often seen in startups and other small businesses.

Clarifying your vision

Before you try to initiate any big change, develop a clear vision of what your organization will look like or how it will operate differently after the change is in place. Your vision should include the purpose for making the change; for example, "To improve our product delivery agility, so we can deliver greater value to our customers faster." Here's one approach for developing a vision for enterprise agility:

1. **Gather all stakeholders or reps from different stakeholder groups in a room for a brainstorming session.**

   This is a great opportunity to bring in people who are likely to resist change, so they have a voice, and you can address any concerns they may have.

2. **Highlight the problems or limitations with the way your organization currently delivers value/product to customers.**

   Ask participants to point out other limitations or challenges in the current system.

3. **Present agile as a solution, pointing out specifically how it can address the limitations or challenges on the list.**

   Ask participants for their input. This is a good opportunity to identify any pockets of resistance you're likely to encounter.

4. **Ask participants to suggest vision statements that describe the way the organization needs to change to more effectively overcome the challenges it faces and to achieve its goal of increasing its enterprise agility.**

   Write down suggested vision statements on your whiteboard.

5. **Engage the group in a discussion until you arrive at a general consensus on the vision statement.**

   Your goal is to walk out of the brainstorming meeting with a vision statement that everyone in the group accepts. An inability to reach consensus on the vision is usually a sign that your transformation will have a difficult time succeeding.

WARNING

Starting without a clear vision guarantees failure. Many organizations don't have a sense of their own culture. They can't envision how agile will fit with their larger organizational mindset. They haven't even considered whether their organization is open to change. Without a clear vision, you're unlikely to be able to overcome the resistance that always accompanies a major change.

Planning for your transformation

After analyzing your existing culture and developing a clear vision of what you want your organization to look like after the change, you have points A and B — your point of departure and point of arrival. All you need now is a map (a plan) that connects the two points. In Chapter 10, I provide detailed guidance on how to develop a plan for implementing an enterprise agile transformation. Your plan may look something like this, which is based loosely on the six-step adoption plan for Large-Scale Scrum (LeSS), presented in Chapter 5:

1. **Choose or develop your own enterprise agile framework.**

   See Chapters 4 to 8 to review the top five enterprise agile frameworks, and choose the framework that's best suited to your organization's existing culture. You generally want to choose the framework that you think your organization will transition to easiest.

2. **Develop an overall strategy for implementing the change.**

   For example, many organizations start small, with a single product and two or three teams. After these teams have successfully adopted the new approach and are satisfied with the results, the change can be extended out to other products or product lines or to other teams.

3. **Establish a time frame for implementing the change.**

   Keep in mind that large organizations tend to take a long time to adopt any new approach. Think in terms of months and years, not days and weeks.

4. **Create a consensus document for everyone who will be involved in implementing the change.**

   Your consensus document must clearly describe the vision and provide all involved with a list of priorities they need to focus on when addressing their changes locally. (See Chapter 10 for details.)

5. **Provide education and training to everyone in the organization who will be involved in and affected by the agile transformation.**

   Your approach to education and training depends on your strategy for implementing the change. If you're planning to roll out the change to the entire organization, everyone needs to receive agile education and training. If you're starting with one product and only a few teams, focus on training those who will be involved from the start.

REMEMBER

   Education and training are important in changing the way people in your organization think about the way they do their work. As they begin to understand and experience the benefits of enterprise agility, they will begin to share their experience with others in the organization, which will help drive the cultural change that delivers the greatest improvements.

6. **Build cross-functional teams.**

   The team is the fundamental unit in agile. Teams must be cross-functional, meaning they have all the knowledge and skills required (design, development, analysis, testing, and so forth) to deliver a product end-to-end to the customer.

7. **Define "product."**

   Your product is anything of value delivered to the customer. Identify the value you deliver to the customer and use it to formulate your definition of "product." Everyone must agree on what the product is before your organization can begin to work on delivering it more effectively to the customer.

8. **Define "done."**

   The definition of "done" (DoD) is a term from Scrum software development that refers to a set of criteria that must be met for a product to be considered satisfactorily completed. For example, a DoD may state that "done" means a feature has been tested and successfully integrated into a working version of the product. Without an agreed-upon DoD, teams may never be able to tell when a product is ready for delivery.

9. **Provide teams with the resources they need to complete their work.**

   In agile, the role of organizational leadership shifts from manager to leader-servant. Leadership sets the mission and overall vision, provides the teams with the resources they need, and then steps out of the way, trusting the teams to deliver the highest quality product to the customer.

TIP

In Scrum, teams conduct two-part sprint planning meetings where they first figure out what needs to be done and then determine how they will get it done. Approach your agile transformation plan the same way. First, figure out what your organization needs to do (or be) and then how your organization will do it (or be it). The vision statement describes what your organization must do. Your plan describes how to do it.

- Using Kotter's eight-step change model for a top-down change
- Changing from the bottom up with the Fearless Change approach
- Overcoming common obstacles to big change

Chapter 10

Driving Organizational Change

Organizations are like cruise ships — they set their course and when they reach cruising speed are slow to change direction. They're likely to remain on course unless a significant amount of directed energy is applied to make them change direction. In an organization, this impetus typically comes from the leadership of the organization (at the top) or from one or more highly motivated and influential groups or individuals working at lower levels of the organization (from the bottom). Ideally, forces at the top and throughout the organization drive the change.

In this chapter, I provide the guidance you need to determine whether a top-down or bottom-up approach to organizational change management is likely to be most effective for your organization, and I describe two formal change management approaches: the eight-step change model designed by John Kotter for driving change from the top and the Fearless Change approach to drive change from the bottom. Finally, I address the obstacles you may encounter as you try to implement a major organizational change (such as enterprise agility) and offer suggestions on how to overcome these obstacles.

Choosing an Approach: Top-Down or Bottom-Up

When you're transforming your organization into an agile enterprise, you have two approaches from which to choose:

- **Top-down organizational change** is driven by the business owner, C-suite executives, or top-level managers — an individual in the organization who has a lot of authority. Choose a top-down approach if your organization has a strong control culture and a leader near the top of the organization who's committed and has the authority to drive the change.
- **Bottom-up organizational change** is driven by teams, individuals, mid-level managers, or outside consultants — an individual or a group that believes passionately in the potential benefits of the change. Choose a bottom-up approach if you're having trouble getting support from your organization's leadership.

REMEMBER

Start the process by trying to understand your organization's culture, as explained in Chapter 9. A top-down approach is generally effective regardless of culture, but if you're unable to recruit an influential advocate at the top of the organization, your only option may be to start small and demonstrate agile's value locally before introducing it to the entire organization.

Soon after the Agile Manifesto, most agile transformations started from the bottom up with software developers who knew about the benefits of agile teams from their colleagues. Most managers stepped back and allowed the agile teams to take the lead, because they saw no reason to resist if the teams improved product delivery. Because enterprise agility requires more coordination among teams, managers have a greater incentive to get involved early on, so enterprise agile transformations are commonly driven from the top down.

REMEMBER

Top-down and bottom-up organizational change are not about who's involved in making the change. Both approaches are effective regardless of whether the transformation is initiated at the top or bottom of the organization. An organization may even use both approaches in tandem; for example, a change leader near the top of the organization may decide that the best way to implement the change is to take a gradual approach with a few teams in one area of the organization and extend it after these initial teams experience some degree of success and are able to serve as evangelists and provide training.

Don't underestimate the work and persistence required. Many organizations approach their agile transformation as a pep rally, bringing in one or more consultants or coaches to communicate their passion for enterprise agility, as if that will be enough to drive the change. That's not how most large organizations change. Instead, they change direction only through a relentless pursuit of small improvements. It's less like a pep rally and more like training for a marathon. You can't run a marathon just by being excited about it; you have to hit the pavement every day (maybe twice daily) regardless of the weather, adopt a healthier diet and lifestyle, and build on small improvements. Likewise, transforming an organization into an agile enterprise involves the day-to-day work of pushing the organization in a new direction. Enthusiasm is great for motivation, but it needs to be combined with hard work.

Driving Change from Top to Bottom with the Kotter Approach

You can find plenty of top-down approaches to organizational change, but the approach I recommend is Kotter's eight-step change model:

1. **Create a sense of urgency around a Big Opportunity.**

   Identify a risk or opportunity and then examine how your organization will be impacted if it fails to respond.

2. **Build and evolve a guiding coalition.**

   Assemble a group with a commitment to change and the authority to lead the effort. This team should work independently of other power structures in the organization.

3. **Form a change vision and strategic initiatives.**

   Envision your organization as one that has the ability to take full advantage of the Big Opportunity you identified, and then develop a strategy for transforming your organization from its current state to your vision of the ideal.

4. **Enlist a volunteer army.**

   Create a group to spearhead the change both by advocating for the change and by adopting and then demonstrating the value of the change. This group needs to lead by example.

5. **Enable action by removing barriers.**

   Remove organizational obstacles standing in the way of change, encourage risk taking, and get people talking about agile.

6. **Generate (and celebrate) short-term wins.**

   Create opportunities to show improvement. For example, you can create a new metric and then work to show improvement on meeting that metric. Recognize and reward others for being part of the improvement.

7. **Sustain acceleration.**

   Build on short-term wins and try to use them as evidence that you can make further changes. Try to create momentum to change structures and remove policies that could undermine the vision.

8. **Institute change.**

   Make the connection between the successful changes and the organization's success. Promote employees who share the vision and are helping to generate the wins into management positions, so they have more authority to drive change.

The creator of this approach, John Kotter, referred to the steps collectively as XLR8 (accelerate), with each step serving as a change accelerator. Kotter's early book was called *Leading Change.* He refined his approach in a later book entitled *Accelerate: Building Strategic Agility for a Fast-Moving World (XLR8)*. Each step flows to the next, almost like a classic waterfall model (see Chapter 1). Most organizations that try the Kotter approach think of it as a big one-time event. It's used as an organizational shakeup, which is why many companies take this approach only if they feel their core business is in danger.

REMEMBER

Change is not a one-time event. As shown in Figure 10-1, change is an ongoing process, and the steps, though sequential, form an ongoing cycle.

Step 1: Create a sense of urgency around a Big Opportunity

For the Kotter approach to be successful, you must be or recruit a strong leader at the top of the organization who has the authority to drive the change, and this leader needs to create a sense of urgency. This person has to convince the rest of the organization that the change being proposed is essential to the organization's continued success. In many ways, the change leader serves as a field commander, rallying the troops and then providing direction, so that they can implement the change.

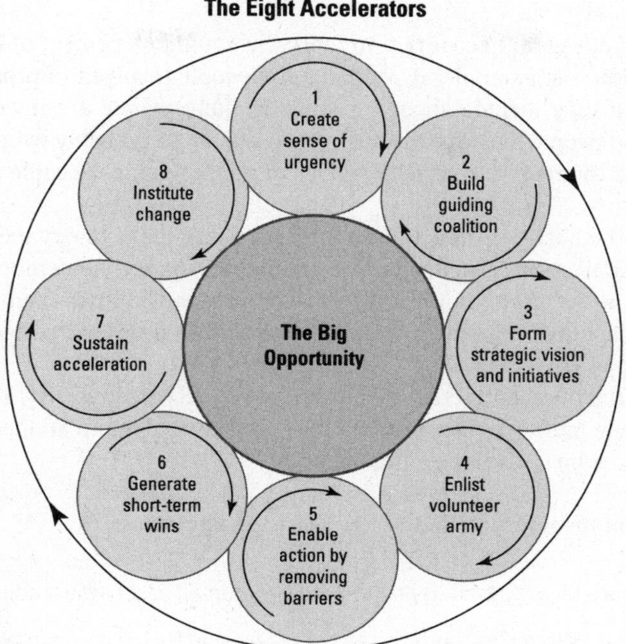

FIGURE 10-1: Kotter's eight-step change model.

The problem is that most organizations don't have field commanders with free time. The types of leaders who need to drive this change are usually CEOs or high-level managers. In large organizations, leadership is almost always tied up with strategic initiatives and financial concerns and is often unaccustomed to leading what they view as changes to operations — something they delegate to lower-level management. As a result, top-level leaders try to outsource this leadership role to outside consultants or change-management firms. Unfortunately, these outsiders, while they certainly have the required expertise, lack the recognition and authority to drive the change.

WARNING

Don't try to delegate change leadership to someone outside your organization, such as an Agile Coach (like me). Instead, choose a leader or build a coalition within your organization and give it the authority to drive the change. This same individual or group will take the lead on all eight steps of the Kotter change management approach.

Step 2: Build and evolve a guiding coalition

A *guiding coalition* is a powerful, diverse, enthusiastic team of volunteers from across an organization that serves as the social leaders of the change initiative. In enterprise agile transformations, the guiding coalition is typically called a center of excellence (CoE). The Scaled Agile Framework® (SAFe®), which is covered in Chapter 4, calls this the Lean-Agile Center of Excellence (LACE).

TIP

Expect your guiding coalition to represent roughly 5 percent of the overall transformation. For example, if you have 100 people involved in product delivery, the coalition may include about 5 people. If 1,000 people are involved, you'll want about 50 people in the coalition, but a group of 50 probably won't get much done, so break them up into smaller groups of no more than 9 people per group.

Divide the coalition into those who contribute ideas (everyone in the coalition) and a small subset responsible for driving the change. Remember that most of the people in the group have other full-time responsibilities. You want to get their opinions, but don't expect them to serve as full-time change agents.

TIP

As you recruit volunteers for your CoE, try to achieve diversity. You want your CoE to include Agile Coaches, practitioners, and some domain and technical experts to connect agile to the larger organization.

Coalition members should follow these guidelines:

- Share ideas without trying to position yourself as an agile leader.
- Work with fellow members to craft ideas and try to solve complex problems about how to increase organizational agility.
- Standardize your ideas so that the organization can have a shared understanding of what the changed organization will look like.
- Align with Lean-Agile principles of continuous improvement and inspecting and adapting. The team should come up with an initial plan that everyone knows will evolve through its implementation.

WARNING

Watch out for HiPPOs (highest-paid-person's opinions)! The CoE's focus should be on learning and on reaching consensus regarding the change initiative. The coalition shouldn't be merely an extension of management that does what the CEO instructs it to do.

Step 3: Form a change vision and strategic initiatives

The first order of business for the CoE is to create a mission statement. Keep it short and simple, as in the following example:

> Sandwich Shop Enterprises is an organization that develops a software program to compare the menus of different restaurants. We've created a Lean-Agile Center of Excellence (LACE), which is a full-time, cross-functional, self-organized team that is

driving the change to improve our organization's Lean-Agile mindset. We will provide guidance on Lean-Agile to the rest of the organization related to training, process improvement, tools, culture, and governance.

Next, create a whiteboard with the following three columns and brainstorm the CoE's scope of responsibility in each area:

- **Doing:** List everything the CoE plans to do to achieve its mission; for example, leadership and team training.
- **Not doing:** List areas that are outside the coalition's sphere of responsibility, such as managing teams.
- **Success metrics:** List measurements of success, such as the percentage of people who received agile team training or the number of agile teams.

Reach a high level of agreement on any major decision, such as the mission statement and the coalition's responsibilities. Strong agreement among coalition members ensures consistent messaging to the rest of the organization.

Step 4: Enlist a volunteer army

Kotter's fourth step is about creating a mass movement around your change initiative. How you accomplish this goal largely depends on the size of your organization:

- **Small organizations:** If your organization is small, consider hosting monthly "lunch and learns" — optional meetings during which coalition members give presentations about the overall change vision. Free pizza or sandwiches are usually an excellent motivator to help increase attendance.
- **Large organizations:** In a larger organization (thousands of people), communicating a clear vision across several CoEs can be challenging. Consider establishing a guiding CoE in the largest location, preferably the location with the most managers (not necessarily the most practitioners). Remember that the Kotter approach is top-down, so work on coaching more managers to drive change. The guiding CoE can standardize the ideas among all CoEs to ensure consistency across the group.

Try to keep your CoE meetings fun and informal. Lunches and morning breaks are usually the best times to have productive, creative discussions about organizational change management. Keep meetings festive, as you would an office birthday party, substituting the cake with bagels, pizza, or sandwiches. Avoid scheduling meetings late in the week or late in the workday. Late Wednesday mornings are often a good choice, because they provide everyone with a break in the middle of the workweek.

REMEMBER

Don't overtax your army of volunteers. You're asking people to add to their workload without shirking their regular job responsibilities. They may need to expand their energy and expertise to 120 to 150 percent above current levels, which is what often happens in a well-functioning system, but try to remain consistent with an agile mindset — respect your people, give them the freedom to be creative, and enable them to make an impact.

Step 5: Enable action by removing barriers

When you're driving a change initiative, remove any barriers that may get in the way, including hierarchies and inefficient processes. Kotter recommends creating a dual operating system (see Figure 10-2):

> The basic structure is self-explanatory: hierarchy on one side and network on the other. The network side mimics successful enterprises in their entrepreneurial phase, before there were organizational charts showing reporting relationships, before there were formal job descriptions and status levels.
>
> —Excerpt from *Accelerate: Building Strategic Agility for a Faster-Moving World* by John P. Kotter

Your organization can maintain the traditional hierarchy while your CoE, army of volunteers, and influential members of the hierarchy form a network of entrepreneurs and leaders who work to make large-scale changes. This strategic network doesn't have a typical command-and-control structure. Instead, it focuses on individuality, creativity, and innovation.

In a sense, Kotter is suggesting that you split your organization in two. The one side holds your management, organizational structure, and legacy ideas (hierarchy). The other side should run like a startup organization (network). It should be free to make, and to some extent, break the rules.

REMEMBER

The CoE is part of the network, but be sure to include people who have the authority to make changes.

WARNING

Although you want corporate leadership to be part of the network, don't let the network become the executive arm of the hierarchy, merely following orders. People will be willing to volunteer and take on extra duties when they believe that their ideas will have a real impact on the success of the organization, but they'll be less likely to volunteer if they're being "voluntold" what to think and do.

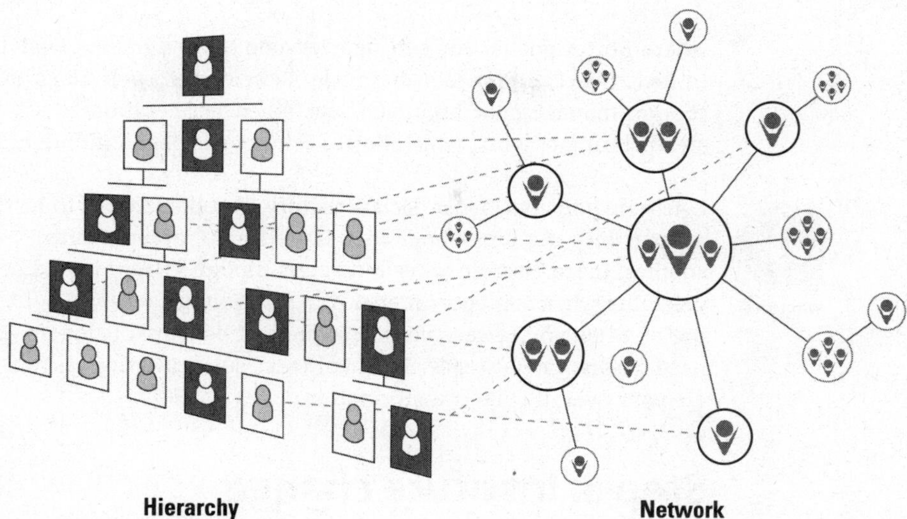

FIGURE 10-2: A dual operating system.

Step 6: Generate (and celebrate) short-term wins

John F. Kennedy popularized the saying that "victory has a thousand fathers but defeat is an orphan." In most organizations, everybody wants to be on the winning team. In fact, if you have a lot of wins, you'll have an easier time recruiting volunteers, even those who were early skeptics. Nobody wants to miss out on a chance to contribute to the organization's success in capitalizing on a Big Opportunity.

Whenever your organization makes even the smallest step forward on its path to becoming more agile, celebrate. This is no time to be modest. On the contrary, have an "arm in the air" fireworks display to communicate your win to the rest the organization. Don't be afraid to fist pump even your modest wins. People have a much higher tolerance for listening to good news and self-promotion than you might think.

Also celebrate individuals and not just the entire team. Call out some of your most valuable contributors as a way to reinforce their commitment to the change. Acknowledging people's contributions is one of the easiest ways to keep people motivated and engaged.

Step 7: Sustain acceleration

After a few wins, a team begins to gain momentum, but many CoEs become satisfied with their contributions and take their foot off the accelerator. They may even disband before they make a real impact on the organization. It's at this stage where Kotter pushes for getting everyone thinking about sustained acceleration. In fact, this is one reason he made "accelerate" such a big part of his updated change management approach. Sustained acceleration is about maintaining a steady string of wins, which Kotter refers to as "sub-initiatives."

WARNING

Celebrate wins but never declare victory. You don't want to be the team to throw a party with the big banner that says "Agility accomplished!" Instead, focus on smaller, more discrete wins and act as though victory is just beyond your grasp. Celebrate when someone in your organization has received agile leadership training or when you release your first product delivered using an agile mindset. You need to celebrate a steady stream of these sub-initiatives as fuel that will accelerate your overall agile transformation.

Step 8: Institute change

As the network part of your dual operating system gathers momentum, point out the connections between the new ways of thinking and working and the organization's success, so the changes you've implemented become strong enough to replace old habits. It's at this point your change initiative transitions from becoming a movement to becoming the organizational culture. Think of it as achieving critical mass — the minimal size or amount of something to spark change and maintain its momentum. Your CoE should begin to push these agile principles, values, practices, and behaviors into the very culture of your organization.

CASE STUDY

SETTING THE WRONG TONE

I once worked for an organization that met disaster when trying to update one of its existing software applications. The teams worked tirelessly to fix a product that was teetering on the edge of the abyss. They had a shared workspace that they used as their war room. With gallows humor, one of the team members put a sign on the door with a toxic waste symbol and the name of the project.

When the organization started its agile transformation, leadership decided to locate the CoE in the vacated room, but everyone associated the room with that doomed project. They even named the room after the project. Even mentioning the room brought groans of agony from others in the organization. After a few months, the CoE decided to move the group into a windowless conference room on the ground floor. It was a dismal room, but it wasn't associated with a losing battle, which made it easier for everyone to start thinking he was on a winning team.

REMEMBER

Maintain your organization's dual operating system. You can keep your organization's hierarchy in place while nurturing networking through communities of practice to ensure that the dialog that drives change in your organization continues. If the networking part of your organization's operating system disbands, all you'll be left with is a hierarchy, which tends to lean toward a control culture that resists change.

TIP

Remember that organizational changes are always uphill and against the wind. The best change agents usually have more patience than passion. Respect others and work to make small incremental improvements. Above all, enjoy the process. People are much more likely to join your effort if they see you having a good time.

Improving your odds of success

If your organization is using the Kotter approach or something similar, here are a couple tips for improving your odds for success:

- Make sure the agents of change have the authority to make changes. What often happens is that an executive delegates the change initiative, which works only if the organization has a strong control culture. If your organization is more collaborative, people will have a tough time accepting one person as the change leader.
- Think of change as ongoing. People who use the Kotter approach often think of it as eight sequential steps at the end of which you have a big change, almost like a deliverable. In reality, change is something that constantly churns throughout an organization.

  REMEMBER

  Don't think of change as one big event; think of it instead as a part of the normal workflow.

Driving a Grass-Roots Change: A Fearless Approach

In their book, *Fearless Change: Patterns for Introducing New Ideas,* Linda Rising and Mary Lynn Manns examine several different patterns that emerge when large organizations try to implement major changes. They point out that one of the big sources of resistance is fear — fear of the future and of the unknown. Their Fearless Change approach recommends that organizations try to instill faith in the organization — a belief that the change will be good for the organization and good for its employees.

DON'T FIGHT FEAR

I've always been a bad swimmer. Over the years I've been on many swim teams and tried different styles, but it doesn't matter; I'm just not a very good swimmer. When I was 15, I joined my first swim team. My coach decided to put me in a race where I competed in the breaststroke. He helped me onto the dive platform and I got up in front of dozens of families. My wiry legs trembled on the cold platform as I stood in my tiny blue swimsuit. He put his hand on the platform and said, "Don't fight your fear, it's your body's way of telling you you're ready."

I'm not sure I agree with my coach that fear is your body's way of telling you're ready, but his advice to not fight the fear was great. The more you fight it, the more fearful you become, because you're focused on fear. Only by *not* fighting it, by turning your attention to something else, can you overcome it.

When transitioning to enterprise agility, you can often help people in your organization overcome their fears by engaging them in the change. As they get lost in the work of implementing the change, they shift their focus from fear.

People mistakenly think change requires a strong leader with a clear vision. They think everyone will listen to the leader and bravely fall in line behind the change. In reality, an organizational change is more like group therapy. You have large groups of people who fear the change. They're not afraid for the health of the organization; they're afraid for themselves. Organizational change often casts doubt on the employee's future, making the person wonder how the change will impact his job.

People don't want to be fearful. They want to feel empowered to move forward, even if they have to do so unwillingly at first. Instead of a strong leader, you may need a leader who's empathetic and reassuring.

WARNING

Don't ignore the fear factor. If you do, you'll be blindsided by those who want to stall or undermine your change initiative.

Recruiting a change evangelist

To take a fearless approach to change, you need to recruit a change evangelist who can establish an emotional connection with the others in the organization the change will impact most. Look for someone who has the following characteristics:

- Someone within the organization, not an outside coach or consultant. An insider is much better positioned to connect emotionally with others in the organization.

- Empathizes with those who may be the biggest skeptics. Someone who has a history with the organization, has seen changes succeed and fail, and understands the emotional factors that have led to past success and failure is likely to have the requisite empathy.
- Is respected and well-liked by her peers.
- Is passionate about the change being considered (in this case, transforming the organization into an agile enterprise).

REMEMBER

A change evangelist makes an emotional connection. She understands both why people are likely to resist the change and why they should embrace it. She acts as a bridge from skepticism to faith, which is a difficult role to play.

CASE STUDY

GETTING AN INSIDE CONNECTION

I once worked for an organization where I was hired as an Agile Coach. One of my first jobs was to create a sense of urgency. I needed to communicate to everyone the importance of having a more agile mindset. I tried to recruit people for the first Scrum team. I was trying the Kotter approach by creating a sense of urgency and building a guiding coalition.

I was having a lot of trouble connecting with the different teams. They'd seen a half-dozen coaches before talk about the value of big changes. These coaches had come and gone, and the organization continued to plod along, so people didn't feel a sense of urgency. They also had a few Scrum teams that started and failed, so no one really wanted to be part of a guiding coalition.

I was trying to be a change leader, but what the organization really needed was a change evangelist. Instead of trying to fly solo, I partnered with someone who'd been inside the organization for several years. She had been evangelizing the agile mindset and was having trouble getting anything going. I offered her the opportunity to spin up a new Scrum team. Then she gave me some of the help I needed to make an emotional connection.

In the very next meeting, she started out by connecting with the teams. She explained to them that she understood their frustration. An army of consultants like me had come through and not made much progress. Nevertheless, she believed this change would help the company. These new Scrum teams would help them produce better software and attract younger developers. She encouraged the rest of the teams to take this leap of faith.

She said this in a way that could come only from an evangelist inside the organization. As an Agile Coach I may have been qualified to lead the change, but I needed someone inside the organization to evangelize new ideas. You need someone whose faith convinces others of the value in the change.

Changing without top-down authority

In many ways, Fearless Change is much more realistic than top-down methods, regardless of whether the change is being driven from the top or bottom. Why? Because top-down change often fails for the following reasons:

- **Lack of executive buy-in:** Other members of the leadership team don't believe in the change, so the change initiative lacks impact. One of the only surveys on this topic suggests that the lack of executive buy-in is one of the most common reasons for a failed transformation. (See the later section, "Seeing how culture can sink agile.")
- **Lack of follow-through:** The CEO or other change leader initiates the change and then gets busy doing other things. With nobody in place to drive the momentum, the change stalls. Even in a strong control culture, people respond to change on an emotional level. The people who have the authority to make big changes don't have the time to evangelize to individual teams.

REMEMBER

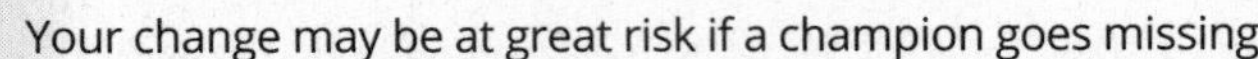

Your change may be at great risk if a champion goes missing!

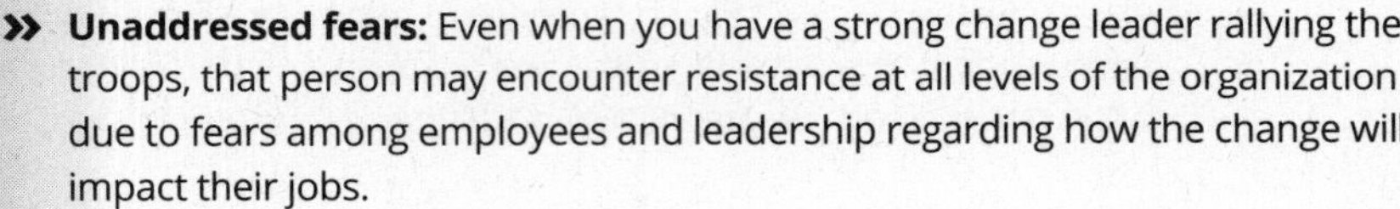

- **Unaddressed fears:** Even when you have a strong change leader rallying the troops, that person may encounter resistance at all levels of the organization due to fears among employees and leadership regarding how the change will impact their jobs.

Regardless of whether you have a strong change leader in the upper echelon of the organization, Fearless Change may be the best approach. You can connect with people on an emotional level and use that connection to gain acceptance and start to recruit advocates.

Making change a self-fulfilling prophecy

Ovid's *Metamorphoses* includes a poem about a young sculptor named Pygmalion, who created a statue so beautiful that he fell in love with it. When he tried to kiss the statue, the goddess Aphrodite willed his beautiful sculpture to life. In the poem, Pygmalion created something beautiful, and his expectations brought the sculpture to life.

When you're making a large organizational change, you can benefit from the same "Pygmalion" effect. You can create a self-fulfilling prophecy where your enthusiasm helps recruit others to make changes. This is one of the key roles of change evangelists. They need to have a contagious excitement that wills the change into existence.

CASE STUDY

LEVERAGING FEAR TO OVERCOME IT

I once worked for a large retailer that was trying to start a change to enterprise agility. This organization had a strong control culture. Each department had dozens of different roles that created a very clear hierarchy of managers and employees. Everyone knew for whom he worked and everyone knew who worked for him. Each group sat together in clusters of power.

Many managers quickly realized that the more people they had, the more influence they had. This led to bloated departments and almost comically confusing titles. The person who was responsible for the agile transformation had the title, "Lead Assistant Senior Special Director for Business Quality Assurance."

This organization had failed a dozen times trying to start a change. The main reason was fear. The organization spent decades creating complex hierarchies and convoluted management structures. There was a lot of organizational "cruft" (a term used in software development to describe overly complicated or badly designed code that often festers over time). There were countless roles that managers created as a way to increase their influence. The people in these roles were afraid. They understood that positions could easily be consolidated and their position eliminated.

The meetings they had about the agile transformation were very intense. How do you explain to a team of 40 business analysts the benefits of having one product owner? Even more challenging, how do you explain the benefits of a self-organized team to a group of mid-level managers?

Many people believed that the best way to confront the challenge was with communication, flexibility, and courage. The problem, however, was that many people were understandably afraid. The organization couldn't become lean and remain bloated at the same time, and trimming the fat was going to impact their positions. Telling them not to be afraid would only deepen their fears.

Instead, we leveraged that fear. We identified the people who were most afraid of the change (those who had the most to lose). Then we created a transformation workgroup that laid out plans for how the organization could move forward. The workgroup focused on taking that negative energy from their fear and turning it into positive energy to drive the plan. They were writing a future for themselves, which helped eliminate their own fears and doubts.

REMEMBER

Your change evangelist is the key player in Fearless Change. Look for someone who has the enthusiasm to bring the vision to life.

Looking for change patterns

In their book *Fearless Change*, Rising and Manns describe several *change patterns* — how people respond to change — and they present various techniques to address these patterns. Here, I present two change patterns I've found to be common in the organizations I've helped with agile transformations.

Accepting change at different rates

People accept change at different rates. You may present an idea to a large group and have people leave the presentation with varying degrees of enthusiasm. Some in the audience will be convinced after seeing the first two slides, while others will see the full fireworks show and still walk away unimpressed.

Connect with both fans and skeptics. If you talk only to the people excited about the change, you'll get the mistaken impression that the transformation will be easy. Even worse, you won't know the source of resistance.

The diffusion of innovations theory

Fearless Change relies on a 50-year-old diffusion of innovations theory created by Everett Rogers, an assistant professor of rural sociology at Ohio State University. He identified five groups of people who respond differently to innovations:

- **Innovators** quickly embrace new ideas.
- **Early adopters** are interested in new ideas but like to hear a little more before they decide.
- **Early majority** like to see what other people think before they make up their minds.
- **Late majority** accept an idea only after the majority of people accept it.
- **Laggards** must be dragged kicking and screaming into any new change.

These groups aren't good or bad. An organization needs laggards as much as it needs early adopters. The company would be in chaos if everyone adopted every new change. At the same time, the company would probably not be around very long if it didn't make any changes. You shouldn't try to sort these groups into good and evil. There are no heroes and villains, but you need to take a different approach when introducing the change to each group.

Recruiting innovators and early adopters

TIP

One strategy to accelerate change is to recruit innovators and early adopters and have them convince the late majority and laggards. The late majority is usually swayed by greater numbers of people, but anyone who resists change is likely to be more receptive when hearing about it from an enthusiastic supporter.

After turning a skeptic into a believer, recruit your new convert to become an advocate for change. Newly converted employees may be your most enthusiastic supporters.

Tailoring your message

As you speak with different groups and individuals, tailor your message to your audience. Don't continue to sell to innovators and early adopters who are already on board. You may need to shift from sales to education and training or to recruiting your new advocates to help spread the word.

When presenting to the late majority and to the laggards, find out why they're resisting the change. Maybe similar initiatives have failed in the past and they're convinced that "nothing's going to change," or they're afraid of how the change will impact them. After figuring out the reason behind their resistance, tailor your message to show that you understand and empathize and then present information that addresses their concerns. Let them know that it's okay to be hesitant about the change.

Don't ignore, dismiss, or make light of people's concerns. However unrealistic the concerns, they're still valid, because they reflect how people feel. Your job is to provide information and insight that alleviates the concern.

TIP

You can help convince the laggards by showing them that the proposed change is actually the best option (or the least unpleasant option).

Steering clear of change myths

In *Fearless Change*, Rising and Manns present several change myths (misconceptions) that can impair your ability to transform your organization. In this section, I present six change myths you're likely to encounter as you start to transform your organization into an agile enterprise.

REMEMBER

Keep these change myths in mind when you're starting your enterprise agile transformation so you'll be less likely to succumb to their influence.

Thinking change sells itself

The first change myth is the notion that if you have something that adds value to the organization, it'll be easy to convince others to accept the change. To avoid falling victim to this myth, keep in mind the following two points:

- Not everyone will see value in your change.
- Even those who see value in the proposed change may not agree that the change is right for the organization; for example, someone may say something like, "I'm sure agile works fine for companies like Google, but this is an office supply business."

The change won't sell itself. You need a change evangelist to sell it and to keep selling it until you get enough people on board and enough energy to overcome any remaining resistance to the change. You may give yourself a headache repeating the value of the change, but that's a necessary discomfort of being a change evangelist. You may not convince everyone that the proposed change is best, but it will at least give people the opportunity to oppose it for the right reasons.

Thinking people knowing about the benefits is enough to change

Educating people on the benefits of change isn't always enough. Some organizations encounter this challenge with their Agile Coaches. The coach spends considerable time training and developing an effective plan but far too little time giving employees a forum for expressing their concerns. The employees end up knowing what to do, but having little motivation to do it.

Organizational change requires a combination of training and group therapy. Big change results in emotional upheaval as much as it requires a reorientation to process. If you fail to address the emotional factors, you'll end up with well-trained employees who are reluctant to change.

Believing change requires charm and PowerPoint

I've worked in several large organizations where agile transformations failed because the most influential people were apathetic about the change. I would give presentations about the agile mindset and they would respond like Bill Murray in the movie *Groundhog Day*, in which his character was forced to live the same day over and over again. I could tell they'd seen it all before. They wouldn't oppose the change, but they weren't excited about it either.

TIP

If you're the change evangelist, try not to rely too much on personal charm and PowerPoint presentations. Instead, position yourself as an approachable outsider — someone who's knowledgeable but not overly friendly. Let people know you're aware of their concerns. For example, you may say something like, "I know you've probably heard this all before and nothing ever seems to change, but . . . ." Then try to recruit these longtime employees and see if you can drum up some excitement.

Trying to steamroll over skeptics

Many change leaders try to steamroll over the skeptics to push change through the organization without addressing their concerns. This approach often increases resistance instead of reducing it. When you're starting an organizational transformation, try to see your skeptics as a positive force in the organization. In many organizations, the skeptics are the ones who are most likely to be right. Always try to engage them in open forums. In most organizations, skeptics are like icebergs. The ones you see often represent a small portion of the group that's actually there.

Encourage the skeptics to open up, so you know the source of their resistance and can address their concerns. Your skeptics can be a valuable resource in helping you choose changes that have the highest chance for success.

Relying too much on one change agent

Rarely can a single change leader push change through an organization, even in an organization that has a strong control culture. The myth that a single person can make or break an organization comes from stories about legendary executives who turned their companies around, such as Steve Jobs (Apple), Lee Iacocca (Chrysler), and Dan Hesse (Sprint).

The problem with these stories is that very few executives have what it takes to become a legend or they're working under entirely different circumstances. Effecting big change as an individual requires a rare combination of vision and authority. Most change evangelists will never enjoy anything close to that level of authority.

Believing people will stay convinced

Perhaps the most dangerous change myth is that once you convince people they'll stay convinced. An agile transformation is almost like trying to maintain a healthy lifestyle. You may lose 50 pounds, but trying to keep it off requires persistence. You may convince most people in your organization that change is needed, but they may have deeply ingrained work habits that take a long time and a lot of effort to change. If you stop pumping energy into your change initiative, people are likely to drift back to comfortable behaviors.

Overcoming Obstacles Related to Your Organization's Culture

Your organization's existing culture can create a great deal of inertia that your organization needs to overcome in order to change direction. In fact, an inability to change an organization's culture is one of the leading causes of failed enterprise agile transformations. In this section, I explain how cultural factors can undermine an enterprise agile transformation, and I provide guidance on how to overcome cultural inertia.

Seeing how culture can sink agile

According to an annual survey conducted by VersionOne on the state of agile, the number one challenge companies face when they attempt an enterprise agile transformation is "Company philosophy or culture at odds with core agile values" (see Figure 10-3). Number four on the list is a "General organization resistance to change." Further down at number six is "Insufficient training."

Most organizations understand and are willing to embrace a more agile mindset. The real challenge is overcoming cultural inertia. The organization wants to adopt enterprise agility, but agile conflicts with a deeply engrained incompatible mindset.

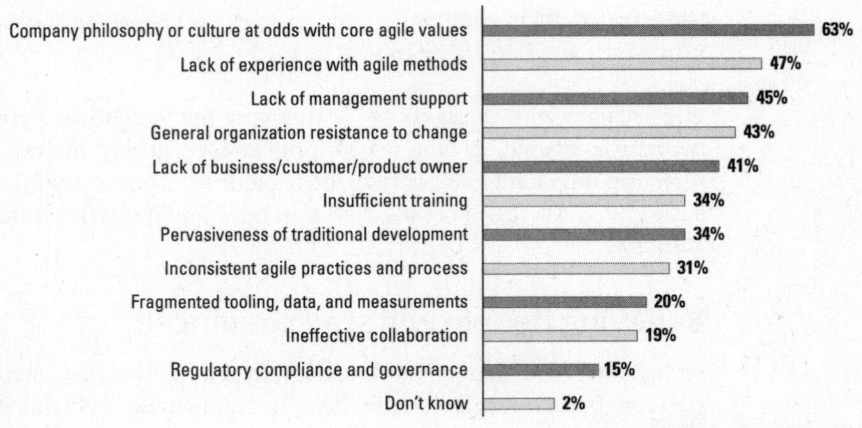

FIGURE 10-3: The top challenges in an agile transformation.

Acknowledging the challenge

The first step to overcoming cultural inertia is to confront it. Many teams try to change culture through training. They think that once individuals understand agile they'll be more likely to embrace it. Unfortunately, more training is rarely the solution. Even when all employees in the organization understand agile and appreciates its potential benefits, they often feel that it's not a solution that'll work in their organization. They lack *faith.*

If you think about it, this feeling makes a lot of sense. A lot of organizations have a strong control culture. Some of agile's key values may be in direct opposition to long-established practices. A culture that puts a lot of emphasis on hierarchy and accountability, for example, is going to have a tough time embracing self-organized teams and distributed authority.

Prioritizing the challenge

When you start your agile transformation, make culture your number one priority. Agile teams always begin with the highest value items first. Training is number six on the list of common challenges, and culture is number one. It's clear that you need to start with culture. Your effort here will make or break your enterprise agile transformation.

CASE STUDY

TALK IS CHEAP, TRAINING ONLY SLIGHTLY LESS SO

I once worked for an organization that was starting out with enterprise agility. It spent the majority of its budget training on an enterprise framework. It figured that if everyone in the organization knew more about enterprise agility, excitement would overcome any cultural inertia, and the cultural challenges would just drift away.

Unfortunately, the opposite happened. People were excited about the idea of trying the new system. They just didn't believe it would work for them. One common theme I heard was, "This is absolutely a great way to work, it will just never work here."

The organization would have been better off learning less and doing more. Its approach was, "Let's all learn enterprise agility and see if it works for us." A better approach would've been "We're making this cultural change, now let's work together to make it happen."

Build on your success. If you're considering an enterprise agile transformation, you already have at least one agile team in your organization, and now you're looking to scale agile to work on larger projects. Leverage the success of your existing agile team(s) to drive cultural change throughout the organization.

Gaining insight into motivation

Managers and developers often clash on the enterprise agility battlefield because their motivations differ. While management often embraces big organizational change and enterprise agile frameworks that promise improved productivity, quality, and customer satisfaction, developers often want management to get out of their way so they can do their best work.

Management

High-level managers are the first to embrace big changes. It's not because they're less conservative or more adventurous. It's because they're evaluated by how well they improve the organization's processes. When they can take a group of people and change the process to improve results, they see that as good management and strong leadership. Large frameworks, such as Scaled Agile Framework (SAFe) and Large-Scale Scrum Huge (LeSS Huge) are like catnip for these high-level managers.

Developers

On the other side, software developers and engineers see themselves as craftsmen. They want to build something that's elegant and satisfying, and they often view a large framework as a way for management to gain more control over their work. If you're a craftsman, the last thing you want to do is create something ugly because someone forces you to make a quick fix.

Large-scale organizational changes often create a tension between managers who want to rewire the machine and developers who want to create a world with fewer wires. Developers want agile, and they may think of enterprise agile as an attempt by management to make them *less* agile.

When you're starting your enterprise agile transformation, take a long objective look at each of these groups' motivations. If you have a manager who wants to make big changes, prepare yourself for a lot of communication and pushback from many of the developers. If the change is driven by developers, be prepared to convince the managers that this is a worthwhile change.

People often assume that others share their motivation. Managers assume everyone wants a big framework, while developers assume that everyone in the company wants (or should want) to deliver beautiful, elegant software. The truth is that the two aren't mutually exclusive. You can have a large framework that provides developers with the creative freedom they crave.

Whether you try the Kotter approach or Fearless Change, think about your particular organization and how each group feels about the change. Both of these approaches push you to better understand everyone's motivations so you can mitigate resistance and avoid unpleasant surprises.

- » Tackling the cultural aspect of a big change
- » Getting everyone in your organization to start thinking Lean
- » Selecting an enterprise agile framework
- » Making lasting changes

Chapter 11

Putting It All Together: Ten Steps to an Agile Enterprise

Enterprise agile transformations involve numerous variables, including the size of the company, its culture, the framework it chooses, the products it creates, and its existing agile competency, so each organization may approach its transformation in a unique way. However, if you're not sure how to get started, consider the following ten-step approach:

1. Identify your organization's culture.
2. List the strengths and challenges with changing your culture.
3. Select the best approach to organizational change management.
4. Train managers on Lean thinking.
5. Start a Lean-Agile Center of Excellence (LACE).

6. Choose a high-level value stream.
7. Assign a budget to the value stream.
8. Select an enterprise agile framework.
9. Shift from detailed plans to epics.
10. Respect and trust your people.

In this chapter, I explain each of these steps in detail.

Think of these steps only as a great way to get started. After you have an enterprise agile framework in place, any additional changes to improve the system will be more targeted to address areas that need improvement.

Step 1: Identifying Your Organization's Culture

The first step toward transforming your organization into an agile enterprise is to size up its existing culture, so you know what you're up against. In Chapter 9, I describe the four corporate culture types presented by William Schneider in his book, *The Reengineering Alternative* — control, competence, collaboration, and cultivation. However, placing your organization into one of those four culture types is challenging for two reasons:

- **As an insider, you may not be the best judge.** You may see your organization as you want it to be instead of as it really is, or you may be unable to see how your organization differs from others.
- **Your organization may have elements of two or more cultures.** For example, your organization may have a control culture with pockets of collaboration and cultivation cultures. What's most common is to have a dominant culture type and then a few characteristics of another type.

Often you can figure out your organizational culture model by touring your organization, observing behaviors, and asking yourself the following questions:

- **What's the office dress code?** For example, a formal dress code is more characteristic of a control culture.
- **How do people decorate their work area?** For example, if people hang copies of their diplomas, certifications, and awards, you're probably dealing with an organization that has a strong competence culture.

- **Where are people sitting?** If people are working in cubicles, then you're likely looking at a competence or control culture. If the cubicle area is surrounded by offices with doors, you're most likely looking at a control culture. If groups share work areas and can see one another's screens, you're probably dealing with a collaboration culture.
- **Where are people meeting?** If people are meeting in groups in the middle of an open floor plan, the organization probably has some aspects of a collaboration culture.
- **Who's calling the shots?** Do employees make decisions or do they receive their marching orders from the top down (as in a control culture)?
- **Do people look happy?** People are generally happiest when they're able to contribute to express themselves and when their opinions matter, as in a collaboration culture. In a strictly controlled environment, people show up for work, put in their time, and go home.
- **What's the noise level?** A noisy environment is more typical of a collaboration culture, but you can have a very noisy office in which everyone is working independently; for example, an office full of real estate brokers.

TIP

As you gather and analyze your evidence, follow these tips and cautions to make a more objective assessment:

- Gather plenty of evidence and look for patterns of behavior. Don't draw your conclusion based on only one or two pieces of evidence.
- Assemble a group of three or more people to make the assessment, so it's not based on one person's opinion. Make sure everyone agrees about the evidence, and then have everyone cast a ballot for the culture type he thinks is predominant in the organization. Approach this vote as you would play a round of planning poker: Vote and then discuss the reasons each person voted the way he did. Continue this cycle of voting and discussing until you reach consensus. Work toward ranking the four culture types from strongest to weakest in the organization.
- Keep in mind that your organization may have one dominant culture with characteristics of other culture types.
- Beware of *confirmation bias* — interpreting data based on preexisting beliefs. For example, everyone in your group may think your organization has a strong collaboration culture, so it gathers evidence and analyzes it in a way to show that the organization has a collaboration culture, even though the organization actually has a strong control culture. Make a conscious effort to be objective.

TIP

Chances are good your organization has a control culture or at least some elements of a control culture, because it's the most prevalent culture type. In fact, most organizations have to work hard to adopt something other than a control culture. Up until recently most of the largest companies relied on a pretty strict hierarchy, which spawns some habits that are tough to break.

REMEMBER

No culture is good or bad, better or worse. Every culture is just an underlying system the organization decided to create and reinforce, and it may have a valuable role to play in the organization's success. What's important is that you understand the culture you're dealing with, so you can implement your agile transformation more effectively and efficiently.

Step 2: Listing the Strengths and Challenges with Changing Your Culture

Different elements of your organization's culture may accelerate or hinder your change initiative, so try to identify these elements early on. One way to identify potential assets and liabilities within your organization is to assess your culture's strengths, weaknesses, opportunities, and threats (SWOT). You can then take advantage of your strengths and try to minimize the impact of your weaknesses.

Create a SWOT diagram as shown in Figure 11-1. At the top of the diagram, write the dominant culture in your organization followed by the secondary culture type (if any). Create a box for each of the SWOT categories — Strengths, Weaknesses, Opportunities, and Threats.

Collaborate with your group to identify specific strengths, weaknesses, opportunities, and threats inherent in your organization's culture that are relevant to your enterprise agile transformation. Record the items your group identifies in each of the relevant boxes, as shown in Figure 11-1.

Your SWOT diagram can be a valuable tool in your agile transformation. For example, one of the strengths identified in the SWOT diagram shown in Figure 11-1 is "Strong PMO" (*PMO* stands for project management office). You can leverage the power of a strong, supportive PMO by using it to drive your enterprise agile transformation.

Dominant Culture: Control

Cultural Elements: Competence

Strengths	Weaknesses
Mandatory Training Executive Buy-in Strong PMO	Risk Averse Next-New-Thing Fatigue
Opportunities	**Threats**
New CIO Great Coaches	Well-Established Hierarchy Functional Managers

FIGURE 11-1: A SWOT diagram of your company's culture.

WARNING

Keep in mind that one organization's strengths may be another organization's weaknesses. If your PMO doesn't support agile, then "Strong PMO" would go in the Threats box, and you'd have to figure out a way to address this potential source of resistance.

Spend extra time on the Opportunities category, because opportunities often provide the impetus to overcome resistance within the organization. Opportunities give people a good reason to embrace change. Look for opportunities in your agile transformation that failed change initiatives from the past didn't have. When you present your SWOT analysis to the organization, you can then use these opportunities to answer the question, "Why will this change initiative succeed when so many others have failed?" You may even want to address specific change initiatives from the past to explain why they failed.

REMEMBER

Think of your SWOT diagram as an analytical tool for developing your game plan. You're identifying your team's strengths and weaknesses, so you can leverage your strengths and minimize the impact of your weaknesses. For example, if you identify strong corporate leadership as a threat and your development teams as a strength, you may decide that a bottom-up approach to your agile transformation would be best, as explained in Chapter 10.

CASE STUDY

A MISTAKEN CULTURAL ASSESSMENT

I once worked for an organization that was convinced it had an open collaboration culture even though the evidence suggested it had a well-established control culture. The organization was divided into functional areas, and each person knew her place in the organization. Managers were often promoted based on the number of "direct reports" they had on their teams. But the people on their agile transformation team had a very strong confirmation bias. They thought that a control culture sounded too cold and harsh. It didn't reflect their values as an organization.

The agile transformation team created a SWOT diagram of the organization's strengths and challenges, but it didn't reflect the reality in the organization. Team members thought that their primary challenge was getting everybody through training and that their strength was working together in teams.

When the time came to choose a change management strategy, they based their choice on a lot of misinformation. They chose to go with Fearless Change, because they thought it was the best approach for collaborative organizations with a strong drive to work together in teams.

When they started their agile transformation, they quickly encountered serious obstacles. Many of the managers didn't want to loan out their team members to this grassroots effort. The managers were afraid that if they were stripped of their direct reports they would not be promoted (or worse), so they only allowed team members to participate only when they had nothing else on their plates. Of course, for many of the team members that was just a euphemism for *never*.

This organization would have had a much easier time had it matched its change management strategy with the reality of the organization and chosen the Kotter approach. The agile transformation team could've worked with executives to create a top-down change management strategy. Executives could've collaborated closely with managers to maintain their functional hierarchy. In Kotter's language, they could still run their own organizational "operating system."

The moral of this story is that you must be very careful when you identify your culture and your organization's strengths and challenges. If you're mistaken in your cultural assessment, you're likely to choose the wrong change management strategy and doom your transformation in the earliest stages.

Step 3: Selecting the Best Approach to Organizational Change Management

After you've identified your organization's culture and conducted a SWOT analysis, choose a change management technique, such as one of the two approaches presented in Chapter 10:

- **Kotter's eight-step change model (top down):** If your organization has strong leadership that supports the enterprise agile transformation, the eight-step Kotter approach is probably best.
- **Fearless Change (bottom up):** If you have influential groups within the organization that enthusiastically embrace enterprise agility and resistance or apathy at the top, driving change from the bottom up may be the most effective approach.

For example, if your organization has a strong PMO, the Kotter approach is likely to be best. A strong PMO has the logistics in place to drive a major transformation, including the reporting structure, in-house training, and relationships with key executives. The PMO would be well-positioned to create and maintain a dual operating system (see Chapter 10) that maintains the functional hierarchy while creating a more flexible team-based network.

On the other hand, if your organization has a stronger competence culture, you may be better off trying Fearless Change. Remember that competence cultures value knowledge and skills. A highly competent culture is likely to have more authority to make big changes, so an enterprise agile evangelist can have significant impact. She could become an expert in enterprise agility and convince others to make big changes.

REMEMBER

Your decision is not an either/or choice. Although the Kotter approach initiates change from the top, it includes bottom-up support through the use of an "army of volunteers." Likewise, although Fearless Change drives change from the bottom up, it relies on a change leader with some level of authority. You can certainly mix and match, choosing elements from both approaches. Your decision is whether to initiate change *primarily* from the top or bottom.

Step 4: Training Managers on Lean Thinking

For any enterprise agile transformation to succeed, top-level managers need to understand that enterprise agility is built on the foundation of Lean thinking — organizing activities in a way that eliminates waste to deliver optimum value. You can use the Simple Lean-Agile Mindset (SLAM), as I explain in Chapter 3, to show the system-level optimizations that are essential to successful enterprise agile transformations.

REMEMBER

Discourage your organization's leadership from thinking of enterprise agility as just a few new process improvements or as a collection of practices, such as small teams and daily stand-up meetings. Enterprise agility is bigger than that. By focusing on Lean thinking, you increase the scope of enterprise agility beyond processes and practices to a mindset. The focus is on delivering value to the customer in the most efficient manner possible.

One fact that top managers often have difficulty accepting is that local optimization differs from system-level optimization. For example, a super-productive employee can actually slow down a system, just as a star player can ruin a team. Instead of hiring and rewarding superstars, organizations need to look for people who have the knowledge, skills, and characteristics to complement the team.

Executives and directors are accustomed to thinking of the organization as broken into different functional areas with each functional area broken down into teams. They may have a difficult time imagining a team of superstars being slower than several teams of average performers. One team turning out too much work too fast can actually create a bottleneck that slows the entire process. Having a balanced system with everyone working at the same pace is most efficient.

REMEMBER

Many of the organizational improvements behind your enterprise agile transformation include system-level optimization, so managers need to grasp the concept and appreciate the value of system-level improvements. Be prepared to spend plenty of time training managers, so they understand the benefits and are ready to make big changes.

CASE STUDY

PLAYING THE PENNY GAME

I was training a group of executives and directors who were having trouble accepting the concept that they could achieve system-level optimization at the expense of local optimization. They kept saying, "I can't have my best workers slowed down so the rest of the organization can catch up." So, I decided to run an exercise called the penny game.

I divided the group into employees and managers so that each employee had a manager. I gave each employee a work queue of ten pennies and instructed them to flip the pennies over one at a time and then pass all ten pennies to the next employee. The manager timed how long it took the employee to turn over all ten pennies and pass them to the next employee.

I repeated the cycle reducing the queue size each time from ten to five and then two. For example, in the second round, the employee received the ten pennies in two batches of five. After flipping over five pennies, he would pass them along to the next person to flip. In the third round, the employee received pennies in five batches of two. After flipping over just two pennies, he passed them to the next employee. For each cycle, the manager recorded the time it took each employee to flip all ten pennies.

As you would expect, each employee required more time to flip and pass the pennies when the batch sizes were smaller. What's surprising, however, is how quickly the first and last batches moved through the system and were delivered (metaphorically speaking) to the customer (see the following table). Although smaller batch sizes reduced apparent local productivity for each employee — BA, Dev1, Dev2, Dev3, and so on — it increased system-level productivity with reduced lead time, faster cycle time, and improved production throughput.

	Batch Size		
Team Member	**10**	**5**	**2**
BA	17	19	22
Dev1	19	17	20
Dev2	22	23	25
Dev3	15	16	18
Dev4	30	22	23
UX/UI	18	17	20
QA1	25	24	22
QA2	26	22	28

(continued)

(continued)

	Batch Size		
Team Member	**10**	**5**	**2**
UAT	25	26	28
Customer First	**3:35**	**1:42**	**37**
Customer Last	**3:35**	**1:55**	**1:08**

For example, it took BA 17 seconds to flip and pass a batch of ten pennies. It took 22 seconds when that same BA flipped and passed ten pennies in batches of two. However, when pennies were flipped and passed in batches of two, the customer received the first batch of pennies in only 37 seconds compared to three minutes and 35 seconds when the pennies were flipped and passed in batches of ten. The smaller the queue size, the faster the customer received value. Perhaps even more important, by processing the pennies in batches of two, all pennies passed through the system in less than one-third the time as when they were processed in batches of ten!

By keeping work moving smoothly through the system, you reduce wait times and achieve system-level optimization even though local optimization suffers.

Step 5: Starting a Lean-Agile Center of Excellence (LACE)

Whether you initiate change at the top or bottom, create a Lean-Agile Center of Excellence (LACE) to transition the entire organization to a Lean-Agile Mindset (see Chapter 10). A Center of Excellence (CoE) is a group of enthusiastic and knowledgeable people who promote change throughout the organization.

To create your LACE, recruit an individual within the organization who has the knowledge, enthusiasm, and charisma to bring others on board. (This may be you.) Provide this individual with the resources she needs, including a meeting room, a budget, and, most important, the authority to make changes.

As you form your LACE and run your meetings and events, follow these guidelines:

- Create a fun group that's passionate about improving the organization. Recruit the type of people who are always looking for new ways to shorten their commute to work and to manage their email more efficiently.

- Recruit doers, not just talkers. Look for people who persevere in the face of adversity. Impatience is okay, but they need to be in it for the long haul.
- Develop a LACE mission statement, goal, and objectives. Formulate a vision of what the organization will look like after it becomes an agile enterprise, and develop a plan for how your LACE will help the organization achieve that vision.
- Charter the group with authority from the top to spearhead change. Your LACE will disintegrate quickly if all its efforts are shut down by middle managers. The LACE should realize that it will encounter some resistance, but its members shouldn't begin to feel that their endeavors are fruitless.
- Maintain a meeting and event calendar with a cadence of regularly scheduled meetings and events. Without a schedule, people are likely to lose interest and stop attending meetings. A predictable cadence helps people plan other commitments around these events, reducing potential conflicts.
- End every event with consensus and an action plan. Never "agree to disagree." Instead, give all participants the opportunity to argue their ideas, but at the end of the event, the group should have consensus and an action plan. Feel free to have a show of hands if you can't reach consensus.

TIP

Find the sweet spot between fun and effective. Remember that most of the people in your LACE are volunteers. They could be working on other projects, and they have a life outside of work. They usually join the LACE out of an interest in improving the organization. Make events festive and productive, so your volunteers look forward to meetings and feel as though the LACE is making a positive impact on the organization. If you give a one-hour PowerPoint presentation about the benefits of the Lean-Agile Mindset, you'll quickly find yourself with many empty seats.

REMEMBER

If your CoE is staffed with volunteers, know that getting real work done with a volunteer army is always a challenge, especially when you're working on an initiative that's likely to encounter resistance. By finding the sweet spot between fun and effective, you can draw the crowds while making a rewarding impact.

Step 6: Choosing a High-Level Value Stream

Your LACE should collaborate with upper management to identify value streams, as I explain in Chapters 4 and 8. (A *value stream* is a series of steps for building solutions that deliver value to a customer continuously.) Value streams come in two types:

- **Operational value streams:** Steps to provide goods or services to customers internally or externally to generate revenue for the organization. For example, an organization may have a value stream for selling and delivering a product to a customer.

» **Development value streams:** Steps to design and build new products, systems, and services capabilities, such as a software application, a driverless car, or an internal process. For example, the process used to create a product sold to a customer would be a development value stream.

To make your organization Lean, you eventually want to optimize both operational and development value streams, but I recommend starting your agile transformation with a development value stream for two reasons:

» Optimizing a development value stream is easier, because you can focus on a system for developing a single product.

» Your work will be more interesting and rewarding, providing greater motivation for everyone involved in your enterprise agile transformation.

Focus on a development value stream that's a key part of the business. Look for a value stream that meets the following four overlapping criteria:

» **It has leadership's support.** You're more likely to rally leadership support for your enterprise agile transformation by improving development of a product that leadership values.

» **It is clearly high level.** Choose a value stream that everyone in the organization understands and appreciates. If people know the product and appreciate its value to the organization, explaining the benefits of enterprise agility will be easier, and your wins will be more visible.

» **It crosses functional areas.** Choose a product that requires collaboration across functional areas, such as business analysis, design, programming, and testing, so you'll need to create one or more small, cross-functional teams.

» **It poses a real challenge or opportunity.** Choose a value stream that has an opportunity for significant improvement, so that your success delivers real value to the organization. A big win will rally the entire organization around future extension of enterprise agility to other areas of the organization.

Step 7: Assigning a Budget to the Value Stream

With enterprise agility, you need to stop budgeting for projects and start budgeting for value streams. Instead of carefully defining the scope of a project, as is common with project budgeting, the scope remains flexible, and the development team integrates functionality into the product incrementally according to an ever-evolving *product backlog* (a prioritized list of work items).

Value stream budgeting moves away from focusing on what the project will do and instead puts all the emphasis on what *value* the product provides.

Think of it this way. Sometimes you walk into a restaurant and you have a complete notion of what you want to order. Maybe you have a favorite sandwich or a dish you've ordered in the past. Other times you walk into the restaurant with a set budget in mind (maybe you don't want to spend more than $30) and a general notion that you just want to get something delicious to eat. In the first example you're funding a project. You know exactly what you want to buy and you know how much it will cost. In the second example you're funding your value stream. It's valuable to you to have something delicious to eat. When you went to the restaurant you don't really know the final product, you just want it to be delicious.

The advantage of value stream budgeting is that it more closely aligns with the enterprise agile mindset. You're giving the teams flexibility to narrow down the highest-value features and work to deliver a high-quality product. You don't have a complete picture of what their product will be when it's finished. Instead, your teams work closely with the customers to zero-in on what they want. Your aligning your organization and agreeing on the highest-value parts of your product.

PROJECT BUDGETING

Most organizations still budget their work as *projects.* They have a budget based on the *project management triangle* (also referred to as the *iron triangle*):

- **Scope:** The product's features or requirements
- **Resources:** Money, personnel, equipment, and so on
- **Time:** The schedule or deadline

Each of these three points in the iron triangle is a constraint. Generally, a change in any of these constraints impacts the other constraints and the overall quality of the product. For example, if you broaden the scope by adding features, the product is likely to cost more and require more time to complete.

CASE STUDY

SHIFTING BUDGETS FROM PROJECTS TO VALUE STREAMS

I once worked for an organization that developed a payroll processing system. It wanted to increase its organizational agility, but was accustomed to funding projects, not value streams. It would work with the customer to develop a list of requirements and a schedule for delivery. Then, it would develop a budget based on the resources and the amount of time required.

Budgeting was a major challenge, because the organization operated in silos, and each project required pulling people from different functional areas. They needed developers, database engineers, business analysts, graphic designers, testers, and so on. The team had a project manager, and each team member had a manager from his own functional area. To get people to work on a project, the project manager had to coordinate with the functional area manager, and if the project took longer than expected, the project manager had to struggle to keep the person on the team before that person got pulled to work on another project.

When the customer requested a new feature (a way for employees to view their paychecks from their smartphones), the organization decided to budget for the value stream instead of for the project.

The organization created a cross-functional team to deliver the new feature and assigned it a budget based on the team's estimate of how long it would take to deliver. The team figured it could deliver a solution in four weeks, so the budget needed to account only for the cost of the team over that four-week time frame. The team had no list of requirements, because the solution was uncertain; for example, the team could create an app or just add an area to the customer's website that employees could access using a mobile web browser.

The organization assigned a budget to the value stream and left it up to the customer and cross-functional team to develop a satisfactory solution.

Step 8: Selecting an Enterprise Agile Framework

Prior to initiating your enterprise agile transformation, choose one of the agile frameworks presented in Part 2, or mix and match elements from various frameworks to tailor your own solution. Refer to Figure 11-2 for guidance:

- **Along the horizontal x-axis:** From left to right, frameworks range from highly prescriptive to more empirical. A highly prescriptive approach, such as the Scaled Agile Framework® (SAFe®), has more roles, practices, and guidance. More empirical frameworks, such as Large-Scale Scrum (LeSS) and the Spotify Engineering Culture, encourage experimentation, measurement, and learning.
- **Along the vertical y-axis:** From bottom to top, frameworks differ depending on the change management strategy — whether change is initiated at the bottom (team) level or is driven from the top (enterprise) level down. Note that SAFe, Disciplined Agile Delivery (DAD), and LeSS all tend to be frameworks that require a top-down change management style to implement.

Use Figure 11-2 to match your organization's existing culture to a suitable framework. For example, if you have a strong control culture, consider a prescriptive framework that you can use to drive change from the top down, such as SAFe. On the other hand, if you have a strong competence culture, you may be better off using a more empirical framework with a greater emphasis on teams, such as LeSS, which gives teams more flexibility in how they do their work and enables you to leverage their expertise in improving the process.

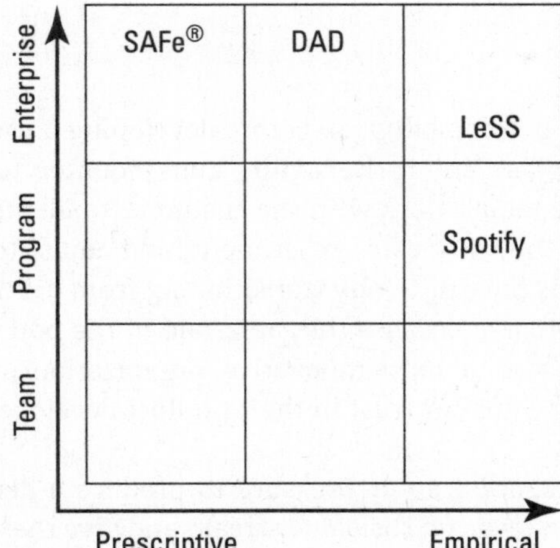

FIGURE 11-2: Characteristics of the top enterprise agile frameworks.

WARNING

Choosing an enterprise agile framework that clashes with your organization's culture can lead to disaster. For example, trying to force the Spotify Engineering Culture on an organization with a strong hierarchy would be very disruptive. A company with a deeply ingrained hierarchy is likely to resist a system that reorganizes everyone into squads, tribes, chapters, and guilds. Such a change would also push a lot of responsibility for process improvement down to small squads of employees, which would introduce far too much uncertainty for high-level management to accept.

WARNING

Don't choose a framework just because it worked well for an organization you admire, because that framework may not be the right match for your organization. For example, many organizations choose a framework merely because it worked for Google, Facebook, Apple, or Microsoft, but when they try the same approach, they fail miserably, because the framework clashes with their organization's existing culture. To make it even more tempting, many consulting firms that promote a given framework try to sell it on the basis that it worked for a few top-performing and well-known companies. Avoid the temptation. Think instead about how suitable the framework is for *your* organization.

REMEMBER

Also remember to choose a framework based on the type of organization you are, *not* the organization you want to be. Compare your transformation to performance training. If you're terribly out of shape, you don't adopt a training program designed for world-class, long-distance runners. Instead, you choose a training program that's better suited to your existing physical condition. After you achieve a certain fitness level, you can step up to a more aggressive program.

Step 9: Shifting from Detailed Plans to Epics

Large enterprises favor predictability, so before developing a product, they insist on having a detailed plan. Enterprise agility runs counter to this traditional approach. Instead, agile teams work with the customer to identify what the customer needs, and then they innovate, experiment, and adjust to develop a solution. Many organizations have difficulty transitioning from detailed planning to a more creative agile approach, because they're afraid of the potential for negative outcomes. However, to become more innovative, organizations must reduce their aversion to risk and place greater trust in their product developers.

TIP

If people in your organization apply pressure to produce a detailed plan, push back. Encourage them to focus on the value stream and give the agile teams creative license to innovate solutions. For example, suppose your organization manufactures breakfast cereals. Your customer wants a tasty low-carb alternative. Leadership demands research and planning. They want a complete list of ingredients, nutritional values, and even the name of the new cereal before even one flake is toasted. But that's not agile. In such a case, you need to push back and have the organization turn the project over to the team in the form of an *epic* — a lightweight business case for creating the product.

Instead of handing the team a detailed list of product requirements, you give the team an epic, such as "Create a nutritious and delicious low-carbohydrate breakfast cereal that will blow the competition off the shelves." The team can then start experimenting with different recipes to lower the carbohydrate content while improving the cereal's flavor and texture. The customer would taste each product increment and provide feedback about how to improve it. The team may even send samples out to some of the customer's more influential social media fans to obtain additional feedback. Over the course of several product iterations, the team would eventually arrive at the winning recipe, and the customer could deliver the product to its market.

The whole point to having agile teams is to optimize value by allowing teams to innovate. Giving teams detailed product requirements undermines the purpose of enterprise agility — to improve value through innovation.

Step 10: Respecting and Trusting Your People

As organizations strive to become more agile enterprises, they often focus on frameworks, roles, and practices and lose sight of the more important aspects of enterprise agile transformations — principles and people. Innovation is a product of the mind. It's the ideas people come up with when they have the knowledge, skills, and resources to do their jobs and the respect and trust to think independently. Otherwise, people simply do what they're told, which stifles innovation.

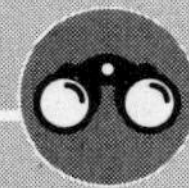

A LONG WAY TO GO

I was coaching a large organization that was trying to change its cubicle structure to an open workspace. I was walking the floor with one of the top executives, explaining the advantages of an open workspace. We stopped to chat next to someone working diligently in his cubicle. The executive rested his elbow on the corner of the cubicle as I explained the benefits of face-to-face communication and how it impacts collaboration. He pointed down to the person in the cubicle and asked me, "How many resources like this do you think we'll be able to fit in this open space?"

I immediately realized that the concept of an open workspace was three or four steps ahead of where the organization was in its understanding of agile. Likening people to resources, such as computers and printers, was a far cry from the Agile Manifesto. I had to go back to Step 4 to make sure the executives and managers were trained on Lean-Agile thinking.

As your organization embarks on its agile transformation, remind everyone of the Agile Manifesto (see Chapter 1). Highlight the first value: "Individuals and interactions over processes and tools." Reinforce that value among executives and all levels of management, so they know that the source of innovation is found in the organization's employees and their interactions with one another and with the organization's leaders and its customers.

REMEMBER

Respect for people is more than just an organizational optimization. It's a wholesale rewrite of how many executives view their workforce. In his book *Drive*, Daniel Pink highlights the three elements that motivate people at work:

- **Autonomy:** Most employees have an inherent desire to do quality work and have a positive impact on the organization's success. They need to feel that they're trusted to do a good job without a great deal of oversight and management intrusion. Unfortunately, many organizations value predictability over autonomy, and they end up stifling innovation and discouraging employees from taking initiative.
- **Mastery:** People like to feel as though they're great at their jobs, and most are willing to spend time outside of work and even invest in their own professional development to achieve mastery. Your organization's leadership would be wise to feed this desire for mastery by supporting personal and professional development.

  Your organization can encourage mastery by supporting communities of practice (see Chapter 5), a center of excellence (see Chapter 10), and guilds (see Chapter 7). For an additional investment, your organization may consider paying for employees to attend seminars or conferences, and it may provide tuition reimbursement for certain classes. The return on investment in terms of increased employee retention and improved knowledge and skills is well worth it.
- **Sense of purpose:** Employees want to feel as though they're having a significant positive impact on the organization's success. Seeing an idea come to life and significantly improve the end user's experience is a huge reward. It's what makes people want to jump out of bed in the morning eager to get to work.

Enterprise agility requires a culture of mutual respect and trust, and it nurtures such a culture. As soon as you transition to small, self-organized, cross-functional teams and stop providing teams with detailed product requirements or specifying *how* to build the product, employees naturally begin to look for ways to improve the product and the process for creating it. Management can help in two ways:

» **Get out of the way.** Although management traditionally assigns and supervises work, in an agile enterprise, it needs to get out of the way. The product owner maintains a product backlog (a prioritized list of work items), and the team draws from this list to determine what must be done. How it gets the work done is up to the team.

» **Serve the teams.** Management should regard themselves as *enablers.* They should provide the teams with whatever they need to excel, whether it's hardware and software, training, agile coaching, specialized tools, or something else entirely. That kind of support will maximize the potential value created by the team.

REMEMBER

Look for ways to continuously improve your organization's workforce and the systems it uses to deliver value to the customer. These two Lean-Agile practices will drive much of your organization's continuous improvement.

Part 4
The Part of Tens

IN THIS PART . . .

Recognize ten common reasons organizations fail in their enterprise agile transformation attempts and how you can avoid becoming the next casualty.

Spot ten common obstacles to making big changes and look at various ways to overcome these obstacles.

Find the motivation you need to keep moving forward by reminding yourself of ten ways enterprise agility improves product delivery and makes everyone's job easier and more fun.

IN THIS CHAPTER

» Avoiding common pitfalls

» Getting started in the right direction

Chapter 12
Ten Reasons Enterprise Agile Transformations Fail

Every organization that succeeds in transforming into an agile enterprise does so in a unique way. Organizations that fail often do so for similar reasons. In this chapter, I point out the ten most common reasons enterprise agile transformations fail. By knowing the most common reasons for failure, you have a better chance of avoiding disaster.

The Organization's Culture Clashes with Agile Values

Many organizations have a disconnect between what they are and what they'd like to be. They may see themselves as nimble, high-tech companies, when in reality they have a strong command-and-control culture. Having a strong control culture is fine. In fact, large organizations with well-established functional areas often do very well. However, organizations often struggle to implement big changes when they overlook their control culture as a challenge to overcome. They don't have any interest in changing their core values; they want agile to "fit in."

CASE STUDY

ENTERPRISE AGILITY IN NAME ONLY

I once worked for an organization that had a strong command-and-control culture. During a presentation, I was trying to describe how enterprise agility is a step in a new direction. The audience was skeptical. The internal agile transformation lead said, "We run our own version of agile here that doesn't involve a change in our management structure." Unfortunately, while the organization did have an enterprise agile framework, it wasn't benefiting from it, because it clashed with the organization's control culture. The company simply had teams that did what they were told.

An enterprise agile transformation is a radical organizational change. While you may be able to retain the corporate hierarchy, that hierarchy must give its agile teams more power to innovate and develop solutions. Using the Kotter approach to drive change from the top down (see Chapter 10), an organization with a strong control culture can create a dual operating system that maintains the hierarchy while establishing an autonomous agile network that delivers innovative products. However, if the hierarchy insists on controlling the network, the organization will have enterprise agility in name only.

Teams Aren't Interested in Making Changes

Many teams just don't have much incentive to change. In his book *The Five Dysfunctions of a Team*, Patrick Lencioni points out that many teams lack commitment or don't have a high degree of trust with each other or the organization. Trust may be lacking for several reasons, including the following:

- The organization has a strong competence culture. Team members are reluctant to share knowledge because their competence gives them greater authority in the organization.
- Management treats employees like "warm bodies," instead of treating them with respect.
- The organization suffers from a lot of turnover, so employees aren't around long enough to build a culture of mutual respect and trust.
- The organization has a lot of contract workers on its development teams. They have no incentive to change the way they work, because they know that as soon as their contracts expire, they'll be moving on.

Prior to embarking on an enterprise agile transformation, make sure you have at least a few long-term employees to anchor your teams and an organization-wide commitment to create a culture of mutual respect and trust. Without stability, respect, and trust, you'll have a tough time motivating people to invest the hard work necessary to achieve enterprise agility. If you don't have those three essentials (stability, respect, and trust), consider delaying your transformation and working on shoring up those areas first.

Executive Support Is Lacking

Executives and managers typically delegate the enterprise agile transformation to directors and team managers and get updates during quarterly meetings. Executives may step in for product demonstrations and offer some words of encouragement. When they leave they offer their tacit approval of the process and congratulate everybody on trying this new approach. Unfortunately, acknowledging the change is not the same as supporting it. Leadership usually believes that the organization will continue to operate the way it always has, just a little better.

You want your executives to be fully involved in many of the details of the change. Remember that enterprise agility is a radical organizational change. It's much different from how most organizations currently deliver products. Work hard to try to frame it that way to help keep your executives involved in the process. If you can't change your executives' expectations, then the changes you implement will be very vulnerable the first time executives get something different from what they're used to seeing.

Key changes must also be made at the highest levels of the organization. If the organization doesn't support value stream budgeting (see Chapter 4), it can be difficult to get your teams to deliver predictable increments of customer value. That is why you want to be careful not to frame your enterprise agile transformation as just a bunch of updated engineering practices. This is an organizational change that will impact your budgets, culture, and overall organizational mindset.

REMEMBER

You actually want your managers and executives to be a little uncomfortable with the change. Their discomfort shows that they understand the scope of the transformation. A lot of people in your organization will have to be retrained. You may even see a short dip in productivity as the organization tries to optimize its own process. You want your managers and executives asking tough questions and pushing back on some of your assumptions. If they don't have this level of involvement, you'll likely get a lot of pushback the first time you hit a real obstacle. Corporate leadership may even encourage you to go back to the way things were until you figure out how to make everyone happy. If that happens, your organizational change will be derailed indefinitely.

The Proposed Change Is Too Radical

Transforming an entire organization into an agile enterprise is a major undertaking. Before you start, evaluate your organization's track record for implementing change. If your organization has a poor record for making big changes, you may want to take a more gradual approach. Instead of aiming for a home run, just try to get on base.

REMEMBER

Being incapable of making a radical organizational change isn't necessarily bad. What's bad is discovering the fact after you started the transformation.

If you doubt your organization's ability to undergo a major transformation, you can still improve your organization's agility by making small changes, such as the following:

- Use Kanban and Lean, as explained in Chapter 8, to reduce waste, optimize workflow, and nudge your organization in the direction of adopting a more Lean-Agile Mindset.
- Try forming one or two agile teams to handle a product or a system within the organization where you think an agile team could offer some value.
- Start a Lean-Agile Center of Excellence (see Chapter 11) to encourage people in your organization to start thinking about an agile transformation and to support them in their efforts to implement changes.
- Break one or more functional areas into small self-organized, cross-functional teams and build slowly on their success.

The Customer Won't Cooperate

An enterprise agile transformation changes not only how your organization delivers value to customers, but also how your customers are involved in the process. Some customers may be reluctant to change. If your customers have grown comfortable with coming up with an idea and then "throwing it over the wall" to your organization to complete, they may not want to invest the time and effort in collaboration. Just as you need to sell your organization on the benefits of agile, you may need to sell your customers on the concept of agile product development.

Until your customers are on board, avoid embarking on your enterprise agile transformation. Without close collaboration with your customers, you're likely to struggle with your enterprise agile transformation. You'll end up with agile teams being handed a list of product requirements, and you'll get very little benefit from your enterprise agile transformation.

Leadership Refuses to Invest in Training

One easy way to tell whether your organization is invested in making a large-scale change is to look at leadership's commitment to training. If your managers balk at the cost of training, they're likely to neglect other key elements, such as coaching, workspace design, and the expenses involved in greater face-to-face communication.

Training is a key to a successful enterprise agile transformation. As more people in your organization are trained and begin to adopt the Lean-Agile Mindset, everyone begins to see the tangible benefits, which motivates both leadership and employees to invest more in the transformation.

An added benefit of training sessions is that they act as a town hall meeting, enabling attendees to voice their concerns or reservations about enterprise agility, which is helpful in breaking down resistance. If the naysayers aren't given an opportunity to express their concerns, their resistance to change will only deepen and spread. This benefit alone is often worth the cost of training.

The Developers Insist on Requirements

Some software developers enter the profession because they like the idea of quietly solving problems in their own workspace. They may not like the idea of working in close collaboration with the customer. They may not even like the idea of working closely with other developers. This is especially the case if they've been able to work from home for years on their own special corner of the product. Bringing these people into the office and getting them to collaborate can be a difficult transition.

Many developers still believe that software development is a solitary activity. They see it as a struggle between one person and a larger problem; their job is to come up with an elegant solution. Unfortunately, software products are becoming too large for this type of product delivery, and no organization can afford to have a single individual in charge of a critical function of its product.

CASE STUDY

PROGRESS HELD HOSTAGE

I once worked for an organization that had a developer who worked for years creating his own middleware between the website and the database. He worked from home and communicated with the rest of the team only during early-morning meetings. He spent the rest of the day optimizing the software and slowly adding features. He insisted on using his own requirements document — a simple list of the new features and a requested completion date. This person had built the middleware from the ground up, so no one else in the organization knew anything about how to develop it.

When the organization tried to switch to a more collaborative approach, this person threatened to quit. He said he couldn't spend time explaining his software to the rest of the team. He wanted to work solely off of requirements and didn't like the idea of collaborating to improve the overall value of the software. Because the organization was scared of losing this key person, it indefinitely postponed the team's transformation.

WARNING

If you have a developer who's not interested in collaboration, then work hard to change that person's perspective and see the value in closer teamwork. If that's not possible, then work to get him off your team. As Netflix CEO Reed Hastings said, "Do not tolerate brilliant jerks. The cost to teamwork is too high."

Each Team Wants to Do Its Own Thing

Some organizations have agile teams long before they embark on their enterprise agile transformation. Often the teams develop independently of one another. Each team inspects and adapts and creates its own version of agile team practices. You may have one Scrum team that uses a project manager as its Scrum Master and other Extreme Programming team that doesn't really have a customer representative.

Having an eclectic collection of modified agile teams is one way to begin an enterprise agile transformation, but such an approach can actually slow down product delivery. Remember that most enterprise agile frameworks promote systems thinking. What works well for one team may actually slow down the rest of the organization (see the sidebar in Chapter 11, "Playing the penny game"). To conduct an effective enterprise agile transformation, some teams may need to unlearn what they've been doing in order to adopt a more uniform approach.

TIP

If you have a mix of agile team practices throughout the organization, you can get all your teams on the same page by providing uniform agile training:

- Provide the same agile training to all teams.
- Break up existing teams and form new teams. If you send a seasoned agile team through training as a unit, its members may have a confirmation bias that makes the team less receptive to new ideas. By breaking up your teams and creating new teams, you can reduce this bias and give your teams a fresh start. Keep in mind that newly formed (or re-formed) teams require time to adjust and achieve a new performing equilibrium. Team stability (the "stable teams" pattern) is widely regarded as a major precondition for higher performing teams.
- Spread team members across different training sessions to further reduce the risk of confirmation bias and to minimize the impact of training sessions on the teams' daily work.

Nobody Has a Plan to Measure Improvements

Prior to embarking on your enterprise agile transformation, you should have metrics in place to measure progress and a system in place for gathering and analyzing relevant data. Otherwise, your organization may have no way of knowing whether the transformation is having the desired results. Consider using a tool such as Agile Transformation's AgilityHealth Radar, shown in Figure 12-1.

If you decide to use your own system, first figure out how you're going to measure enterprise agility success and the type of data you need to collect, such as the following:

- Customer satisfaction
- Team output
- Workflow optimization
- Waste reduction
- Number of defects/bugs

What's more difficult to measure are overall process improvement and team collaboration. You can give your team questionnaires, but the results may not provide an accurate assessment. After all, with questionnaires, team members are grading their own progress.

REMEMBER

A good indication that team members are collaborating well together on a cross-functional team is team cadence. If everyone on the team is always working on something, and the team is pulling work through the system at a consistent pace, that's a reflection that everyone is working together to get things done. However, if the team is still functioning as a collection of specialists, with one team member focusing on coding, another on testing, another on interface design, and so on, you'll see team members waiting on other team members to complete their tasks.

TIP

Use a Kanban board, as explained in Chapter 8, to visualize workflow. You want to see a steady flow of work going into the system and a steady flow coming out. Bursts of productivity are usually a sign that a team member is specializing, causing a bottleneck. When you spot a bottleneck, encourage teams to become more cross-functional and collaborative. Point out that when team members stick to their areas of expertise, it slows down the system.

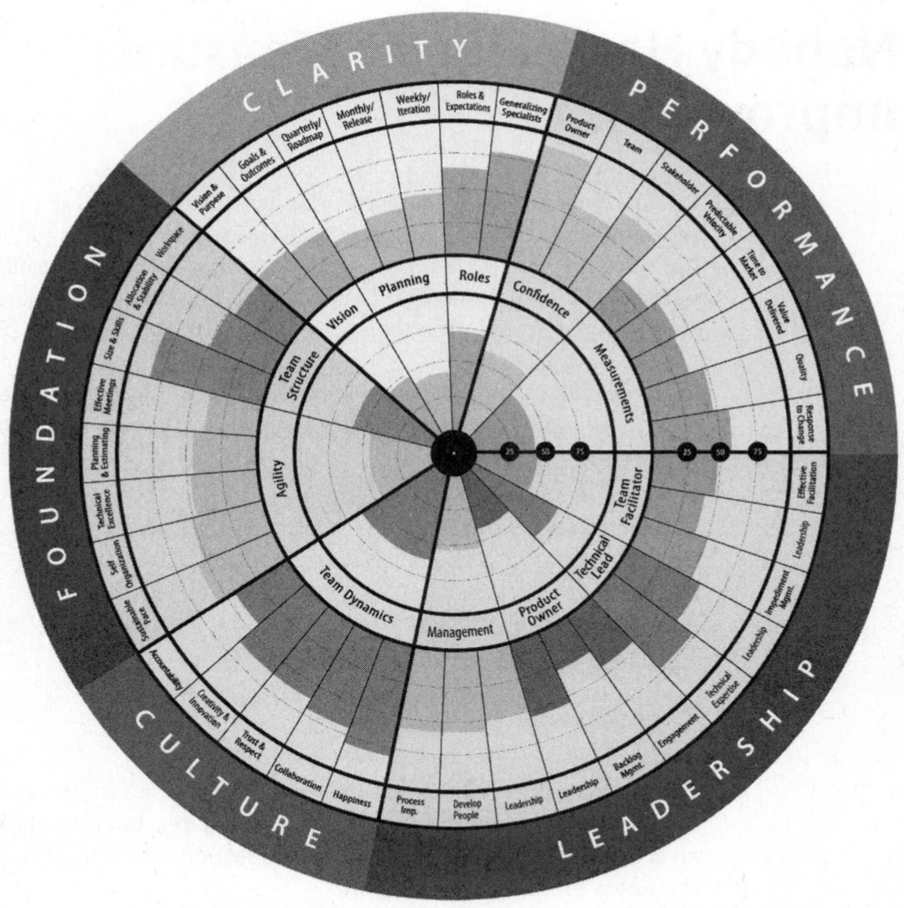

FIGURE 12-1: The AgilityHealth Radar tool.

Image from Sally Elatta, `https://agilityhealthradar.com`. Copyright © 2017 by Agile Transformation, Inc. Reprinted by permission.

The Functional Areas Are Too Deeply Entrenched

When functional areas, such as analysis, coding, and testing, are deeply entrenched, team members may struggle to transition to cross-functional teams even after they've received cross-training. Many team members have trouble accepting the cross-functional approach as a legitimate way to work. They're accustomed to the traditional model: "When you finish your task, I start my task." They need to make a conscious effort to change their mindset; otherwise, they just fall back to that way of working. What often happens is that mini silos form within a team with each team member focusing on certain tasks.

TIP

Where possible, co-locate the cross-functional team members, so they aren't living in a functional "camp" based on their primary technical expertise. Within a team, try various approaches to "pairing" and "swarming" around work items in progress, to get people more used to collaborative development.

CASE STUDY

STRUGGLING TO CHANGE

I once worked for an organization that had about eight agile teams, but they were struggling to deliver at the end of their sprints. When I went to talk to the teams, I soon realized that team members were creating their own silos. Each team member embraced his own functional role. The developers focused solely on development and then passed their work along to the testers, who then passed the product to the UI developers to handle the layout and add buttons and other graphics.

I mentioned that cross-functional teams were supposed to cut horizontally across the different functional areas, that everyone on the team needed to work together to deliver the highest-value work items. I pointed out that their focus needed to be on completing work items and optimizing workflow and not on what each team member knew how to do. I encountered a lot of resistance. The testers weren't interested in developing software. The graphic designers had no interest in learning how to write Java code.

I asked the team to run a couple of experiments during each sprint to see whether they could improve their productivity by having everyone work together. After a few experiments, the teams eventually started to see the benefits of cross-training and collaboration (learning to become "generalizing specialists").

» Rallying leadership to support your enterprise agile transformation

» Using consultants wisely

» Overcoming pockets of resistance

Chapter 13
Ten Tips for Overcoming Common Obstacles

Transforming an organization with well-established functional areas into a collection of small, closely aligned teams requires a major overhaul. In this chapter, I provide ten tips to smooth your path to enterprise agility.

When organizations fail in their efforts to become agile enterprises, they often conclude that enterprise agility isn't the right fit for them. However, the reason an enterprise agile transformation fails can usually be traced back to the organization's approach to change management or its resistance to change, not to enterprise agility.

Develop a Clear Roadmap

Prior to embarking on an enterprise agile transformation, develop a roadmap — a path that leads from point A (where your organization is today) to point B (your vision of what your organization will look like when it's an agile enterprise).

If your organization has a control culture (most large organizations do), then your roadmap may look like a project plan:

1. **Identify the change.**
2. **Analyze the change.**
3. **Convince the stakeholders.**

   Stakeholders must do the following:

   - Agree that the organization needs to change.
   - Agree to start the change.
   - Commit to helping make the change.
4. **Implement the change.**
5. **Monitor the change and make adjustments.**

Form a change management team, complete with a team leader, to implement this five-phase plan.

WARNING

Approaching your enterprise agile transformation as a project is fine, but don't think of the transformation as a one-time event. Projects, by definition, have a beginning and an end, but enterprise agility is an ongoing process.

CASE STUDY

GETTING CUSTOMERS INVOLVED

I once worked for an organization that was in the middle of an enterprise agile transformation. The organization had no trouble getting people to participate in the Scrum events, such as the sprint review, but it struggled to get its customer involved. The customer just wasn't accustomed to the level of collaboration required.

I had a coaching session with an executive at the customer's organization during which I explained that without customer collaboration, the developers would have a hard time meeting expectations. This executive showed up at the next sprint review. When other people in the customer's organization heard about it, they started showing up at sprint reviews as well.

Sometimes, a public display of support from an executive is all it takes.

Engaging in the planning process is more important than having a detailed plan in place. As Dwight D. Eisenhower once said, "Plans are worthless, but planning is everything." The goal of your planning process is to reach consensus on how to start to change. When everyone's on board, you'll have less friction to overcome.

Find Support at the Top

Leadership alignment is one of the key challenges to any big change initiative. Executives and managers must take more than a casual interest. If you're following Kotter's eight-step change model (see Chapter 10), executives should help set the vision. If you're changing from the bottom up, executives should demonstrate their support in ways that are visible to others in the organization; for example:

- Set a budget for the change management plan.
- Invest in training and coaching.
- Provide support for the organization's Lean-Agile Center of Excellence (LACE), as explained in Chapter 11.
- Attend enterprise agile transformation meetings, ask questions, and provide input.

Engaging others in the transformation is much easier when they see the organization's leadership playing an active role. Often just having one of the organization's executives sit in on a meeting is enough to keep your change efforts moving forward. What people see often has much more impact than what they hear.

Set Realistic Expectations

Every big idea comes with big expectations, but transforming a large, slow organization into an agile enterprise doesn't happen overnight. In fact, your agile transformation should be a never-ending process of continuous improvement. If you set your expectations too high, you and others in your organization may give up when you don't see immediate big improvements.

Set realistic expectations and don't try to oversell the benefits. Prepare your organization for a long and bumpy ride. Managing expectations may curb the organization's enthusiasm, but it will improve your likelihood of success. Large organizational change takes time, and you should be skeptical of anyone who tells you otherwise. Steer clear of quick fixes. With enterprise agile transformations, slow and steady always wins the race.

TIP

Establish clear metrics to make progress visible and keep everyone motivated. When change is slow, progress is often difficult to see.

Compensate Employees for Their Investment

An enterprise agile transformation requires a significant investment from employees, but few organizations return the favor. They don't release employees from their usual responsibilities or create time in the workday for change management events. Although executives and managers may not intentionally exploit workers' good will, the oversight can make employees wonder whether they're the only ones sacrificing for the organization's success.

TIP

Create an employee change investment memo that shows the number of hours employees have invested in the enterprise agile transformation in excess of their normal hours. Present the memo to your organization's executives to demonstrate what employees have already contributed and to make the case that with a little investment, employees may be willing to do much more.

Change Minds as Well as Systems

Any effective enterprise agile transformation requires a change in both how people work and how they think about their work. According to some schools of thought, you can change people's thinking by changing their behaviors. Others believe that you can change people's behaviors by changing their thoughts. I recommend doing both:

- **Change the culture.** You can change your organization's mindset by promoting agile values and principles, such as valuing people and interactions over processes. Creating a proactive Lean-Agile Center of Excellence (LACE) can be a great way to start changing minds within your organization.

» **Adopt agile principles and practices.** Creating agile teams and adopting agile practices gets people to change the way they do their work and how they work together. Experiencing enterprise agility reinforces the Lean-Agile Mindset, which helps drive the necessary change in culture.

Be Objective When Assessing Your Organization's Culture

Most organizations have a stronger control culture than they would like to admit. They like to think of themselves as highly collaborative, and they may be very collaborative at certain levels. However, when you look more closely, you can see that people are generally doing what they're told.

When you're trying to identify your organization's existing culture (see Chapter 9), be objective. View your organization as it is and not as you want it to be. Then, choose an appropriate change management strategy (see Chapter 10). If your organization has a control culture and leadership supports enterprise agility, choose a top-down approach, such as Kotter's eight-step approach. Choose a bottom-up strategy, such as Fearless Change, only if your organization is highly collaborative.

Build Broad Consensus on the Reason for the Change

People often have different reasons for wanting enterprise agility, such as a desire for process improvement, better products, waste reduction, or increased collaboration. That's fine when you're just getting started, but lack of consensus on the reason for making the change can dilute the impact of everyone's efforts.

Think of it this way: Organizational change management is about solving problems. This could be a problem with your culture, a low-quality product, or even a hostile workplace. Everyone should have the same understanding of the problem so all can work together to create a solution. If you're the change leader, collaborate with all stakeholders to reach consensus on the greatest challenge and develop a prioritized list of objectives.

CASE STUDY

A LACK OF CONSENSUS

I once worked for an organization that was going through a massive enterprise agile transformation. When I started asking people why they thought the organization was making the change, I got a variety of answers. Some teams thought it would cut costs. Others thought leadership wanted to show that the organization was high-tech. Some believed the organization was trying to be more innovative.

When I asked the managers why there was so little overlap, they said that many of the teams had gone through different training sessions. Management didn't see much of a problem with the lack of consensus because all the teams were steadily improving.

But the lack of consensus was actually a significant challenge. It made it difficult for the center of excellence (CoE) to agree on the highest-priority changes. It also gave employees different expectations on where things would start changing. Some thought they would start going to high-tech conferences, while others thought they would have more opportunities to innovate. This gave everyone a different perspective on how quickly things were changing and what to expect next. The organization would've had a much easier transformation had it helped the employees create a common consensus on the change.

Don't Rely Solely on Outside Consultants to Drive Change

Consultants are great, but they should be used primarily to provide objective third-party insight into your organization. Some organizations misuse consultants by treating them as disposable change agents. They hire a consultant to drive the change and then fire him when it fails. This practice — also known as the "scapegoat" method — persists because it protects managers from shouldering the cost of failure, and it gives consultants interesting work, but it's not good for the organization.

A better approach is to choose a well-respected and longtime employee to drive the change internally with the mindset that the change is inevitable — failure is not an option. A well-respected, longtime employee can do a good job communicating the reason behind the change. She can point out that she's been there for a long time and understands that this will be a challenge. She can speak in a language everyone in the organization understands and use examples that resonate throughout the organization.

TIP

If you use a consultant to drive change, make sure you have one or two longtime employees working alongside her, so they can continue to drive change after the consultant leaves. Otherwise, the change initiative is likely to lose momentum, and the organization may even reverse course.

Encourage Reluctant Executives and Managers to Embrace the Change

You may encounter some of the stiffest resistance to enterprise agility at the top of your organization, because change requires taking a risk — something executives and managers have been trained to avoid or to manage carefully. To ease your organization's leadership into embracing the change, try the following techniques:

- Be completely honest about the potential benefits and risks.
- Raise awareness of the risk of not changing.

CASE STUDY

WHEN SUCCESS POSES A RISK

An executive's past success can pose the biggest threat to your enterprise agile transformation. For example, I once worked for an organization led by an executive who had held his position for over a decade. He had a lot of success with traditional product delivery — a lot of up-front planning and months or even years of product development before the customer saw the finished product.

He struggled with the concept of incremental product delivery and cringed at the idea of the customer seeing an "unfinished" product. He insisted that the only time a customer would see the product was when it was ready for release.

The Agile Coaches tried to explain that product increments would be "potentially shippable" and that customer collaboration during development would improve innovation and increase the value of the product, but the executive wouldn't budge. His insistence that the customer see the product only after it was completed quickly derailed the enterprise agile transformation, and development reverted back to a waterfall approach.

When you're working with executives, keep in mind that they've built their careers on their own successful strategies and will probably be reluctant to stop doing what has made them successful. Be prepared to do a lot of convincing.

- Give more than one choice in how to implement the change.
- Don't let executives overestimate people's desire to change.
- Don't let the executives underestimate their own roles in the process.

Whether you take a top-down or a bottom-up approach (see Chapter 10), your organization's leaders will have a huge impact on the transformation. If leadership is reluctant to change the way it works, you'll have difficulty getting others in the organization to change the way they work.

Listen to the Skeptics

Every organization has skeptics who will resist any major change initiative, and that's not necessarily bad. Employees should be able to voice their opinions about large organizational changes. Listen to the skeptics; they may have some good points that you would be wise to consider.

WARNING

Don't dismiss the naysayers as resisting change merely because they're afraid of the unknown. They may reveal important insights that can make your efforts more successful. In addition, by giving them a voice, you're more likely to get their cooperation and may even convert them into your strongest advocates.

Expect some resistance and prepare strong counter arguments in favor of the change. You may even want to create a resistance management plan, which includes the following:

- A list of reasons why people may be invested in the way the organization currently operates, along with a list of ways these same people may benefit from an enterprise agile transformation. Think carefully about who might be hostile to the change and work hard to come up with solid and consistent responses.
- A list of additional work requirements that will be expected of employees, along with a list of ways the enterprise agile transformation will lighten their workloads or improve worker satisfaction.
- The reason for the change. Making employees change without providing them a reason for the change only makes them feel confused and frustrated. It provides no incentive for them to change.

REMEMBER

Be prepared to answer the skeptics' questions, so you don't fumble when challenged. Work with your change team to brainstorm possible reasons for resisting the change and responses to these reasons, so you're all on the same page. You want everyone on your change team giving the same responses, which will reduce confusion and anxiety.

» Making your workplace more fun and productive

» Increasing customer satisfaction

» Boosting quality while mitigating risk

Chapter 14
Ten Ways Enterprise Agility Improves Product Delivery

When you're trying to convince your organization's leadership or your customers to invest in enterprise agility, you need to highlight the many advantages it has to offer. In this chapter, I list ten of the most valuable benefits.

Increasing Agility

One of the advantages of enterprise agility and iterative, incremental product delivery is that they enable organizations to respond quickly and creatively to all sorts of changes, including the following:

- Evolving customer needs
- New technologies and approaches

- Emerging opportunities and threats
- Changes in the industry and marketplace

Although large organizations can certainly plan ahead to respond to change, change often occurs at a rate that exceeds the ability to plan for it. Modern organizations need to be agile to keep pace with the rate of change.

Boosting Innovation

Enterprise agility drives innovation in numerous ways, including the following:

- Solutions involve collaborative input from customers and developers, who are the closest to the product, opportunistically merging business and technical perspectives.
- Developers work from user stories instead of detailed requirements, so they have more freedom to develop innovative solutions, adapting just in time to current context and new insights.
- Developing in product increments enables everyone to interact with working versions of a product, which sparks more creative ideas. That also enables more responsive "steering" based on current feedback.
- Cross-functional team members have broader knowledge and skill sets, so they can synthesize and contribute ideas beyond their traditional areas of expertise.
- Given more creative freedom and authority to make decisions, developers have a greater personal stake in the product and more motivational drive or incentive to create awesome products.

Enhancing Transparency

Traditional product delivery is almost like a submarine mission. The customer loads a bunch of requirements into development, which disappears below the surface only to resurface months later with a finished product. Most of the hard work happens below the surface and outside the view of the customer and the organization's leadership. The process remains hidden for the most part, so problems are rarely exposed or addressed, and there are missed opportunities for contemporaneous guidance or steering.

Enterprise agility increases transparency in several ways, including the following:

- Customers can review the product at the end of each product development cycle: for example, at the end of each two- to four-week sprint. Customers see their products improve incrementally.
- Small, cross-functional teams work on smaller areas of a product and test the product frequently, so their work is constantly scrutinized.
- Most teams use Kanban or a similar system to visualize workflow, which improves visibility into workflow issues, such as incomplete work items and bottlenecks. (Workflow visualization also enables managers and other stakeholders to monitor progress without requiring teams to waste time building progress reports.)
- Enterprise agile principles emphasize transparency and learning from failure to encourage employees to be more open about mistakes, missed opportunities, and areas that need improvement.

REMEMBER

With traditional project management, you don't really know when a team is struggling until close to the release date. Project managers who've worked with software teams are probably familiar with the 90-percent rule: Teams tell management that the software is 90 percent done 90 percent of the time. With enterprise agility, problems are much easier to spot at any point in the development process.

Boosting Productivity

Enterprise agile transformations almost always result in increased productivity, most of which comes from Lean thinking and systematic, global workflow optimization based on queueing theory (see Chapter 4). Most teams don't realize how much time they spend waiting for others to finish their tasks. No employees in the organization like to look idle, so they engage in other activities, such as reading tech journals or researching ways to improve the product — activities that deliver little or no immediate value to the customer.

CASE STUDY

KEEPING BUSY

I once worked for an organization that was in the middle of an enterprise agile transformation. The teams were having trouble meeting their sprint goals. The Scrum Masters worked with the teams to create more realistic estimates, but the teams still struggled to meet these more modest goals. Just looking at the teams, you'd never guess they were falling behind schedule; everyone was always busy and filled with eager energy.

However, when I took a closer look at what people were doing, I knew immediately why they were falling behind. Most of the team members were researching different ways to improve the product. These improvements could be months or even years off and often were completely unrealistic. One person was looking into what it would take to redevelop much of the core software. Another person was checking out new testing strategies. None of this work was providing any value to the customer. When asked why they were doing this, they said that most of the work was stuck with another team, so they were trying to make the best use of their time until the other team finished.

It was nice that they didn't want to just sit and read tech journals, but from the customer's perspective, it didn't make much of a difference. They weren't working on the product. As soon as I pointed this out to the product manager, he started to look for ways to optimize workflow.

TIP

Strive to reduce dependencies and handoffs. Part of the magic of cross-functional teams is that their self-sufficiency reduces their dependencies on others, and thus eliminating a lot of potential request queueing and wait time. So, break up the functional service teams, and reassemble your people into cross-functional teams. If you're successful, you'll see immediate improvements in productivity, because people will spend less time waiting for others to complete their work. Don't underestimate how well people can make themselves look busy when they're really not delivering any value to the customer. Watch out for teams that have several hours of meetings each day or team members who are working on individual tasks that are not clearly linked to the product.

Making Product Development More Fun and Rewarding

Creating innovative products that enhance people's lives is fun and rewarding, until someone steps in with a "my way or the highway" attitude and sucks the joy out of the process. Enterprise agility makes product development much more fun and rewarding in the following ways:

- Development teams have more creative freedom.
- Teams have less management oversight, spend less time in meetings, and waste less time keeping management posted of their progress.
- Team members are continuously acquiring new knowledge and skills, learning from each other, to improve their mastery and make their teams more cross-functional.
- Team members work more collaboratively, feeding on each other's creativity, leading to more productive synergy.
- Iterative product development gives teams more opportunities to celebrate their wins and learn from their experience. Instead of feeling as though they're pushing a boulder up a mountain, they can celebrate each time they roll a pebble up a hill.

REMEMBER

Most developers like the challenge of coming up with elegant solutions to complex problems. Graphic artists enjoy creating functional, attractive design elements. Testers love to play with software and "break" it. For many professionals, work is like play until someone starts telling them how to do their jobs. With enterprise agility, everyone trusts one another to do his or her job well, which keeps work fun and makes it more rewarding.

Strengthening Customer Relationships

Product development can create an adversarial relationship between your organization and its customer. The customer wants the maximum value at the lowest cost, whereas your organization wants to maximize its profit. Enterprise agility can improve your organization's relationship with its customers in two ways:

- Customers collaborate with developers on the product, so they build a deeper connection.
- Budgeting can be more flexible. Customers and developers collaborate to create a prioritized list of features, which can then be gradually built and integrated into the product as the customer's budget allows.

With traditional product development, budget disputes can often make the customer feel that your organization isn't aligned with its goal of creating a spectacular product. With enterprise agility, everyone agrees that the product should be spectacular and works toward that goal until the money runs out or the customer decides that the product is spectacular enough.

REMEMBER

One of the four values in the Agile Manifesto is "Customer collaboration over contract negotiation." You want to work together to come up with the best solution and not spend all your time trying to box each other into long-term, winner-loser commitments.

Enhancing Product Quality

Several agile practices are designed specifically to boost product quality, including the following:

- **Cross-functional teams** exchange information through open and honest communication, exposing problems instead of obscuring them.
- **Definition of "done"** (see Chapter 2) ensures that the product has been tested and fully inspected by at least two people, for example, and that it has met all agreed business and technical criteria for release.
- **Automated testing** ensures timely and rapid quality verification throughout the development process without any additional time or effort required of the team.
- **Continuous integration** ensures that developers merge their completed work and test it frequently to identify and address integration issues early on.
- **Test-driven development (TDD) or test-first development** deters developers from writing any more code than is required to enable a feature to fulfill its function, ensuring cleaner code. It also encourages everyone to get clarity on acceptance criteria before writing code. By producing just enough, just in time, the savings also accrue to future maintenance costs without the burden of unclear criteria, unnecessary code, or unjustified complexity.
- **Pair programming** (see Chapter 2) requires that programmers write code in pairs, so one programmer can focus on writing the code while the other offers guidance and checks the work. This has a strong, positive effect on code quality. There is also an intangible, yet profound, benefit in the rapid learning from each other with better practices and shared knowledge spreading quickly as team members collaborate.

Making Product Delivery More Predictable

An organization's leaders often fear enterprise agility will make product delivery less predictable because it does away with a lot of the upfront planning. However, developing product increments in short cycles actually makes product delivery *more* predictable. Anyone who wants to see the status of the product development can just sit in on one of the review meetings, or peruse the Kanban boards or other real-time project information radiators.

With traditional product development, organizations often waste a significant amount of time drawing up plans that they later discard when something changes that makes the plan obsolete. In fact, managers often build buffers into a plan, because they're relatively certain that development won't go according to plan and they're likely to miss the deadline by weeks or even months.

There are now many sources of empirical project data confirming that — on the average — agile product development results are more "in control" (in the classical sense of statistical process control) than similar development using traditional waterfall methods.

Reducing the Risk of Failure

Software projects can fail for a number of reasons, but one of the most common is a disconnect between what the customer wanted and what the team delivered. Enterprise agility reduces this disconnect in two ways:

- Short product development cycles, such as two- to four-week sprints, give customers more opportunities to let the development teams know whether the product they're creating is on track, and frequent opportunity to influence and help steer continuing efforts.
- A customer representative or product owner (see Chapter 2) communicates the customer's needs directly to the team. With traditional product development, customer needs are typically relayed to the development teams by someone in the organization who's outside of development. Having an actively engaged product owner as part of the team ensures that the product will meet the customer's needs.

CASE STUDY

AN ABSENT PRODUCT OWNER

I once worked for an organization with a product owner who had formerly served as a business analyst. As a business analyst, he created a detailed list of requirements at the very beginning of the project and then moved on to the next project. He wasn't in the habit of being a part of the team and sticking around to answer questions.

When he started as a product owner, he quickly fell back into his old habits. He wrote hundreds of user stories and then returned to his cubicle in a different part of the building. He answered questions only during weekly project updates and rarely attended sprint review meetings, so he didn't have a strong sense of how the product was developing.

Several months into the product, he attended a sprint review meeting that coincided with a visit from a key executive. In the middle of the sprint review, the executive turned to the product owner and asked several questions about the product. The product owner tried to answer the questions but he didn't really have the information and was awkwardly corrected by the team. The executive was visibly annoyed and encouraged the product owner to make some changes.

The executive said he knew that the product owner was putting the project at risk. Fortunately, the product owner quickly adapted to his new role and became a more engaged team member. He listened to the executive's suggestions and worked closely with the developers to ensure alignment.

Improving Developer Discipline

An agile team must stick closely to the work items it committed to completing during any given product development cycle. Together, the product owner and the team agree upon a group of high-priority work items and then the team decides how to complete those work items. If the team thinks other work is a bigger priority (such as reengineering a database), it must convince the product owner that this work will deliver value to the customer. A good product owner will push back and ask tough questions such as, "Why do you need to do this now?" and "What happens if we don't do it?"

This push and pull between the product owner and the development team keeps everyone honest and makes all of them more focused and disciplined in their work. In the end, this inherent conflict and close collaboration usually results in a higher-quality product.

CASE STUDY

A FRUITLESS ENDEAVOR

I once worked for an organization that was delivering an enterprise-level product using traditional project management. One of the teams decided that it needed to convert the legacy database into a NoSQL datastore. It wasn't a project requirement, but the team argued that it would make the other features much easier to deliver. Team members said the change would improve the overall product and would take less than two weeks. The project manager agreed to the change, and the team got started.

The legacy database server turned out to be much messier than anyone had anticipated. The more the team dug into it, the more sloppy code it encountered. What began as a two-week detour quickly ballooned up into a month and then two months. The project manager was livid. As the third month approached, the project manager demanded that the team reassemble the legacy database server and return to working on the project requirements.

Index

E

F

G

H

I

J

K

L

M

N

O

P

Q

R

S

T

About the Author

Doug Rose has been transforming organizations through technology, training, and process optimization for more than 20 years, and he now specializes in providing agile coaching and training for teams, programs, and organizations. He's especially adept at introducing agile and Lean into organizations that take a traditional project-management approach to product development. Author of the Project Management Institute's (PMI) first major publication on the agile framework, *Leading Agile Teams,* Doug helps his clients improve their organizational agility by coaching, instructing, and facilitating on the Scaled Agile Framework (SAFe), Scrum, Extreme Programming (XP), Kanban, Lean Software Development, Iterative Project Management, User Stories, Use Cases, and Retrospectives.

Doug has a master's degree (MS) in Information Management, a law degree (JD) from Syracuse University, and a bachelor of arts degree (BA) from the University of Wisconsin–Madison. He's also a Scaled Agile Framework Program Consultant (SPC), Certified Technical Trainer (CTT+), Certified Scrum Professional (CSP-SM), Certified Scrum Master (CSM), PMI Agile Certified Professional (PMI-ACP), Project Management Professional (PMP), and Certified Developer for Apache Hadoop (CCDH).

You can attend Doug's lively and engaging business and project management courses at the University of Chicago or online through Lynda.com or LinkedIn Learning.

Doug works through Doug Enterprises, an organization with an office in whatever city he lives. Currently that's in Atlanta, Georgia, where he spends his free time either riding a stationary recumbent bike or explaining the Marvel Universe to his son.

For more about Doug, visit his website at `www.dougenterprises.com`.

Dedication

For Jelena and Leo,

♪ ♫ You're the wind beneath my wings. ♫ ♪

(That song will be in your head now. You're welcome.)

Author's Acknowledgments

When I graduated college, I found out that I had very few marketable skills. I did, however, have an interesting hobby. Instead of working on my term papers I found myself drawn to the beige boxy computers in the library. There I spent many hours exploring the full range of this new technology. But my self-taught computer skills weren't enough to get me an early IT job. So, while working part time in a combination ice cream/burrito parlor, I picked up my first *For Dummies* book. It was the first edition of *Networking For Dummies,* by Doug Lowe.

Doug explained networking in a way that extremely accessible. Nowadays, it's hard to imagine that anyone would ever need to write, "Networking . . . Why bother?" But at the time, networking skills were considered cutting edge. I was so pleased with this book that I picked up a second *For Dummies* book. It was *UNIX For Dummies,* by John Levine. He explained the history of this terrific operating system and how to get around using various "shells."

These two books together gave me a pretty good understanding of how to set up a computer network and even do some basic server configurations. They didn't make me an expert, but they gave me a high-level overview about the language and the concepts, and they helped me land my first IT job working at a computer lab at Northwestern University.

That's why nearly a quarter-century later it's deeply rewarding for me to publish my own *For Dummies* book. In this book I've tried to stick with what I liked about these earlier books. I've tried to keep things informal and accessible, and I don't try to make any assumptions about what you might already know. Learning about new topics is fun. I try to remember that even when the topic is littered with acronyms, jargon, and needlessly obtuse language. These other authors understood that, and I tried to follow in their footsteps.

I'm happy to have the opportunity to thank the people who contributed to this book. First, I'd like to thank Amy Fandrei and the team at John Wiley & Sons, Inc. Amy created this opportunity and was very generous with her time and feedback. Joe Kraynak is simply the best editor I've ever worked with. He masterfully helped me reorganize the information in this book and enhanced the best parts while simultaneously showing me what to cut. I'd also like to thank Katharine Dvorak and Ken 'classmaker' Ritchie. They offered terrific guidance, and I appreciate their excellent suggestions. Also, special thanks to Sharon Kaplan for looking over early drafts. My wife was my first (and most critical) editor. After reading my drafts, she now threatens to teach organizational agility to political science PhD students.

I'd also like to thank the people in different organizations where I've done coaching and training. Without them I wouldn't have had much material for this book and or enough material to keep Doug Enterprises going. Special thanks to Sally Elatta and her team at Agile Transformations. Also thanks to Cox Automotive and The Home Depot. I relied heavily on content and feedback from several enterprise agile framework developers as well. Thanks to Dean Leffingwell, Terri Groh, and Richard Knaster from Scaled Agile, Inc.; Craig Larman and Bas Vodde from Large-Scale Scrum; and Scott Ambler and Mark Lines from Disciplined Agile. Of course, thanks to the agile community for always coming up with new ideas and for having interesting and engaging conferences. Adriana Danaila did terrific work creating some of the graphics around key concepts.

Additionally, I'd like to thank the team at Lynda.com and LinkedIn Learning, where I have several courses on improving organizational agility. The feedback from these courses was instrumental in deciding what to include in this book. Finally, I'd like to thank the University of Chicago and Syracuse University. Both of these great institutions have given me the opportunity to teach agility to graduate students and lifelong learners, whose many questions were always on my mind as I wrote this book.

Publisher's Acknowledgments

Senior Acquisitions Editor: Amy Fandrei

Editor: Joe Kraynak

Project Editor: Katharine Dvorak

Technical Editor: Ken 'classmaker' Ritchie

Proofreader: Debbye Butler

Sr. Editorial Assistant: Matt Lowe

Production Editor: Antony Sami

Cover Image: © Orla / iStockphoto